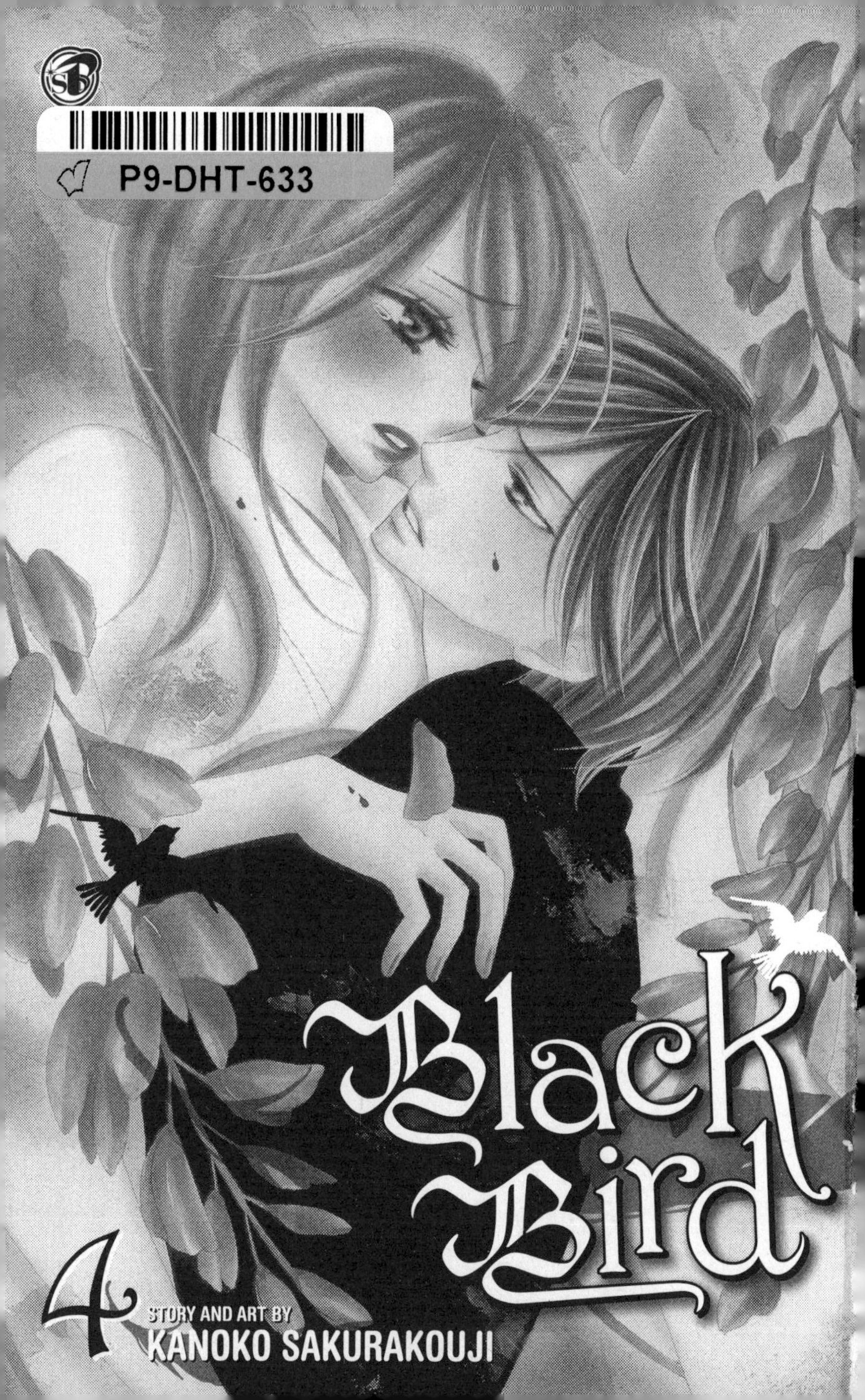
Black Bird
4
STORY AND ART BY
KANOKO SAKURAKOUJI

Black Bird

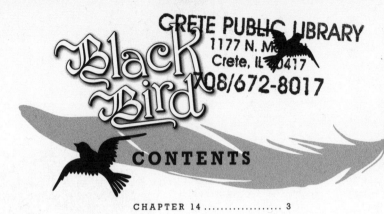

CONTENTS

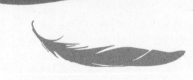

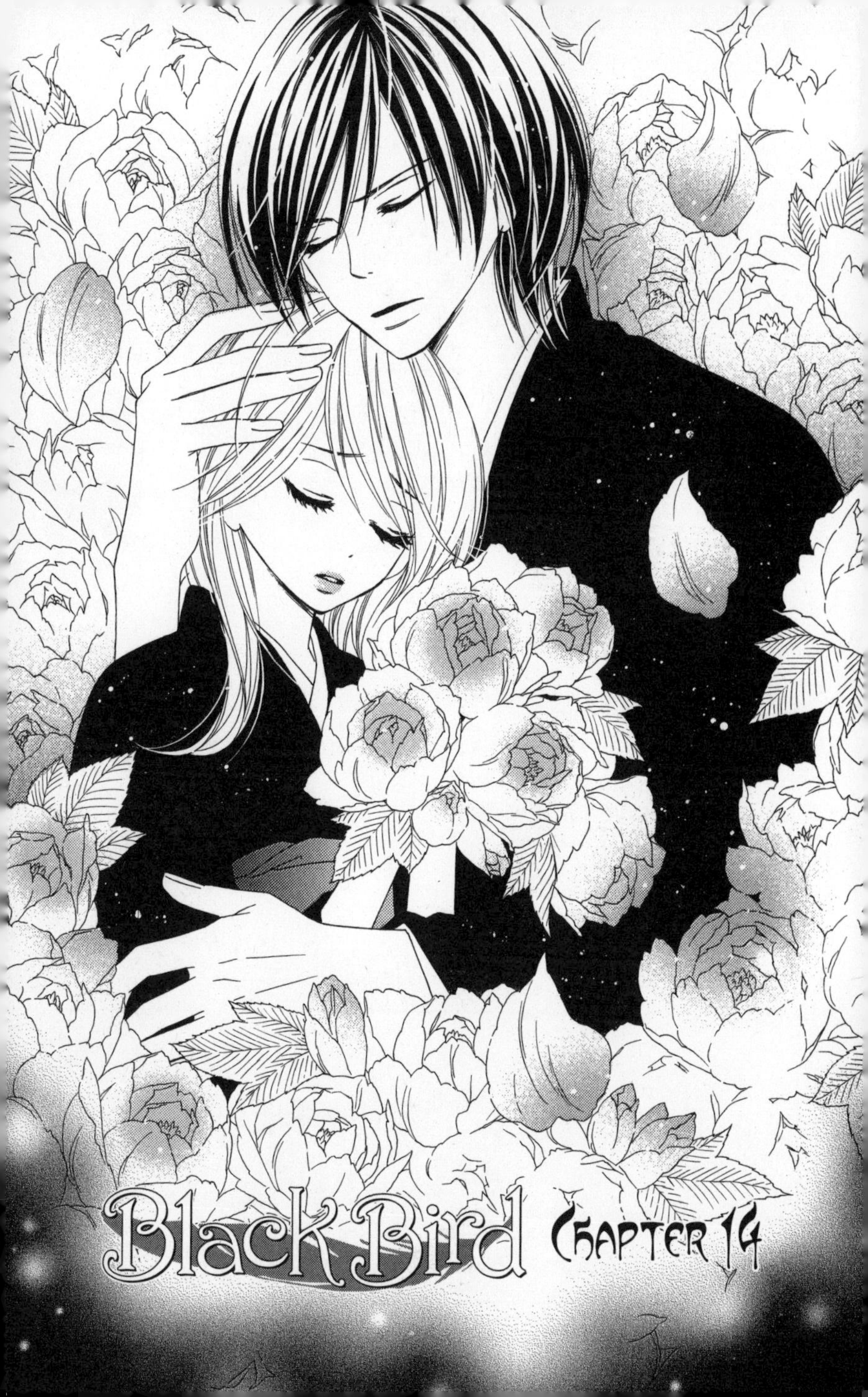
Black Bird
Chapter 14

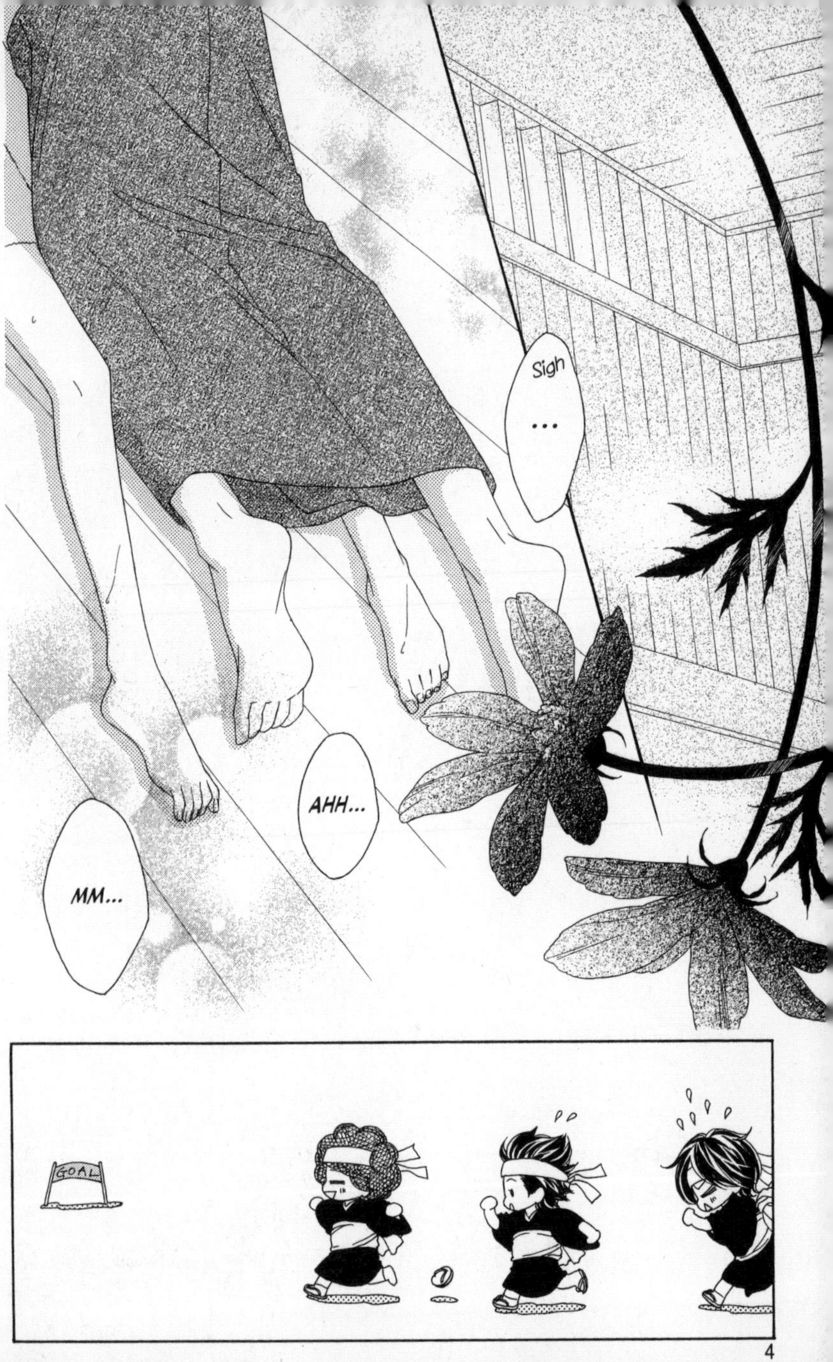
Sigh
...
AHH...
MM...
GOAL

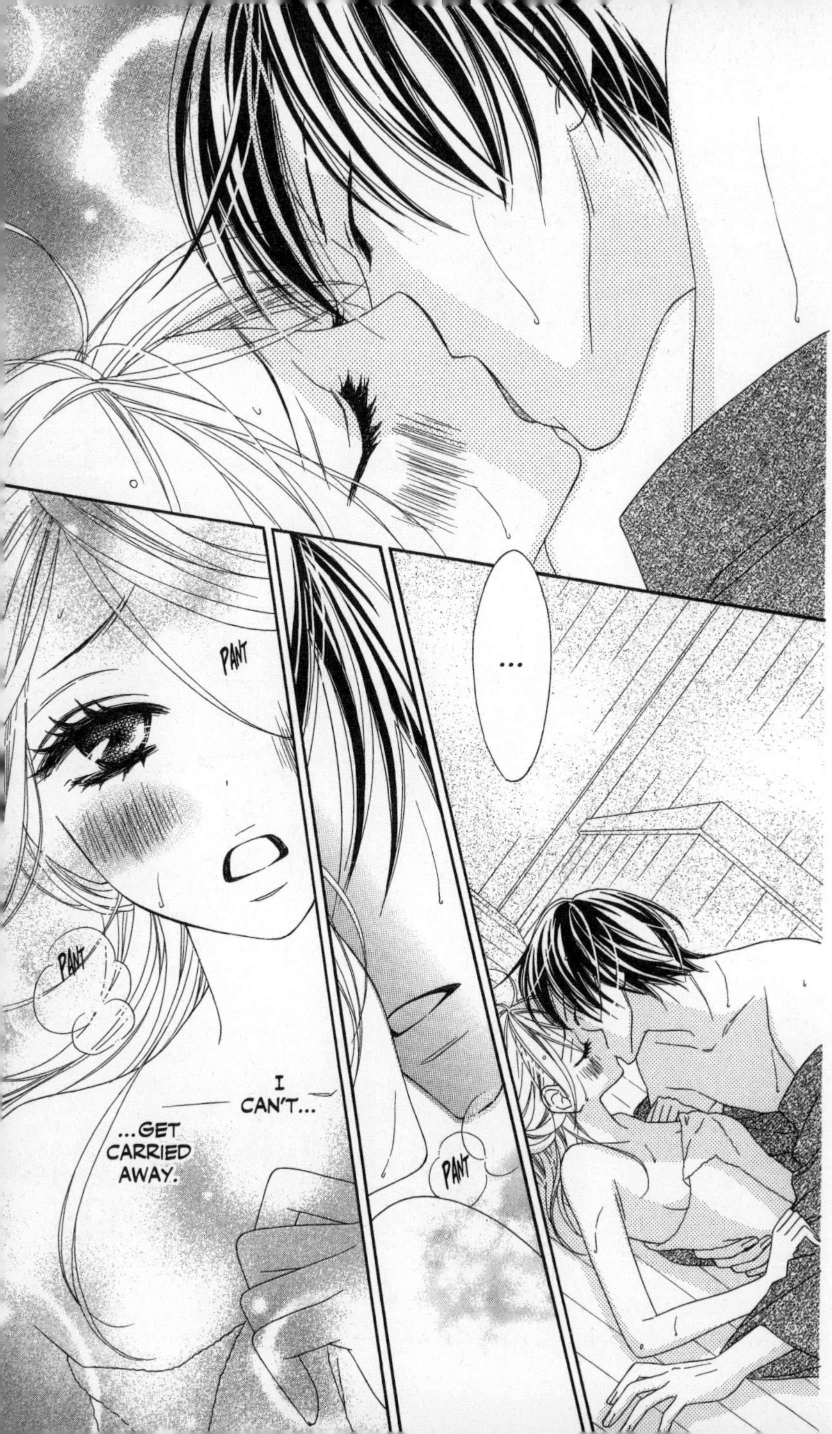
...
PANT
PANT
PANT
I CAN'T...
...GET CARRIED AWAY.

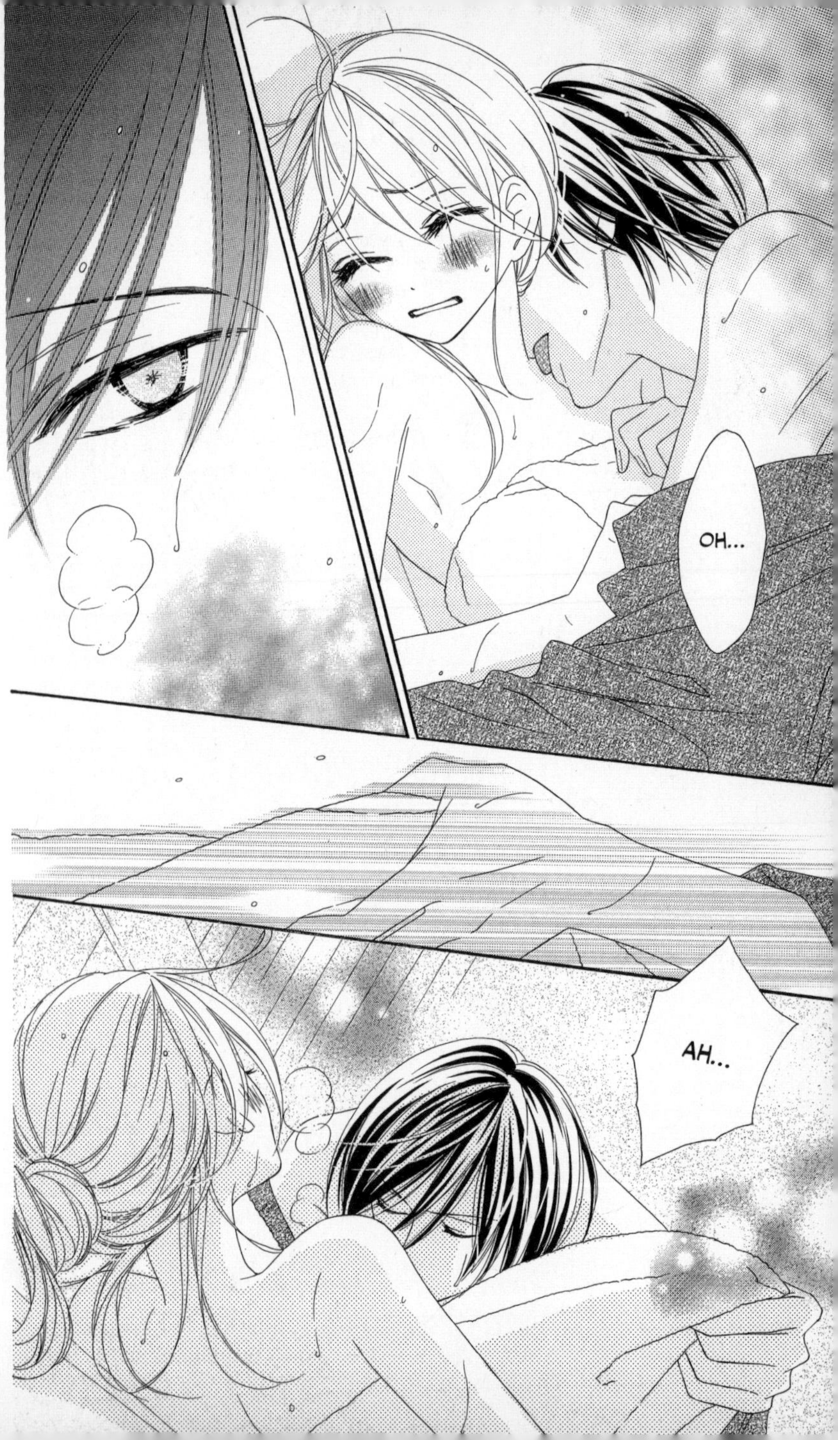
OH...
AH...

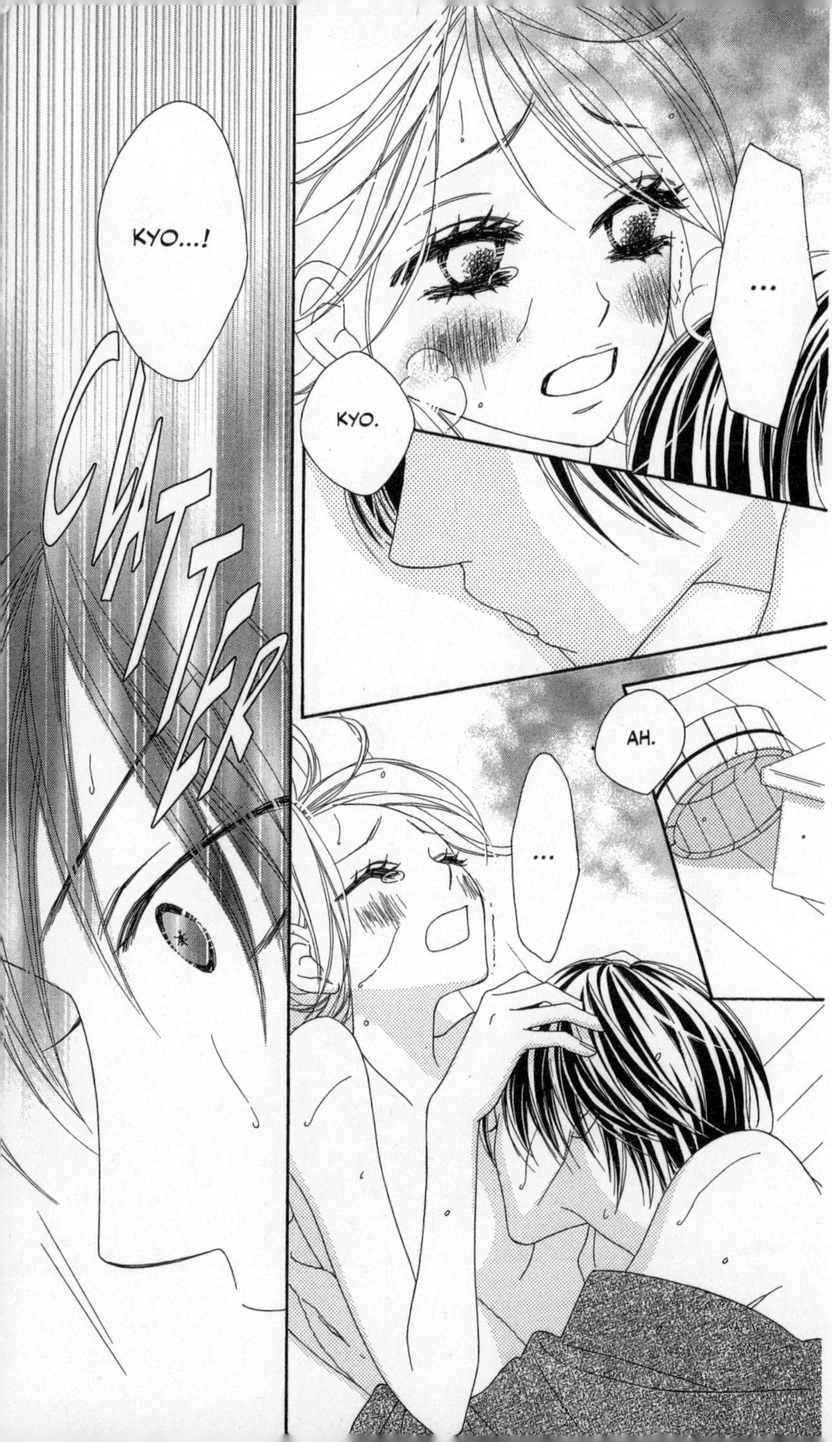
...
KYO.
AH.
...
KYO...!
CLATTER

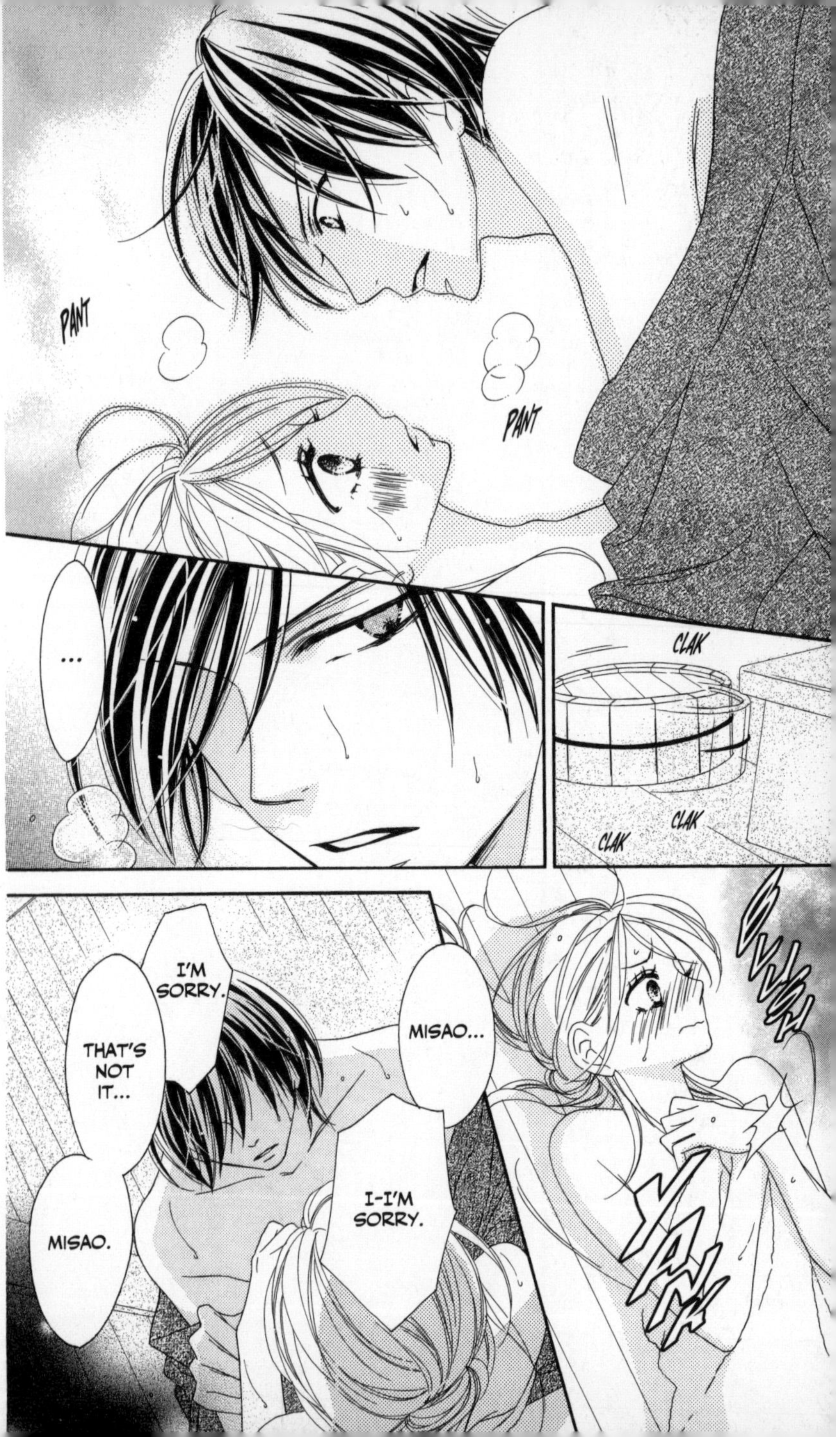
PANT
PANT
CLAK
CLAK
CLAK
...
YANK
MISAO...
I'M SORRY.
THAT'S NOT IT...
I-I'M SORRY.
MISAO.

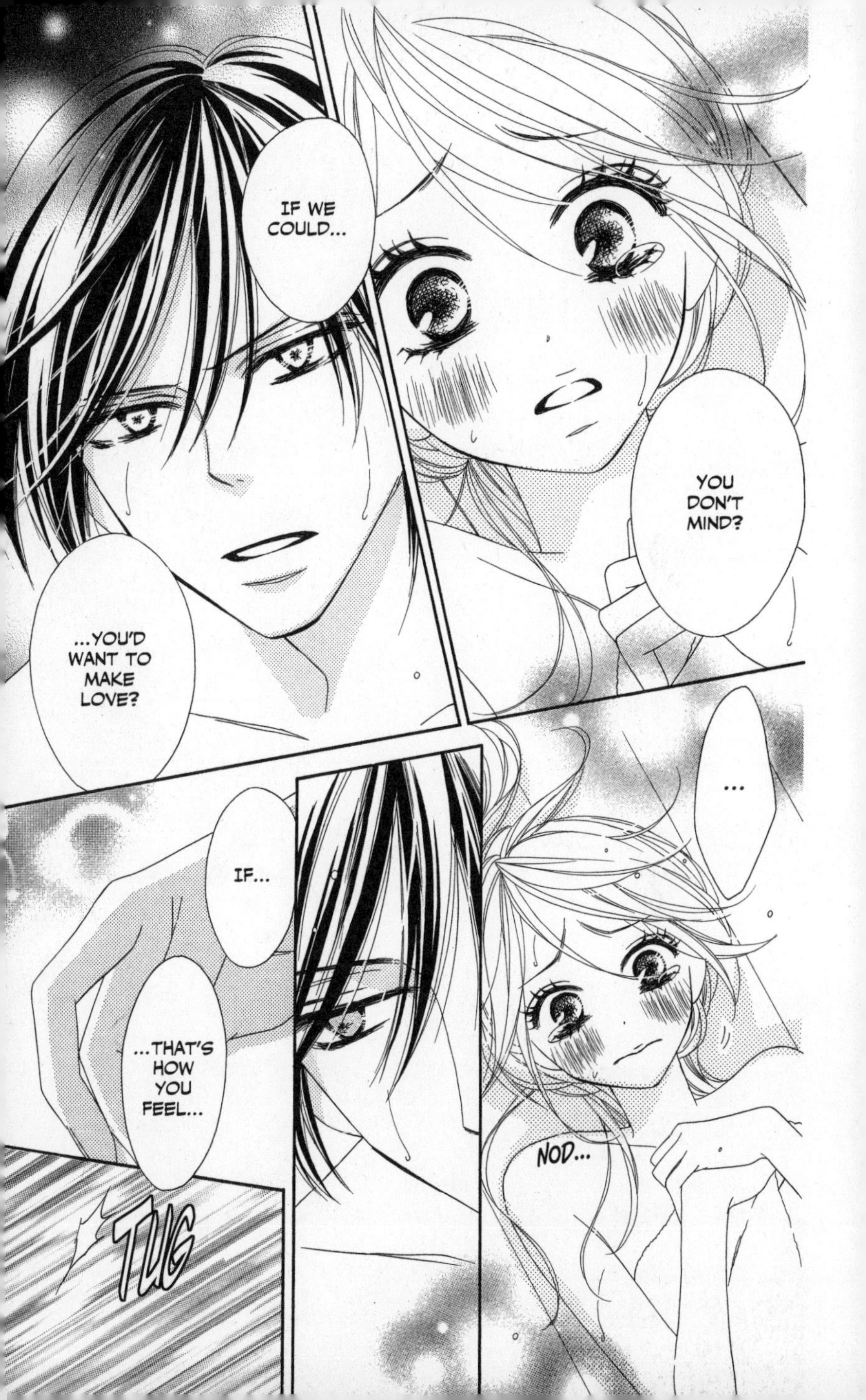
IF WE COULD...
...YOU'D WANT TO MAKE LOVE?
YOU DON'T MIND?
...
NOD...
IF...
...THAT'S HOW YOU FEEL...
TUG

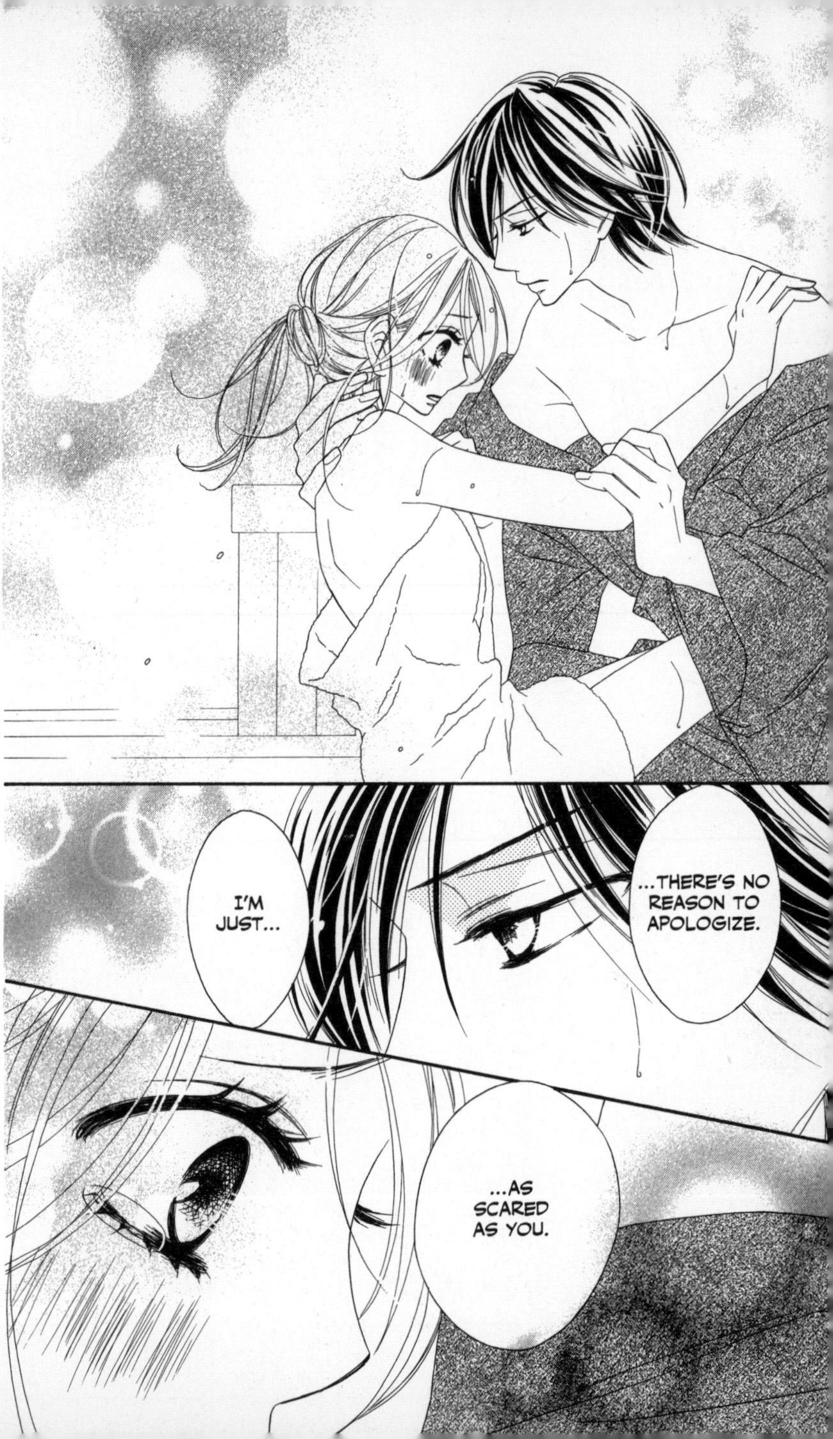
...THERE'S NO REASON TO APOLOGIZE.
I'M JUST...
...AS SCARED AS YOU.

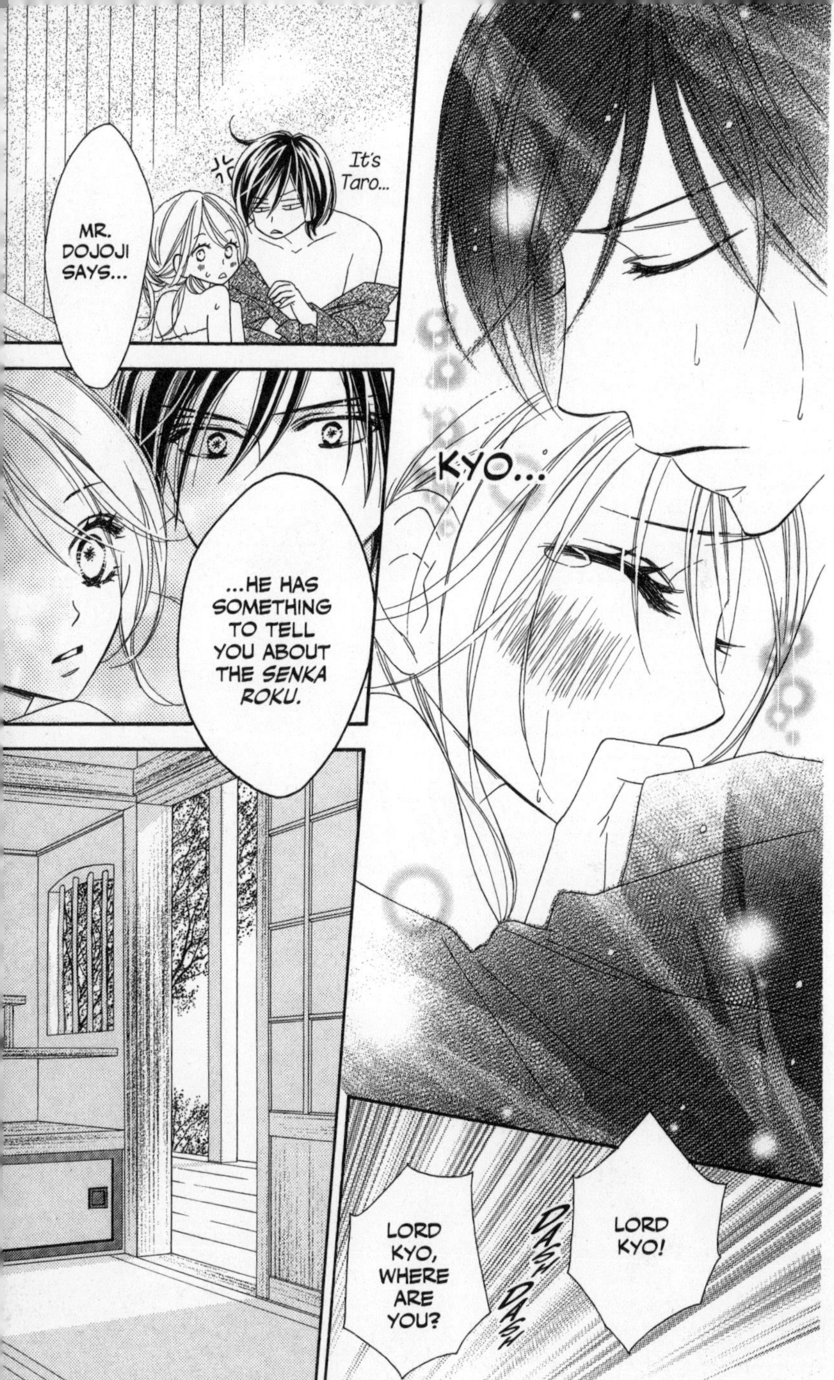
KYO...
It's Taro...
MR. DOJOJI SAYS...
...HE HAS SOMETHING TO TELL YOU ABOUT THE *SENKA ROKU.*
LORD KYO!
DASH DASH
LORD KYO, WHERE ARE YOU?

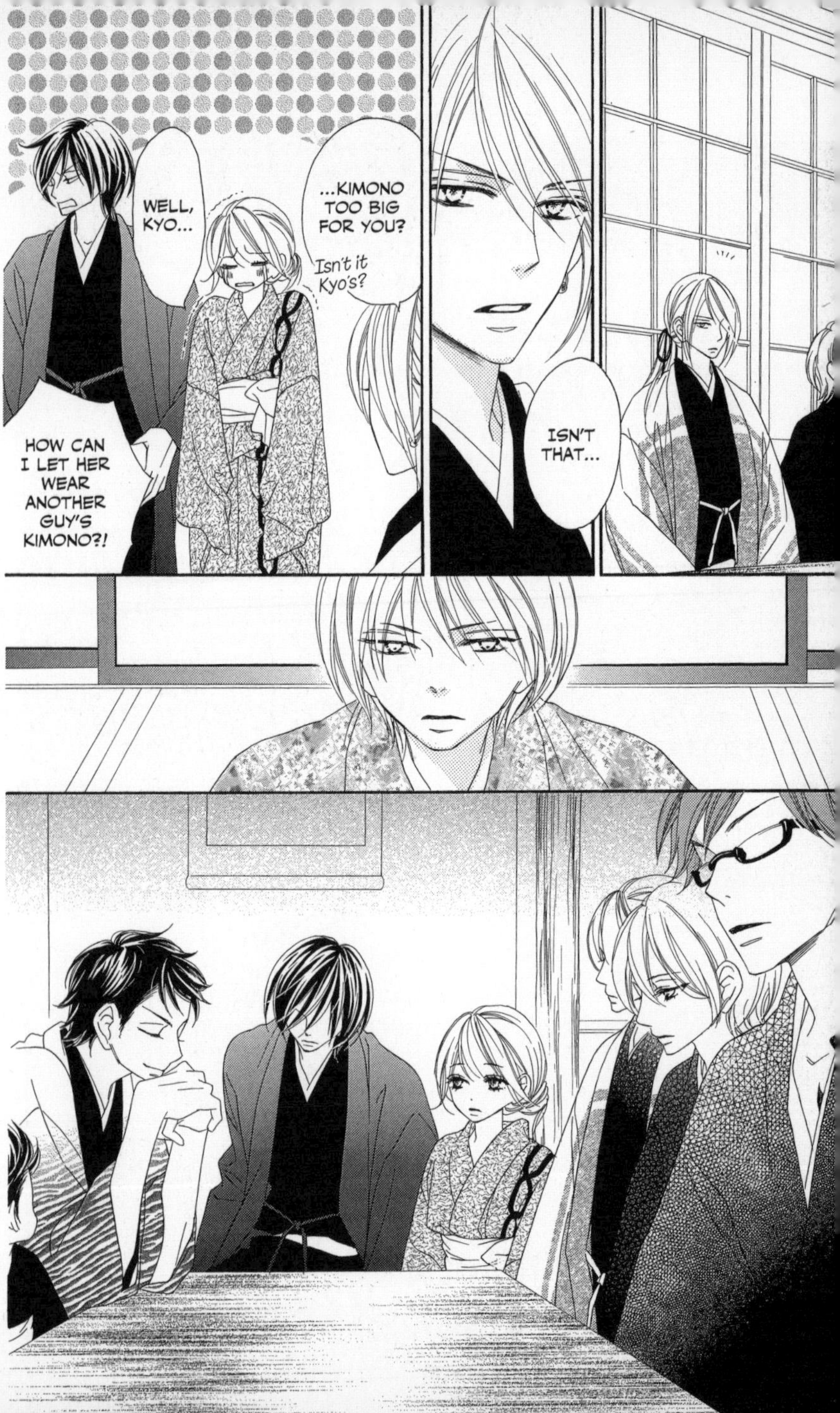
ISN'T THAT...
...KIMONO TOO BIG FOR YOU?
Isn't it Kyo's?
WELL, KYO...
HOW CAN I LET HER WEAR ANOTHER GUY'S KIMONO?!

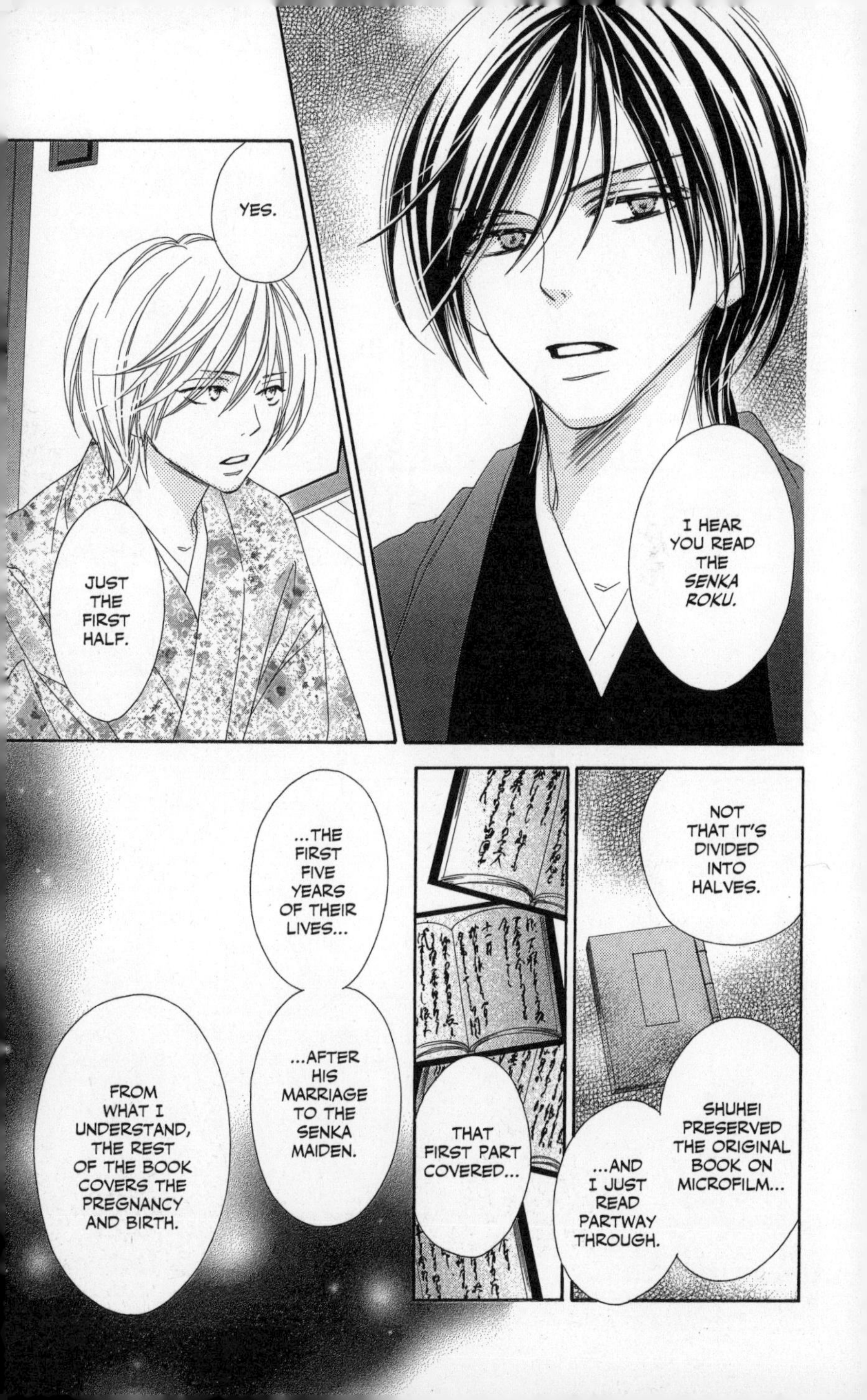
I HEAR YOU READ THE *SENKA ROKU.*
YES.
JUST THE FIRST HALF.
NOT THAT IT'S DIVIDED INTO HALVES.
SHUHEI PRESERVED THE ORIGINAL BOOK ON MICROFILM...
...AND I JUST READ PARTWAY THROUGH.
THAT FIRST PART COVERED...
...THE FIRST FIVE YEARS OF THEIR LIVES...
...AFTER HIS MARRIAGE TO THE SENKA MAIDEN.
FROM WHAT I UNDERSTAND, THE REST OF THE BOOK COVERS THE PREGNANCY AND BIRTH.

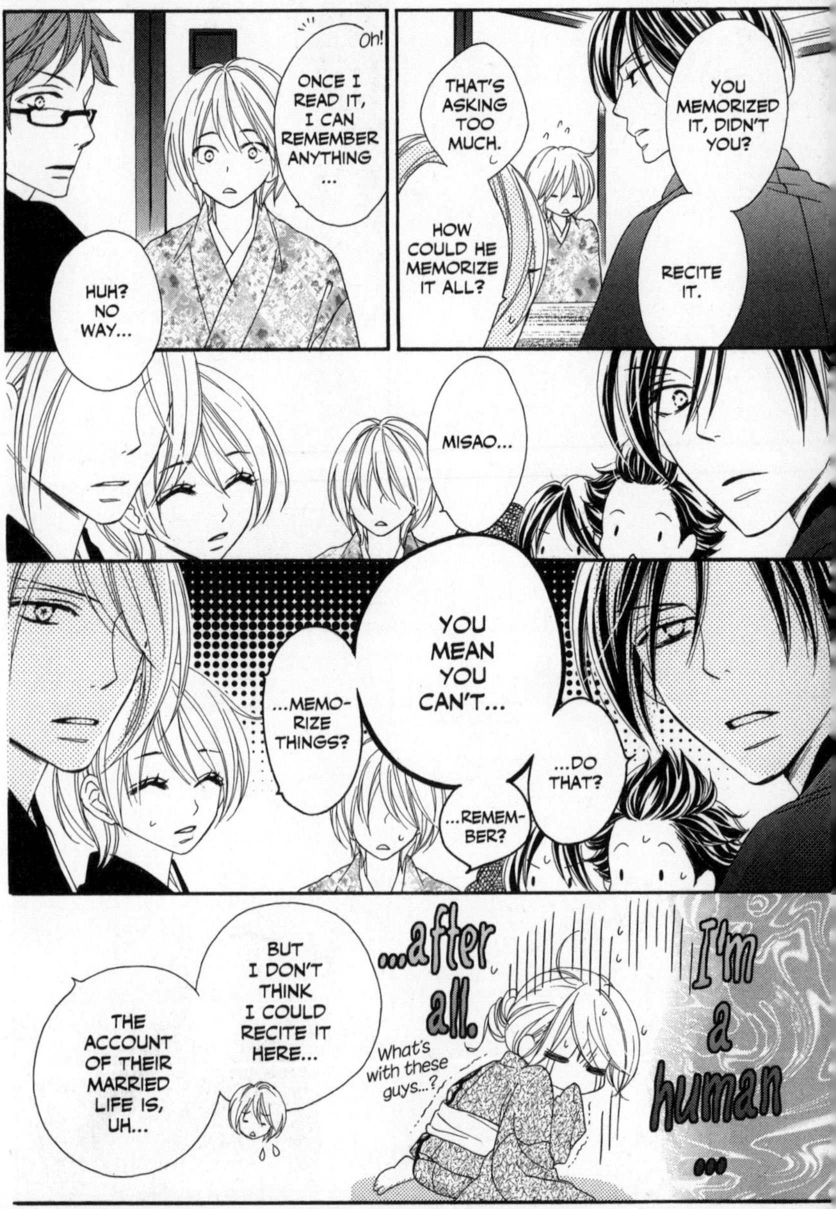
YOU MEMORIZED IT, DIDN'T YOU?
RECITE IT.
THAT'S ASKING TOO MUCH.
HOW COULD HE MEMORIZE IT ALL?
Oh!
ONCE I READ IT, I CAN REMEMBER ANYTHING...
HUH? NO WAY...
MISAO...
YOU MEAN YOU CAN'T...
...DO THAT?
...REMEMBER?
...MEMORIZE THINGS?
I'm a human...
...after all.
What's with these guys...?
BUT I DON'T THINK I COULD RECITE IT HERE...
THE ACCOUNT OF THEIR MARRIED LIFE IS, UH...

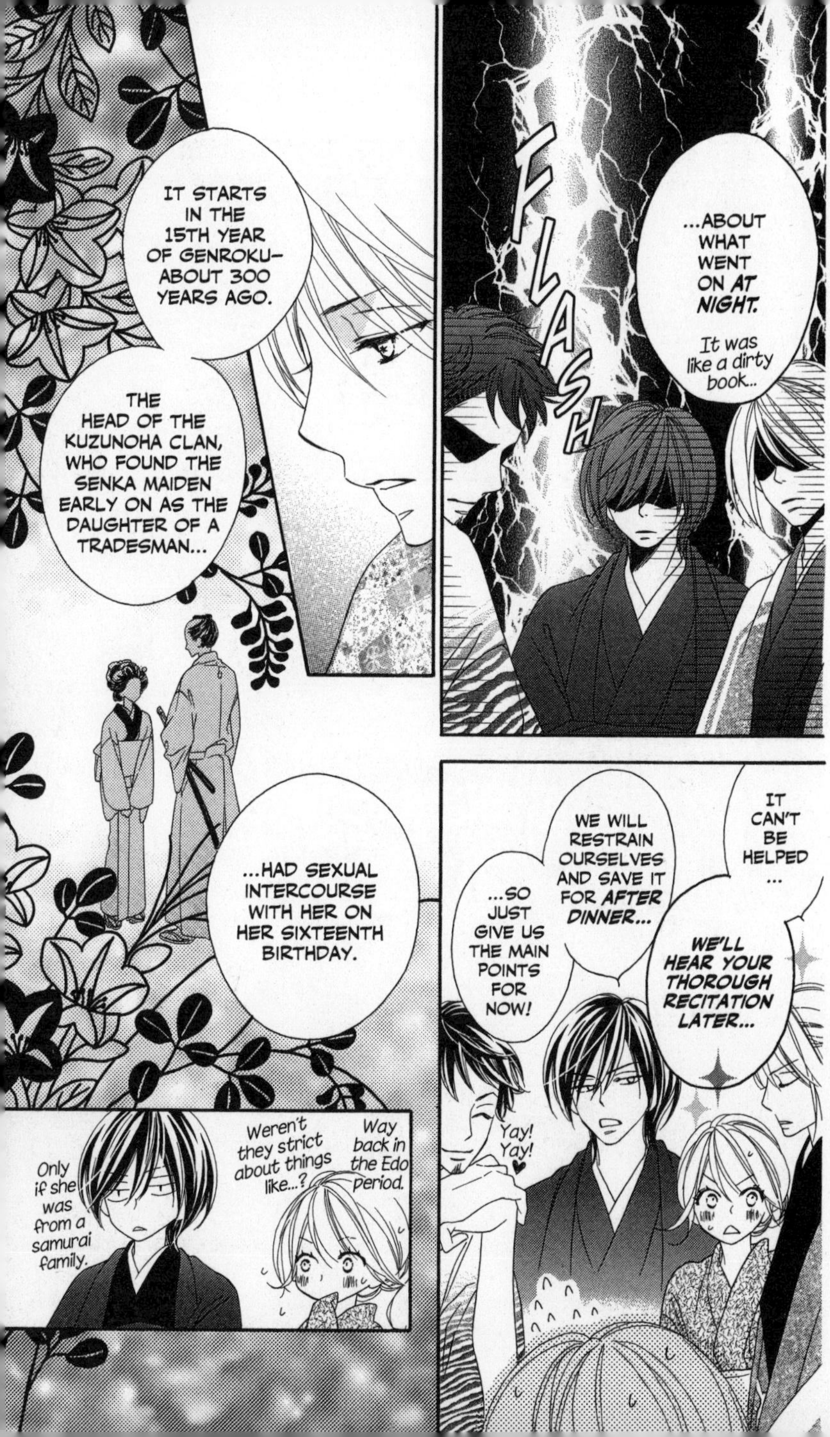
IT STARTS IN THE 15TH YEAR OF GENROKU— ABOUT 300 YEARS AGO.
THE HEAD OF THE KUZUNOHA CLAN, WHO FOUND THE SENKA MAIDEN EARLY ON AS THE DAUGHTER OF A TRADESMAN...
...HAD SEXUAL INTERCOURSE WITH HER ON HER SIXTEENTH BIRTHDAY.
Way back in the Edo period.
Weren't they strict about things like...?
Only if she was from a samurai family.
FLASH
...ABOUT WHAT WENT ON AT NIGHT.
It was like a dirty book..
IT CAN'T BE HELPED...
WE WILL RESTRAIN OURSELVES AND SAVE IT FOR AFTER DINNER...
...SO JUST GIVE US THE MAIN POINTS FOR NOW!
WE'LL HEAR YOUR THOROUGH RECITATION LATER...
Yay! Yay! ♥

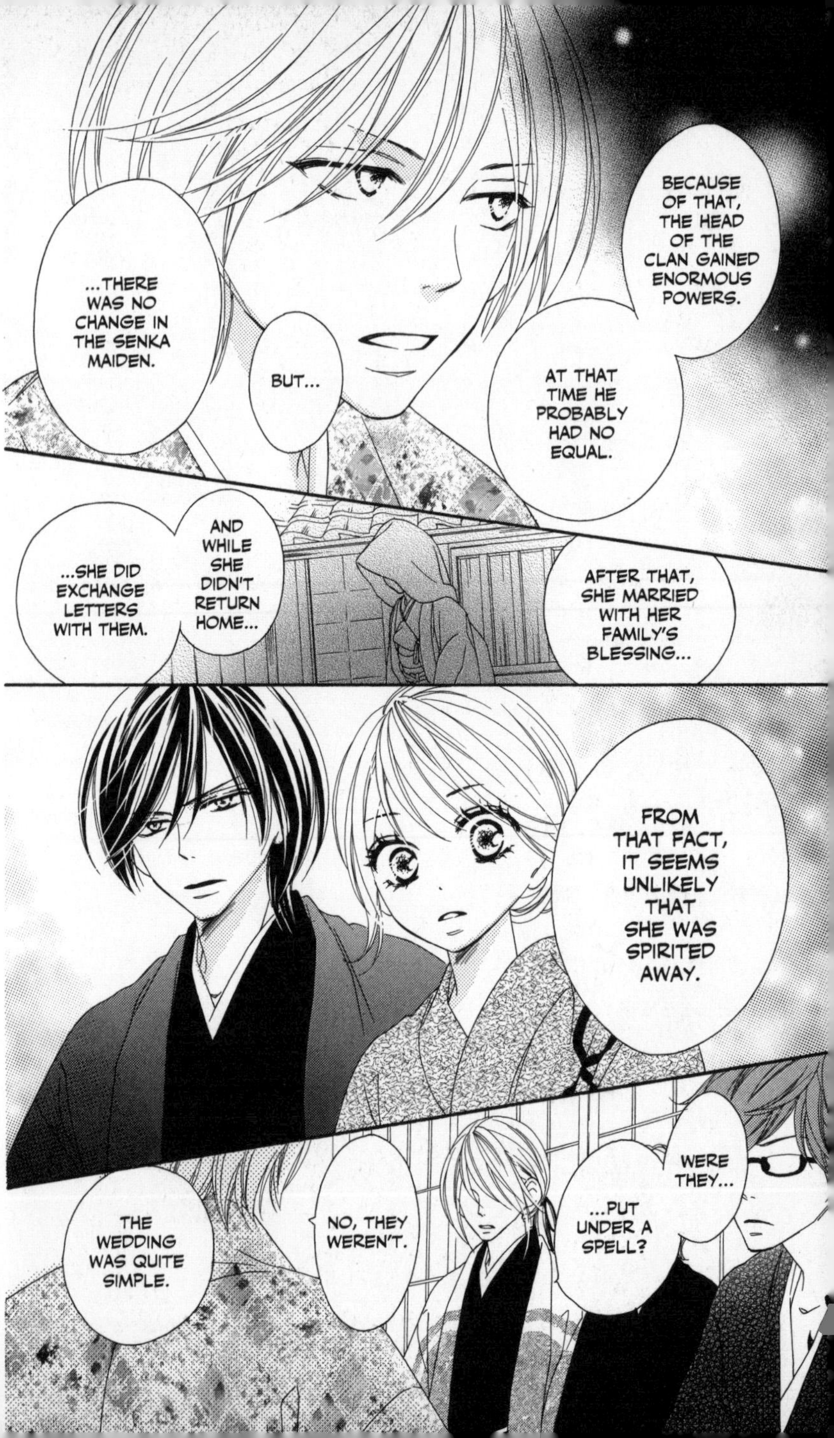
BECAUSE OF THAT, THE HEAD OF THE CLAN GAINED ENORMOUS POWERS.
AT THAT TIME HE PROBABLY HAD NO EQUAL.
BUT...
...THERE WAS NO CHANGE IN THE SENKA MAIDEN.
AFTER THAT, SHE MARRIED WITH HER FAMILY'S BLESSING...
AND WHILE SHE DIDN'T RETURN HOME...
...SHE DID EXCHANGE LETTERS WITH THEM.
FROM THAT FACT, IT SEEMS UNLIKELY THAT SHE WAS SPIRITED AWAY.
WERE THEY...
...PUT UNDER A SPELL?
NO, THEY WEREN'T.
THE WEDDING WAS QUITE SIMPLE.

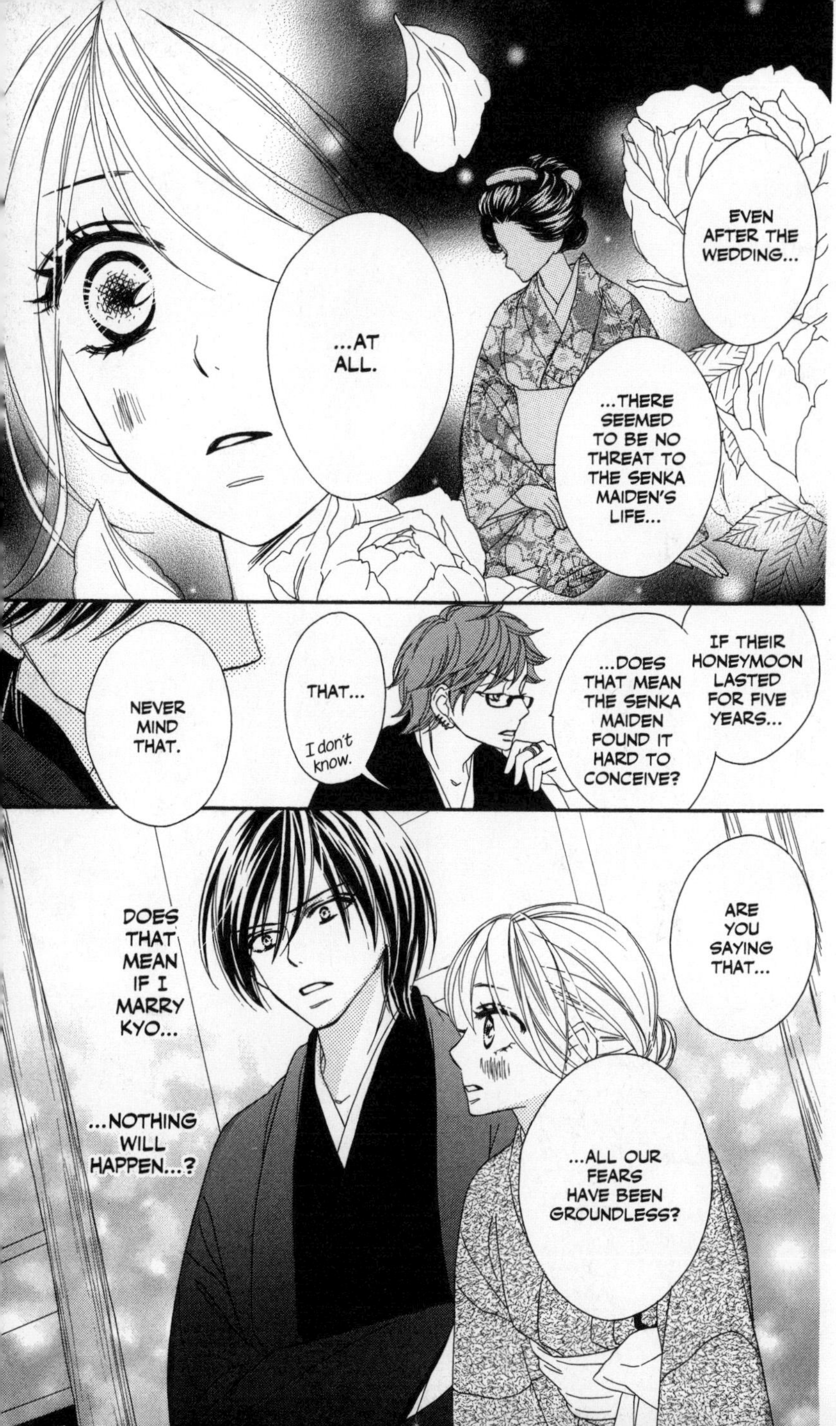
EVEN AFTER THE WEDDING...
...THERE SEEMED TO BE NO THREAT TO THE SENKA MAIDEN'S LIFE...
...AT ALL.
IF THEIR HONEYMOON LASTED FOR FIVE YEARS...
...DOES THAT MEAN THE SENKA MAIDEN FOUND IT HARD TO CONCEIVE?
THAT...
I don't know.
NEVER MIND THAT.
ARE YOU SAYING THAT...
...ALL OUR FEARS HAVE BEEN GROUNDLESS?
DOES THAT MEAN IF I MARRY KYO...
...NOTHING WILL HAPPEN...?

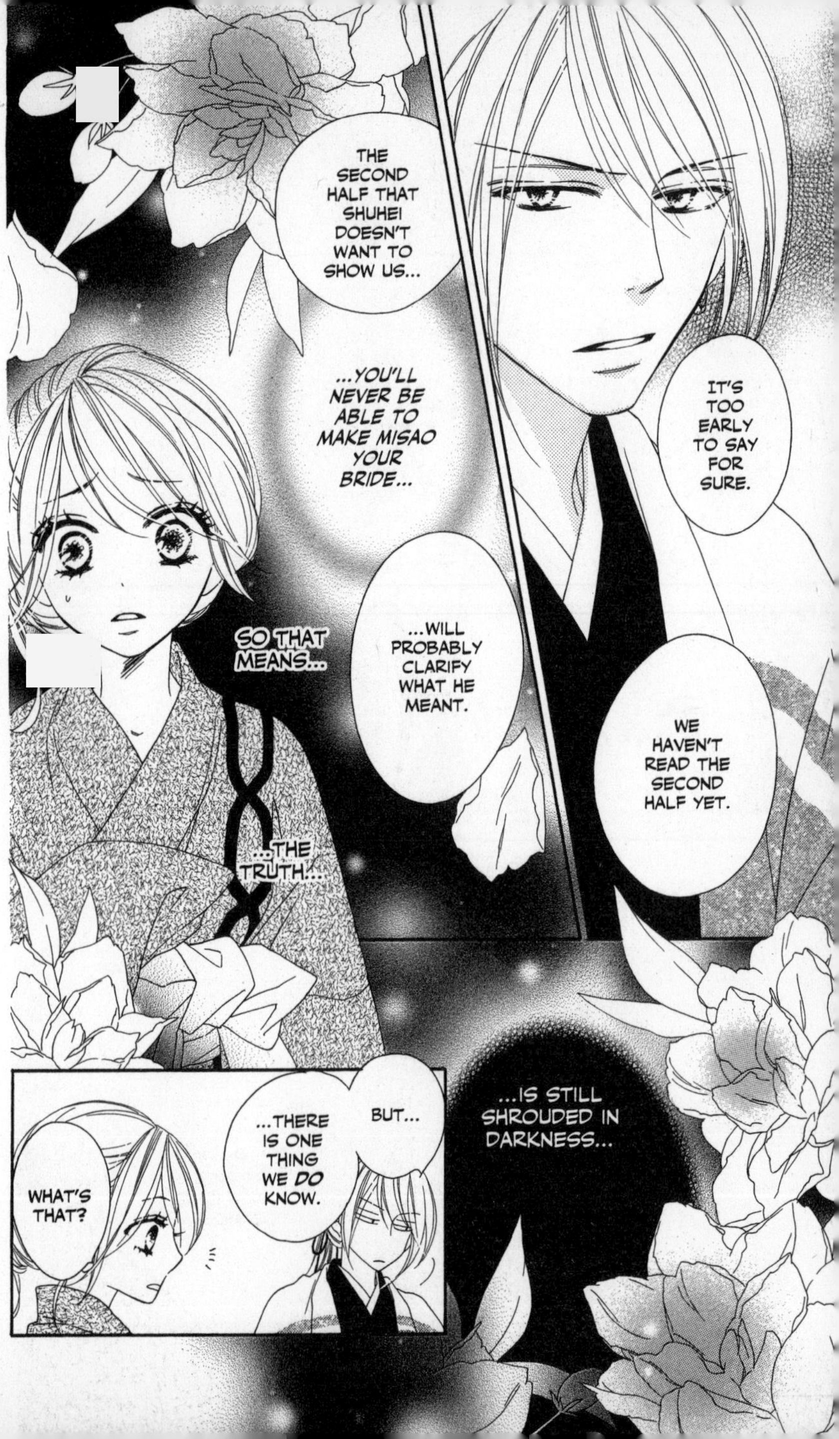
IT'S TOO EARLY TO SAY FOR SURE.
WE HAVEN'T READ THE SECOND HALF YET.
THE SECOND HALF THAT SHUHEI DOESN'T WANT TO SHOW US...
...WILL PROBABLY CLARIFY WHAT HE MEANT.
...YOU'LL NEVER BE ABLE TO MAKE MISAO YOUR BRIDE...
SO THAT MEANS...
...THE TRUTH...
...IS STILL SHROUDED IN DARKNESS...
BUT...
...THERE IS ONE THING WE *DO* KNOW.
WHAT'S THAT?

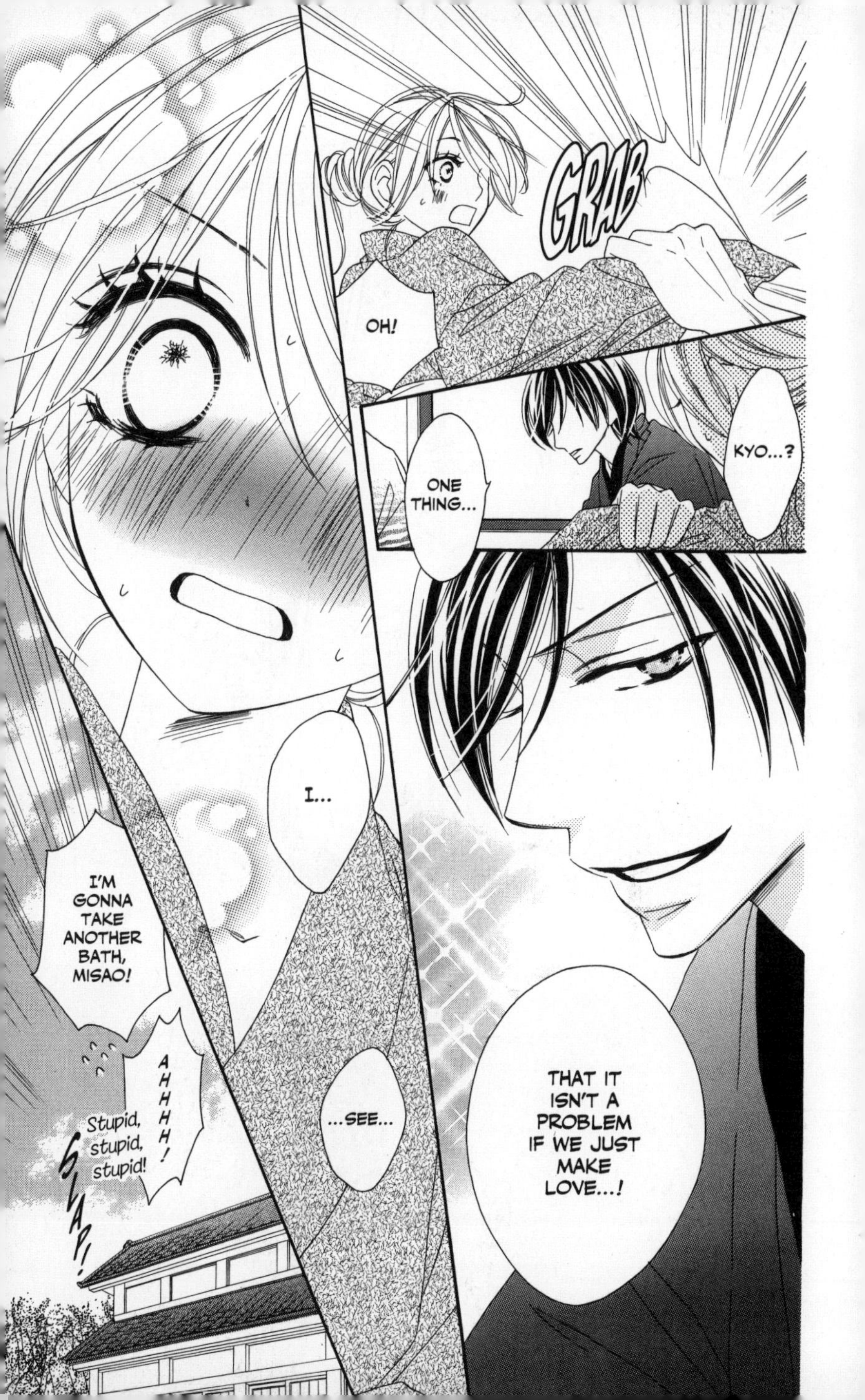
GRAB
OH!
KYO...?
ONE THING...
I...
...SEE...
THAT IT ISN'T A PROBLEM IF WE JUST MAKE LOVE...!
I'M GONNA TAKE ANOTHER BATH, MISAO!
AHHHH!
Stupid, stupid, stupid!
SLAP!

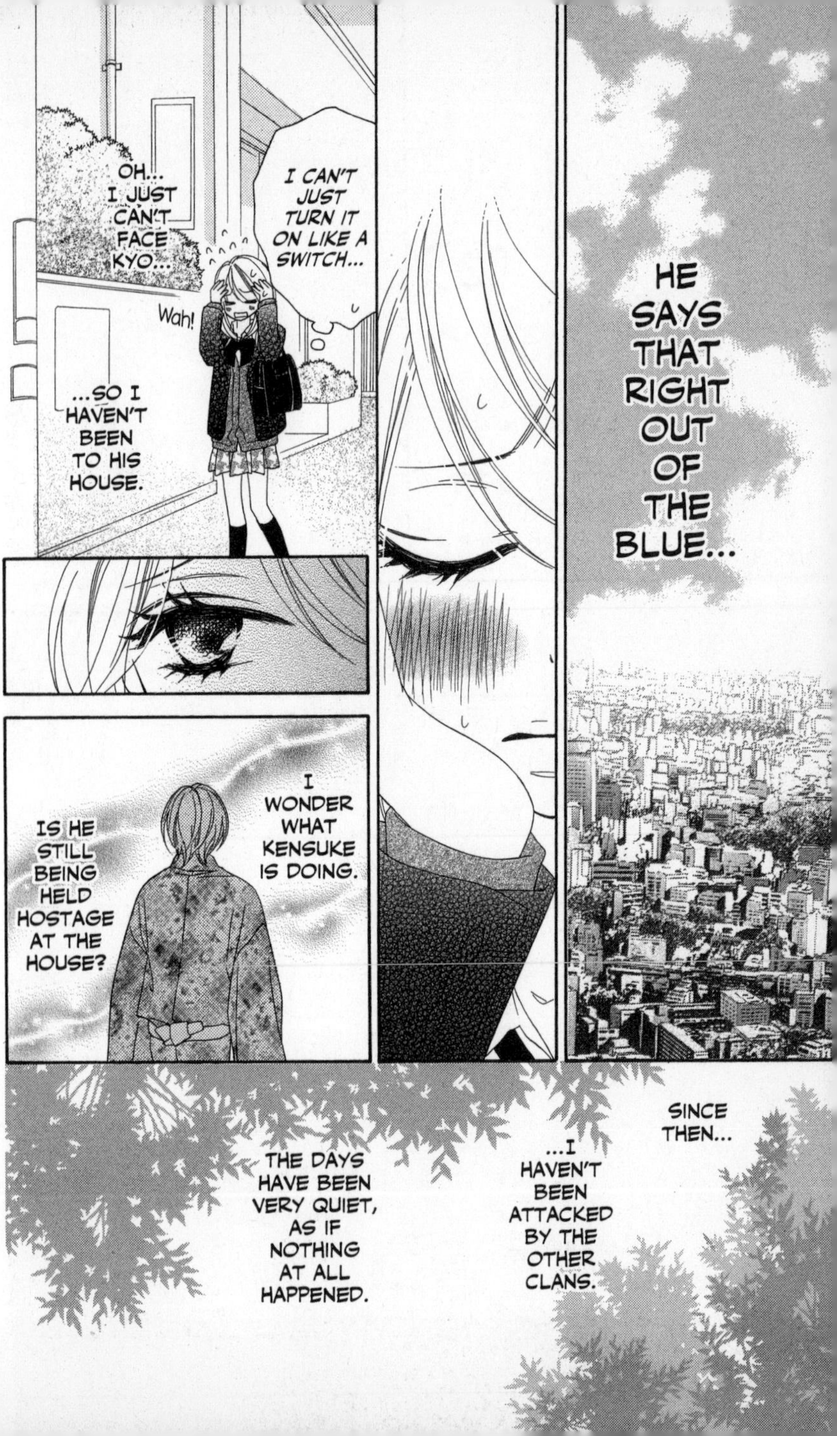
HE SAYS THAT RIGHT OUT OF THE BLUE...
I CAN'T JUST TURN IT ON LIKE A SWITCH...
OH... I JUST CAN'T FACE KYO...
Wah!
...SO I HAVEN'T BEEN TO HIS HOUSE.
I WONDER WHAT KENSUKE IS DOING.
IS HE STILL BEING HELD HOSTAGE AT THE HOUSE?
SINCE THEN...
...I HAVEN'T BEEN ATTACKED BY THE OTHER CLANS.
THE DAYS HAVE BEEN VERY QUIET, AS IF NOTHING AT ALL HAPPENED.

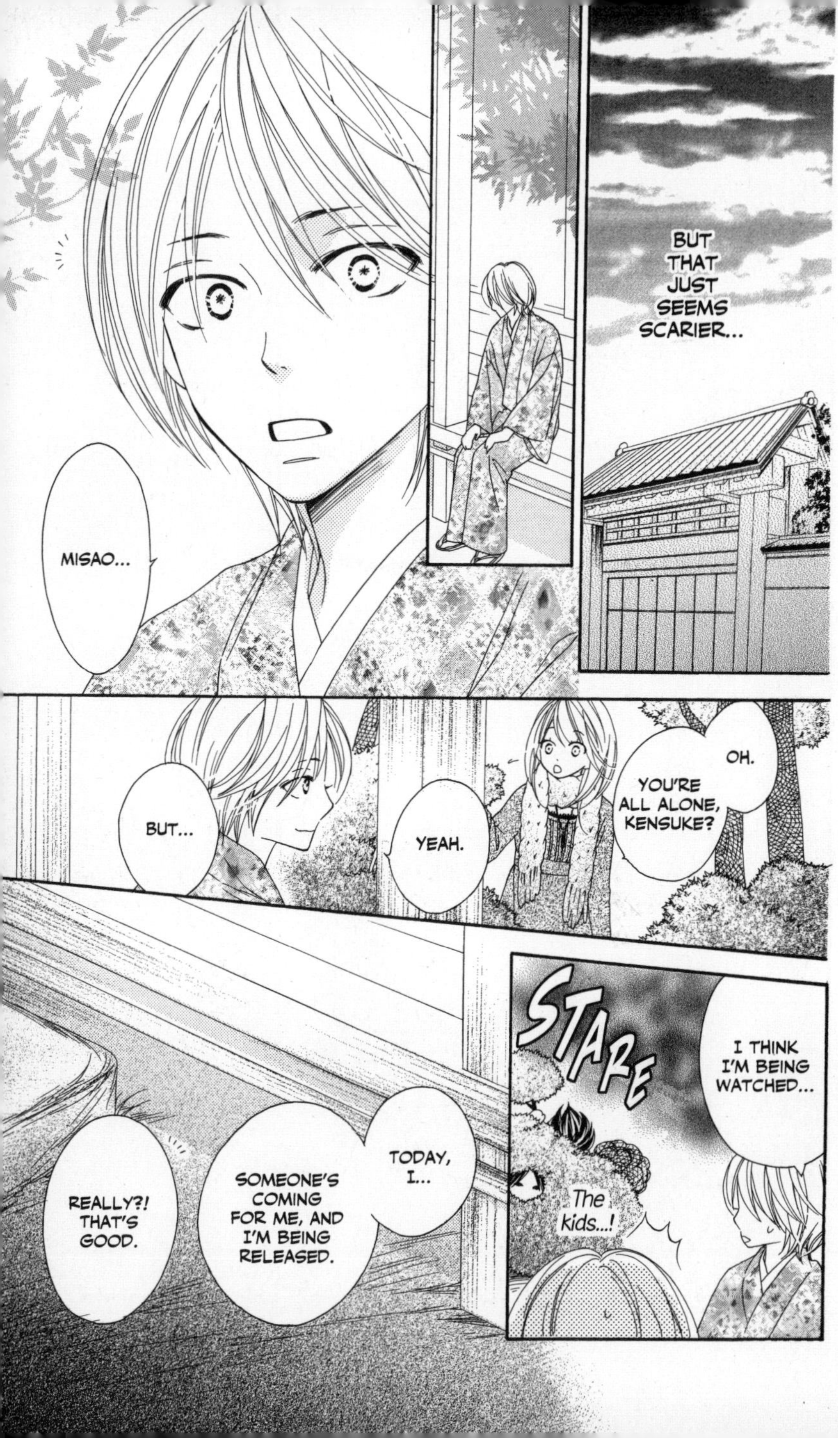
BUT THAT JUST SEEMS SCARIER...
MISAO...
OH.
YOU'RE ALL ALONE, KENSUKE?
YEAH.
BUT...
STARE
I THINK I'M BEING WATCHED...
The kids...!
TODAY, I...
SOMEONE'S COMING FOR ME, AND I'M BEING RELEASED.
REALLY?! THAT'S GOOD.

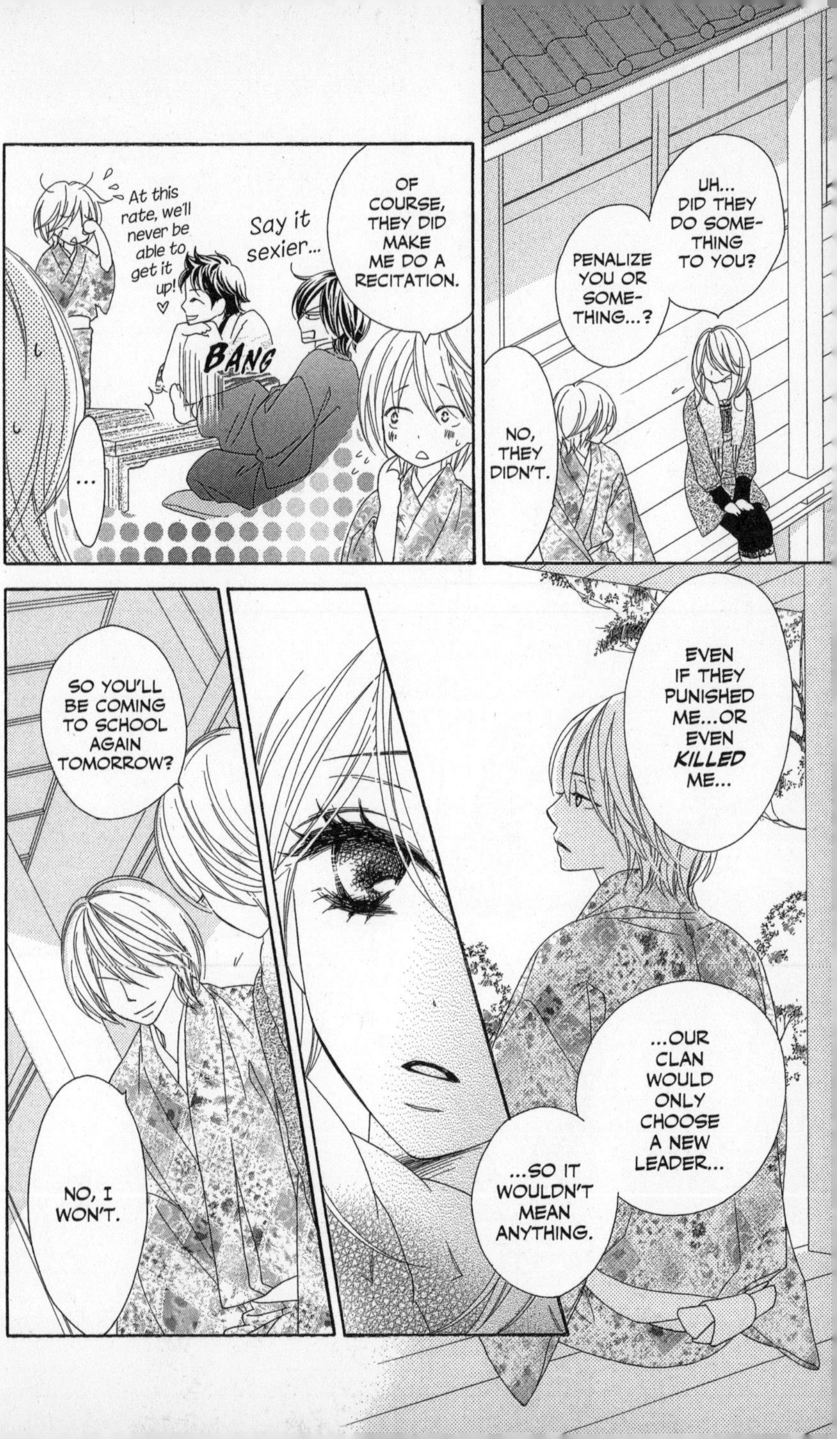
UH... DID THEY DO SOMETHING TO YOU?
PENALIZE YOU OR SOMETHING...?
NO, THEY DIDN'T.
OF COURSE, THEY DID MAKE ME DO A RECITATION.
Say it sexier...
At this rate, we'll never be able to get it up! ♥
BANG
...
EVEN IF THEY PUNISHED ME...OR EVEN KILLED ME...
...OUR CLAN WOULD ONLY CHOOSE A NEW LEADER...
...SO IT WOULDN'T MEAN ANYTHING.
SO YOU'LL BE COMING TO SCHOOL AGAIN TOMORROW?
NO, I WON'T.

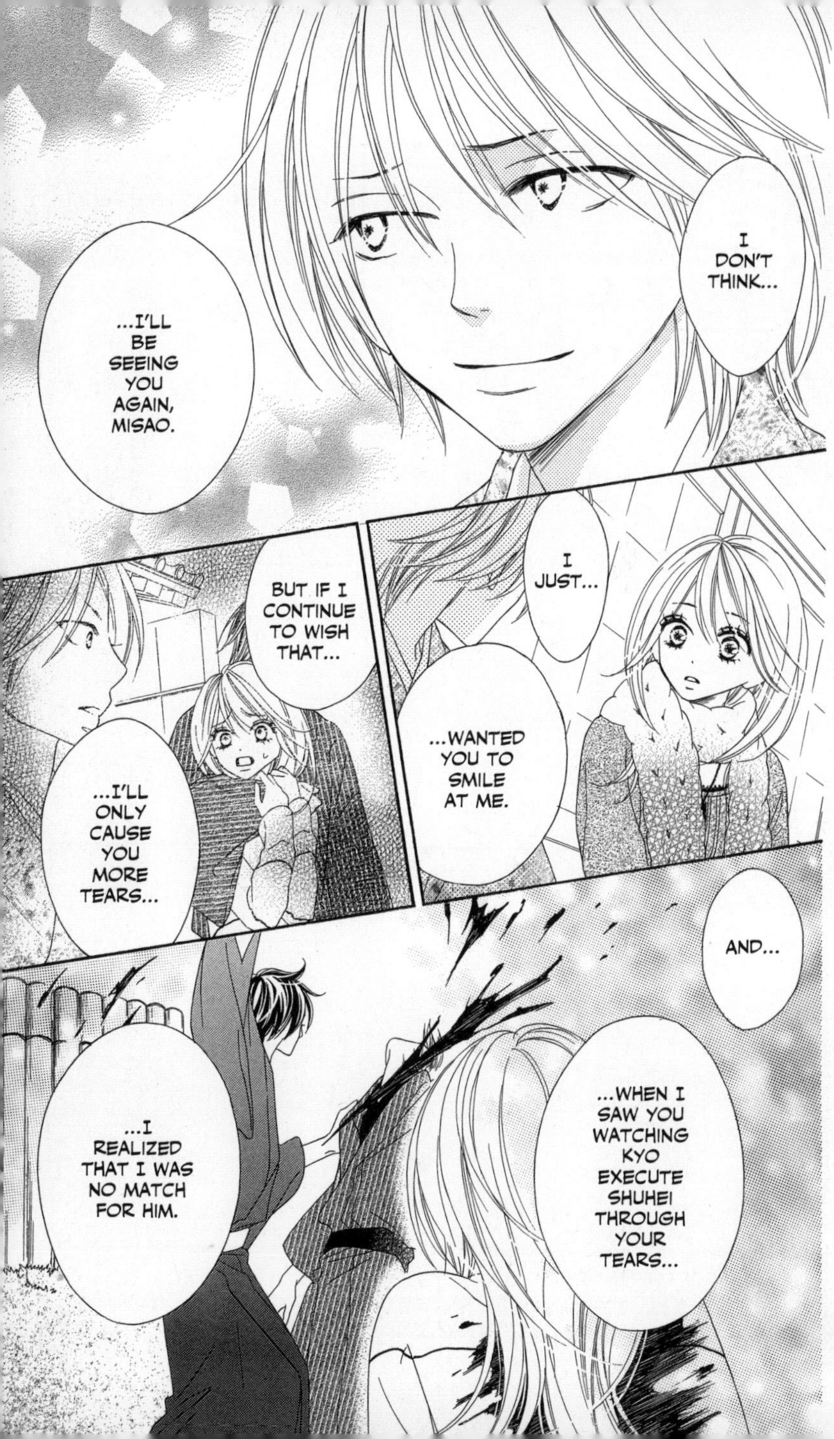
I DON'T THINK...
...I'LL BE SEEING YOU AGAIN, MISAO.
I JUST...
...WANTED YOU TO SMILE AT ME.
BUT IF I CONTINUE TO WISH THAT...
...I'LL ONLY CAUSE YOU MORE TEARS...
AND...
...WHEN I SAW YOU WATCHING KYO EXECUTE SHUHEI THROUGH YOUR TEARS...
...I REALIZED THAT I WAS NO MATCH FOR HIM.

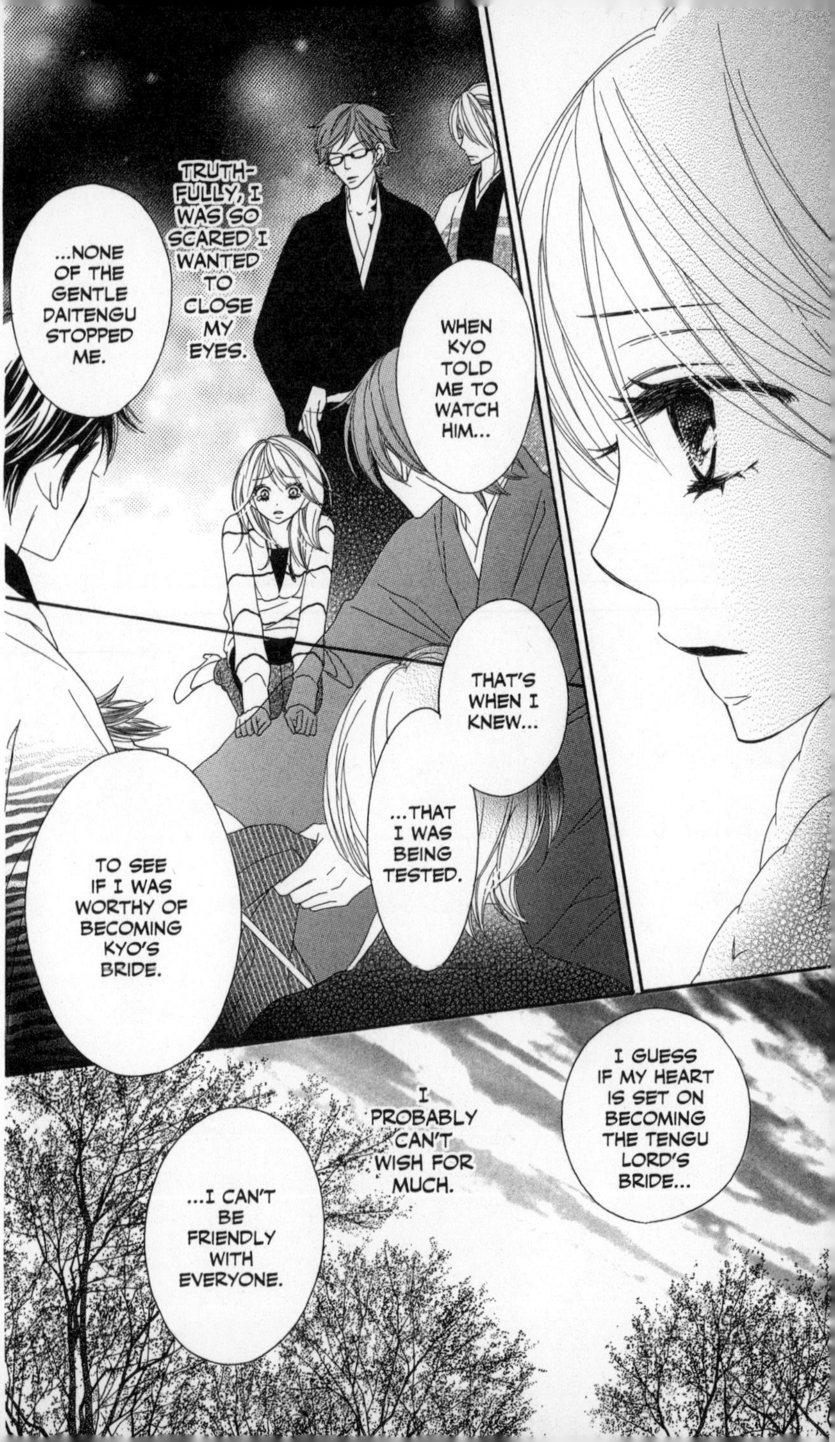
WHEN KYO TOLD ME TO WATCH HIM...
TRUTH-FULLY, I WAS SO SCARED I WANTED TO CLOSE MY EYES.
...NONE OF THE GENTLE DAITENGU STOPPED ME.
THAT'S WHEN I KNEW...
...THAT I WAS BEING TESTED.
TO SEE IF I WAS WORTHY OF BECOMING KYO'S BRIDE.
I GUESS IF MY HEART IS SET ON BECOMING THE TENGU LORD'S BRIDE...
I PROBABLY CAN'T WISH FOR MUCH.
...I CAN'T BE FRIENDLY WITH EVERYONE.

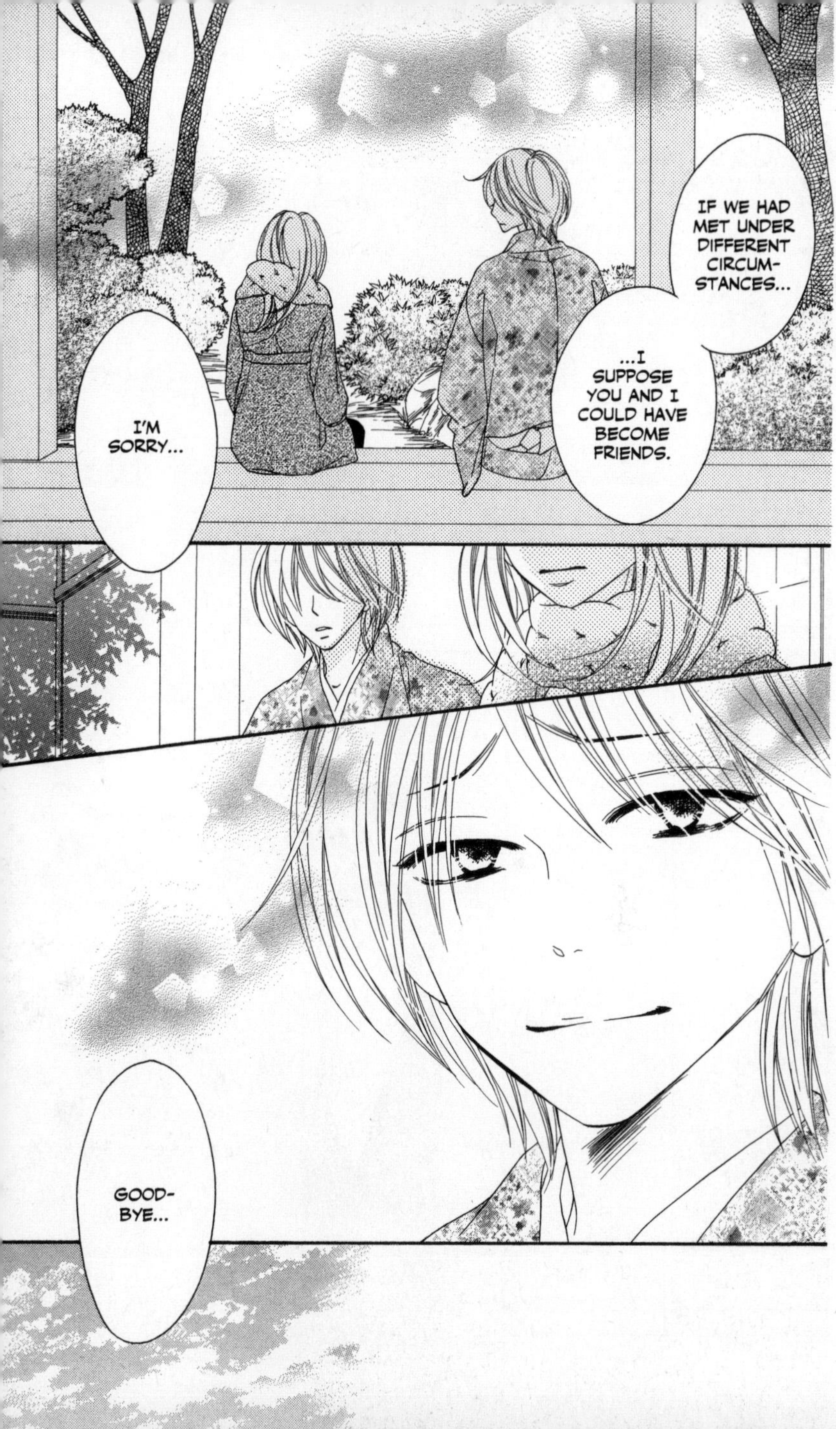
IF WE HAD MET UNDER DIFFERENT CIRCUM-STANCES...
...I SUPPOSE YOU AND I COULD HAVE BECOME FRIENDS.
I'M SORRY...
GOOD-BYE...

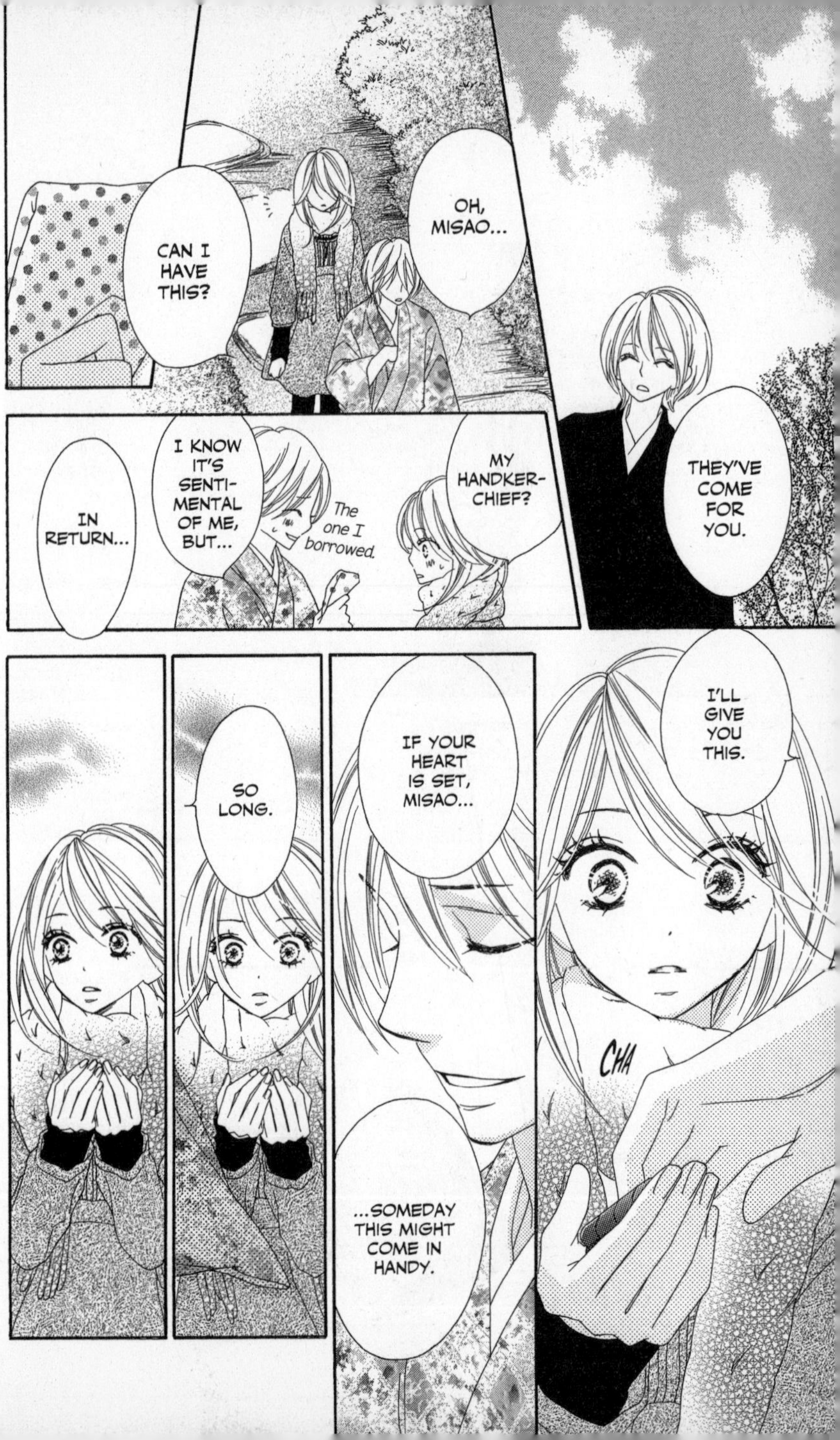
THEY'VE COME FOR YOU.
OH, MISAO...
CAN I HAVE THIS?
MY HANDKER-CHIEF?
The one I borrowed.
I KNOW IT'S SENTI-MENTAL OF ME, BUT...
IN RETURN...
I'LL GIVE YOU THIS.
CHA
IF YOUR HEART IS SET, MISAO...
...SOMEDAY THIS MIGHT COME IN HANDY.
SO LONG.

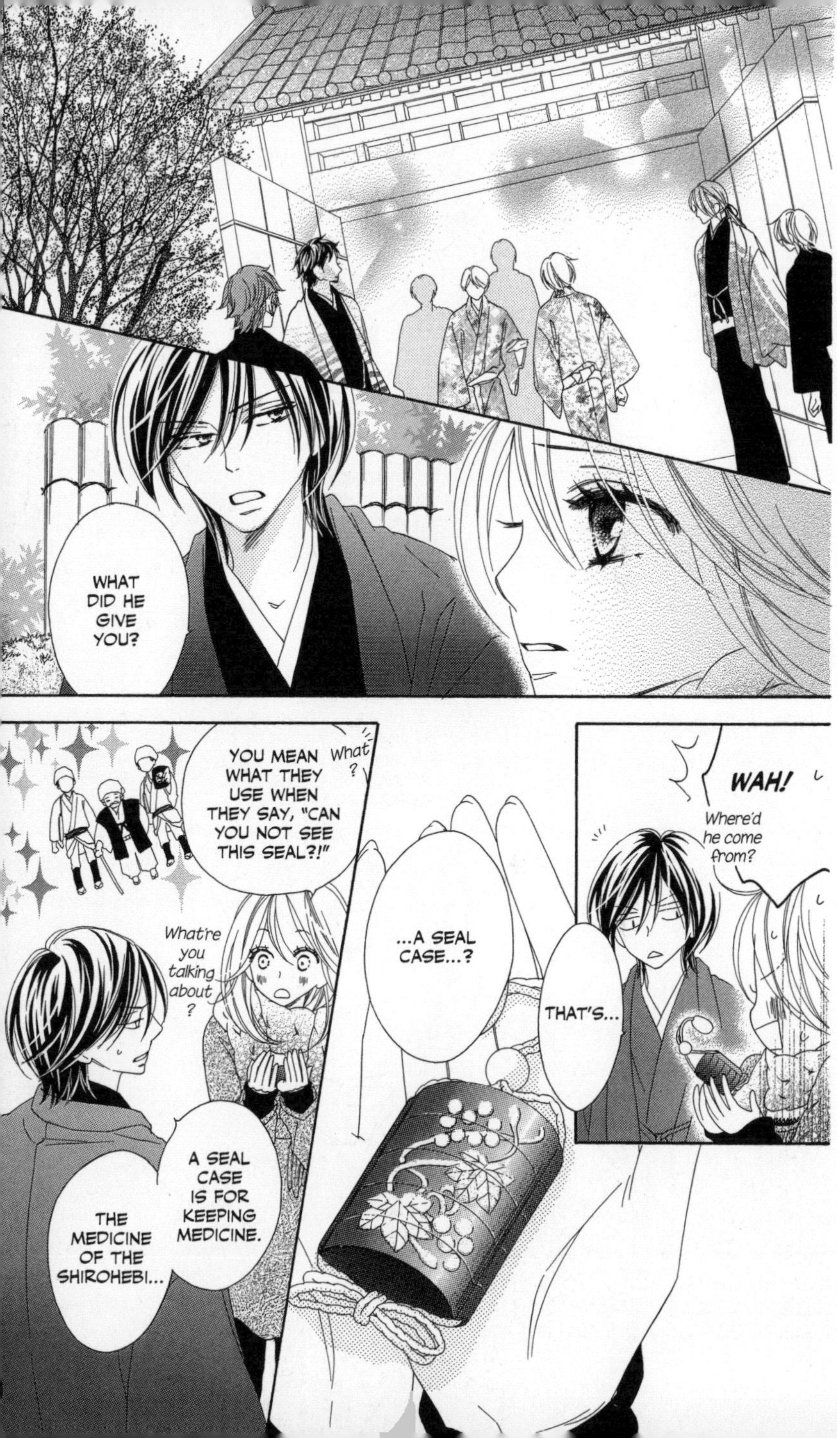

WHAT DID HE GIVE YOU?
WAH!
Where'd he come from?
THAT'S...
...A SEAL CASE...?
YOU MEAN WHAT THEY USE WHEN THEY SAY, "CAN YOU NOT SEE THIS SEAL?!"
What?
What're you talking about?
A SEAL CASE IS FOR KEEPING MEDICINE.
THE MEDICINE OF THE SHIROHEBI...

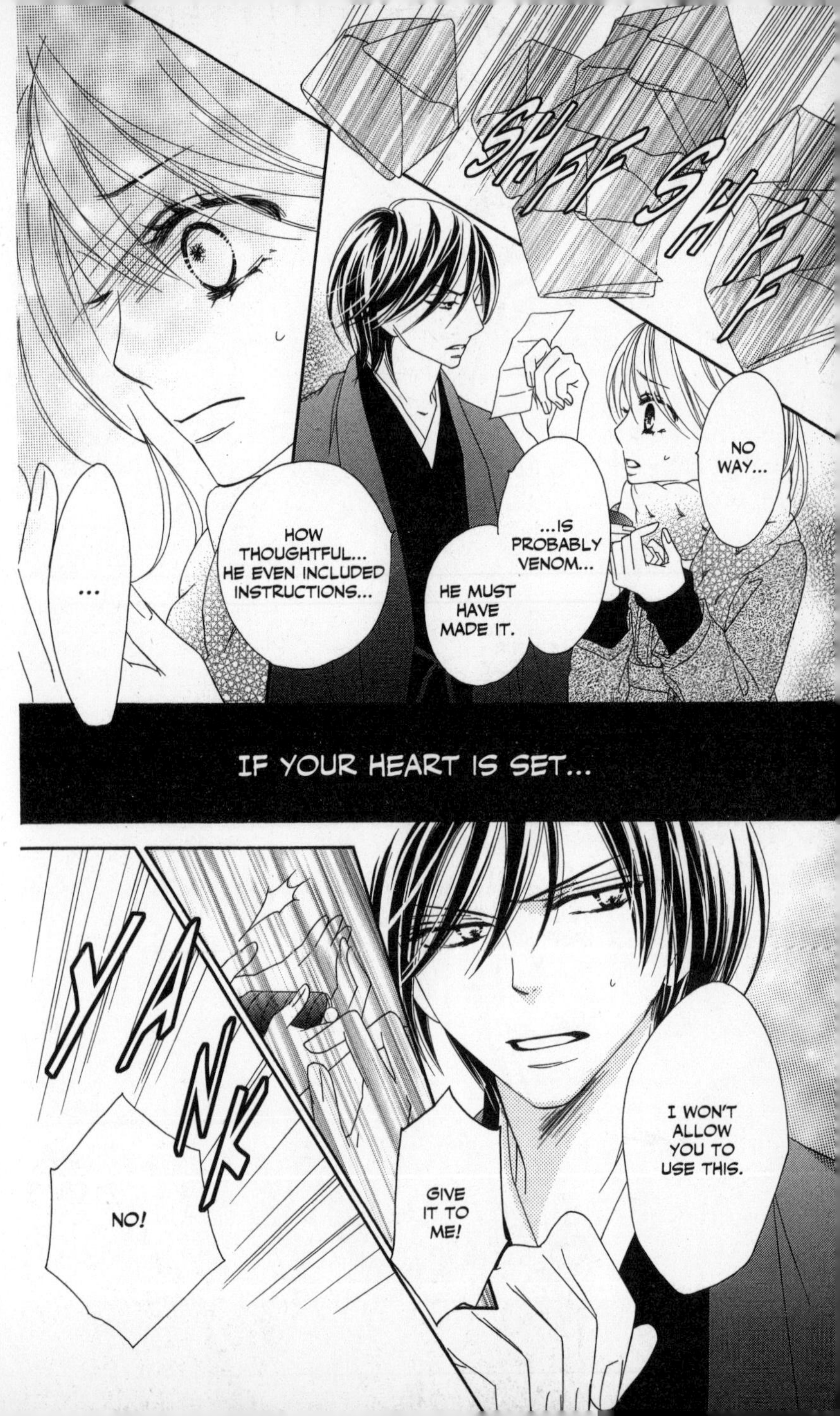
SHFF SHFF
NO WAY...
...IS PROBABLY VENOM...
HE MUST HAVE MADE IT.
HOW THOUGHTFUL... HE EVEN INCLUDED INSTRUCTIONS...
...
IF YOUR HEART IS SET...
I WON'T ALLOW YOU TO USE THIS.
GIVE IT TO ME!
YANK
NO!

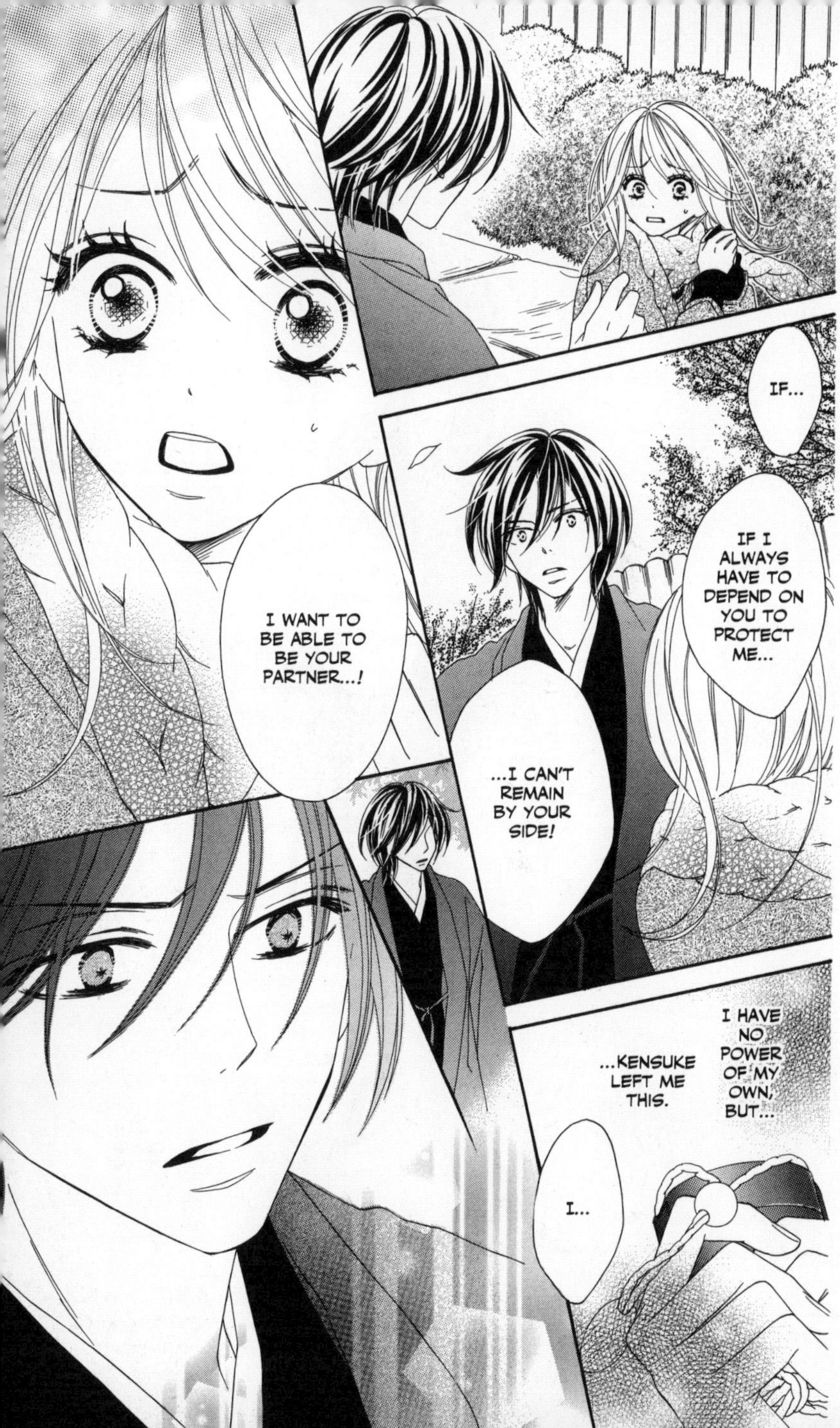
IF...
IF I ALWAYS HAVE TO DEPEND ON YOU TO PROTECT ME...
...I CAN'T REMAIN BY YOUR SIDE!
I WANT TO BE ABLE TO BE YOUR PARTNER...!
I HAVE NO POWER OF MY OWN, BUT...
...KENSUKE LEFT ME THIS.
I...

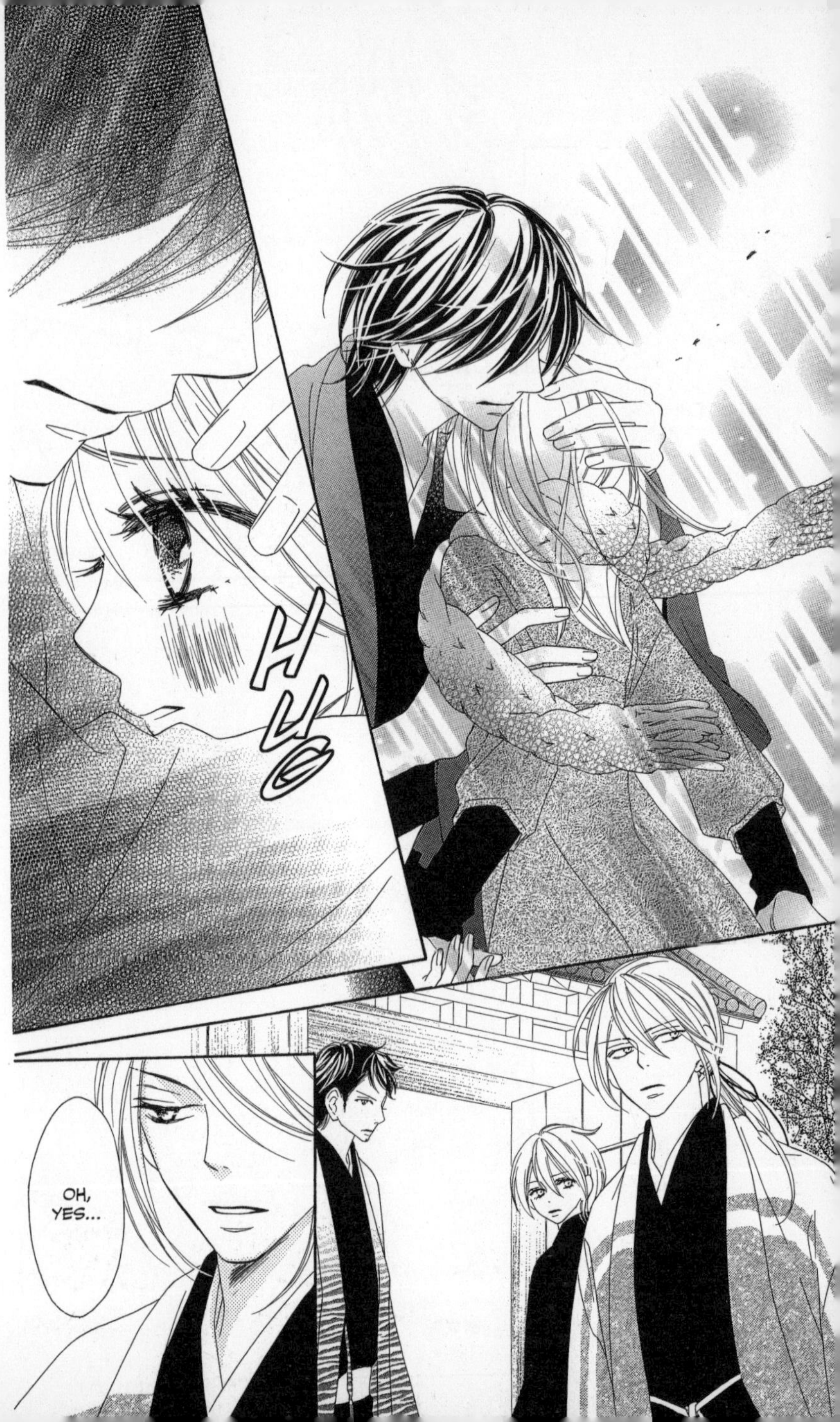
HUG
OH, YES...

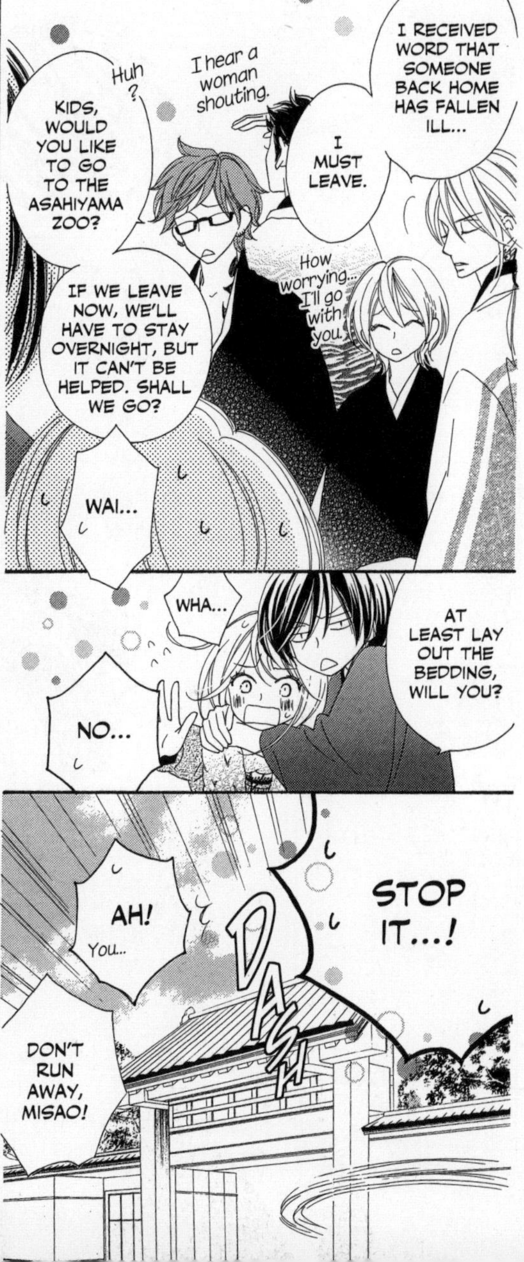
I RECEIVED WORD THAT SOMEONE BACK HOME HAS FALLEN ILL...
I MUST LEAVE.
I hear a woman shouting.
How worrying... I'll go with you.
Huh?
KIDS, WOULD YOU LIKE TO GO TO THE ASAHIYAMA ZOO?
IF WE LEAVE NOW, WE'LL HAVE TO STAY OVERNIGHT, BUT IT CAN'T BE HELPED. SHALL WE GO?
WAI...
AT LEAST LAY OUT THE BEDDING, WILL YOU?
WHA...
NO...
STOP IT...!
DASH
AH!
You...
DON'T RUN AWAY, MISAO!

Hello. It's me, Sakurakouji.

My heart is full of gratitude to all of you who have picked up volume 4 of *Black Bird!*

This is already the fourth volume... That was quick.

I sometimes receive letters asking, "Why are the demons wearing traditional Japanese clothing?" There is just one answer. I, Kanoko Sakurakoji, love men in Japanese clothes!!

I love girls in them too, although Misao wears western clothing.

I'm so happy to be able to draw so many men in Japanese wear.♥ I'm going to continue to draw them, so I hope you continue to enjoy the story...

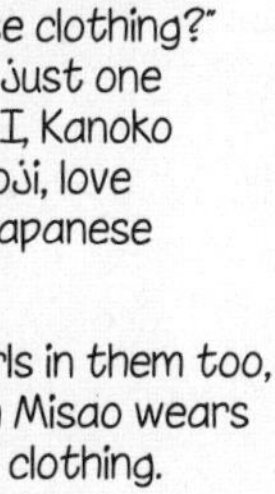

The hakama are nice too, but I love them in kimono with haori jackets.

Kyo wears a long haori jacket.

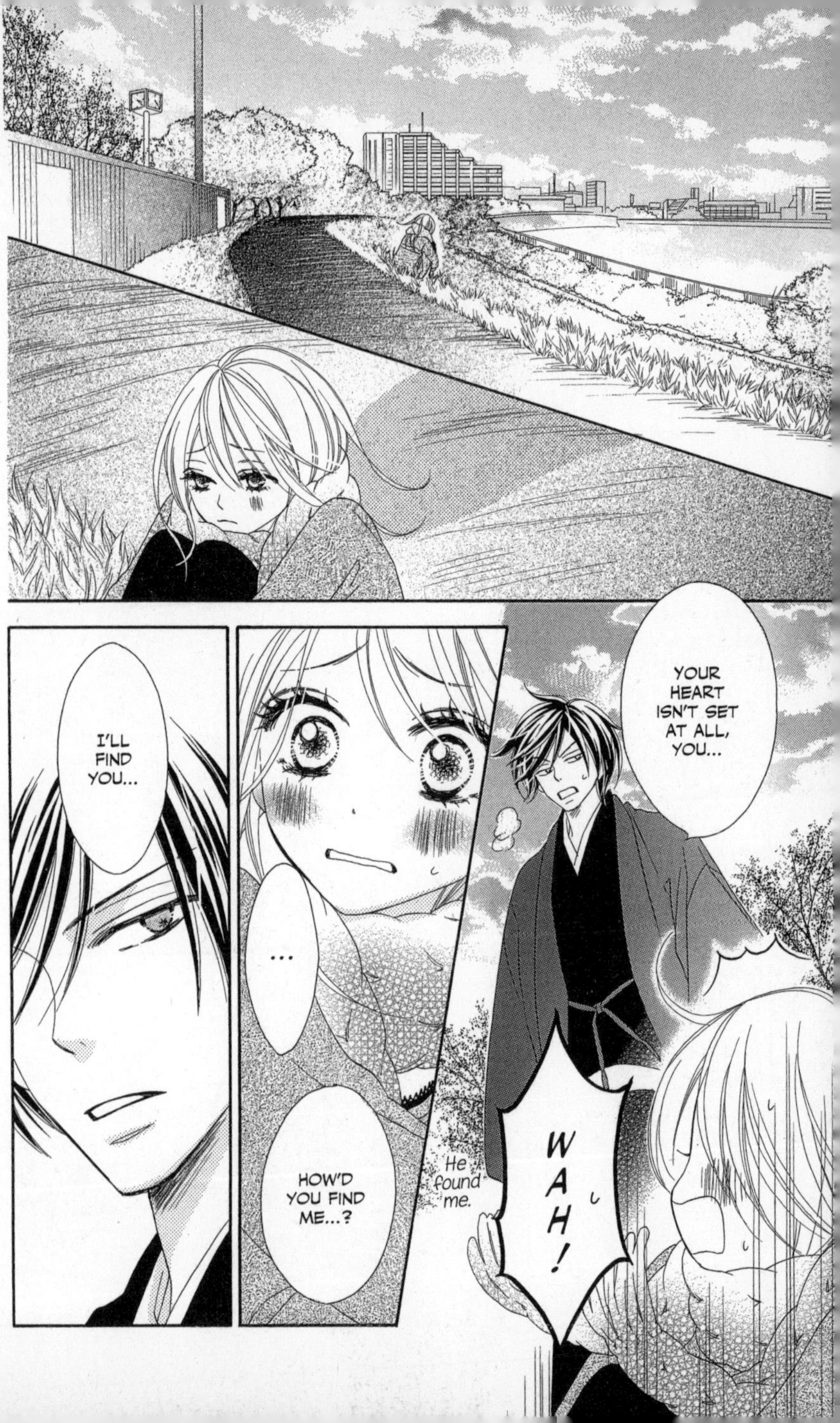
YOUR HEART ISN'T SET AT ALL, YOU...
WAH!
He found me.
...
HOW'D YOU FIND ME...?
I'LL FIND YOU...

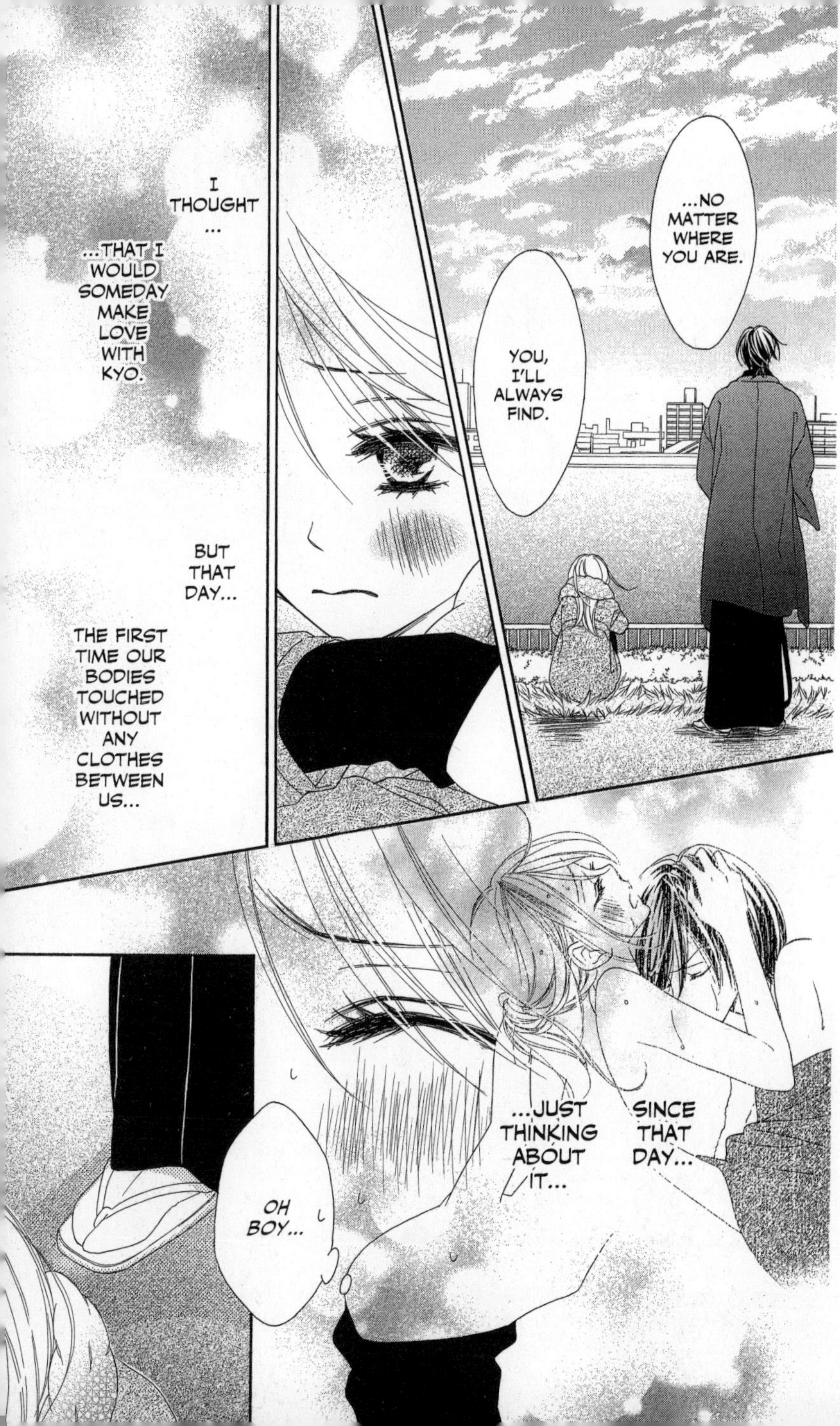
...NO MATTER WHERE YOU ARE.
YOU, I'LL ALWAYS FIND.
I THOUGHT...
...THAT I WOULD SOMEDAY MAKE LOVE WITH KYO.
BUT THAT DAY...
THE FIRST TIME OUR BODIES TOUCHED WITHOUT ANY CLOTHES BETWEEN US...
SINCE THAT DAY...
...JUST THINKING ABOUT IT...
OH BOY...

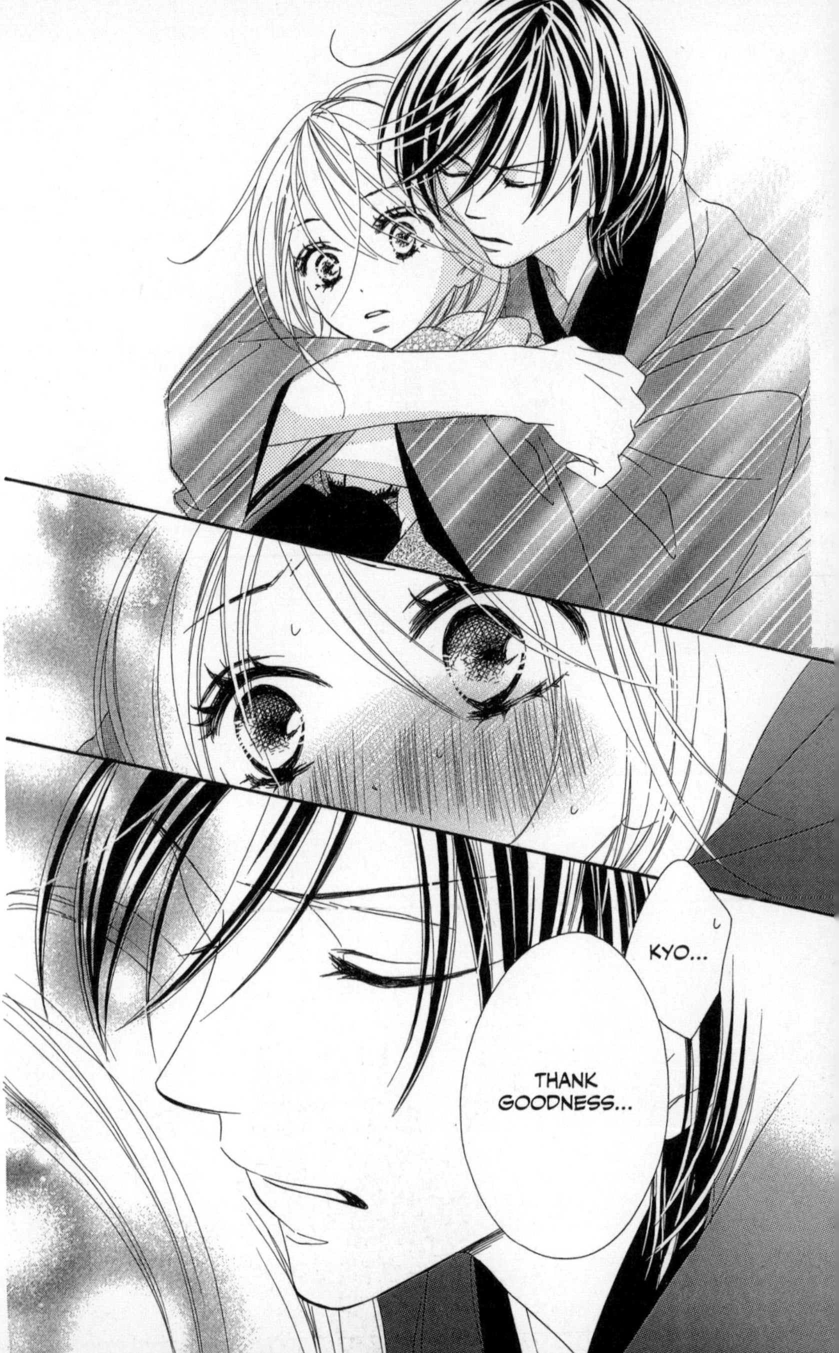
KYO...
THANK GOODNESS...

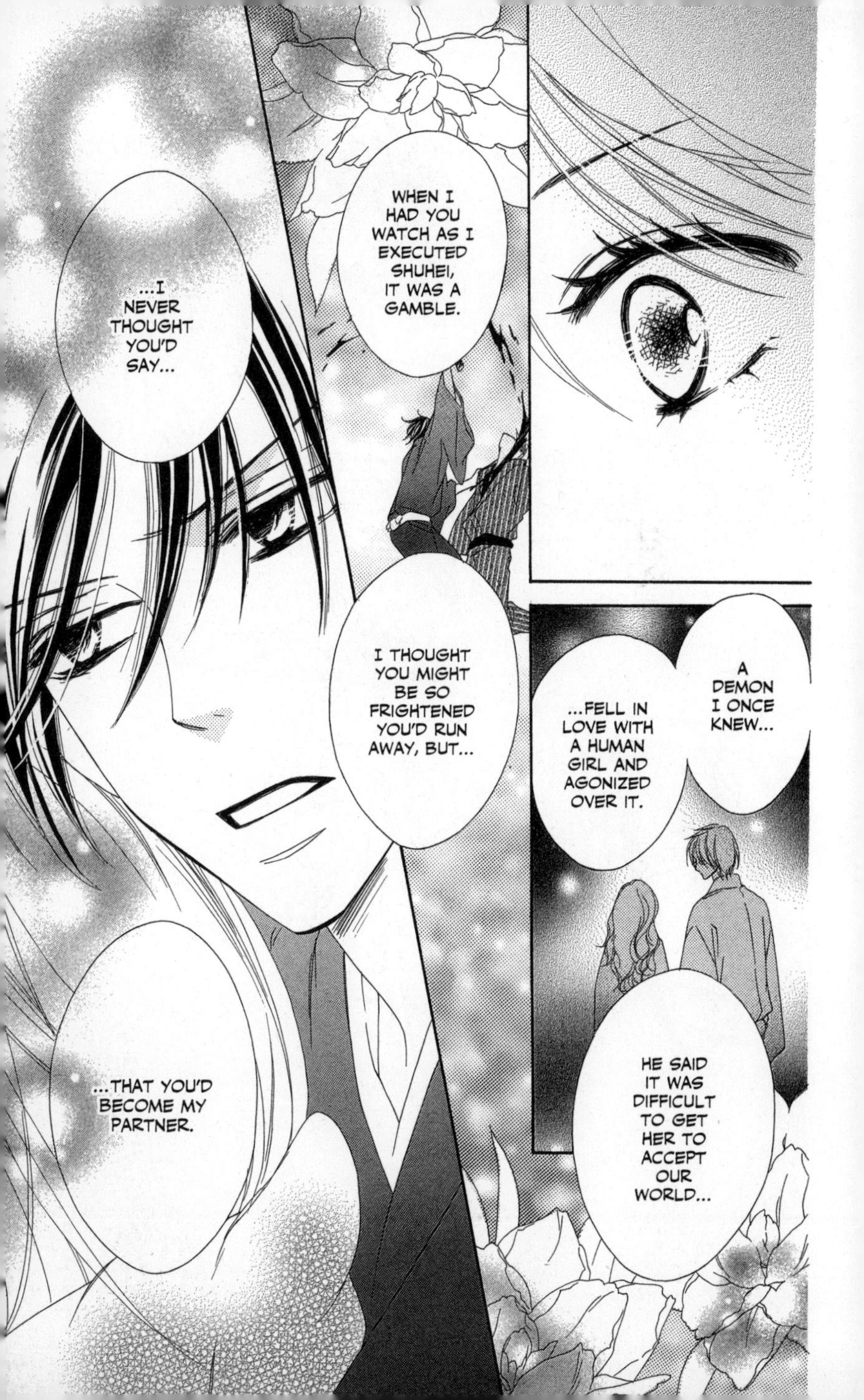
A DEMON I ONCE KNEW...
...FELL IN LOVE WITH A HUMAN GIRL AND AGONIZED OVER IT.
HE SAID IT WAS DIFFICULT TO GET HER TO ACCEPT OUR WORLD...
WHEN I HAD YOU WATCH AS I EXECUTED SHUHEI, IT WAS A GAMBLE.
I THOUGHT YOU MIGHT BE SO FRIGHTENED YOU'D RUN AWAY, BUT...
...I NEVER THOUGHT YOU'D SAY...
...THAT YOU'D BECOME MY PARTNER.

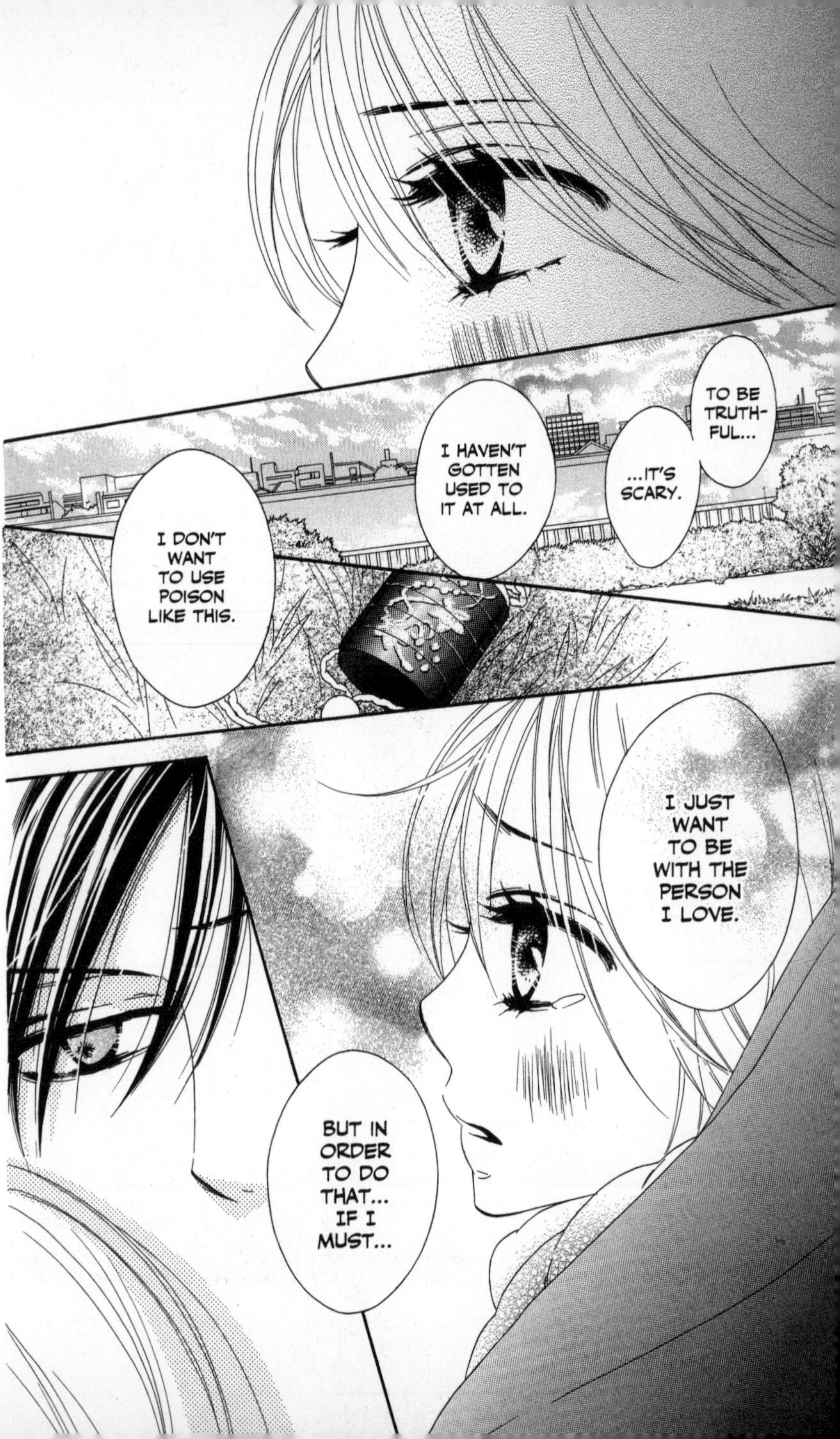
TO BE TRUTHFUL...
...IT'S SCARY.
I HAVEN'T GOTTEN USED TO IT AT ALL.
I DON'T WANT TO USE POISON LIKE THIS.
I JUST WANT TO BE WITH THE PERSON I LOVE.
BUT IN ORDER TO DO THAT... IF I MUST...

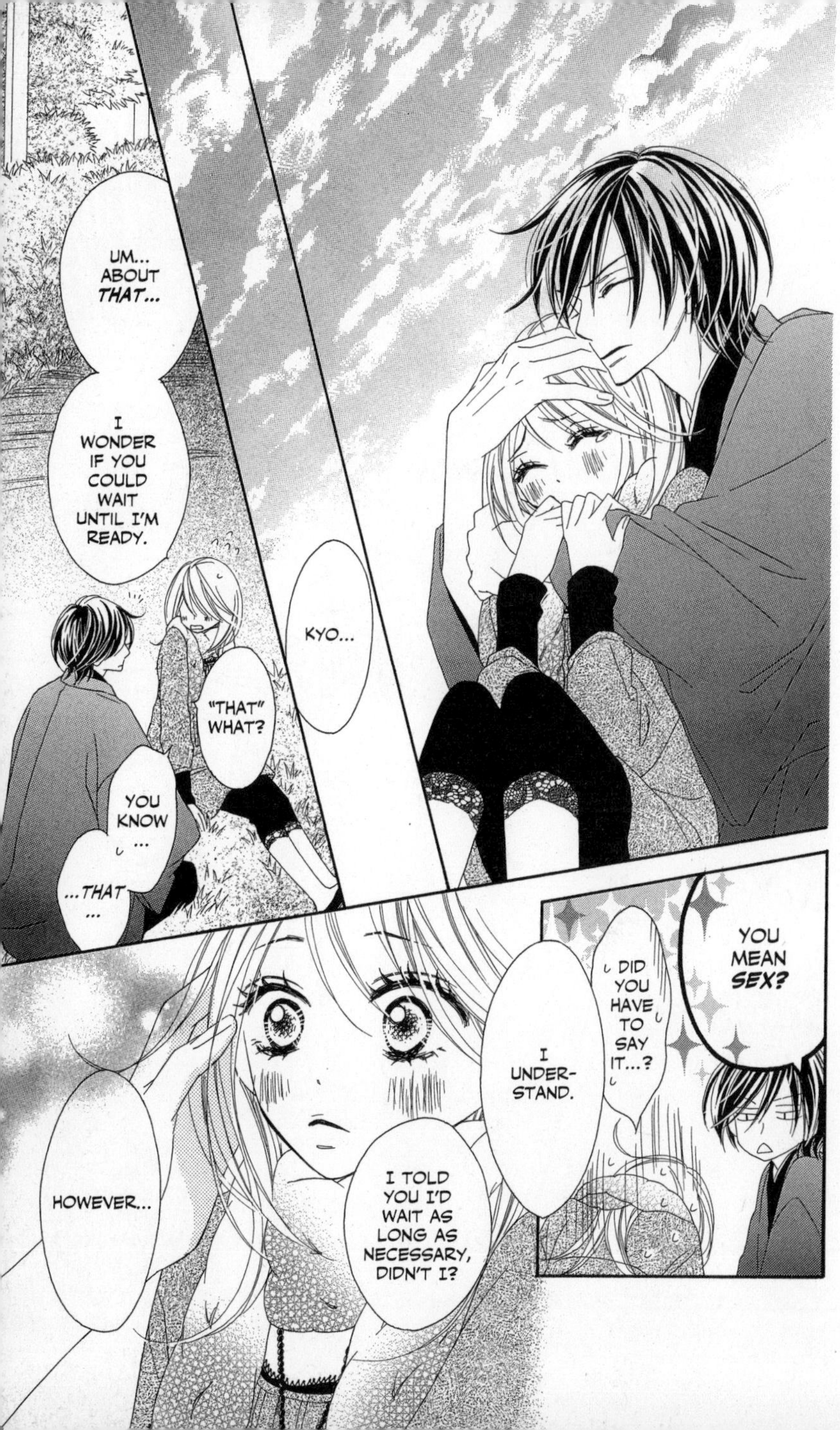
KYO...
UM... ABOUT *THAT*...
I WONDER IF YOU COULD WAIT UNTIL I'M READY.
"THAT" WHAT?
YOU KNOW ...
...*THAT* ...
YOU MEAN **SEX?**
DID YOU HAVE TO SAY IT...?
I UNDER-STAND.
I TOLD YOU I'D WAIT AS LONG AS NECESSARY, DIDN'T I?
HOWEVER...

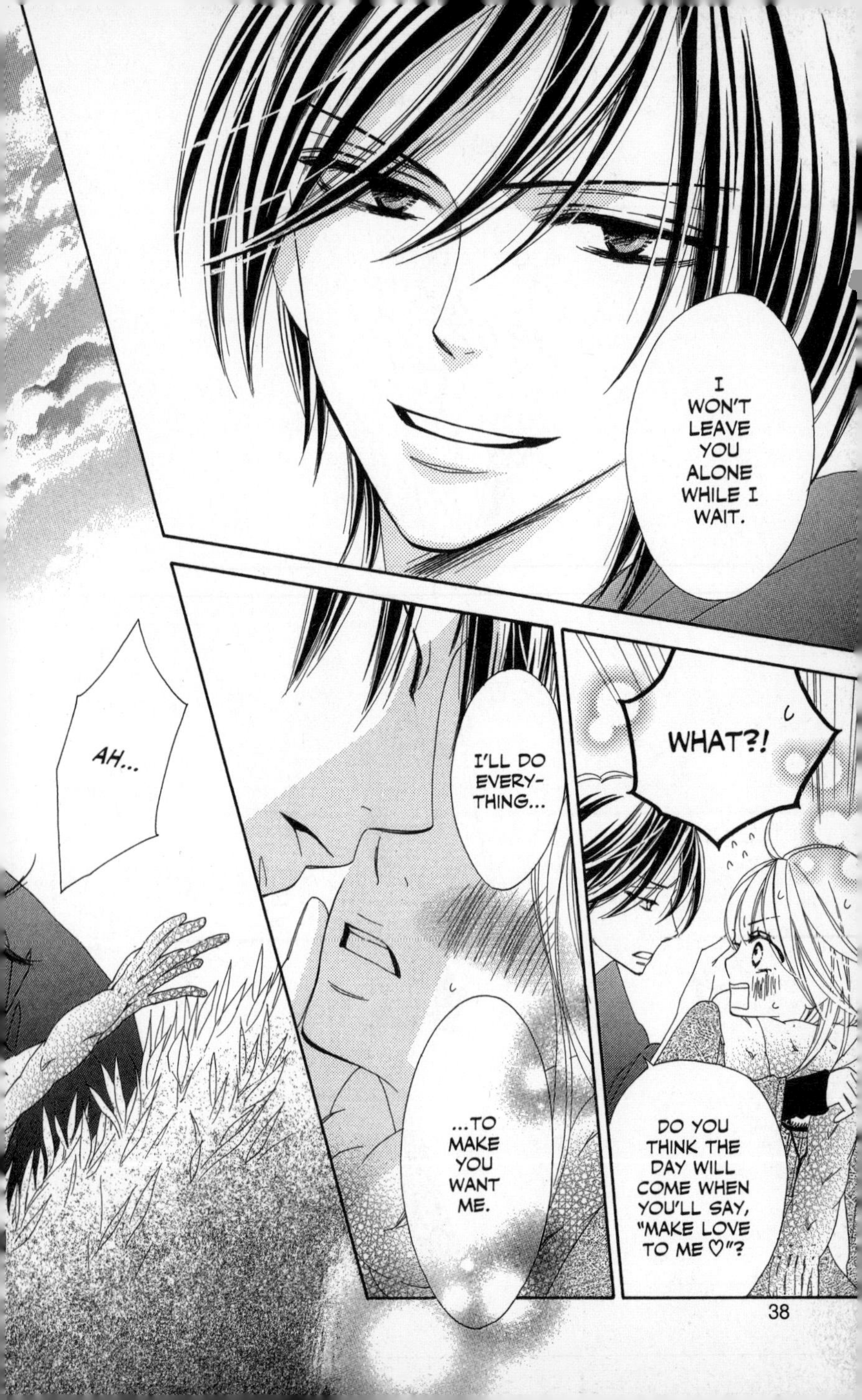
I WON'T LEAVE YOU ALONE WHILE I WAIT.
WHAT?!
DO YOU THINK THE DAY WILL COME WHEN YOU'LL SAY, "MAKE LOVE TO ME ♡"?
I'LL DO EVERYTHING...
...TO MAKE YOU WANT ME.
AH...

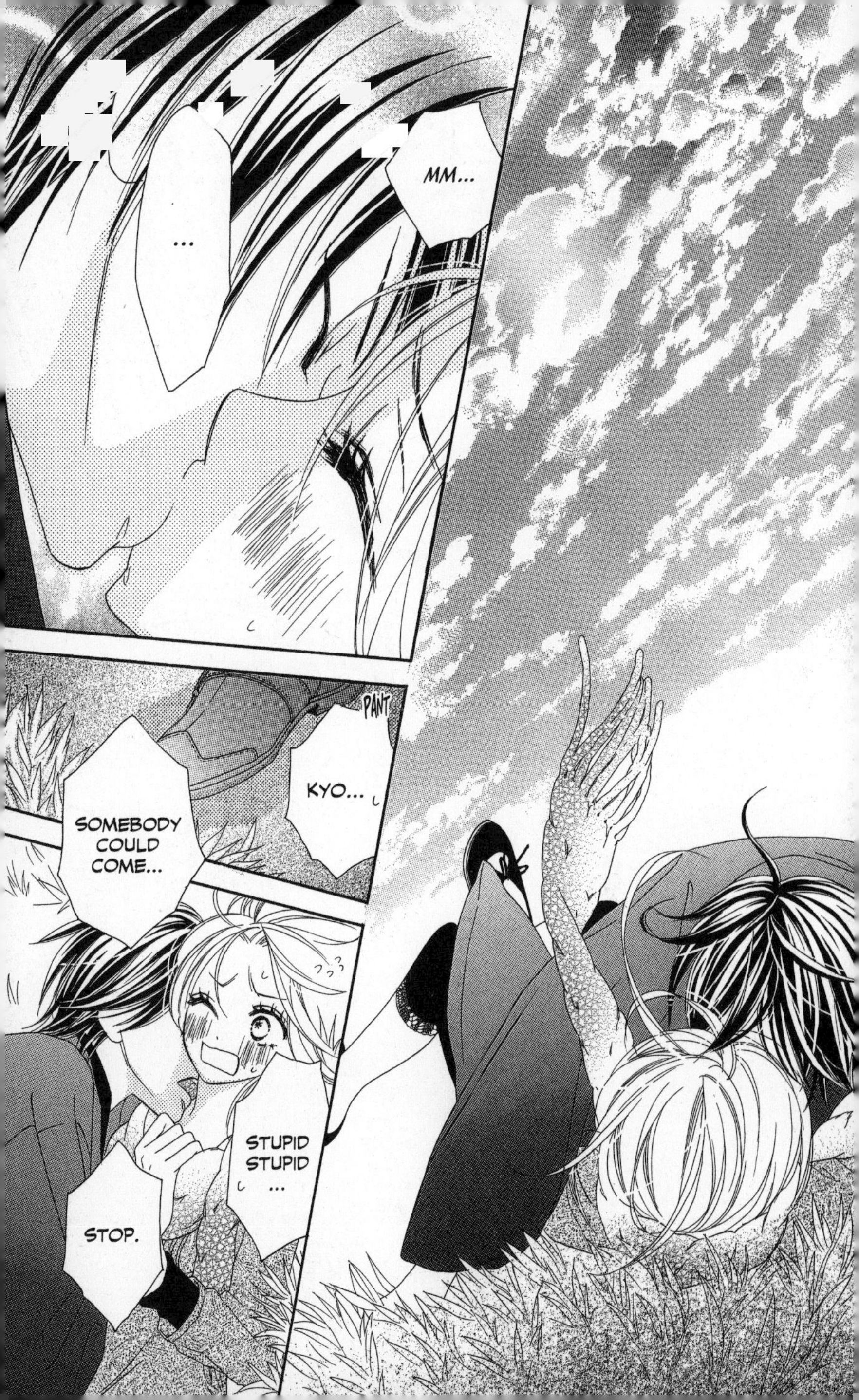
MM...
...
PANT
KYO...
SOMEBODY COULD COME...
STUPID STUPID ...
STOP.

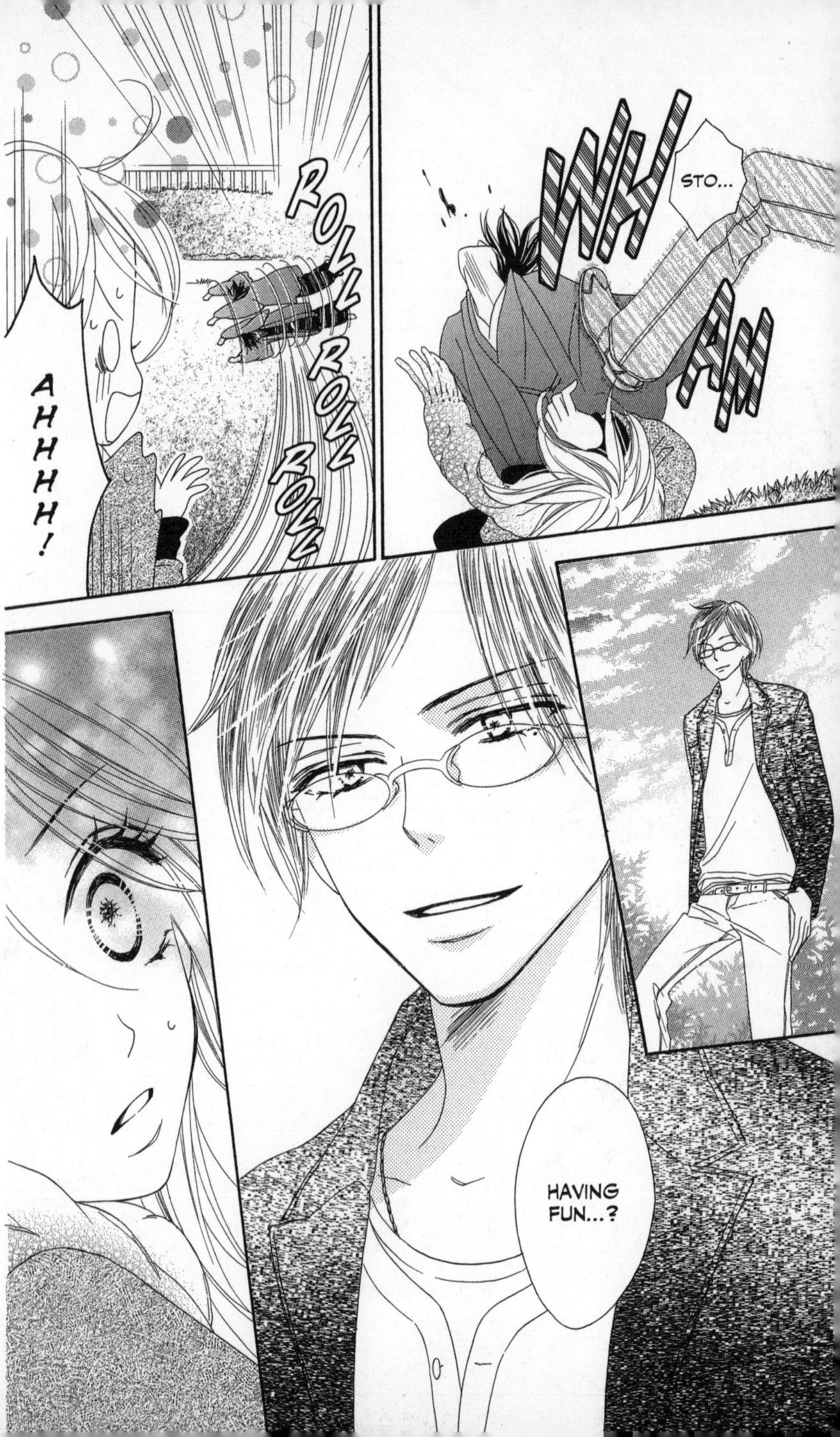
STO...
WHAM
ROLL ROLL ROLL
AHHHHH!
HAVING FUN...?

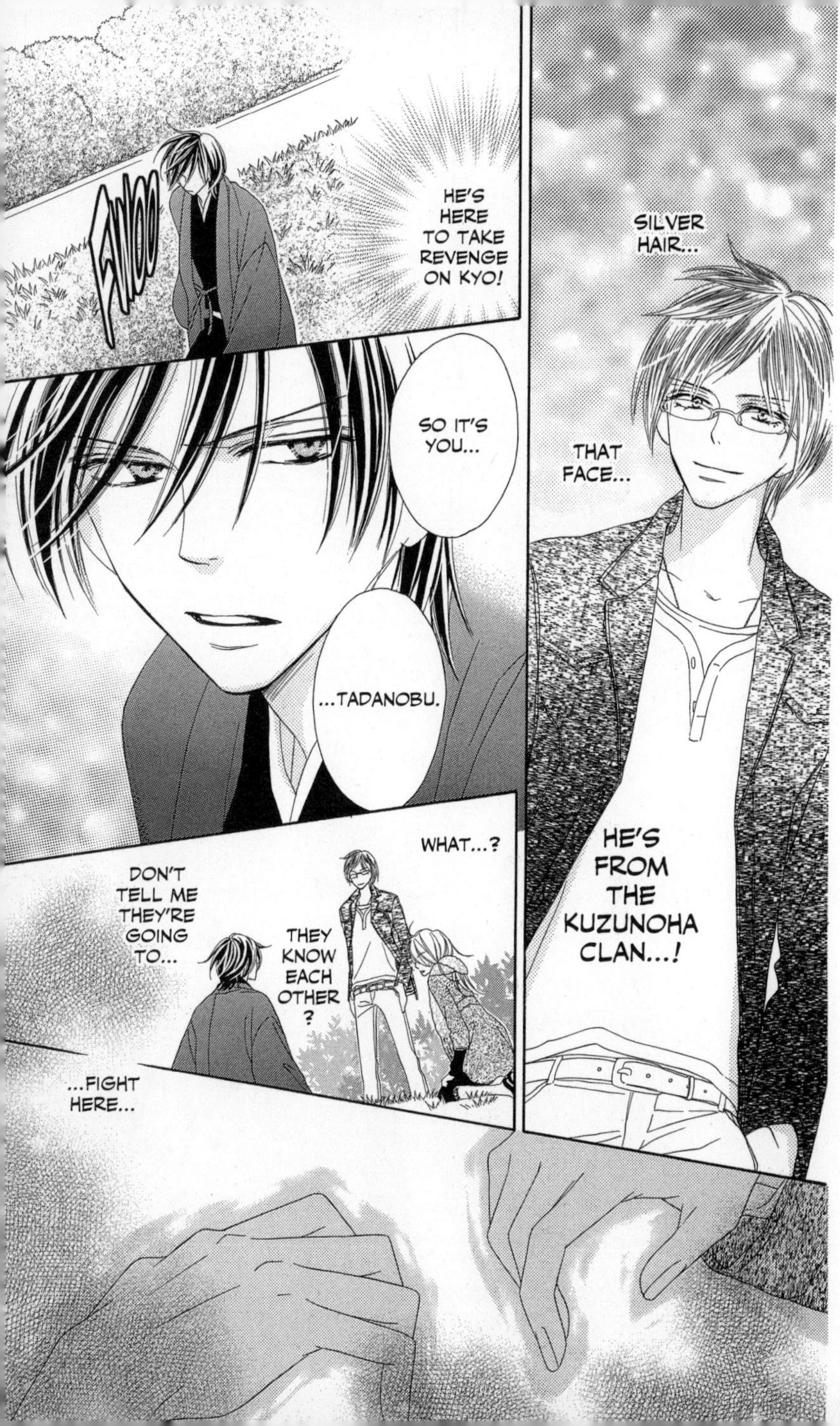
SILVER HAIR...
THAT FACE...
HE'S FROM THE KUZUNOHA CLAN...!
SWOO
HE'S HERE TO TAKE REVENGE ON KYO!
SO IT'S YOU...
...TADANOBU.
WHAT...?
THEY KNOW EACH OTHER?
DON'T TELL ME THEY'RE GOING TO...
...FIGHT HERE...

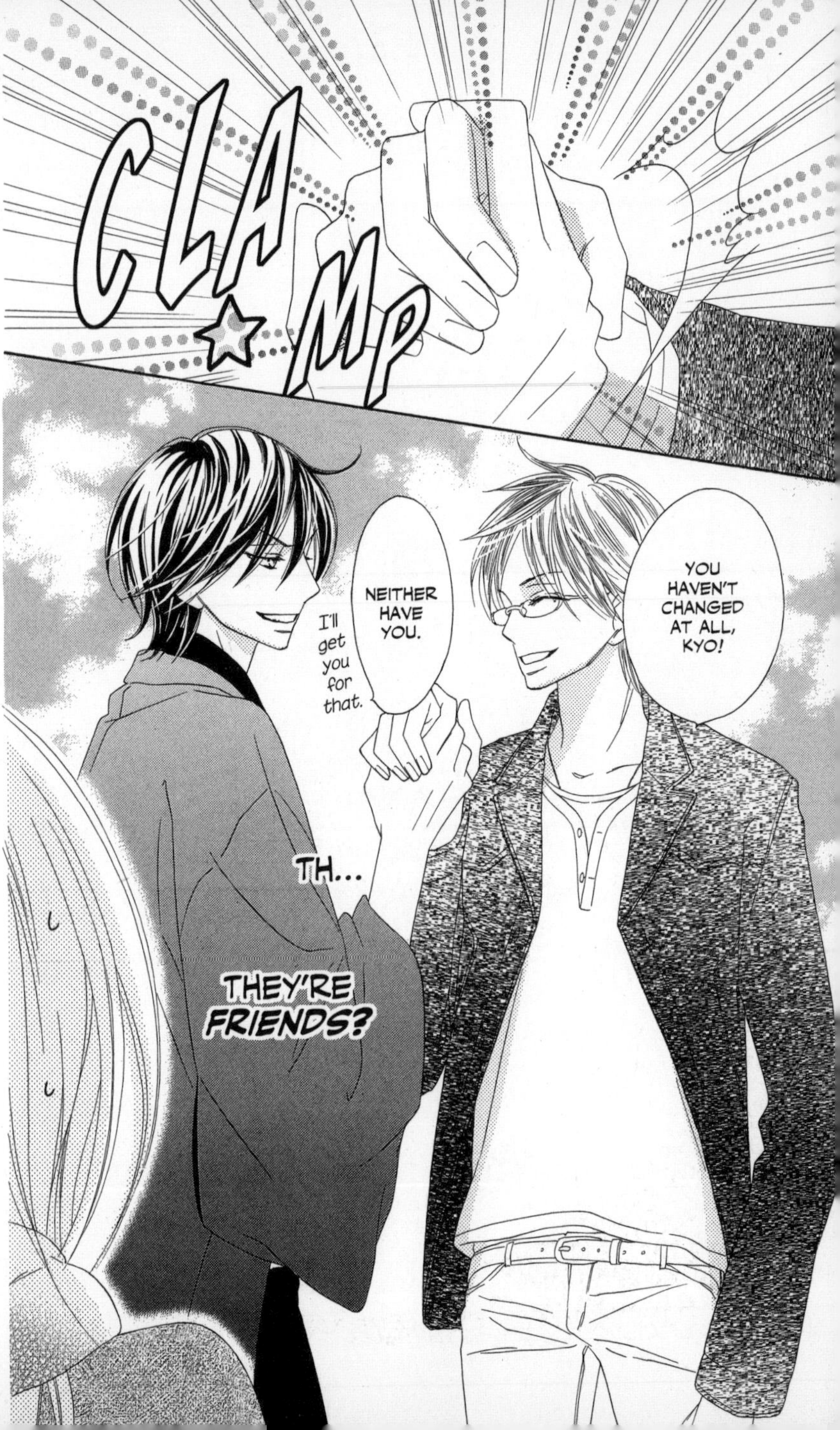
CLAMP
YOU HAVEN'T CHANGED AT ALL, KYO!
NEITHER HAVE YOU.
I'll get you for that.
TH...
THEY'RE FRIENDS?

Illustration Request Number Four

"The triplets should say this."

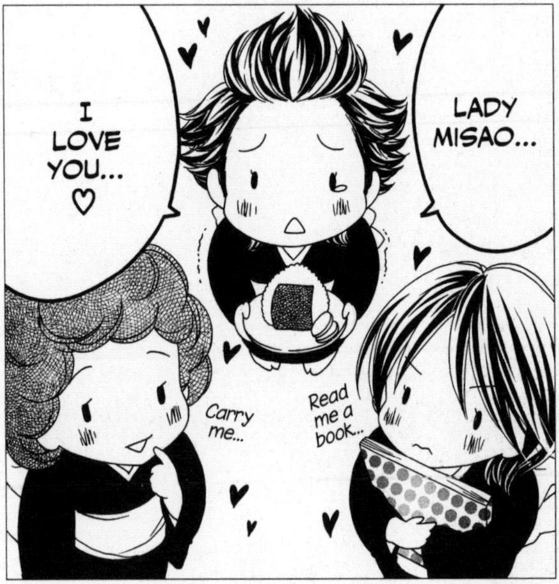
LADY MISAO...
I LOVE YOU... ♡
Read me a book...
Carry me...

The triplets comfort me.

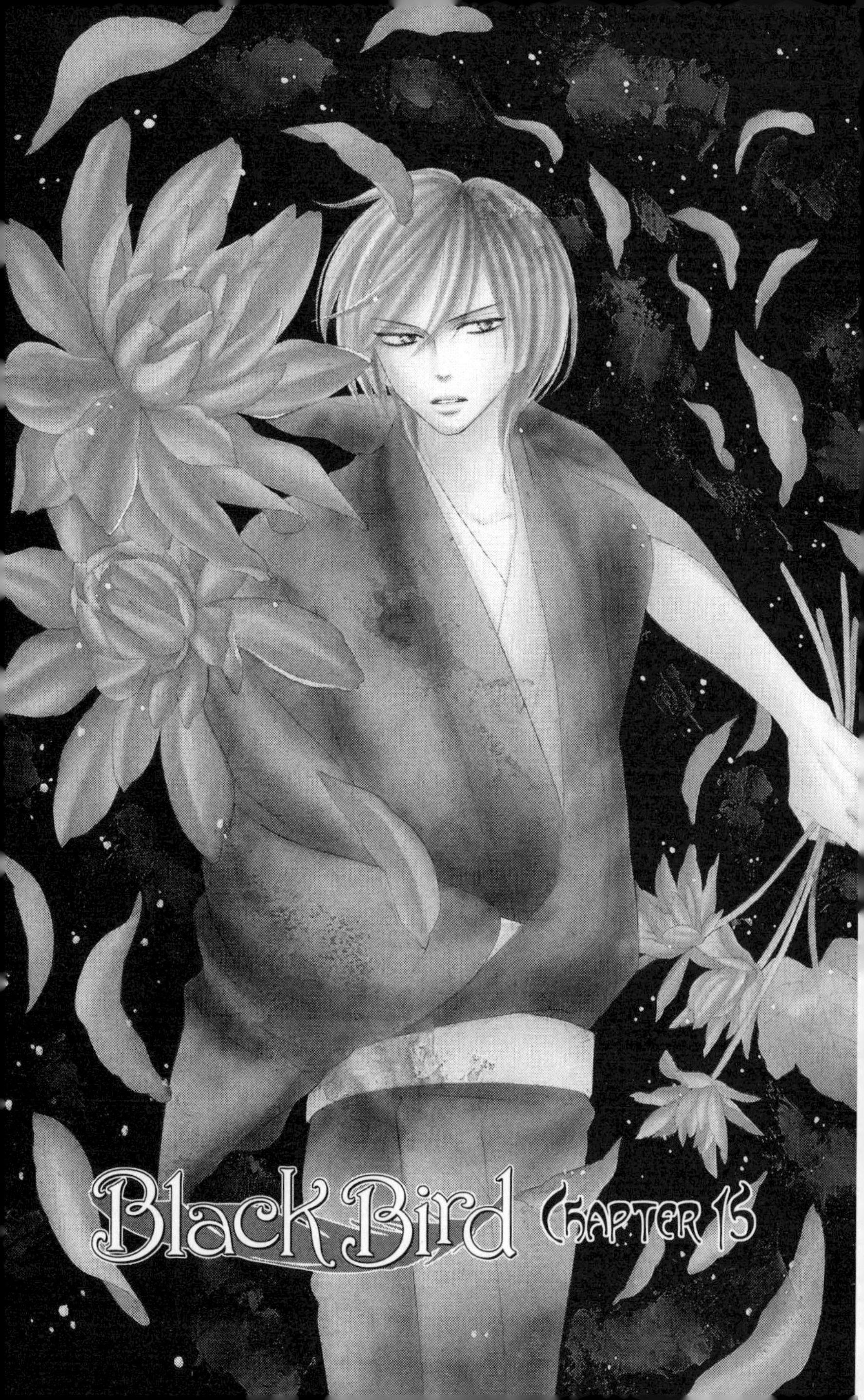
Black Bird
Chapter 15

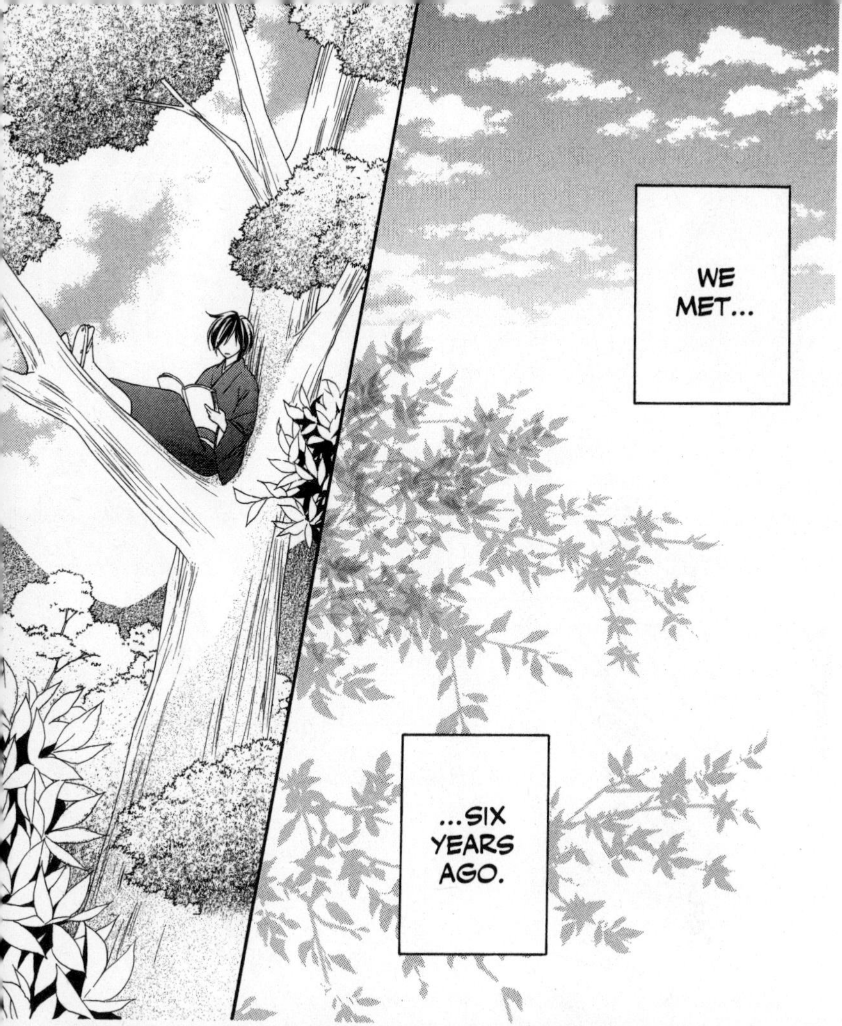
WE MET...
...SIX YEARS AGO.

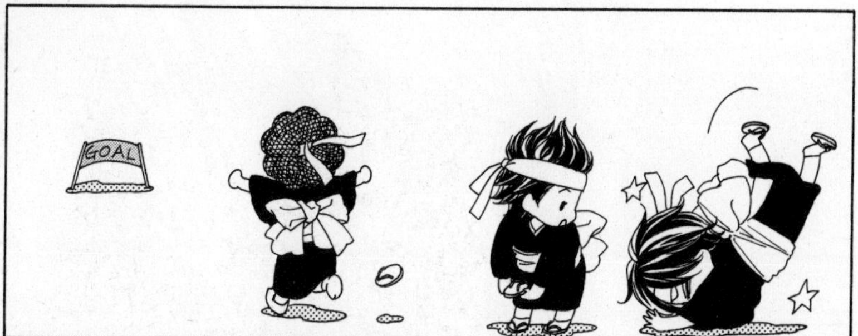
GOAL

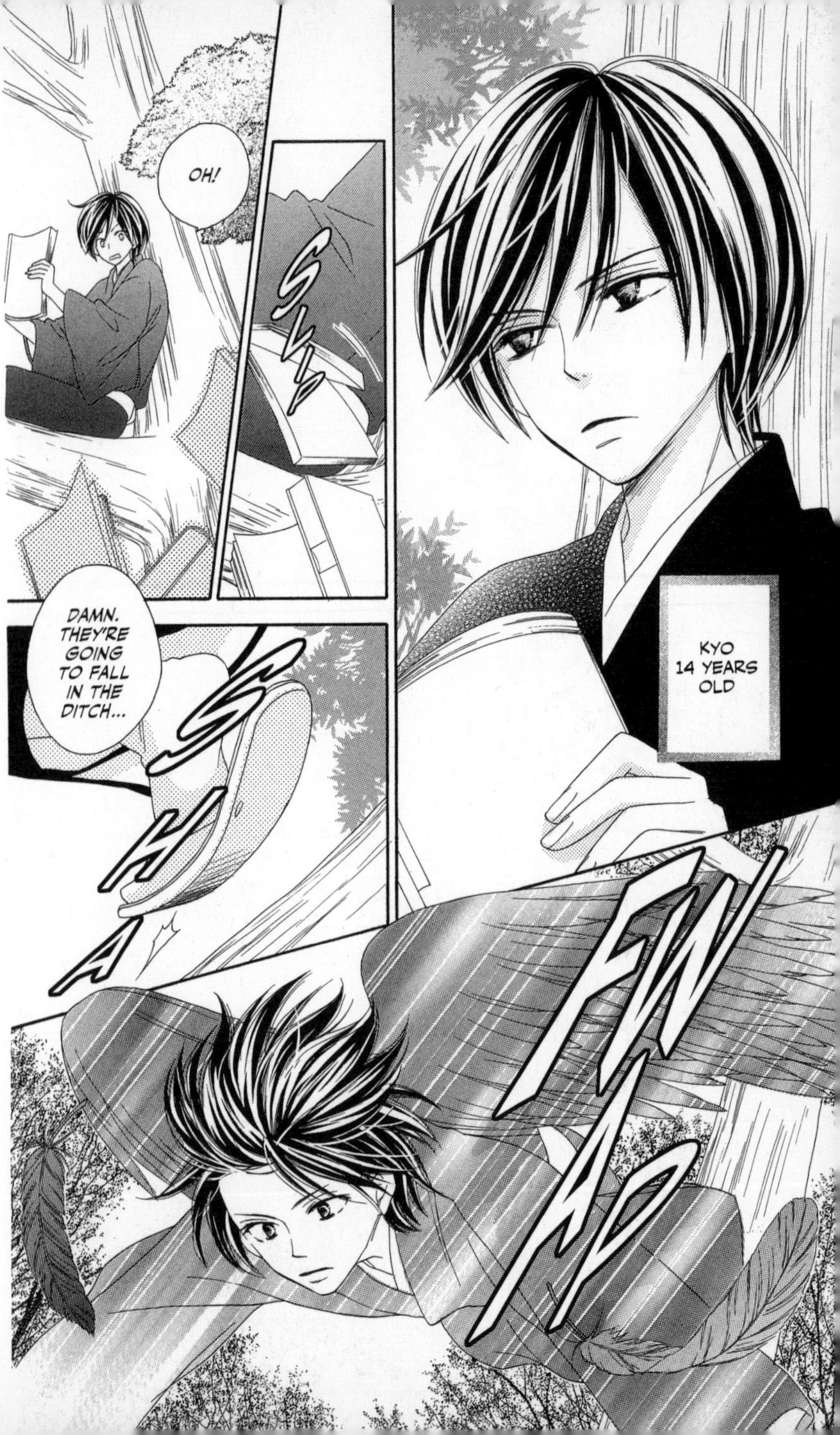
KYO
14 YEARS
OLD
SLIP
OH!
DAMN. THEY'RE GOING TO FALL IN THE DITCH...
SHA
FWAP

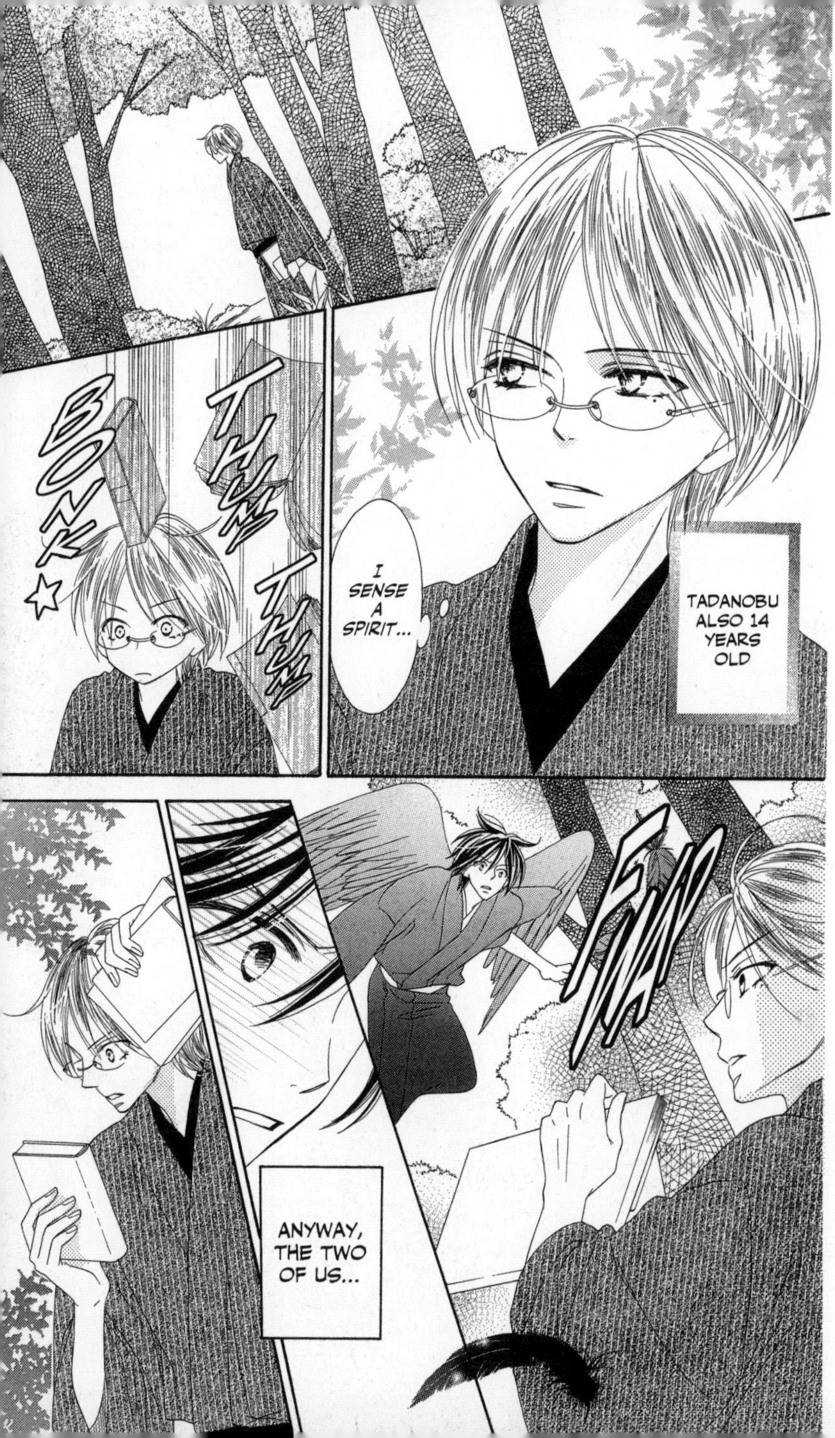
TADANOBU ALSO 14 YEARS OLD
I SENSE A SPIRIT...
THUM THUM
BONK
FWAP
ANYWAY, THE TWO OF US...

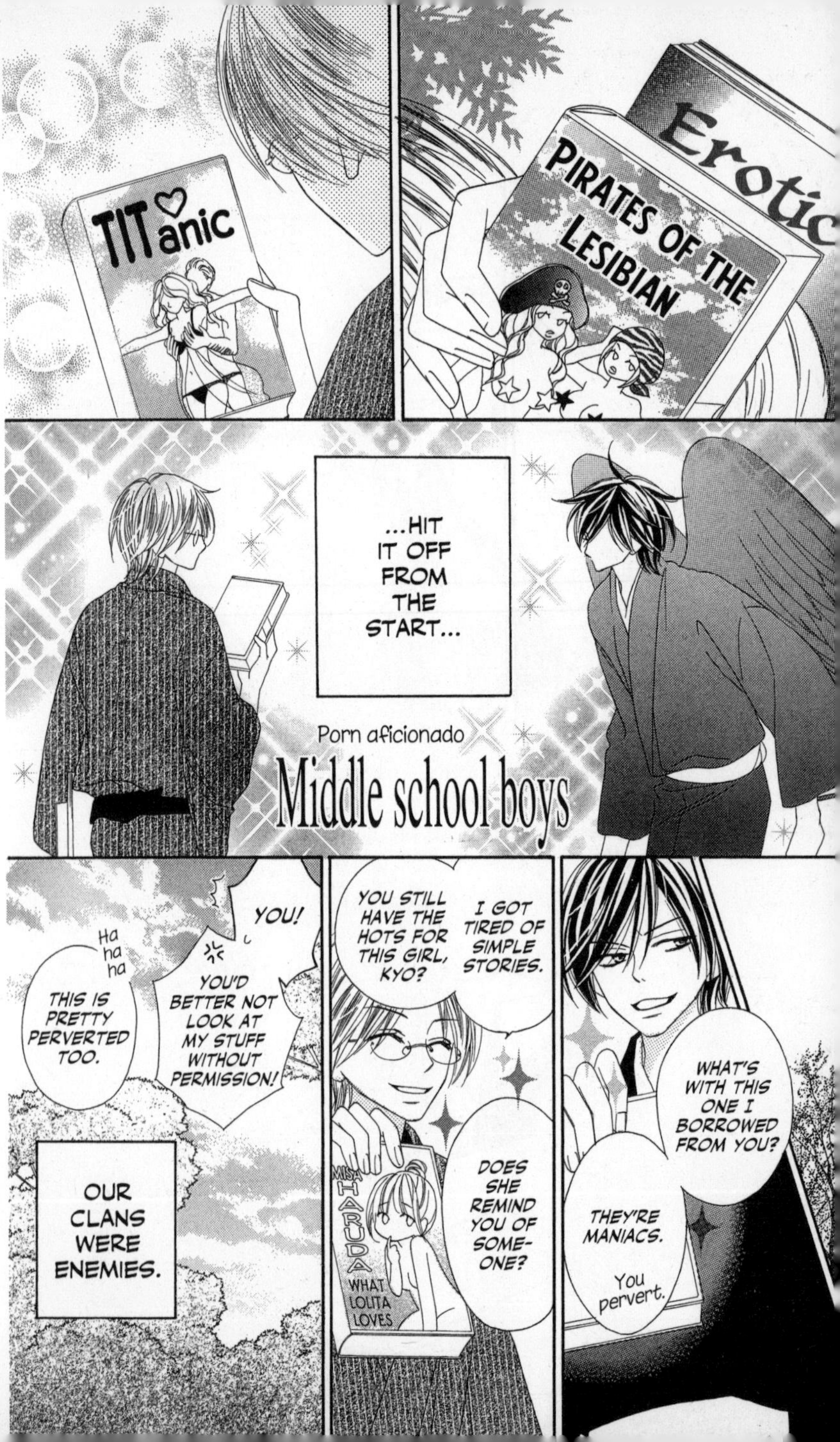
Erotic
PIRATES OF THE LESIBIAN
TIT♡anic
...HIT IT OFF FROM THE START...
Porn aficionado
Middle school boys
WHAT'S WITH THIS ONE I BORROWED FROM YOU?
THEY'RE MANIACS.
You pervert.
I GOT TIRED OF SIMPLE STORIES.
YOU STILL HAVE THE HOTS FOR THIS GIRL, KYO?
DOES SHE REMIND YOU OF SOME-ONE?
MISA HARUDA
WHAT LOLITA LOVES
YOU!
YOU'D BETTER NOT LOOK AT MY STUFF WITHOUT PERMISSION!
Ha ha ha
THIS IS PRETTY PERVERTED TOO.
OUR CLANS WERE ENEMIES.

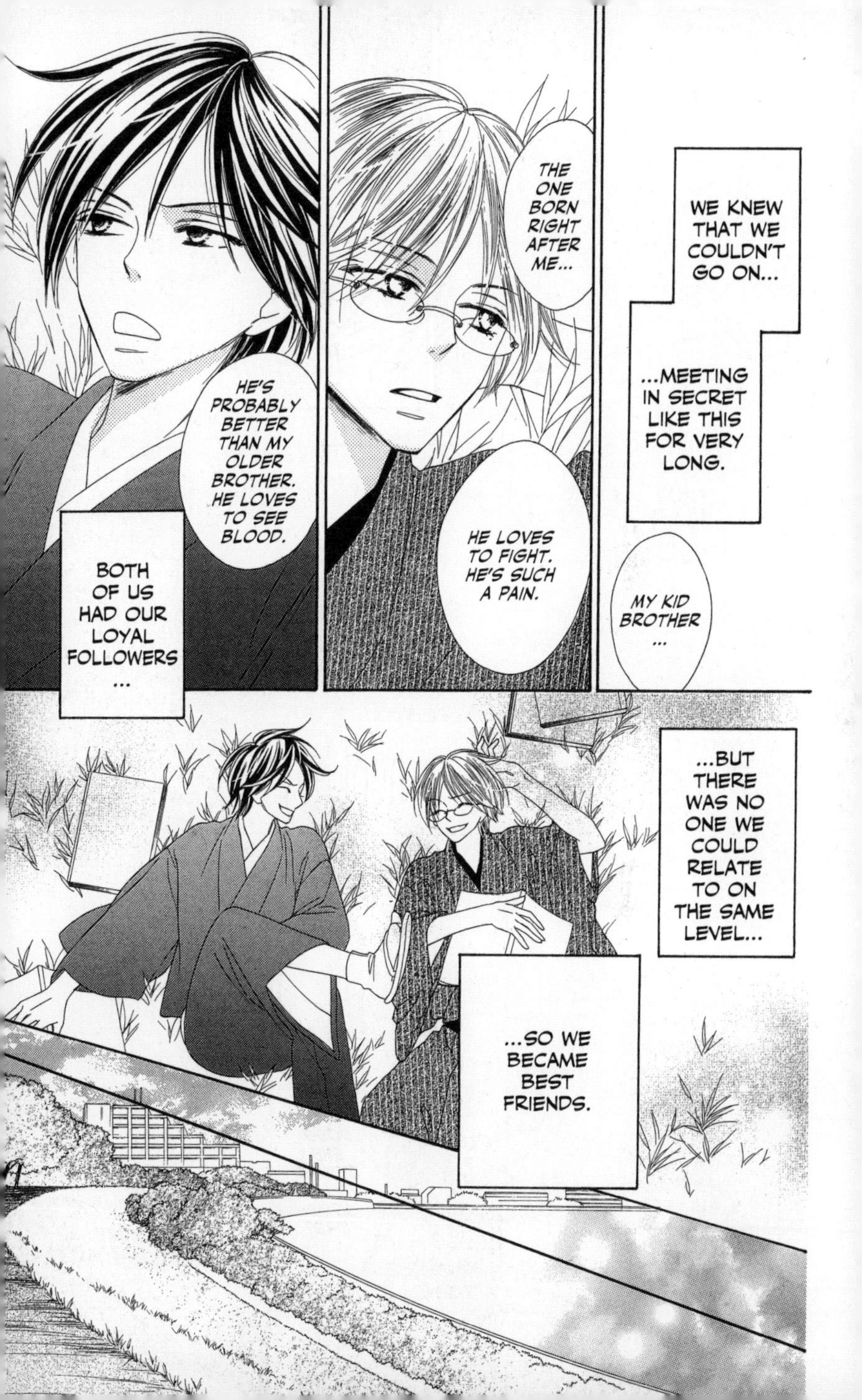
WE KNEW THAT WE COULDN'T GO ON...
...MEETING IN SECRET LIKE THIS FOR VERY LONG.
MY KID BROTHER ...
THE ONE BORN RIGHT AFTER ME...
HE LOVES TO FIGHT. HE'S SUCH A PAIN.
HE'S PROBABLY BETTER THAN MY OLDER BROTHER. HE LOVES TO SEE BLOOD.
BOTH OF US HAD OUR LOYAL FOLLOWERS ...
...BUT THERE WAS NO ONE WE COULD RELATE TO ON THE SAME LEVEL...
...SO WE BECAME BEST FRIENDS.

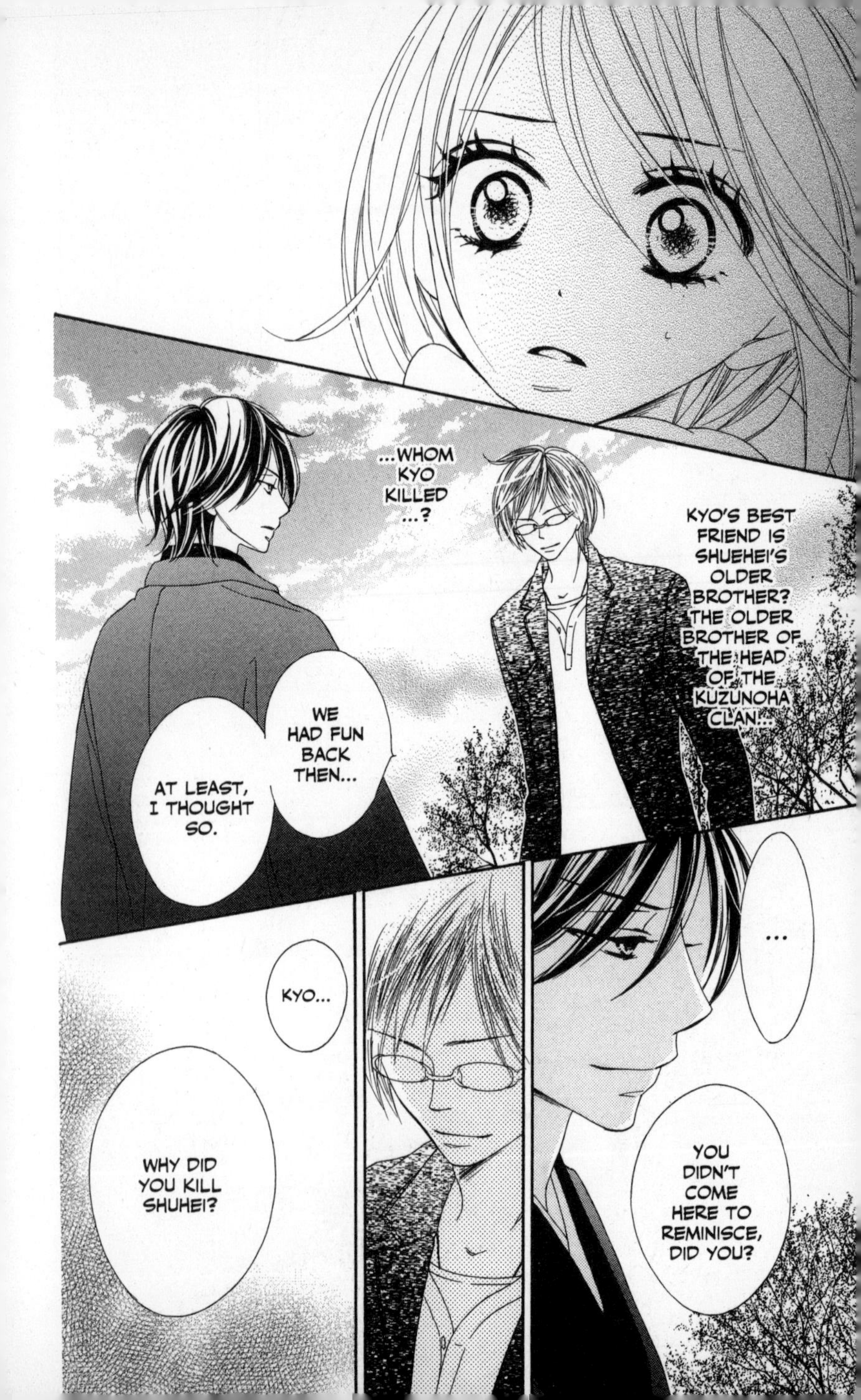
KYO'S BEST FRIEND IS SHUEHEI'S OLDER BROTHER? THE OLDER BROTHER OF THE HEAD OF THE KUZUNOHA CLAN...
...WHOM KYO KILLED ...?
WE HAD FUN BACK THEN...
AT LEAST, I THOUGHT SO.
...
YOU DIDN'T COME HERE TO REMINISCE, DID YOU?
KYO...
WHY DID YOU KILL SHUHEI?

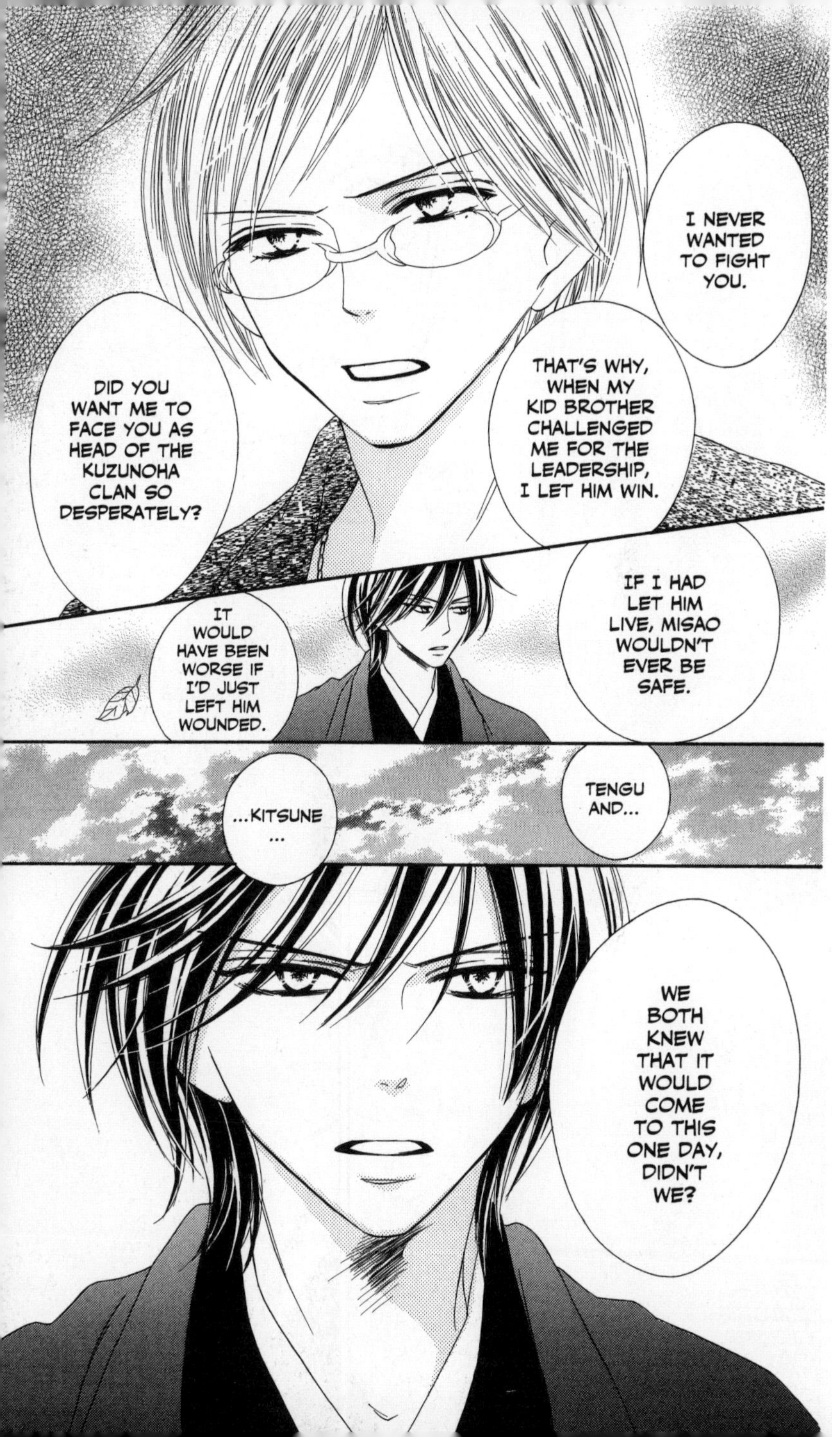
I NEVER WANTED TO FIGHT YOU.
THAT'S WHY, WHEN MY KID BROTHER CHALLENGED ME FOR THE LEADERSHIP, I LET HIM WIN.
DID YOU WANT ME TO FACE YOU AS HEAD OF THE KUZUNOHA CLAN SO DESPERATELY?
IF I HAD LET HIM LIVE, MISAO WOULDN'T EVER BE SAFE.
IT WOULD HAVE BEEN WORSE IF I'D JUST LEFT HIM WOUNDED.
TENGU AND...
...KITSUNE ...
WE BOTH KNEW THAT IT WOULD COME TO THIS ONE DAY, DIDN'T WE?

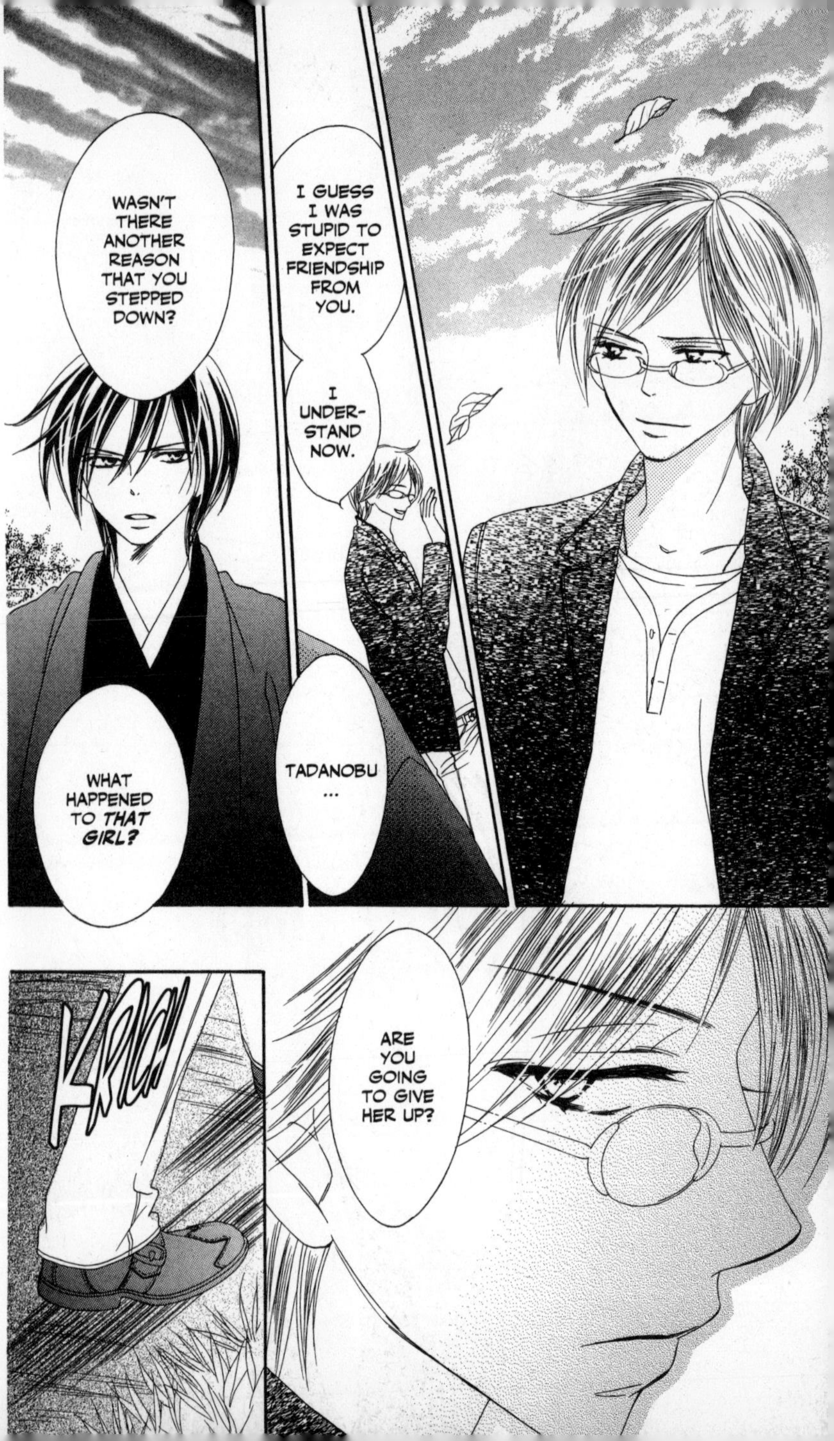
I GUESS I WAS STUPID TO EXPECT FRIENDSHIP FROM YOU.
I UNDERSTAND NOW.
TADANOBU...
WASN'T THERE ANOTHER REASON THAT YOU STEPPED DOWN?
WHAT HAPPENED TO *THAT GIRL?*
ARE YOU GOING TO GIVE HER UP?

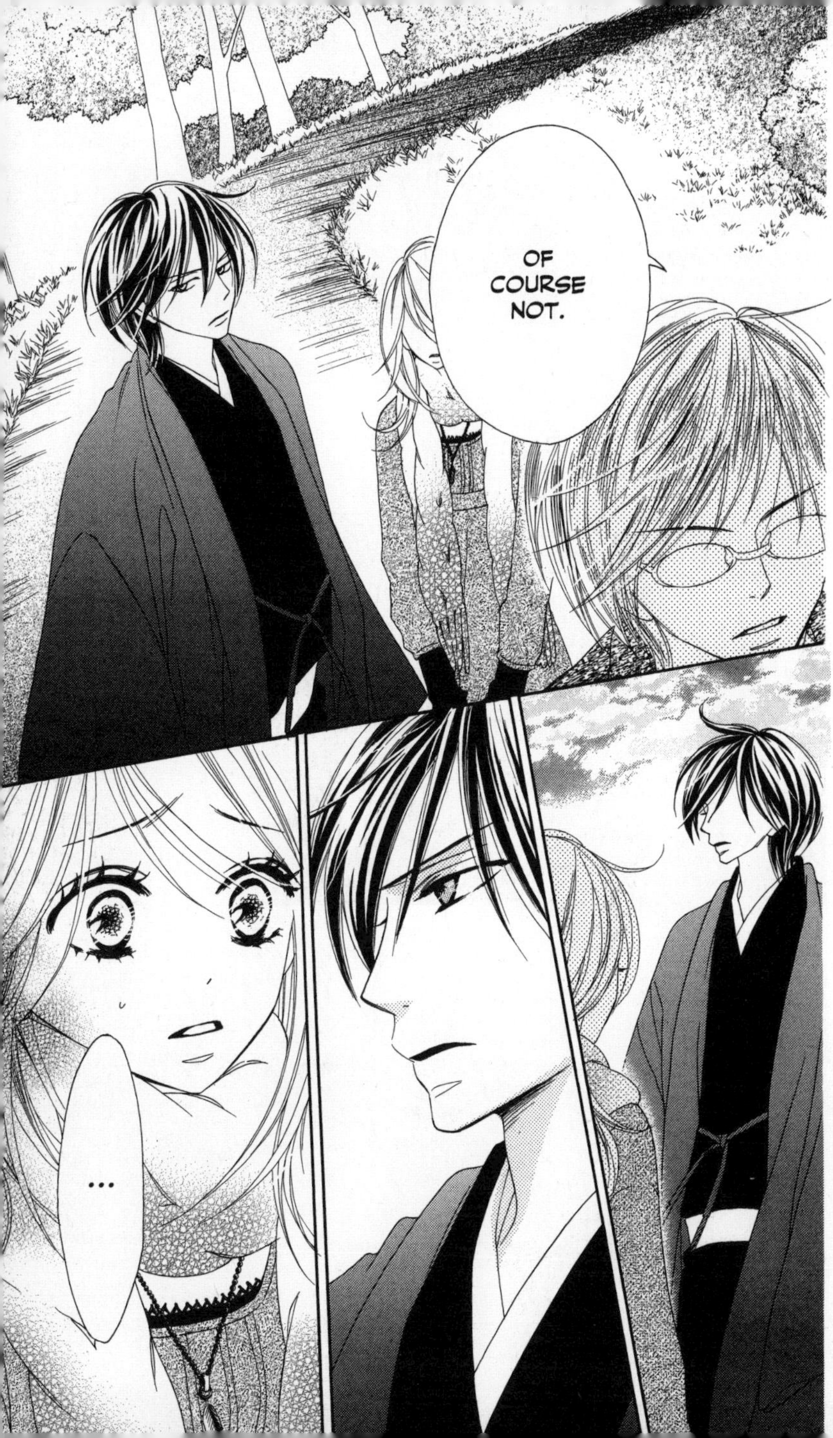
OF COURSE NOT.
...

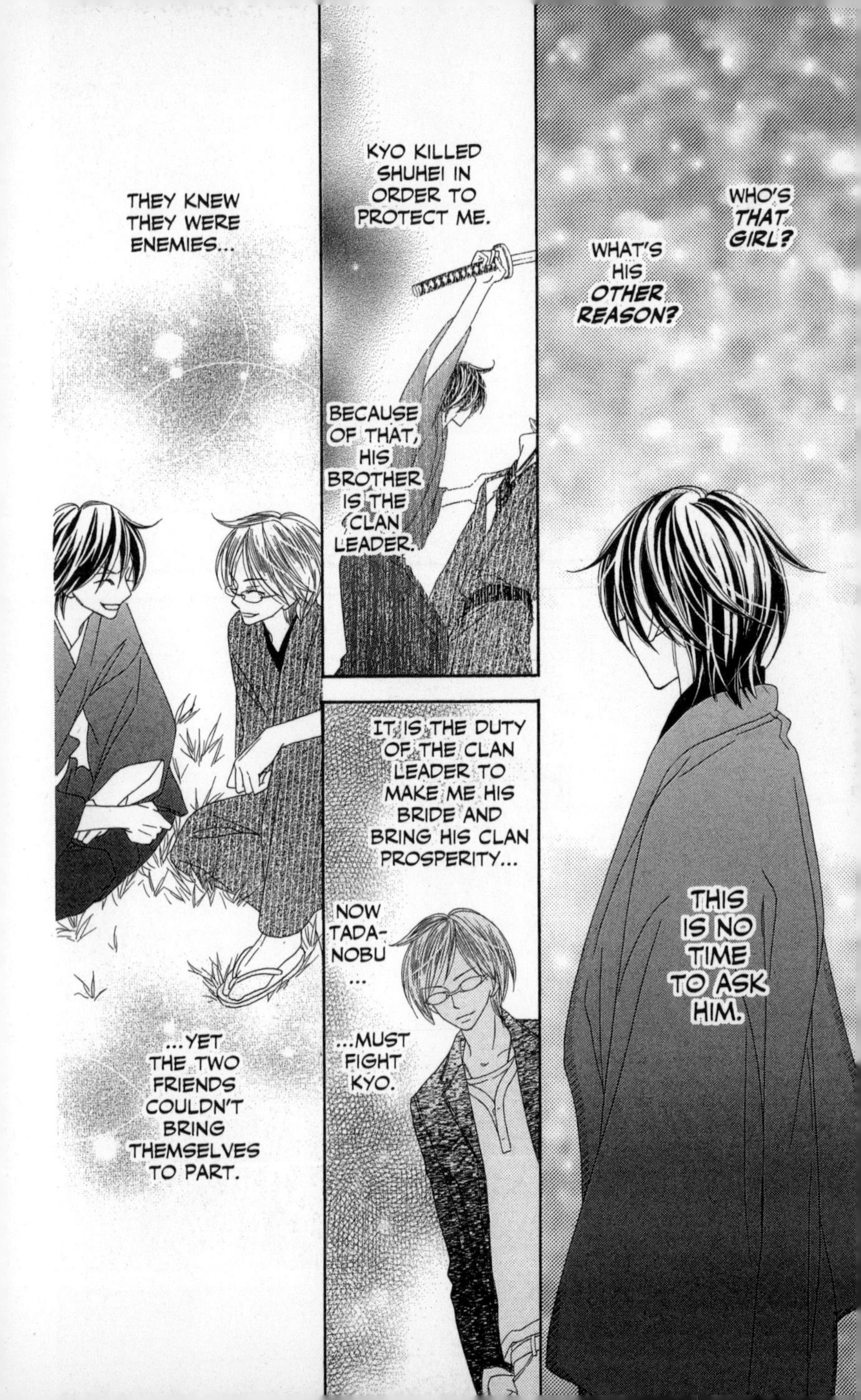
WHO'S THAT GIRL?
WHAT'S HIS OTHER REASON?
THIS IS NO TIME TO ASK HIM.
KYO KILLED SHUHEI IN ORDER TO PROTECT ME.
BECAUSE OF THAT, HIS BROTHER IS THE CLAN LEADER.
IT IS THE DUTY OF THE CLAN LEADER TO MAKE ME HIS BRIDE AND BRING HIS CLAN PROSPERITY...
NOW TADA-NOBU...
...MUST FIGHT KYO.
THEY KNEW THEY WERE ENEMIES...
...YET THE TWO FRIENDS COULDN'T BRING THEMSELVES TO PART.

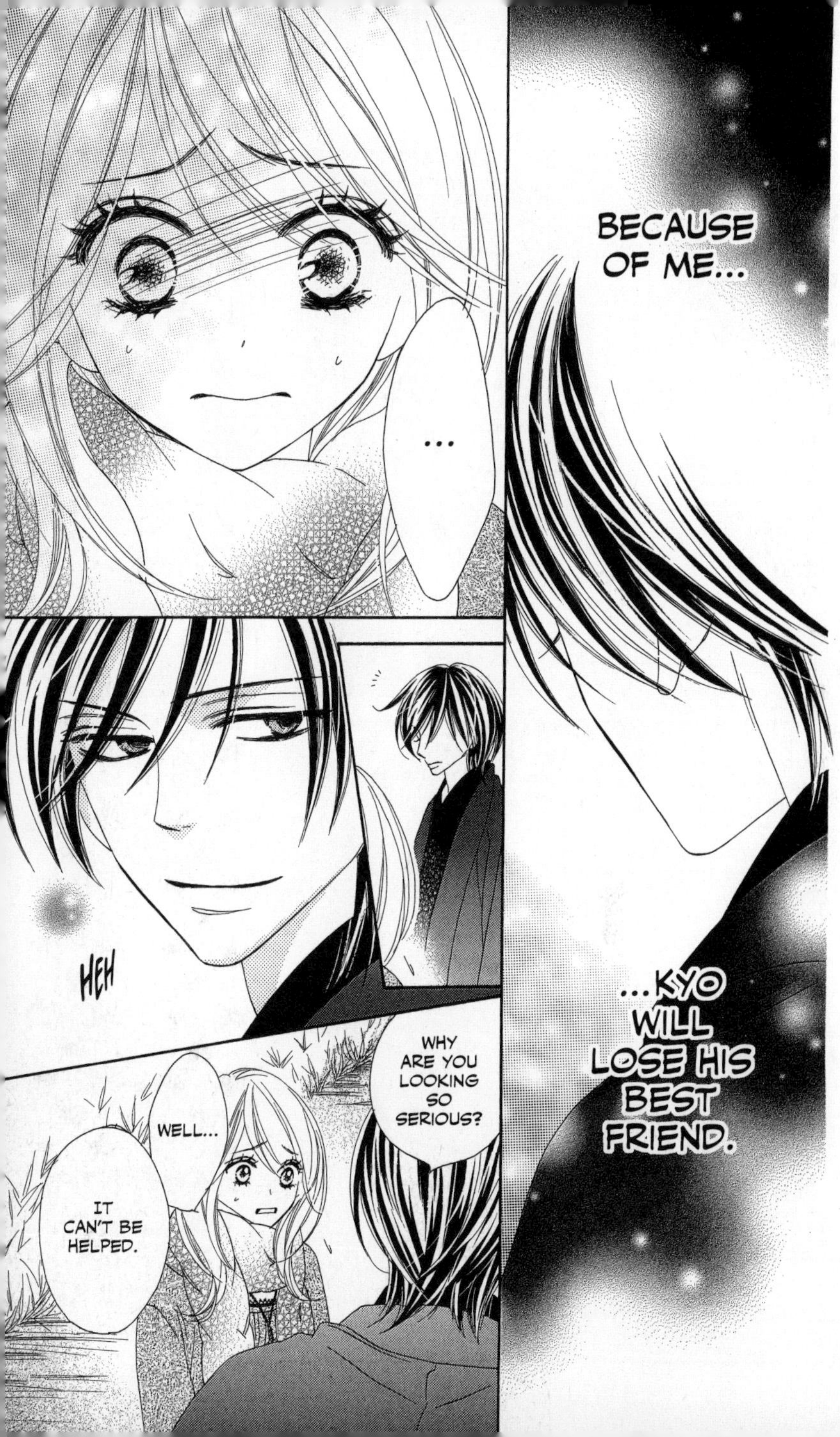
BECAUSE OF ME...
...KYO WILL LOSE HIS BEST FRIEND.
...
HEH
WHY ARE YOU LOOKING SO SERIOUS?
WELL...
IT CAN'T BE HELPED.

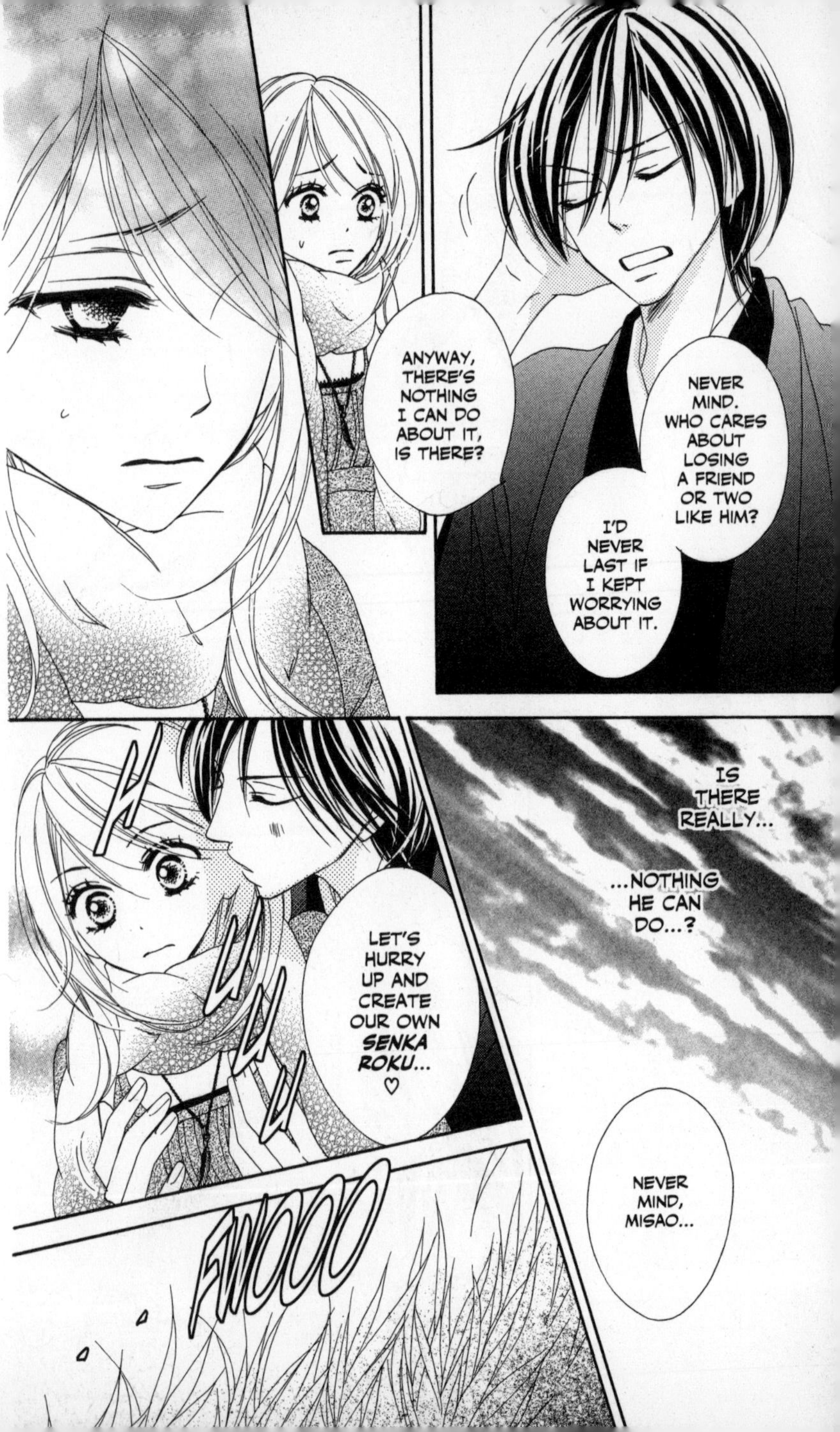
NEVER MIND. WHO CARES ABOUT LOSING A FRIEND OR TWO LIKE HIM?
I'D NEVER LAST IF I KEPT WORRYING ABOUT IT.
ANYWAY, THERE'S NOTHING I CAN DO ABOUT IT, IS THERE?
IS THERE REALLY...
...NOTHING HE CAN DO...?
NEVER MIND, MISAO...
LET'S HURRY UP AND CREATE OUR OWN *SENKA ROKU*... ♡
FWOOO

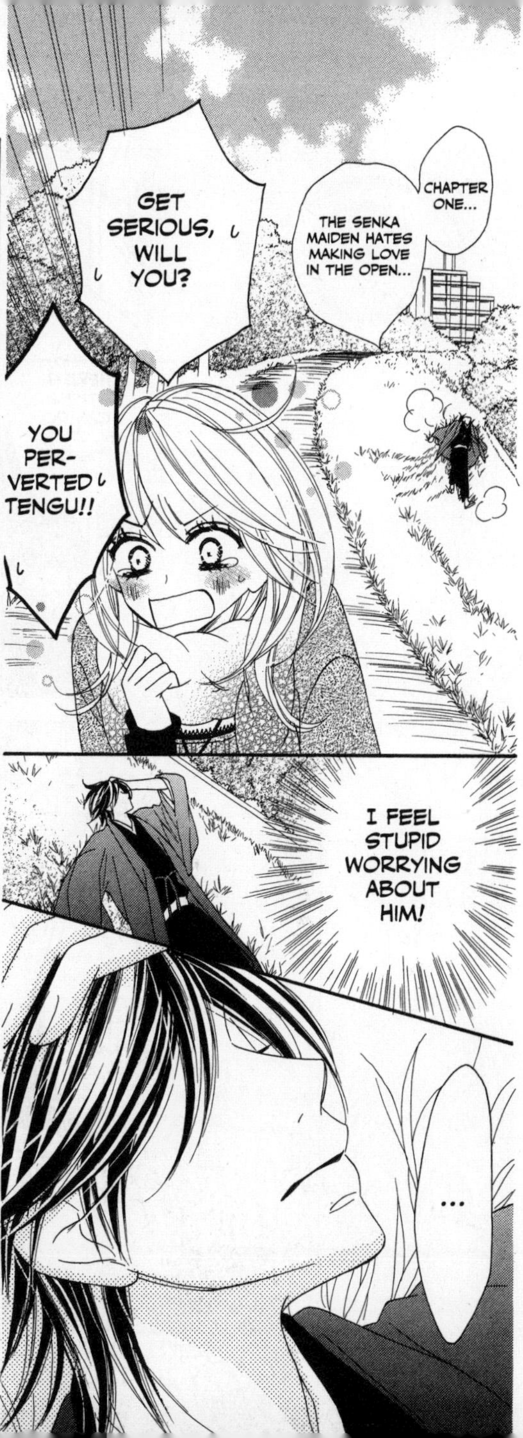
CHAPTER ONE...
THE SENKA MAIDEN HATES MAKING LOVE IN THE OPEN...
GET SERIOUS, WILL YOU?
YOU PER-VERTED TENGU!!
I FEEL STUPID WORRYING ABOUT HIM!
...

Character Introduction

Kensuke Dojoji
age: 16 height: 169cm

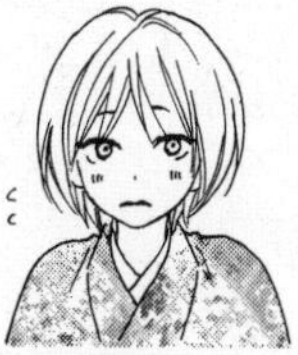

I came up with this name because "Dojoji" brought to mind a temple bell, and the temple bell brought to mind the name "Kensuke." I don't suppose you follow me. I'm talking about a Kabuki play. The name of the character in the play is actually "Gonsuke."

There are so many black hearted villains, so Kensuke was like an oasis to me. Perhaps that is why he is more popular than I expected. It surprised me.

I hope he'll be able to appear again.

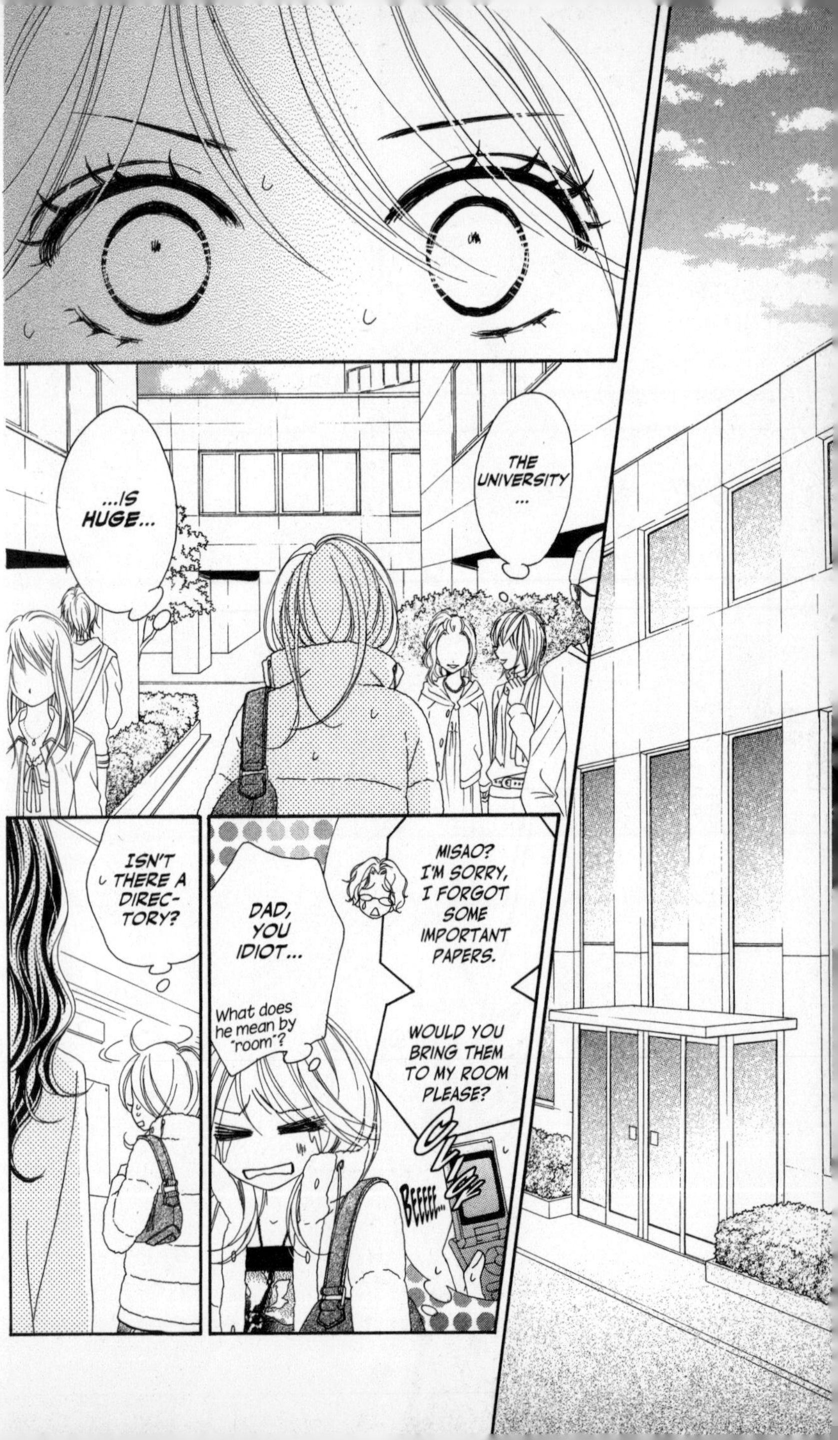
THE UNIVERSITY ...
...IS HUGE...
MISAO? I'M SORRY, I FORGOT SOME IMPORTANT PAPERS.
WOULD YOU BRING THEM TO MY ROOM PLEASE?
BEEEEE...
DAD, YOU IDIOT...
What does he mean by "room"?
ISN'T THERE A DIRECTORY?

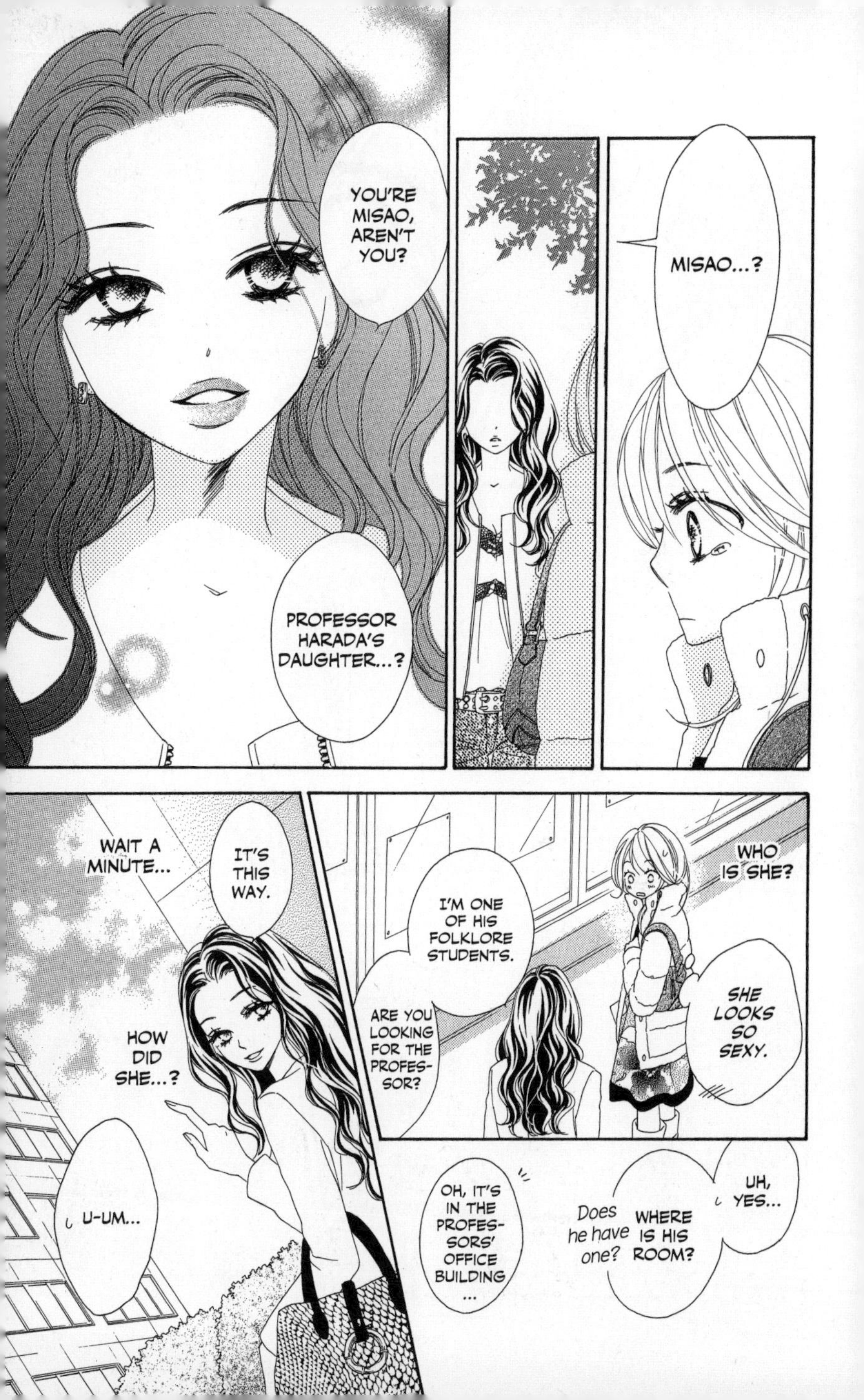
MISAO...?
YOU'RE MISAO, AREN'T YOU?
PROFESSOR HARADA'S DAUGHTER...?
WHO IS SHE?
I'M ONE OF HIS FOLKLORE STUDENTS.
SHE LOOKS SO SEXY.
ARE YOU LOOKING FOR THE PROFES-SOR?
UH, YES...
WHERE IS HIS ROOM?
Does he have one?
OH, IT'S IN THE PROFES-SORS' OFFICE BUILDING...
IT'S THIS WAY.
WAIT A MINUTE...
HOW DID SHE...?
U-UM...

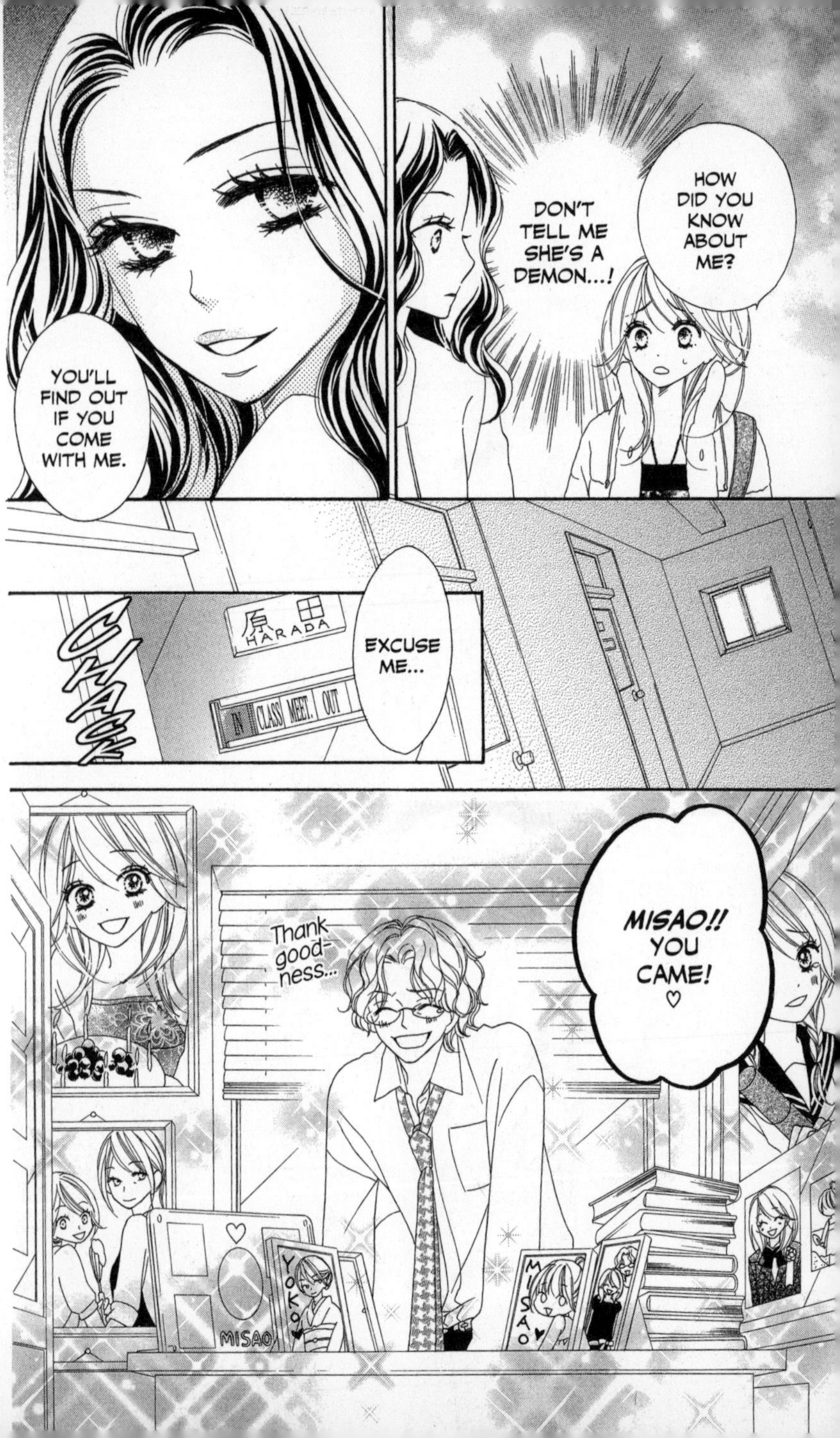
HOW DID YOU KNOW ABOUT ME?
DON'T TELL ME SHE'S A DEMON...!
YOU'LL FIND OUT IF YOU COME WITH ME.
EXCUSE ME...
原田
HARADA
IN CLASS MEET. OUT
CHACHAK
MISAO!! YOU CAME! ♡
Thank goodness...
YOKO
MISAO
MISAO

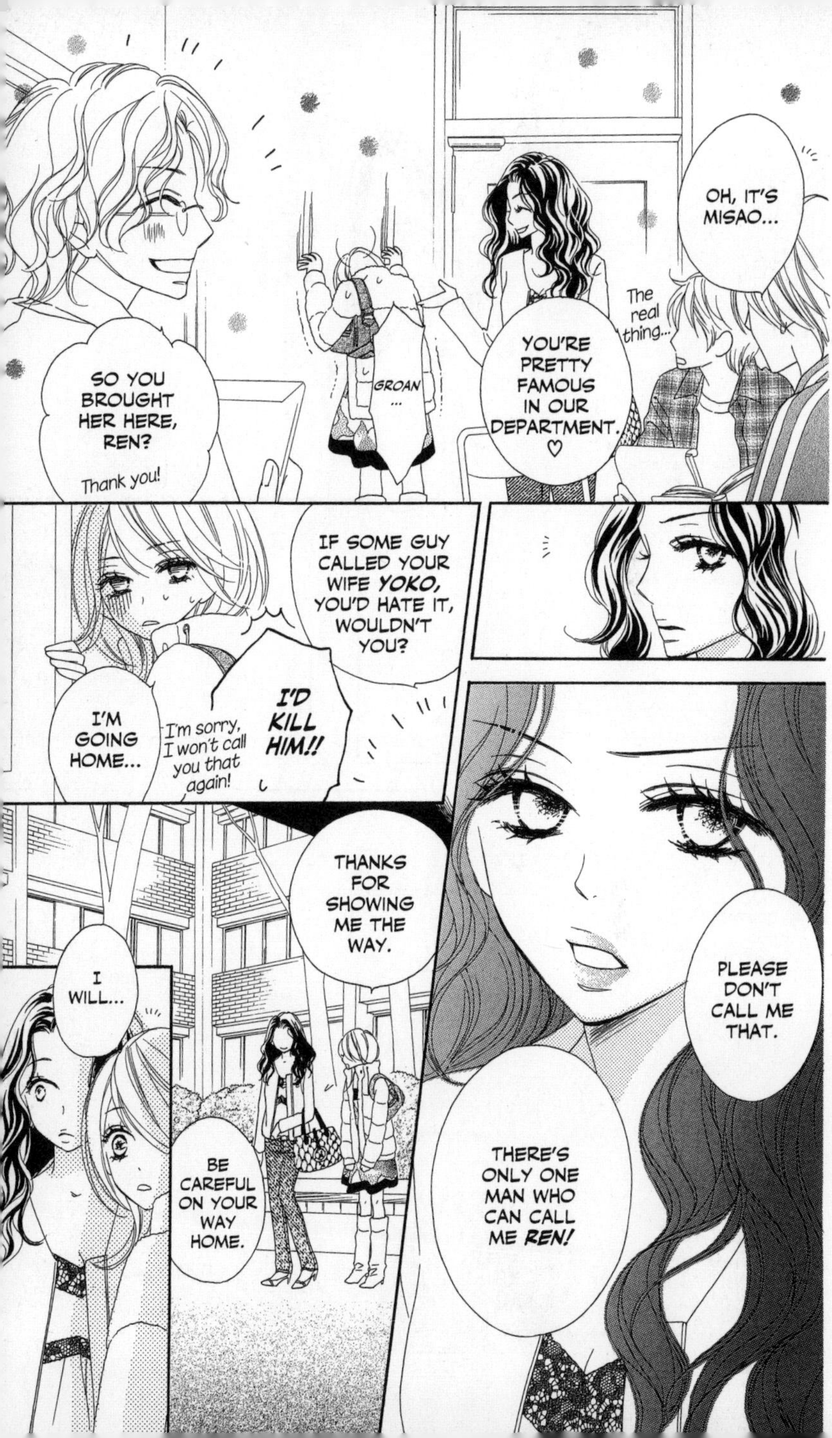
OH, IT'S MISAO...
The real thing...
YOU'RE PRETTY FAMOUS IN OUR DEPARTMENT. ♡
GROAN...
SO YOU BROUGHT HER HERE, REN?
Thank you!
IF SOME GUY CALLED YOUR WIFE *YOKO,* YOU'D HATE IT, WOULDN'T YOU?
I'D KILL HIM!!
I'm sorry, I won't call you that again!
I'M GOING HOME...
PLEASE DON'T CALL ME THAT.
THERE'S ONLY ONE MAN WHO CAN CALL ME *REN!*
THANKS FOR SHOWING ME THE WAY.
BE CAREFUL ON YOUR WAY HOME.
I WILL...

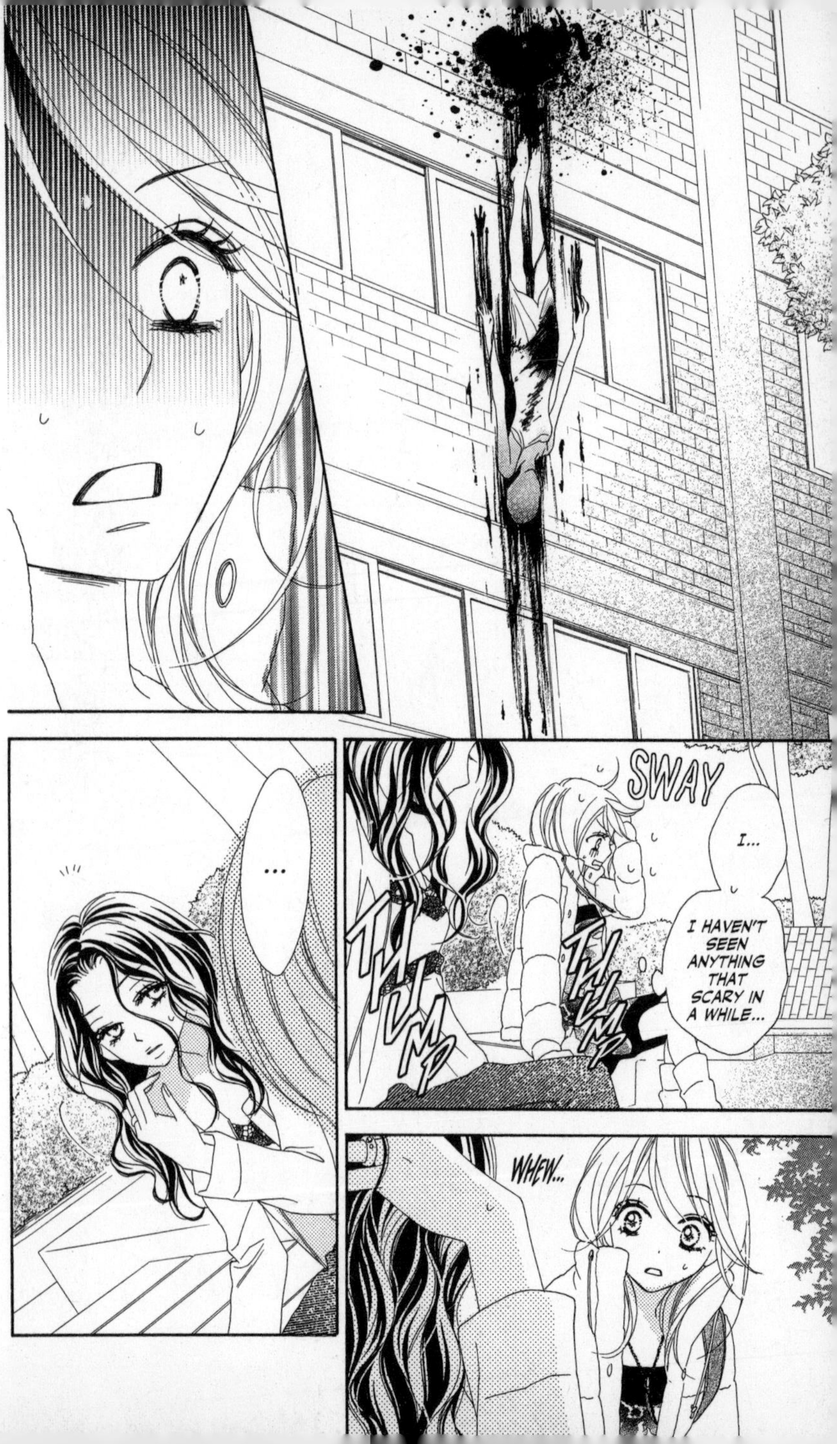
SWAY
I...
I HAVEN'T SEEN ANYTHING THAT SCARY IN A WHILE...
THUMP
THUMP
...
WHEW...

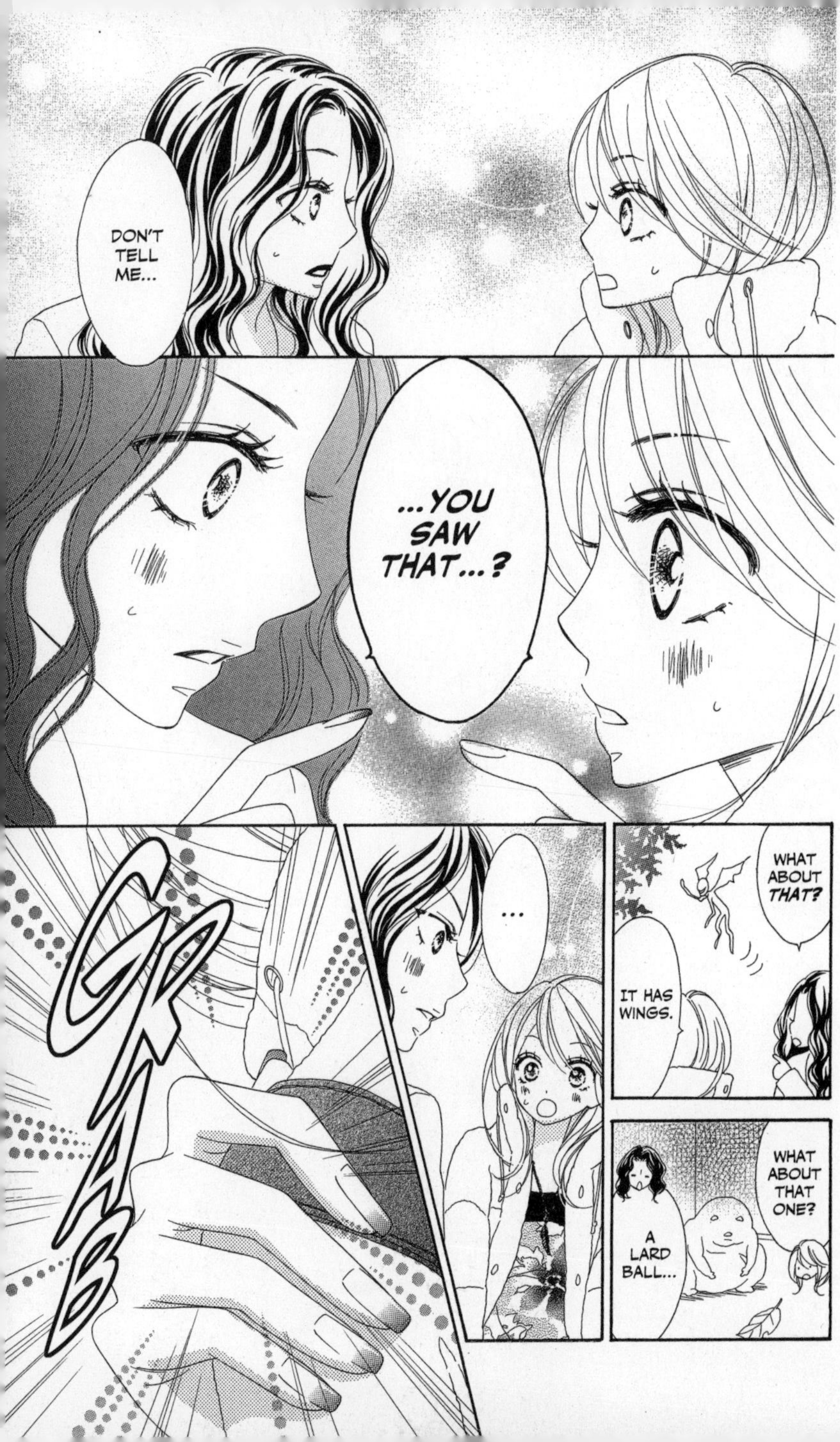
DON'T TELL ME...
...YOU SAW THAT...?
WHAT ABOUT *THAT?*
IT HAS WINGS.
WHAT ABOUT THAT ONE?
A LARD BALL...
...

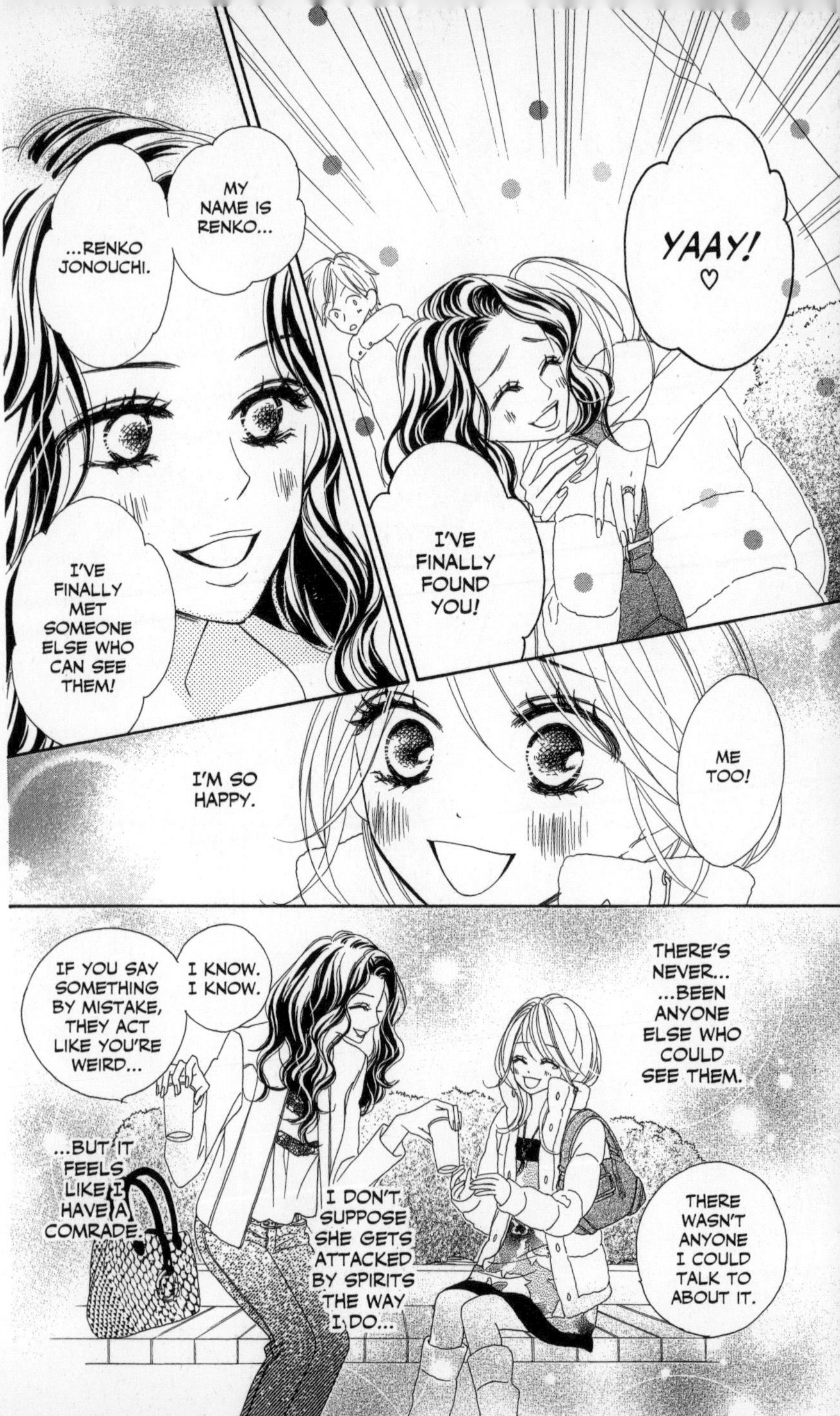
YAAY! ♡
I'VE FINALLY FOUND YOU!
MY NAME IS RENKO...
...RENKO JONOUCHI.
I'VE FINALLY MET SOMEONE ELSE WHO CAN SEE THEM!
ME TOO!
I'M SO HAPPY.
THERE'S NEVER... ...BEEN ANYONE ELSE WHO COULD SEE THEM.
THERE WASN'T ANYONE I COULD TALK TO ABOUT IT.
I DON'T SUPPOSE SHE GETS ATTACKED BY SPIRITS THE WAY I DO...
I KNOW. I KNOW.
IF YOU SAY SOMETHING BY MISTAKE, THEY ACT LIKE YOU'RE WEIRD...
...BUT IT FEELS LIKE I HAVE A COMRADE.

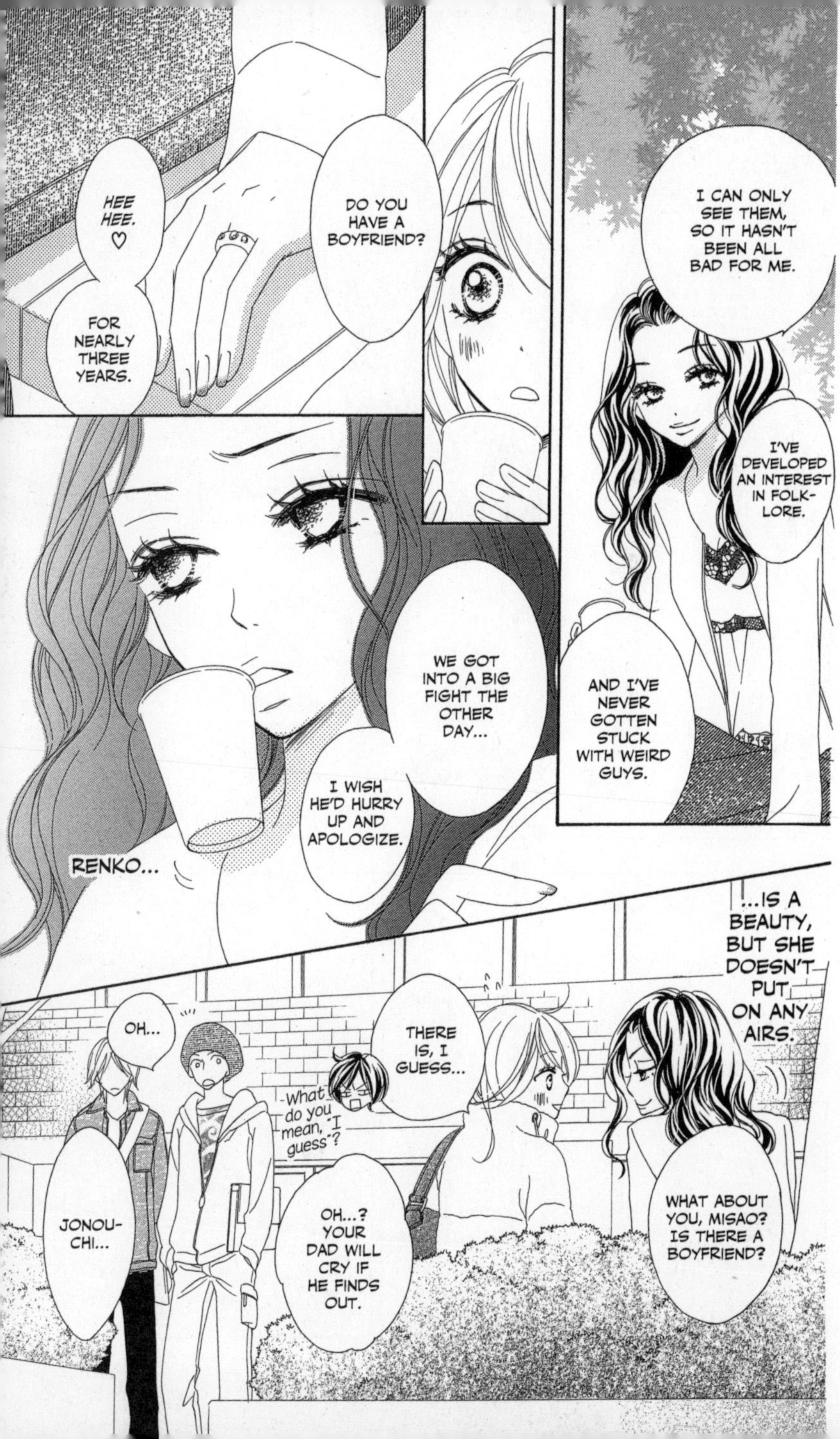
I CAN ONLY SEE THEM, SO IT HASN'T BEEN ALL BAD FOR ME.
I'VE DEVELOPED AN INTEREST IN FOLK-LORE.
AND I'VE NEVER GOTTEN STUCK WITH WEIRD GUYS.
DO YOU HAVE A BOYFRIEND?
HEE HEE. ♡
FOR NEARLY THREE YEARS.
WE GOT INTO A BIG FIGHT THE OTHER DAY...
I WISH HE'D HURRY UP AND APOLOGIZE.
RENKO...
...IS A BEAUTY, BUT SHE DOESN'T PUT ON ANY AIRS.
WHAT ABOUT YOU, MISAO? IS THERE A BOYFRIEND?
THERE IS, I GUESS...
-What do you mean, "I guess"?
OH...? YOUR DAD WILL CRY IF HE FINDS OUT.
OH...
JONOU-CHI...

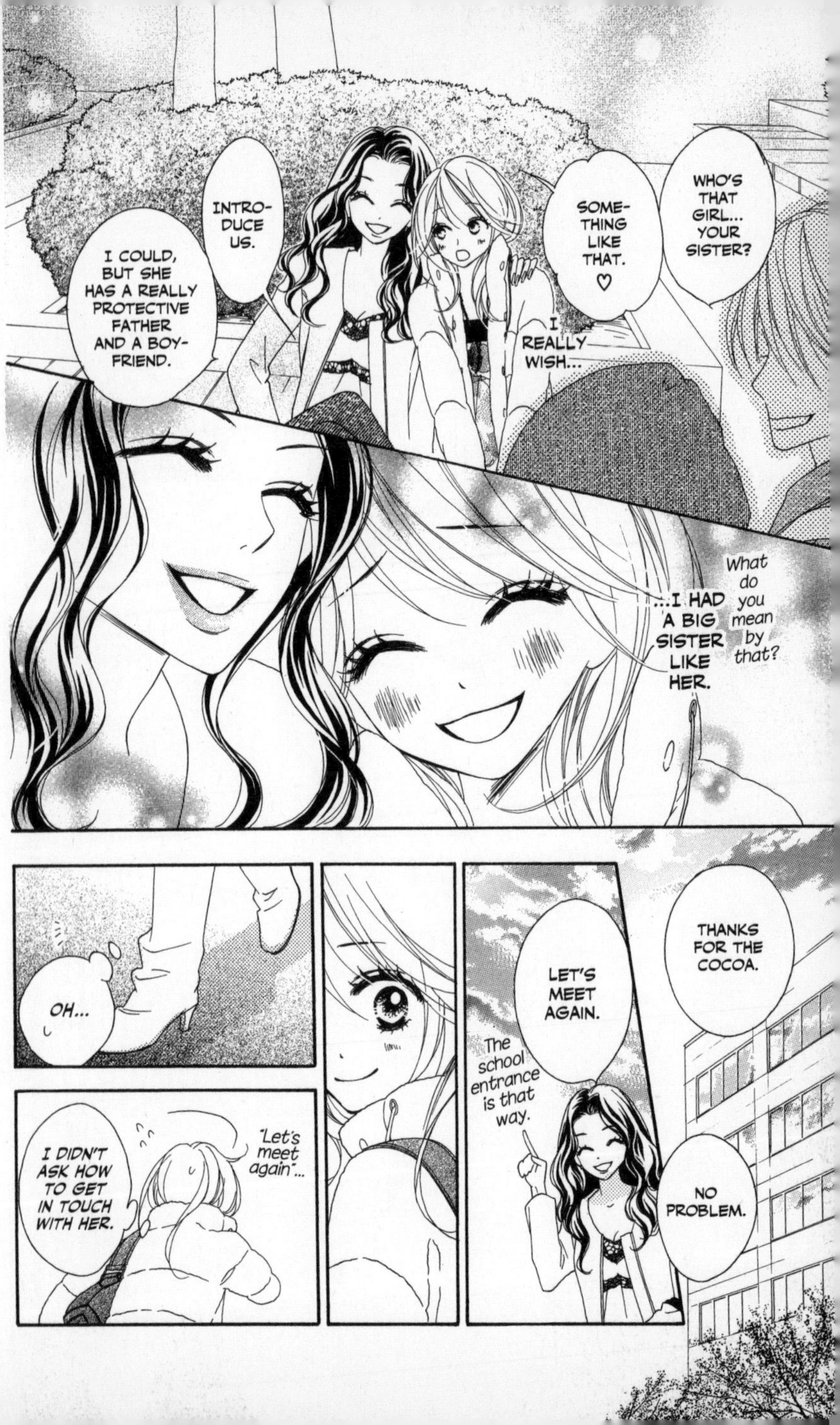
WHO'S THAT GIRL... YOUR SISTER?
SOME-THING LIKE THAT. ♡
INTRO-DUCE US.
I COULD, BUT SHE HAS A REALLY PROTECTIVE FATHER AND A BOY-FRIEND.
I REALLY WISH...
...I HAD A BIG SISTER LIKE HER.
What do you mean by that?
THANKS FOR THE COCOA.
NO PROBLEM.
LET'S MEET AGAIN.
The school entrance is that way.
OH...
"Let's meet again"...
I DIDN'T ASK HOW TO GET IN TOUCH WITH HER.

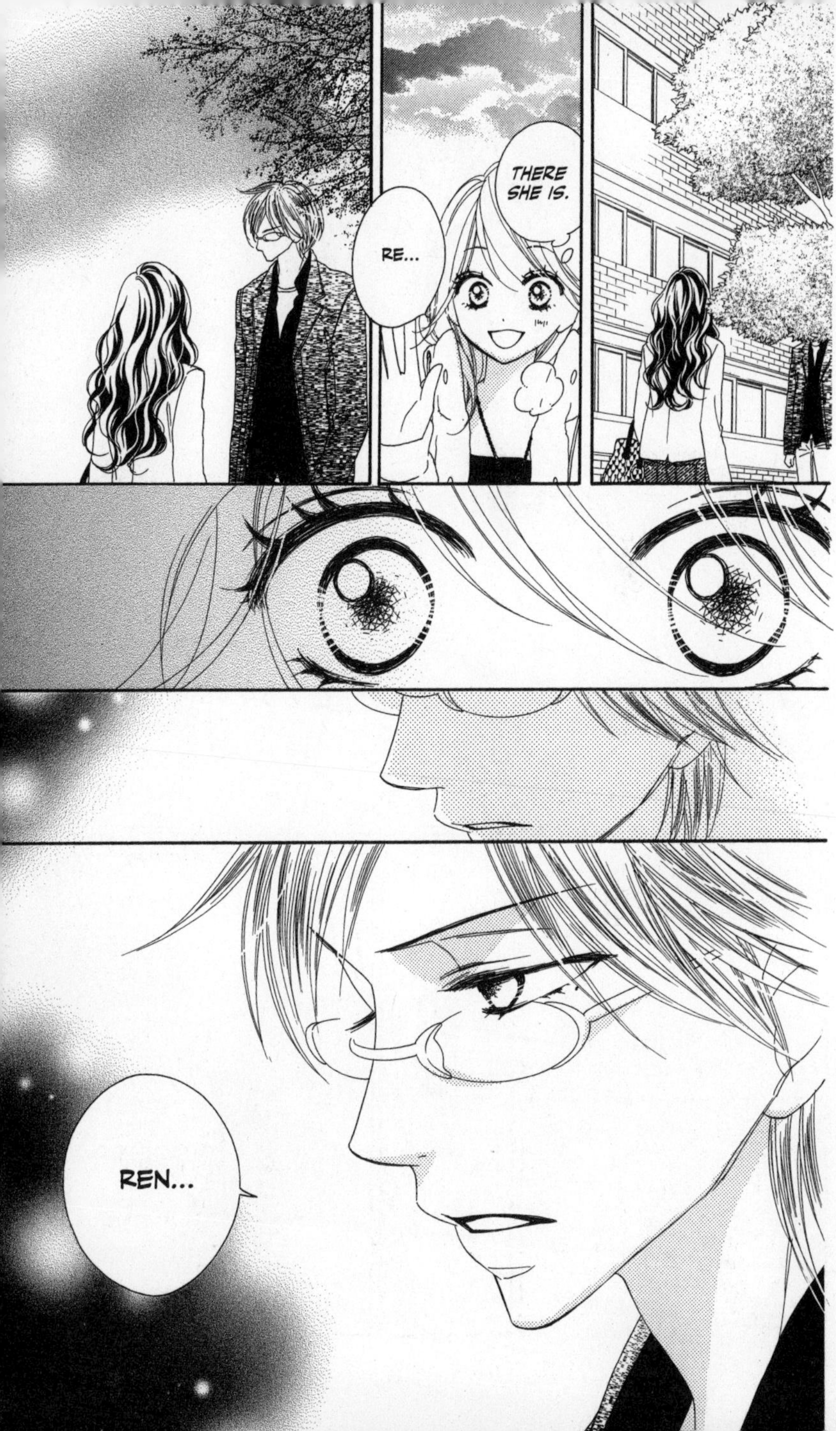
THERE SHE IS.
RE...
REN...

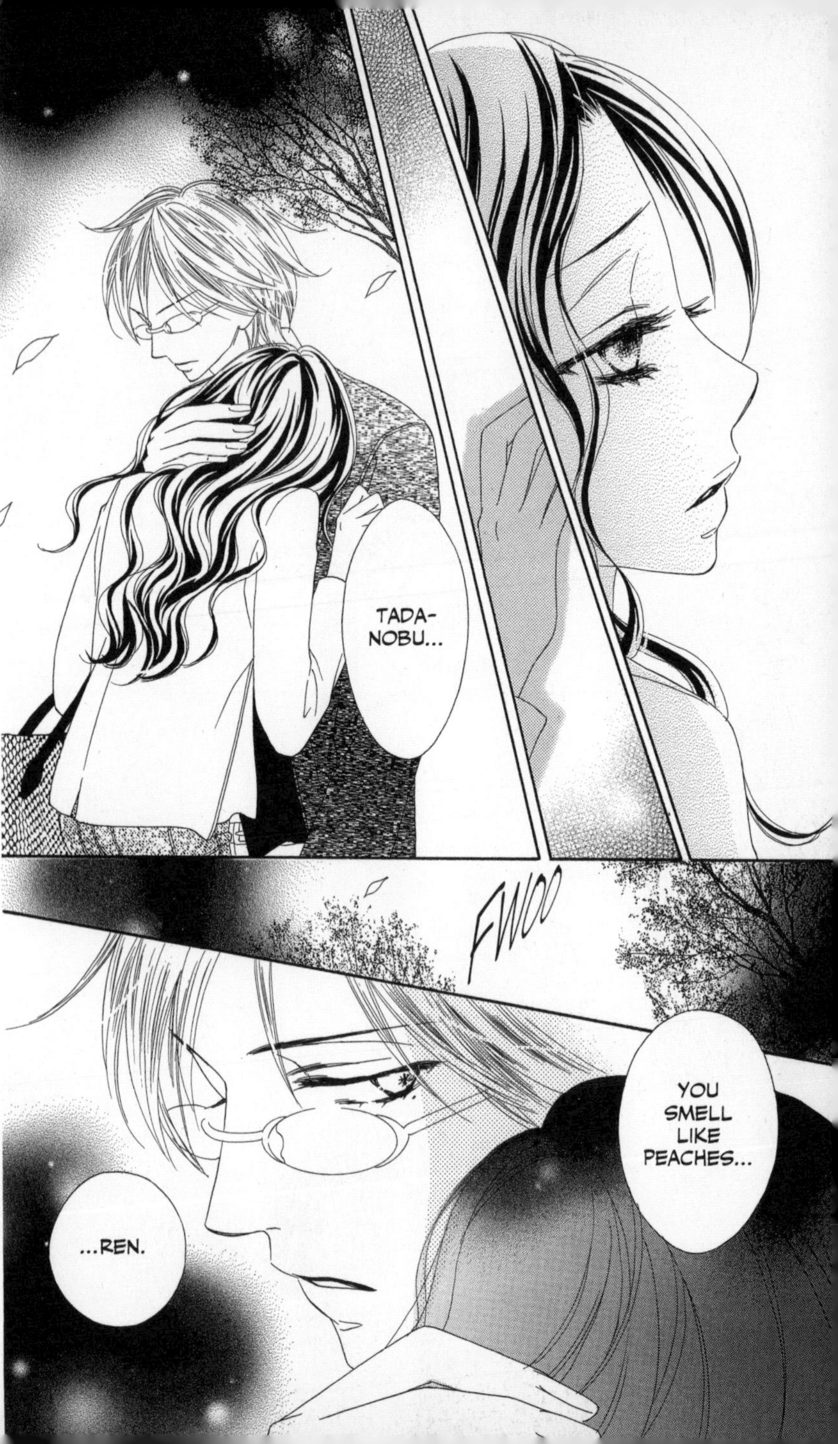
TADA-NOBU...
FWOO
YOU SMELL LIKE PEACHES...
...REN.

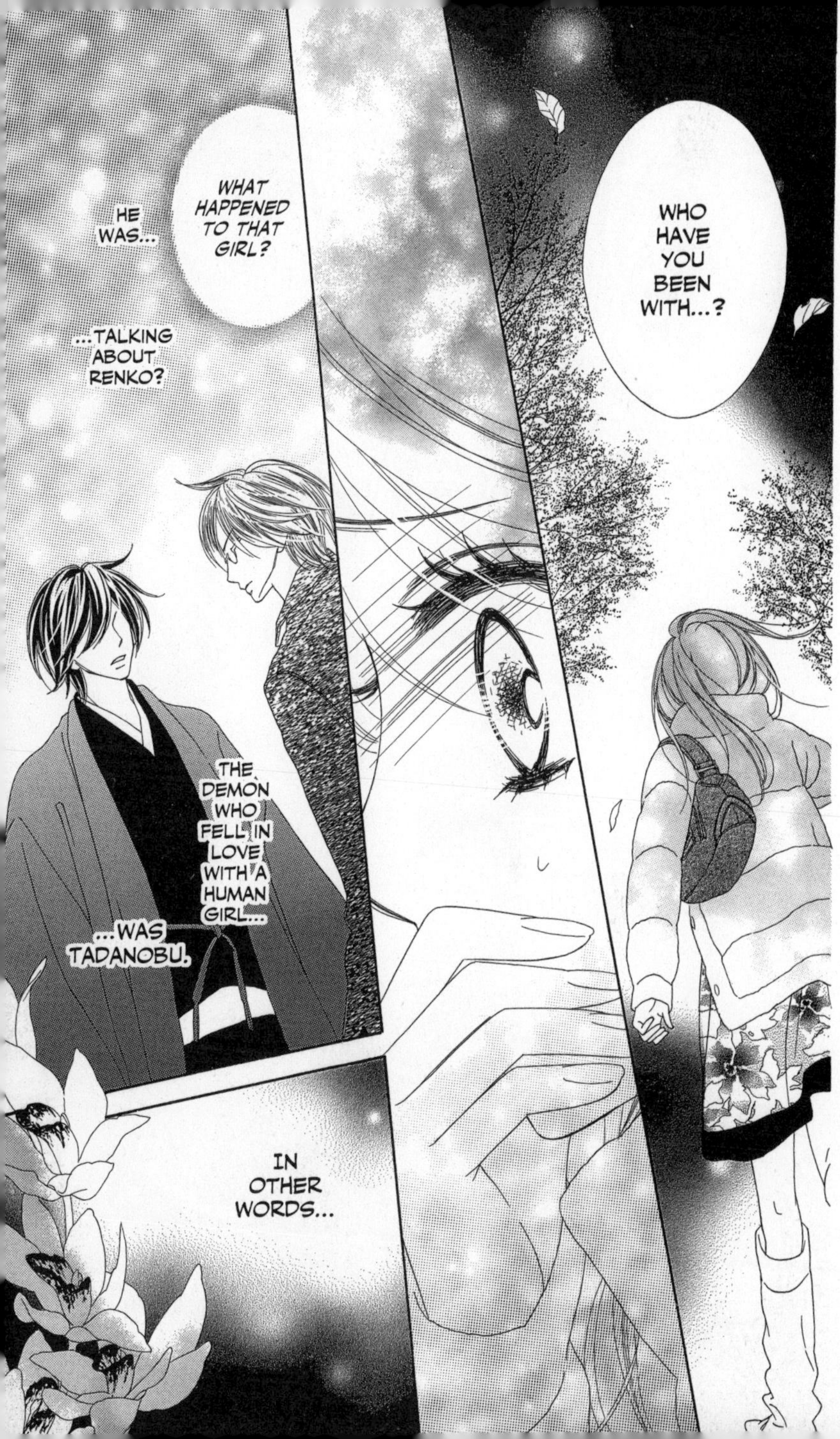
WHO HAVE YOU BEEN WITH...?
WHAT HAPPENED TO THAT GIRL?
HE WAS...
...TALKING ABOUT RENKO?
THE DEMON WHO FELL IN LOVE WITH A HUMAN GIRL...
...WAS TADANOBU.
IN OTHER WORDS...

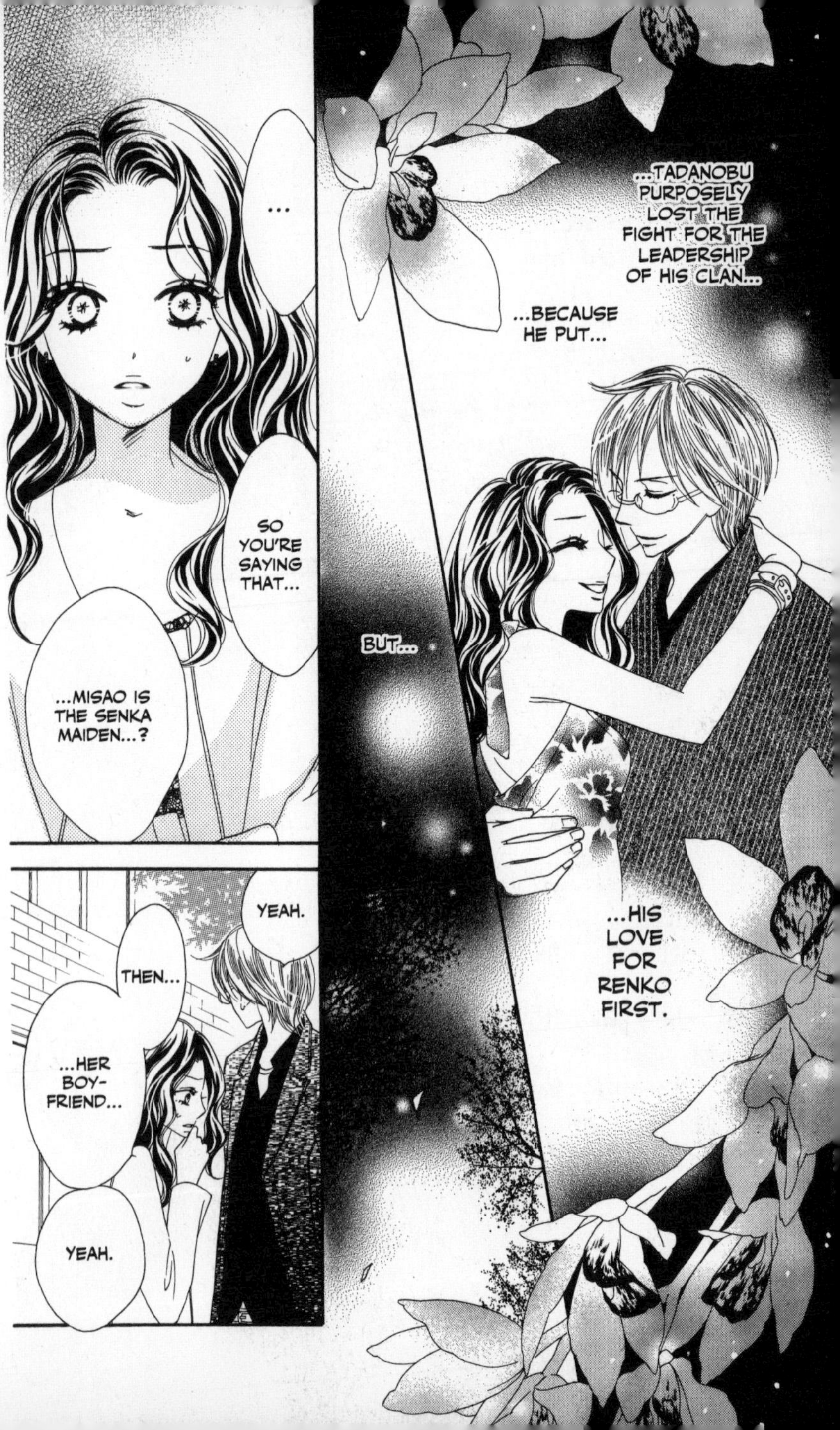

...TADANOBU PURPOSELY LOST THE FIGHT FOR THE LEADERSHIP OF HIS CLAN...
...BECAUSE HE PUT...
...HIS LOVE FOR RENKO FIRST.
BUT...
...
SO YOU'RE SAYING THAT...
...MISAO IS THE SENKA MAIDEN...?
YEAH.
THEN...
...HER BOY-FRIEND...
YEAH.

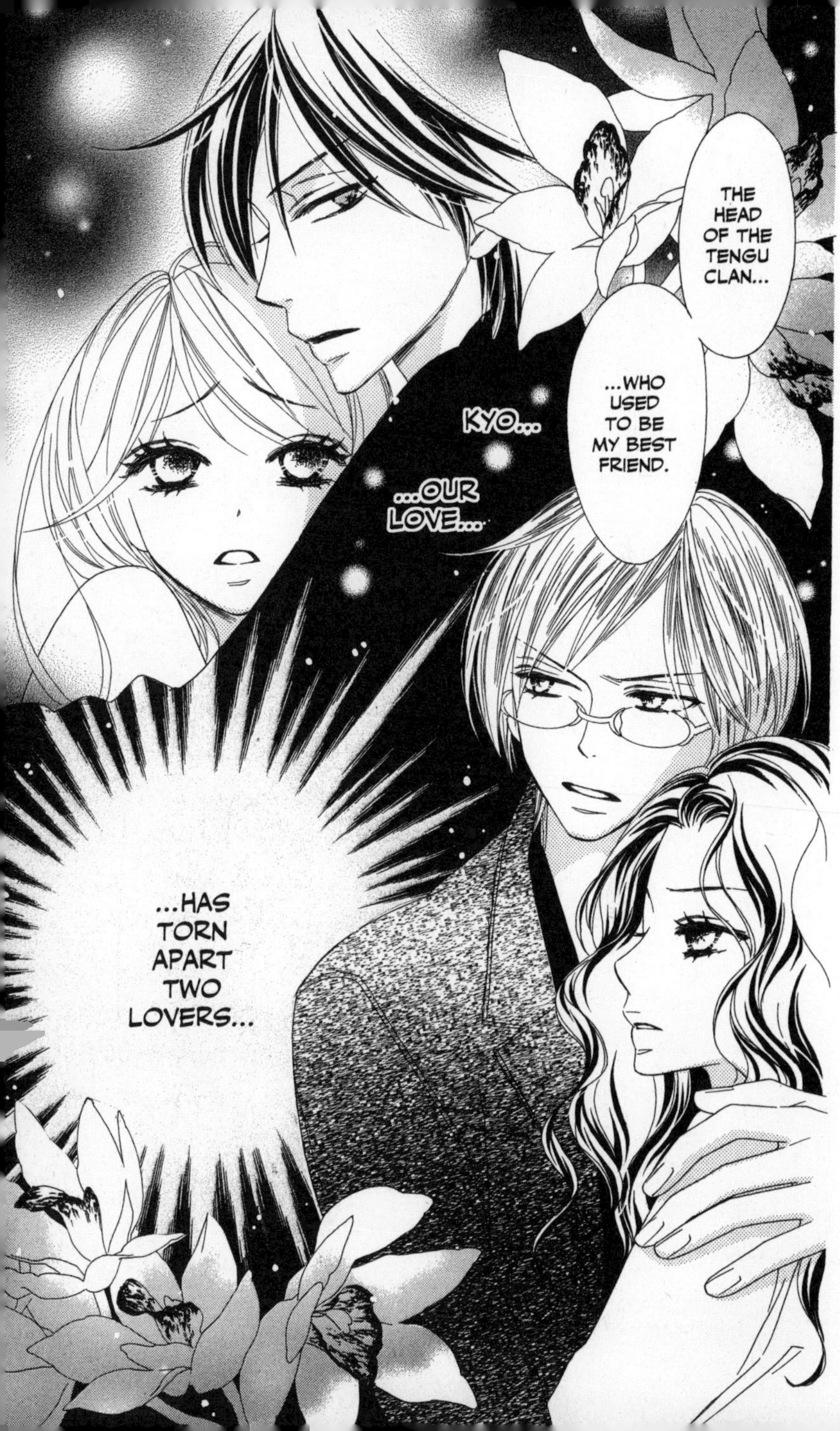
THE HEAD OF THE TENGU CLAN...
...WHO USED TO BE MY BEST FRIEND.
KYO...
...OUR LOVE...
...HAS TORN APART TWO LOVERS...

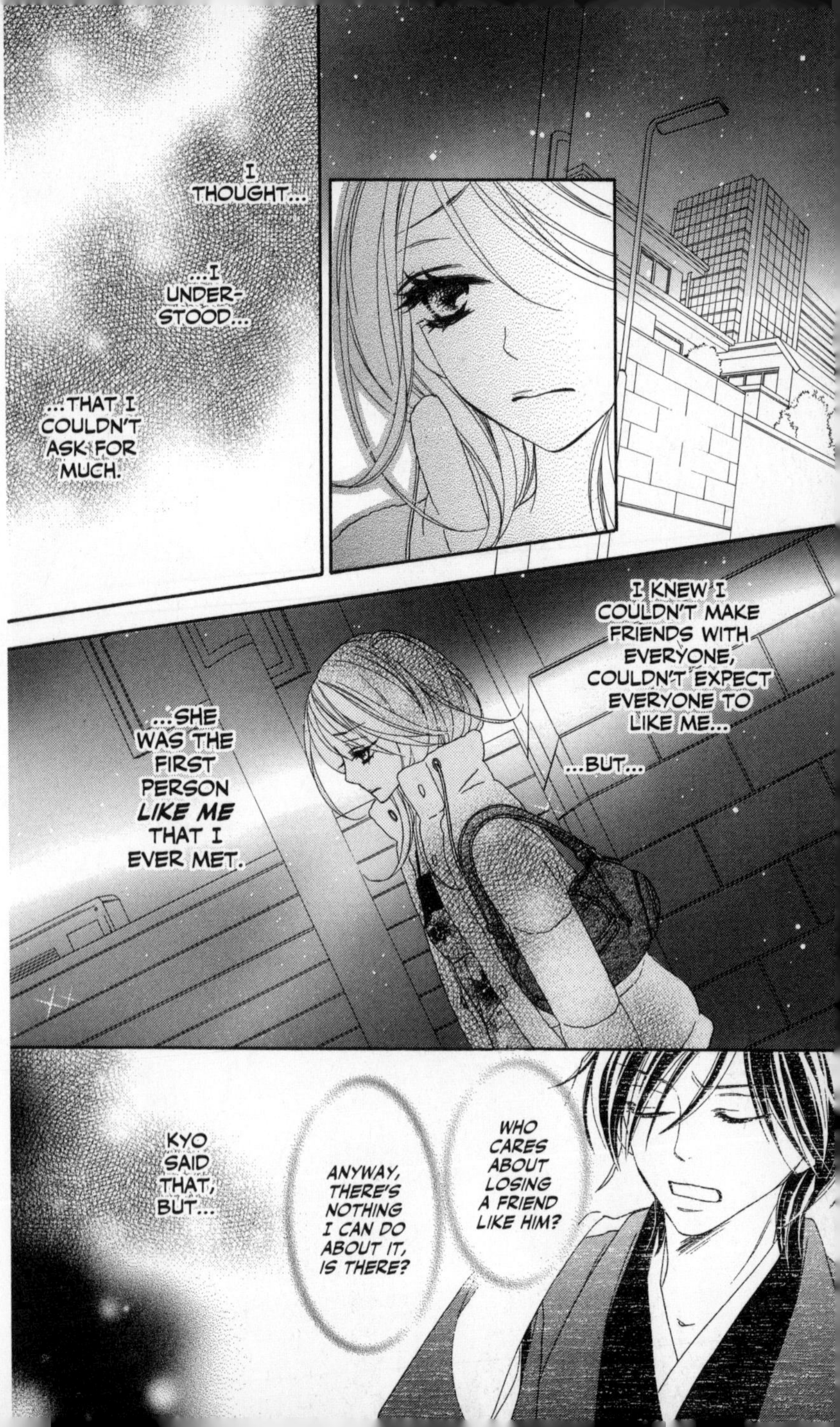
I THOUGHT...
...I UNDER-STOOD...
...THAT I COULDN'T ASK FOR MUCH.
I KNEW I COULDN'T MAKE FRIENDS WITH EVERYONE, COULDN'T EXPECT EVERYONE TO LIKE ME...
...BUT...
...SHE WAS THE FIRST PERSON ***LIKE ME*** THAT I EVER MET.
WHO CARES ABOUT LOSING A FRIEND LIKE HIM?
ANYWAY, THERE'S NOTHING I CAN DO ABOUT IT, IS THERE?
KYO SAID THAT, BUT...

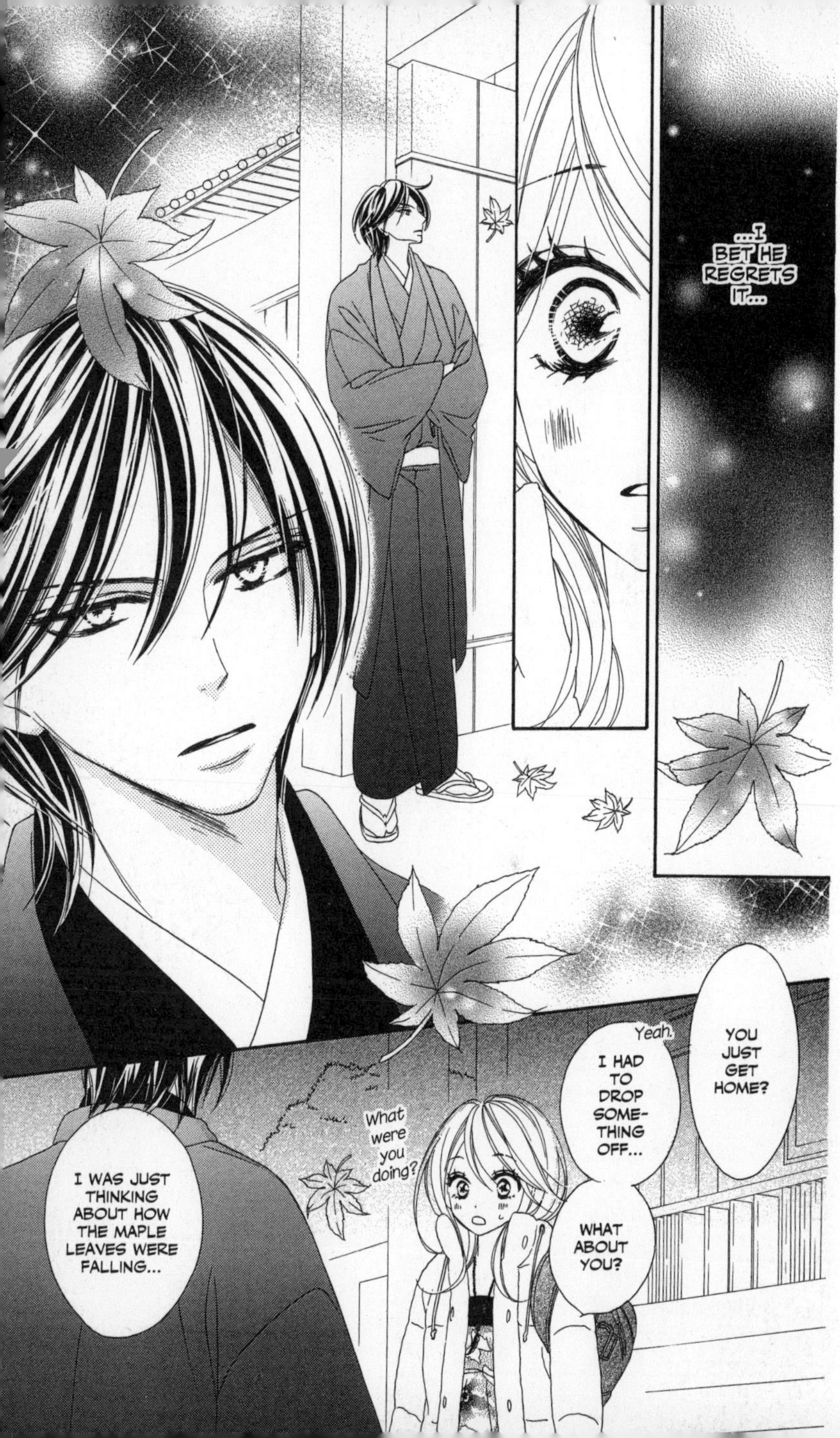
...I BET HE REGRETS IT...
YOU JUST GET HOME?
Yeah.
I HAD TO DROP SOME-THING OFF...
WHAT ABOUT YOU?
What were you doing?
I WAS JUST THINKING ABOUT HOW THE MAPLE LEAVES WERE FALLING...

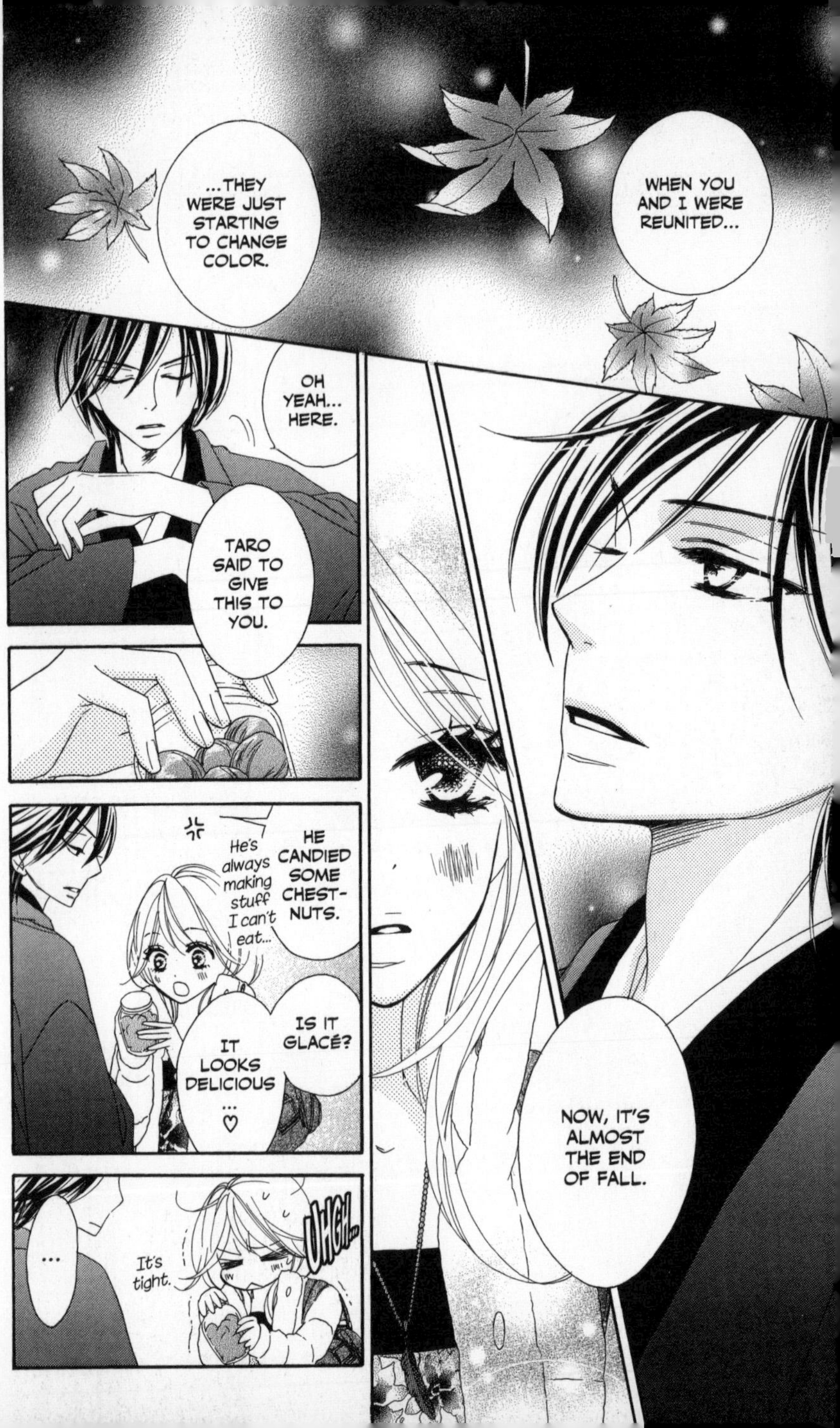
WHEN YOU AND I WERE REUNITED...
...THEY WERE JUST STARTING TO CHANGE COLOR.
NOW, IT'S ALMOST THE END OF FALL.
OH YEAH... HERE.
TARO SAID TO GIVE THIS TO YOU.
HE CANDIED SOME CHEST-NUTS.
He's always making stuff I can't eat...
IS IT GLACÉ?
IT LOOKS DELICIOUS ... ♡
UHGH...
It's tight.
...

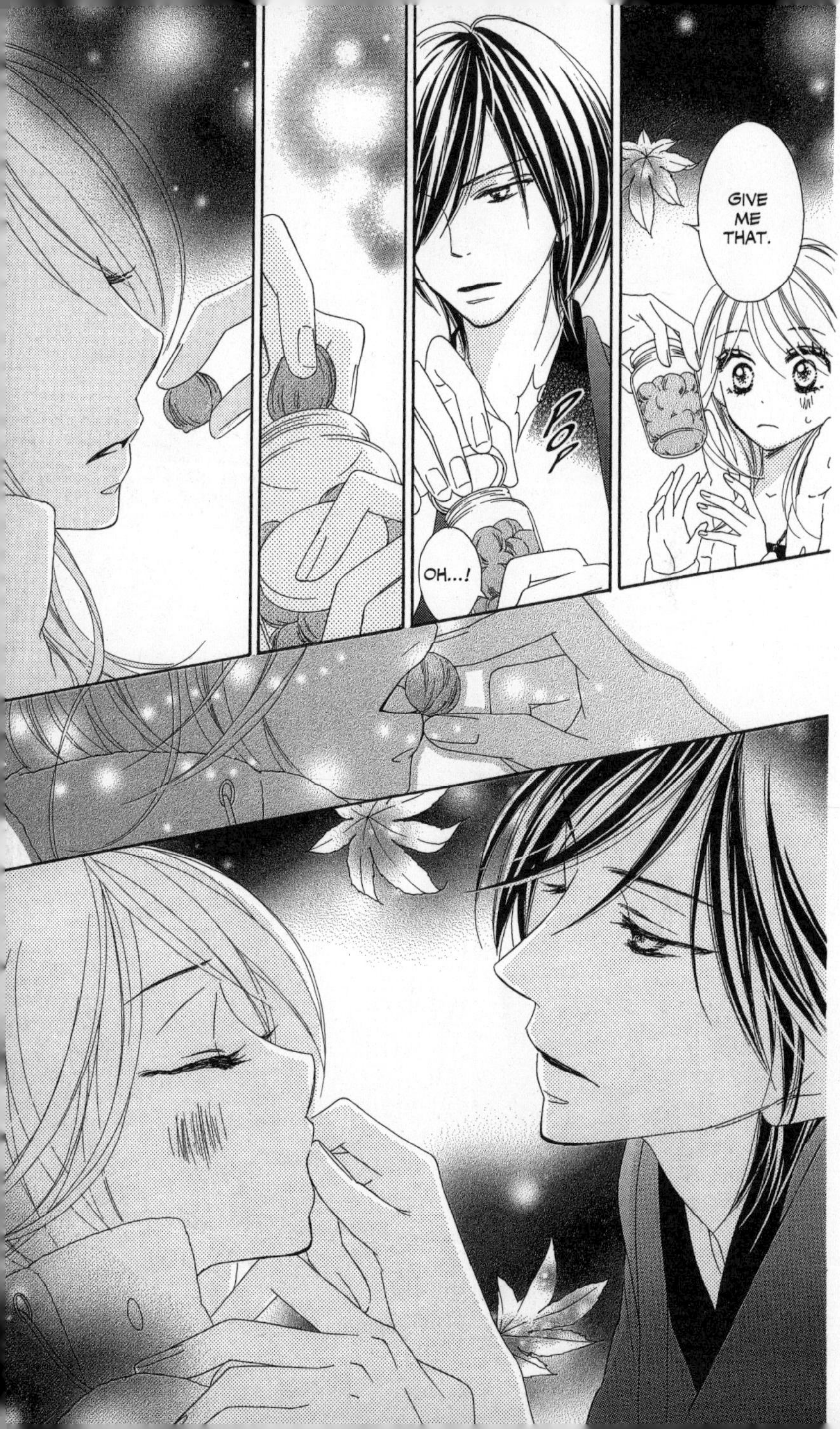
GIVE ME THAT.
POP
OH...!

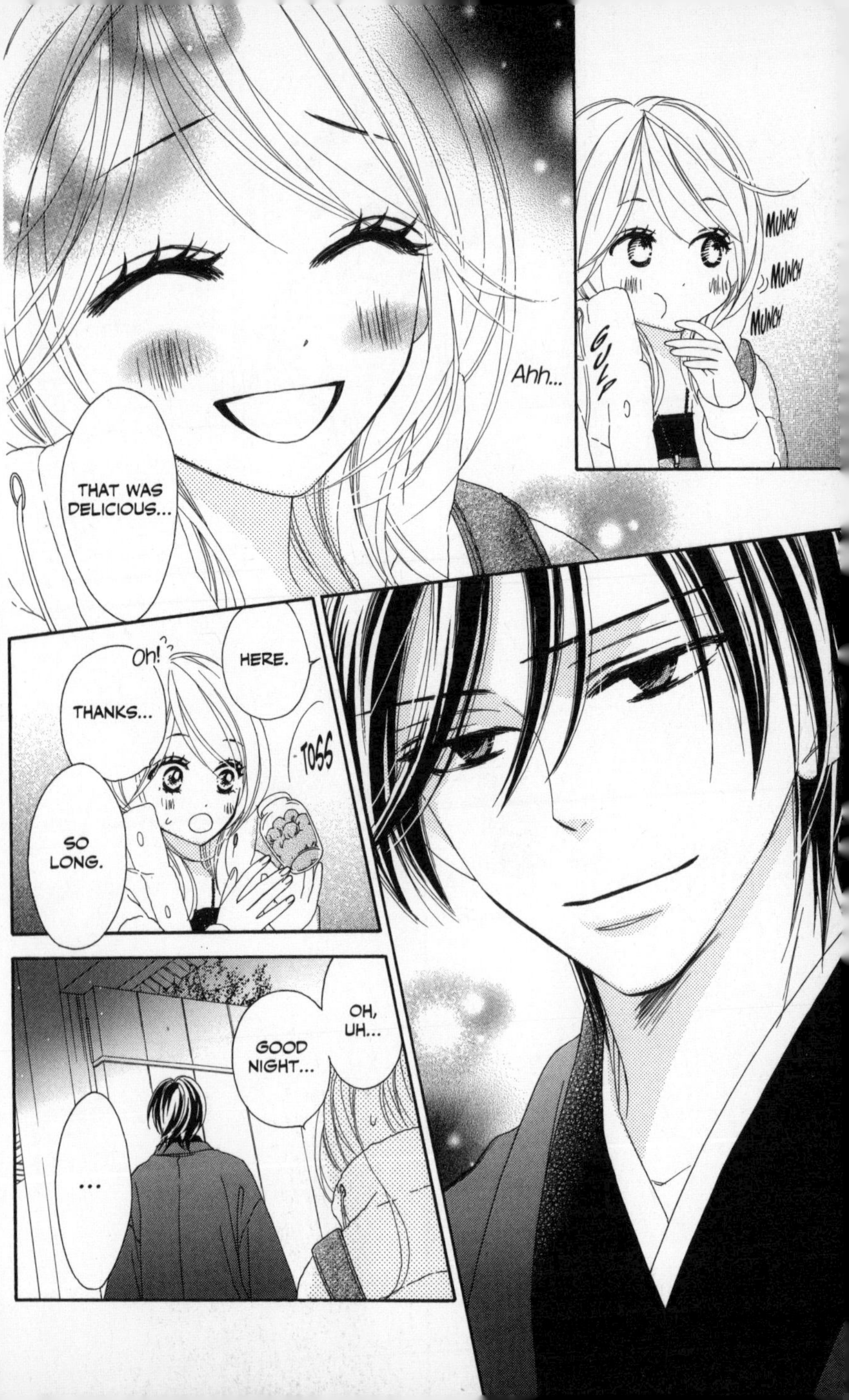

MUNCH
MUNCH
MUNCH
GULP
Ahh...
THAT WAS DELICIOUS...
HERE.
TOSS
Oh!
THANKS...
SO LONG.
OH, UH...
GOOD NIGHT...
...

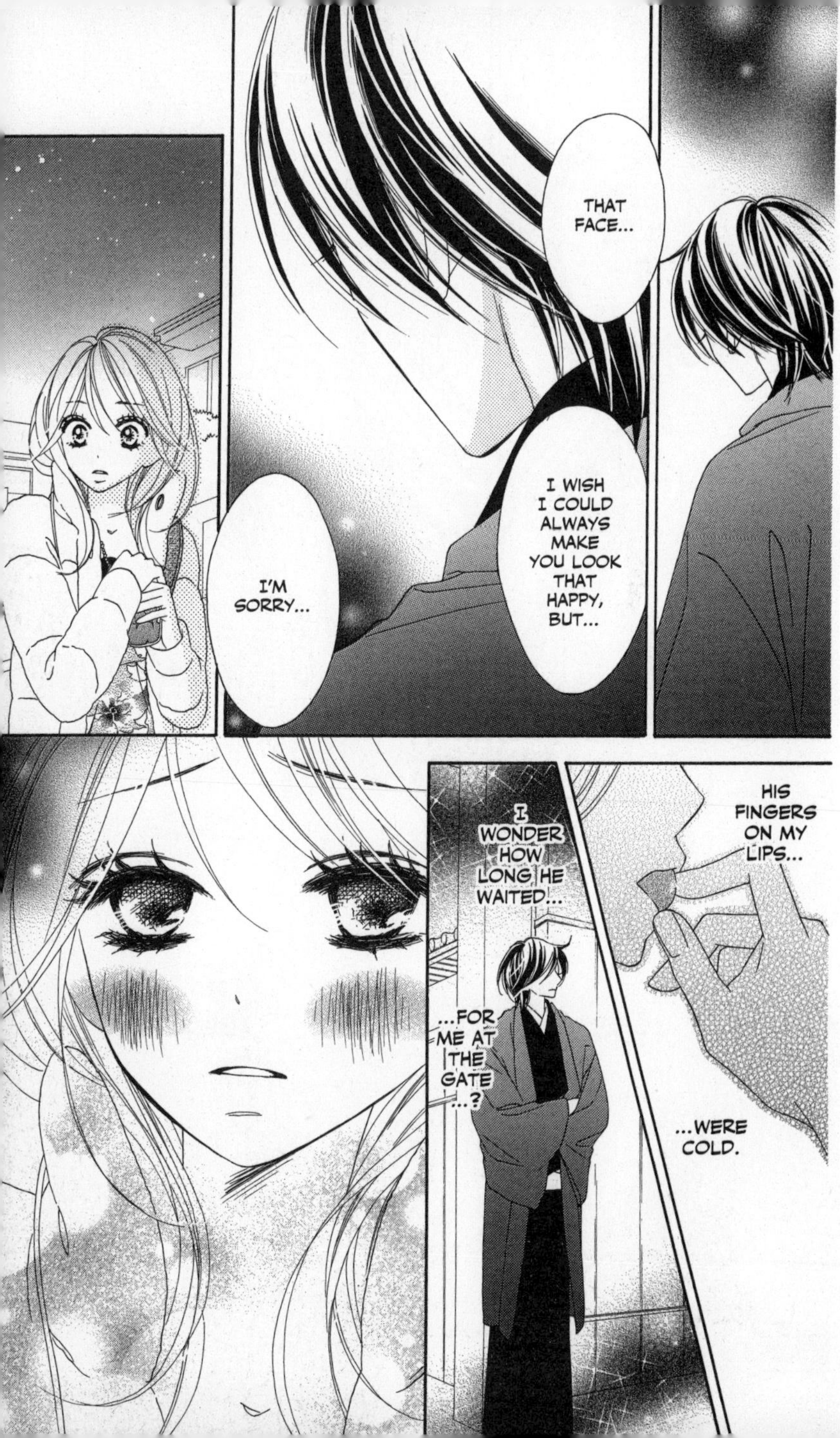
THAT FACE...
I WISH I COULD ALWAYS MAKE YOU LOOK THAT HAPPY, BUT...
I'M SORRY...
HIS FINGERS ON MY LIPS...
...WERE COLD.
I WONDER HOW LONG HE WAITED...
...FOR ME AT THE GATE...?

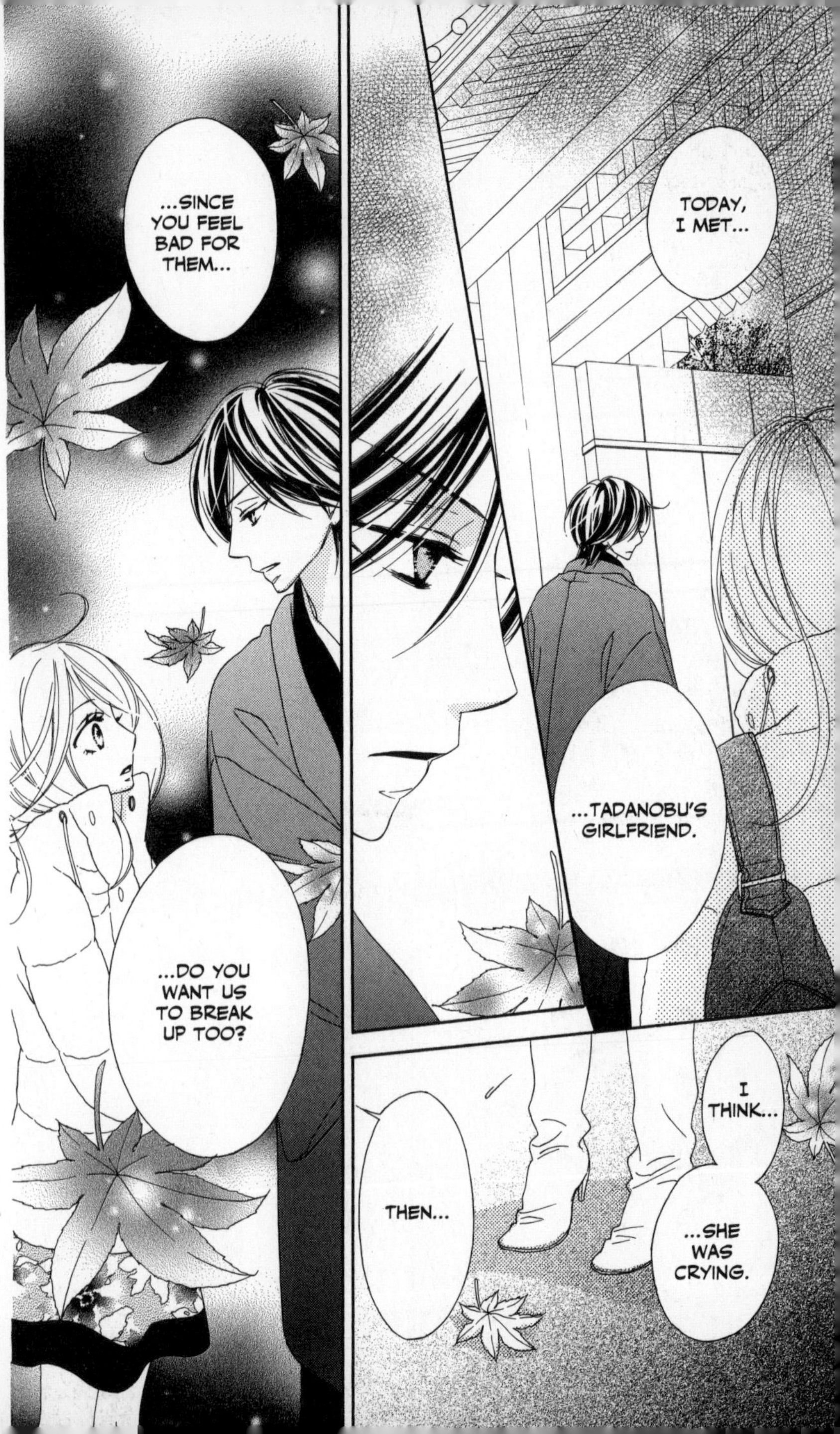
TODAY, I MET...
...TADANOBU'S GIRLFRIEND.
I THINK...
...SHE WAS CRYING.
THEN...
...SINCE YOU FEEL BAD FOR THEM...
...DO YOU WANT US TO BREAK UP TOO?

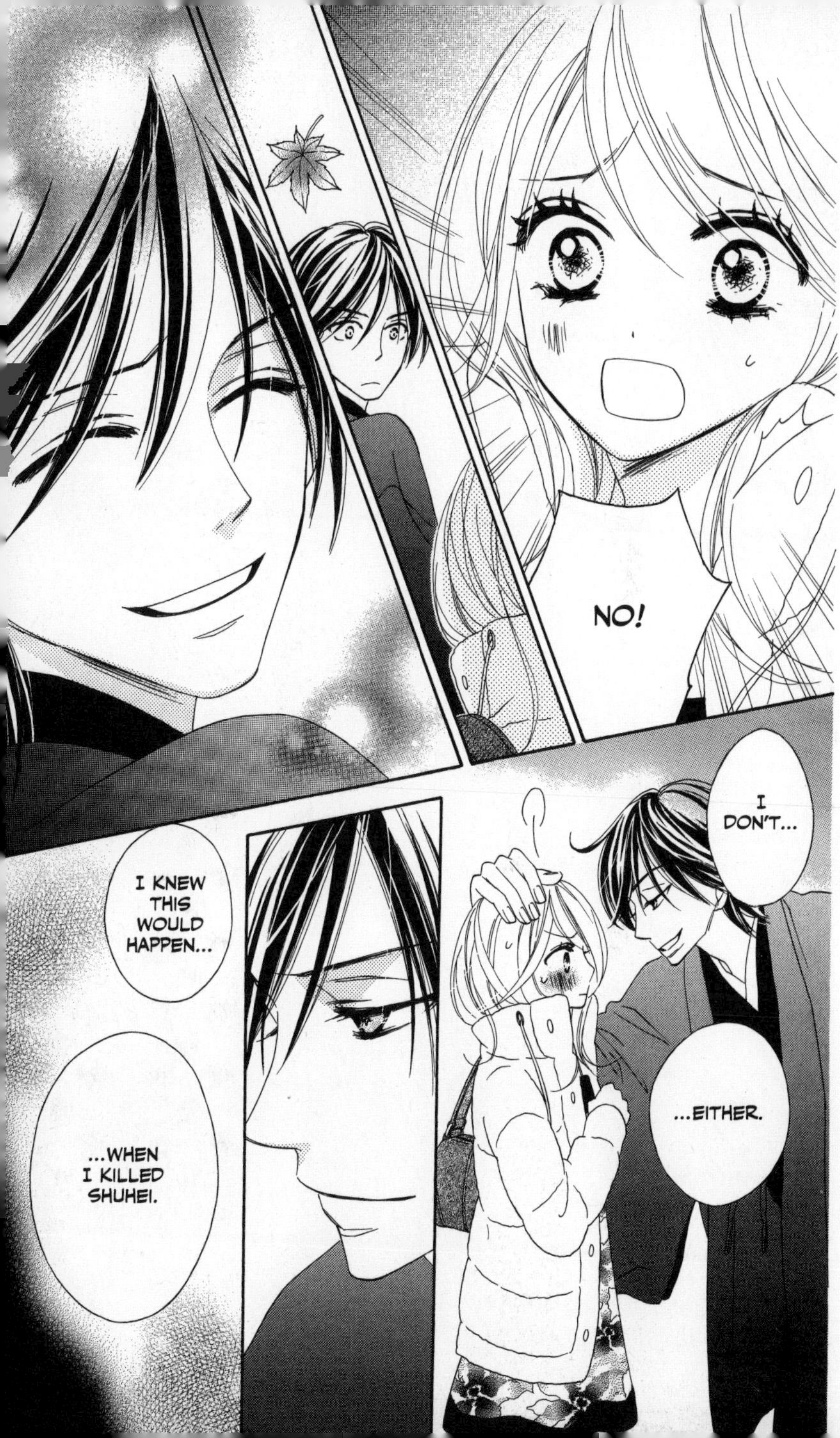
NO!
I DON'T...
...EITHER.
I KNEW THIS WOULD HAPPEN...
...WHEN I KILLED SHUHEI.

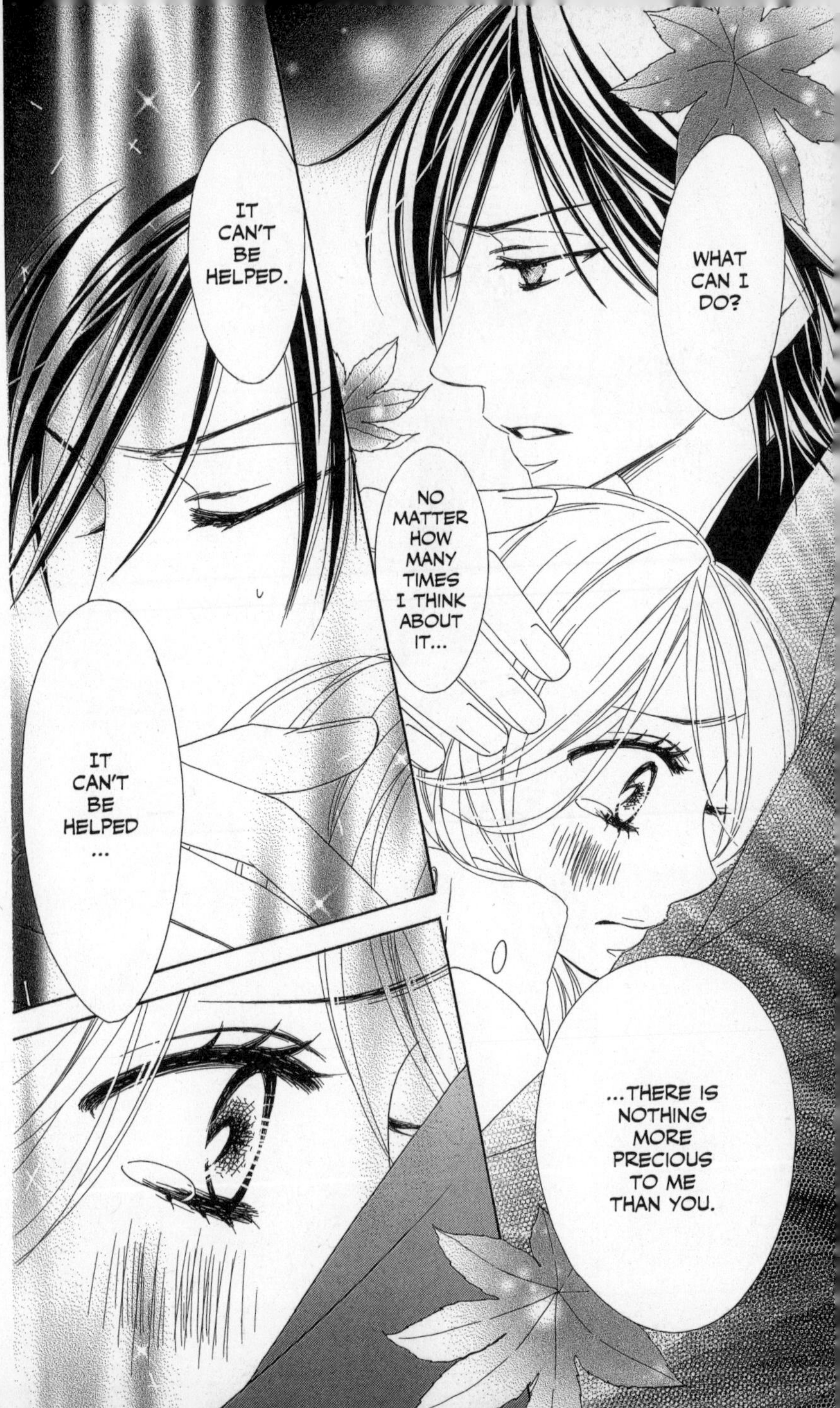
WHAT CAN I DO?
NO MATTER HOW MANY TIMES I THINK ABOUT IT...
...THERE IS NOTHING MORE PRECIOUS TO ME THAN YOU.
IT CAN'T BE HELPED.
IT CAN'T BE HELPED...

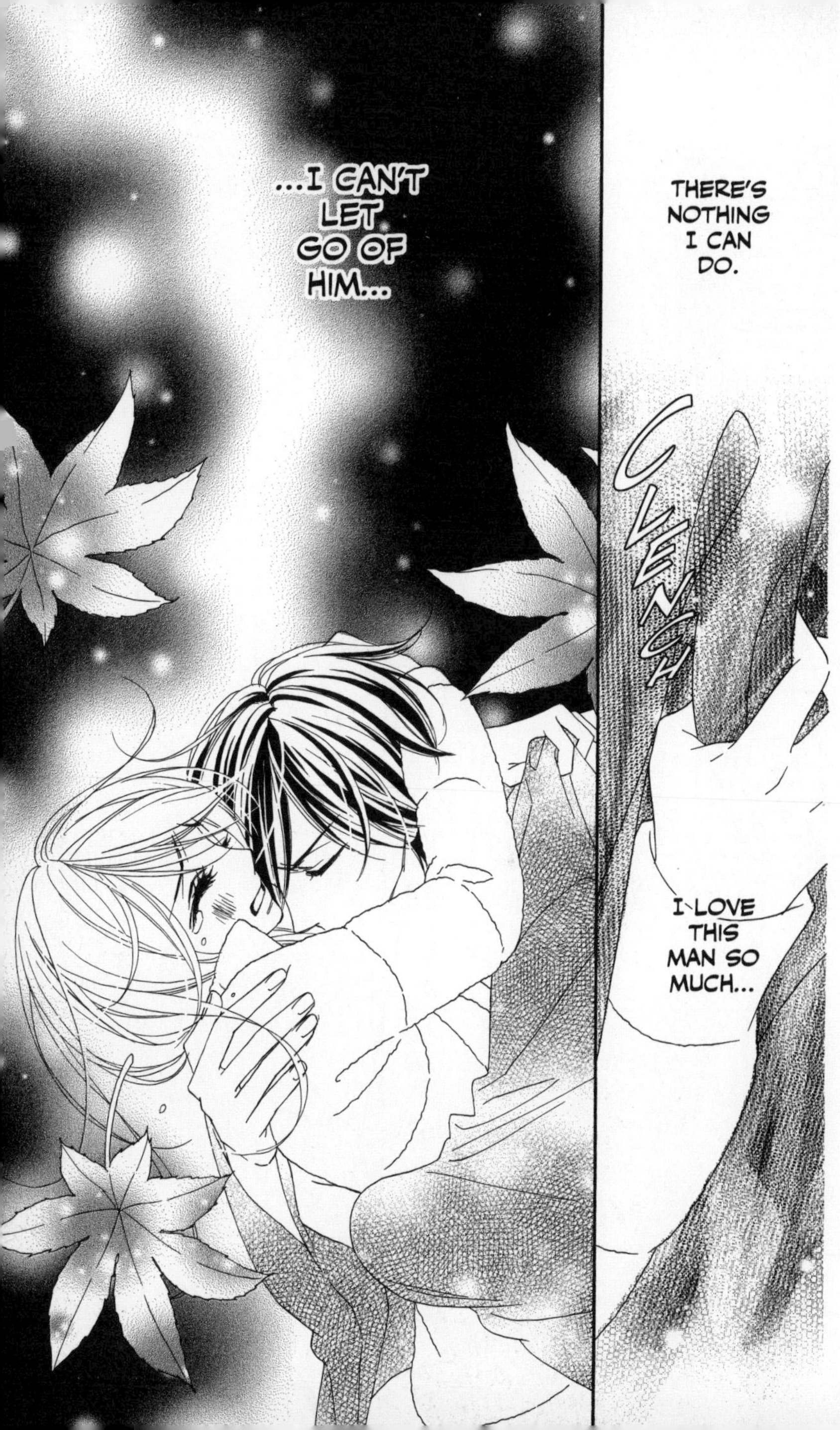
THERE'S NOTHING I CAN DO.
CLENCH
I LOVE THIS MAN SO MUCH...
...I CAN'T LET GO OF HIM...

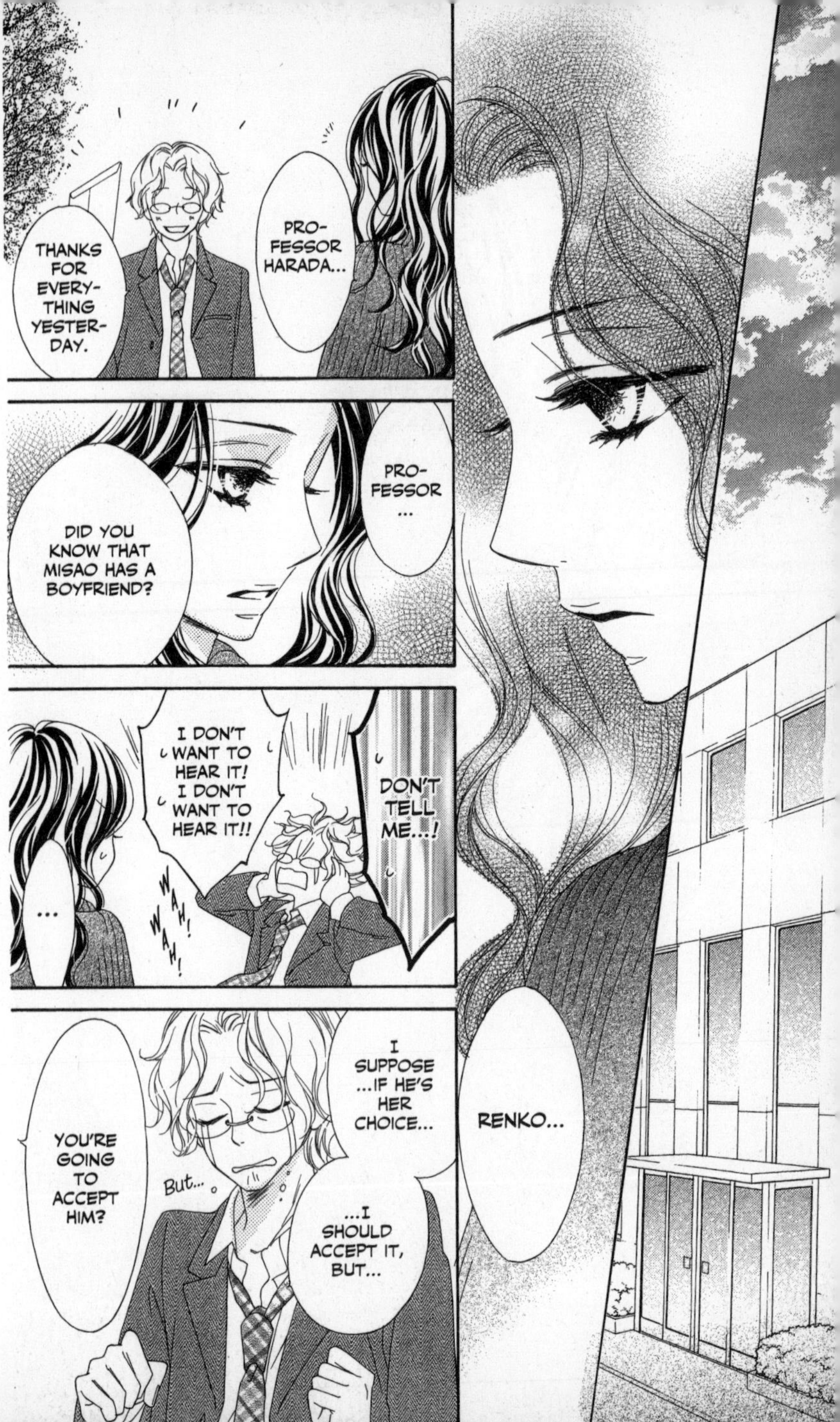
RENKO...
PRO-FESSOR HARADA...
THANKS FOR EVERY-THING YESTER-DAY.
PRO-FESSOR ...
DID YOU KNOW THAT MISAO HAS A BOYFRIEND?
DON'T TELL ME...!
I DON'T WANT TO HEAR IT! I DON'T WANT TO HEAR IT!!
WAH! WAH!
...
I SUPPOSE ...IF HE'S HER CHOICE...
...I SHOULD ACCEPT IT, BUT...
But...
YOU'RE GOING TO ACCEPT HIM?

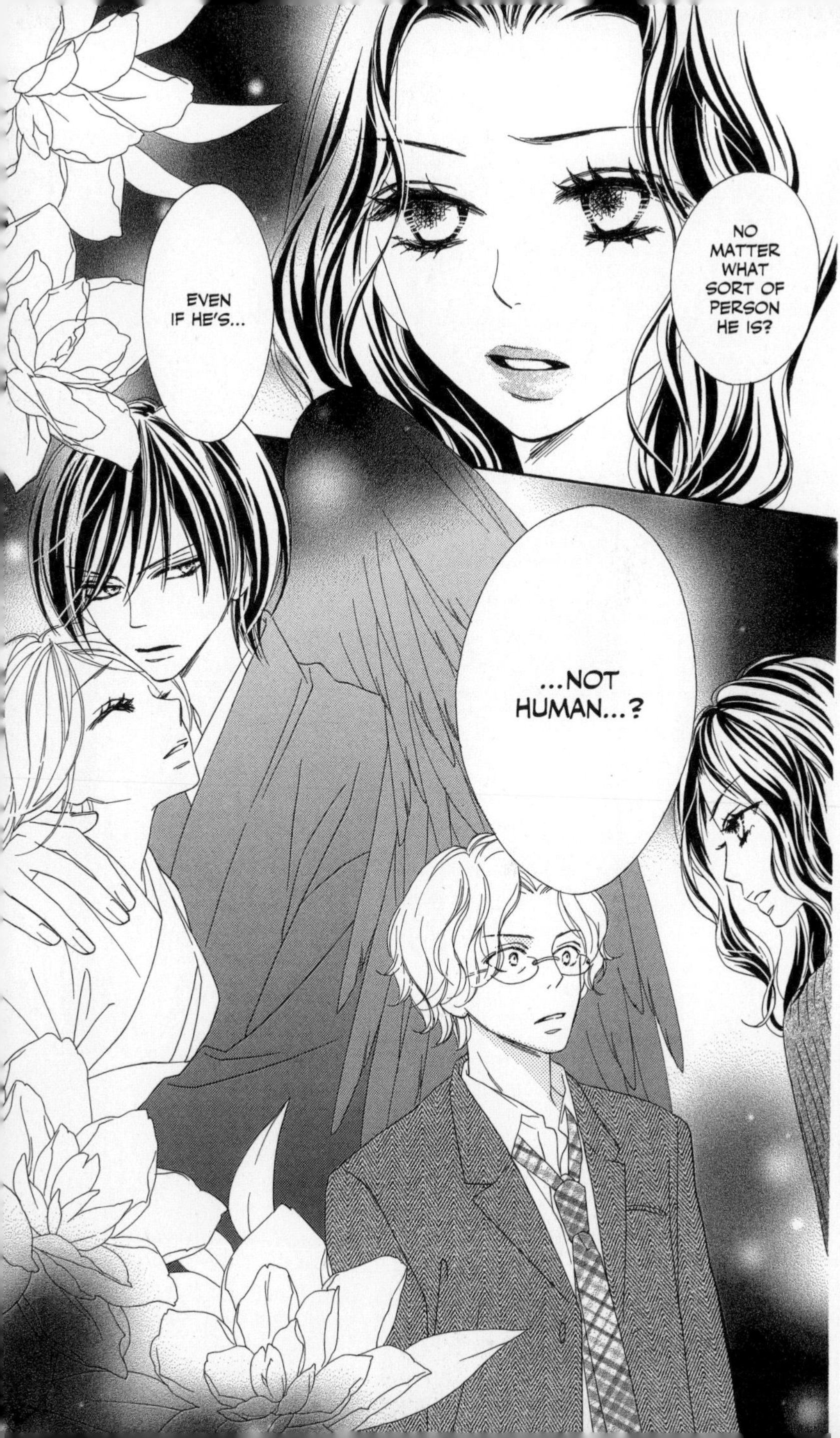
NO MATTER WHAT SORT OF PERSON HE IS?
EVEN IF HE'S...
...NOT HUMAN...?

Illustration Request Number Five

"Buzen the Police Officer"

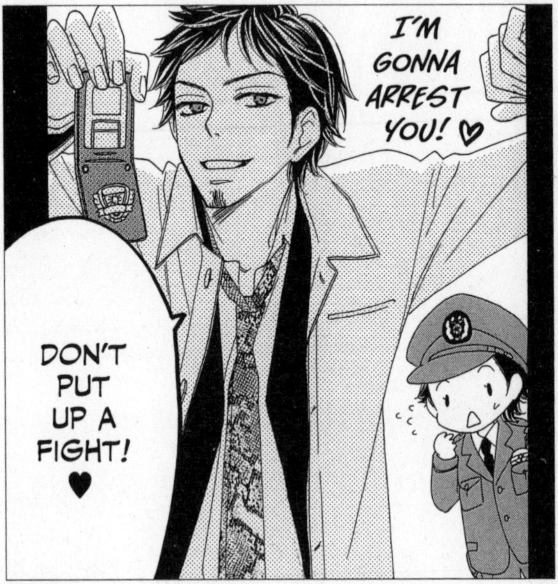
I'M GONNA ARREST YOU! ♡
DON'T PUT UP A FIGHT! ♥

I had the police badge and uniform at home before I even got the request. I love uniforms.♥

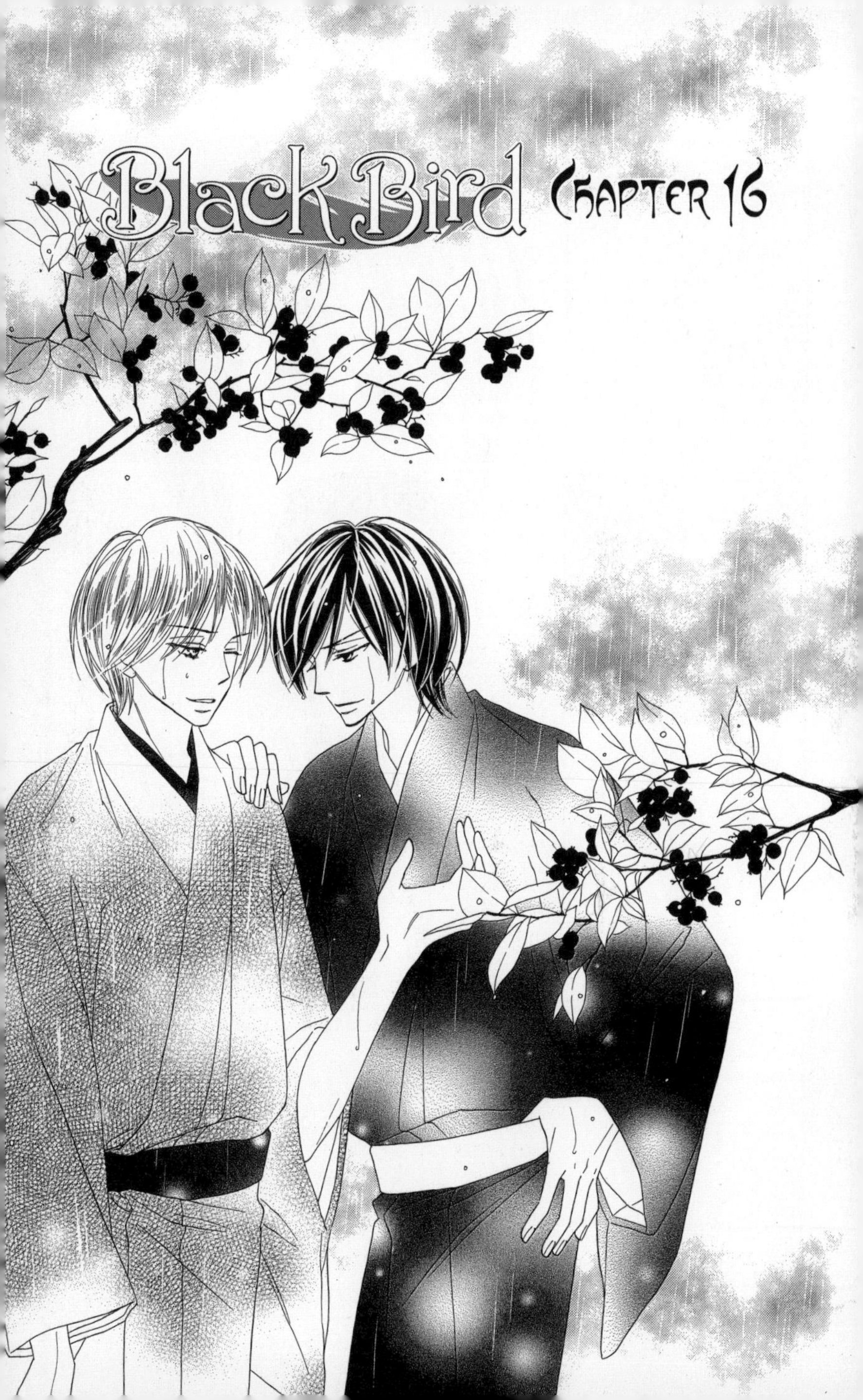
Black Bird
Chapter 16

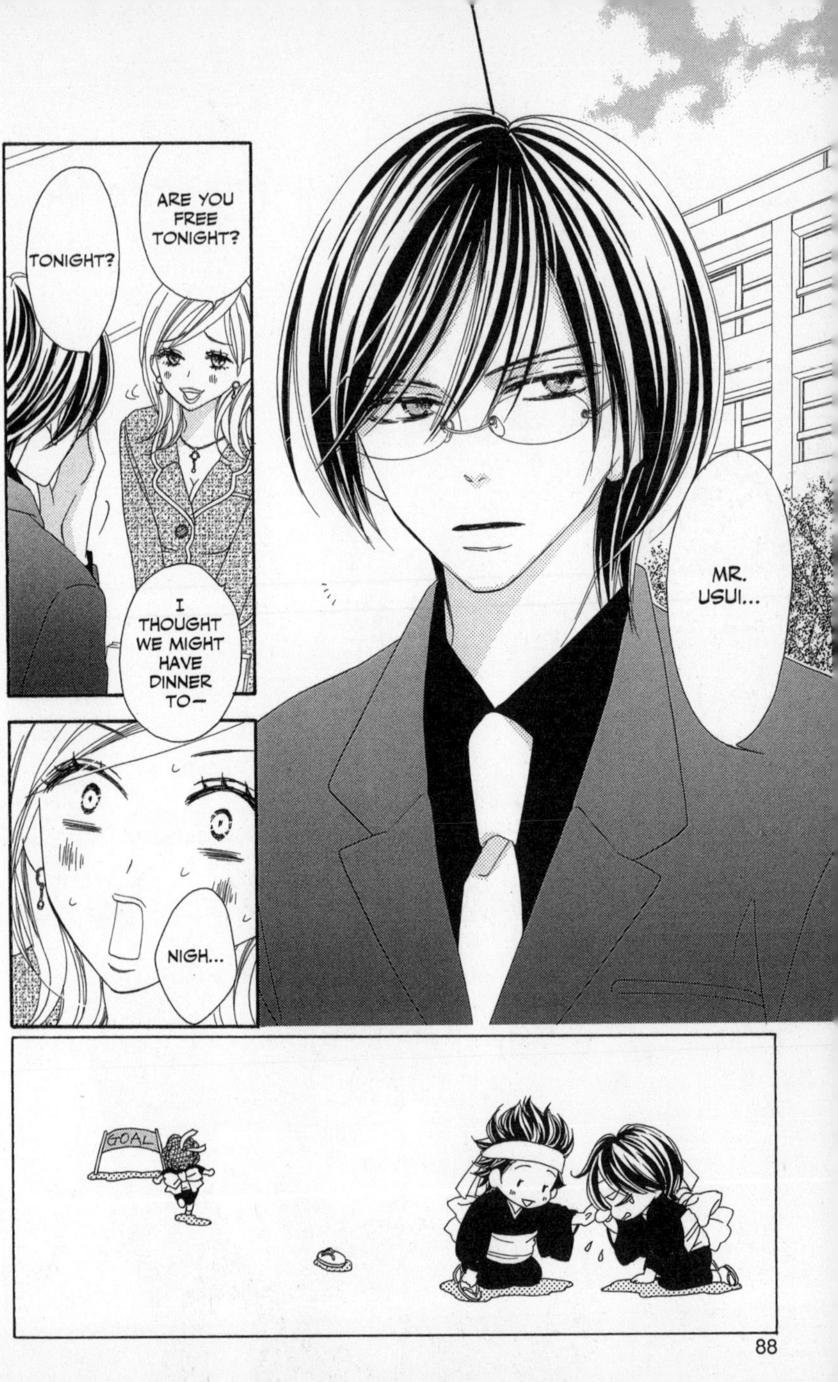
MR. USUI...
ARE YOU FREE TONIGHT?
TONIGHT?
I THOUGHT WE MIGHT HAVE DINNER TO—
NIGH...
GOAL

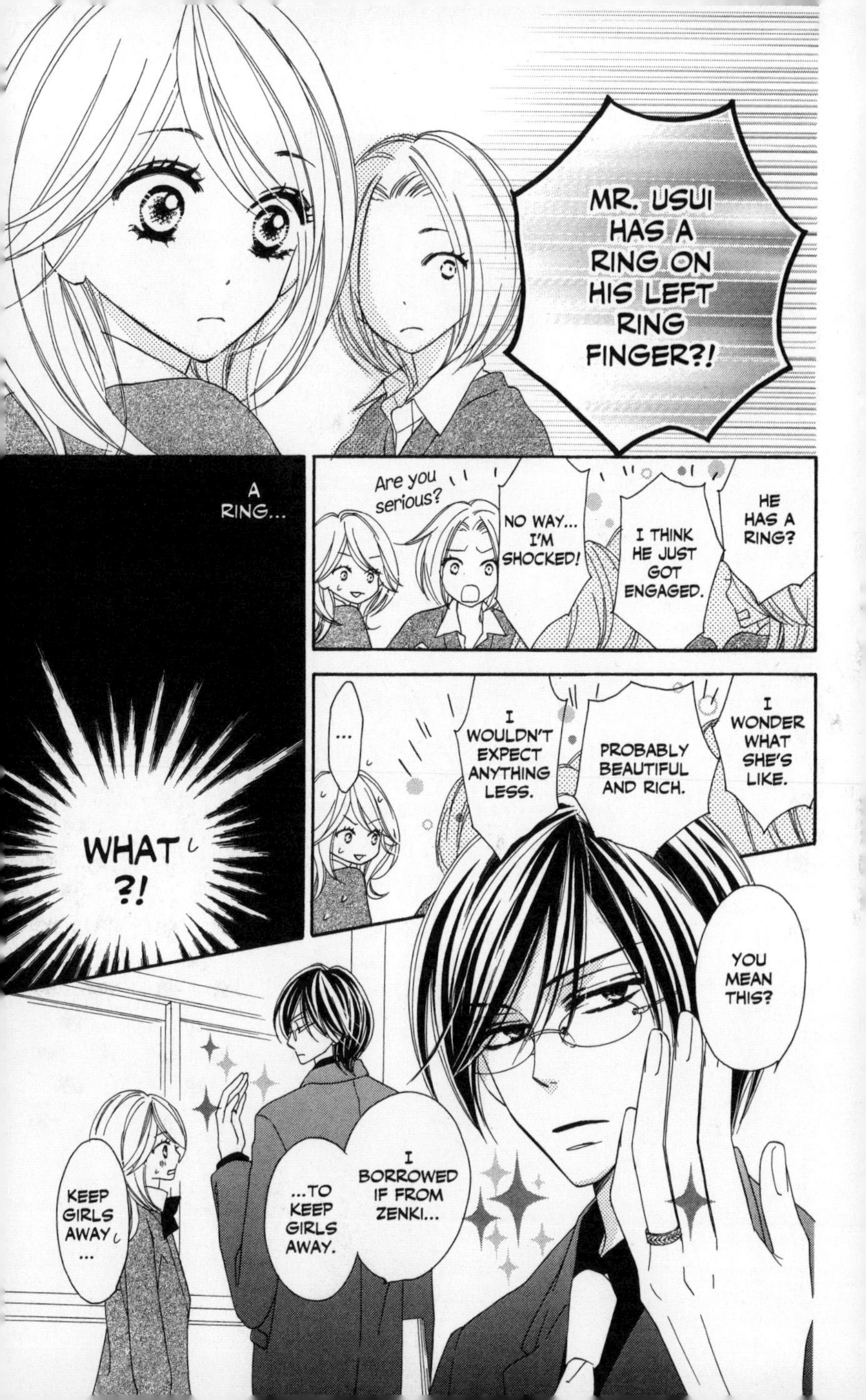
MR. USUI HAS A RING ON HIS LEFT RING FINGER?!
HE HAS A RING?
I THINK HE JUST GOT ENGAGED.
NO WAY... I'M SHOCKED!
Are you serious?
I WONDER WHAT SHE'S LIKE.
PROBABLY BEAUTIFUL AND RICH.
I WOULDN'T EXPECT ANYTHING LESS.
...
A RING...
WHAT?!
YOU MEAN THIS?
I BORROWED IF FROM ZENKI...
...TO KEEP GIRLS AWAY.
KEEP GIRLS AWAY...

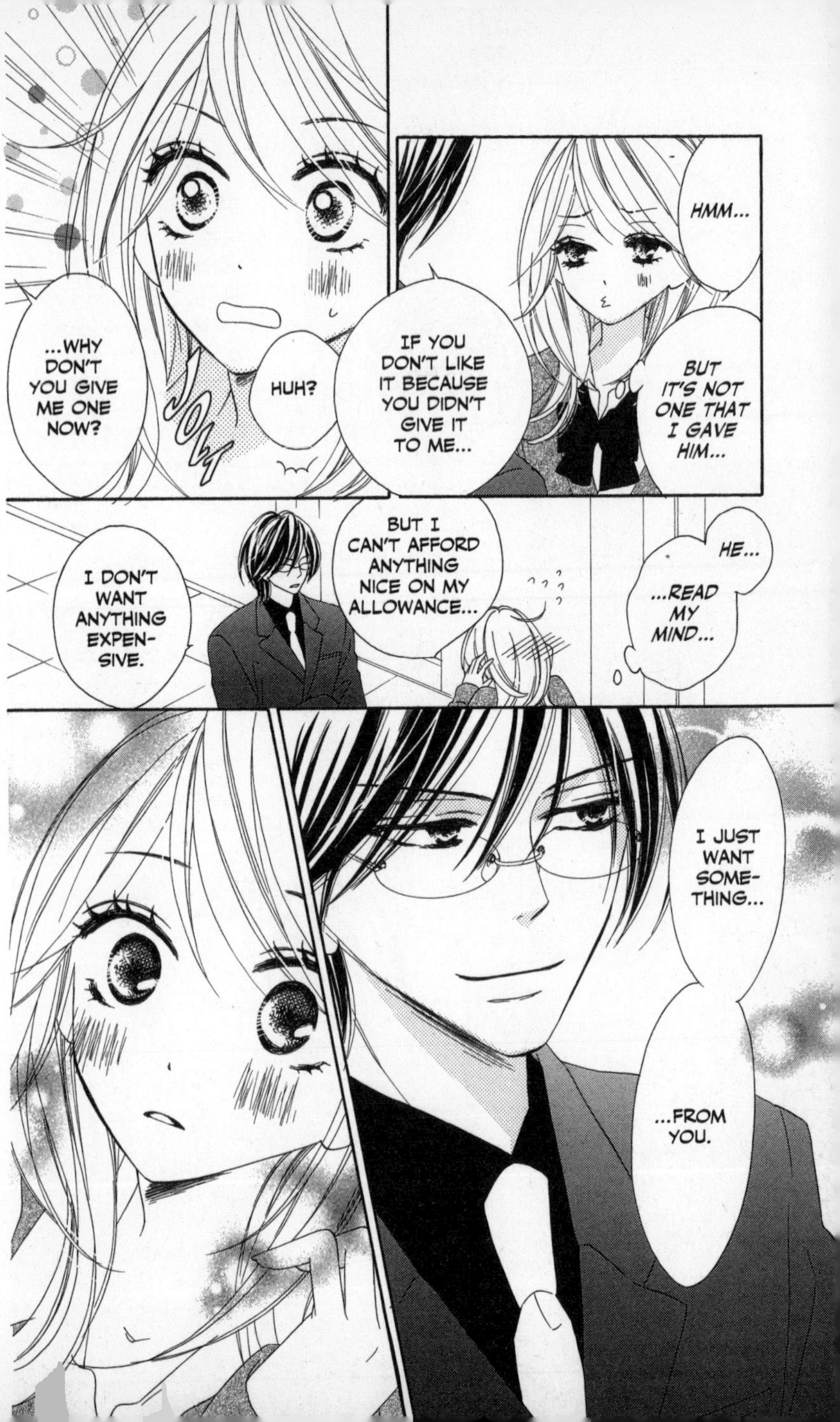
HMM...
BUT IT'S NOT ONE THAT I GAVE HIM...
IF YOU DON'T LIKE IT BECAUSE YOU DIDN'T GIVE IT TO ME...
HUH?
...WHY DON'T YOU GIVE ME ONE NOW?
HE... ...READ MY MIND...
BUT I CAN'T AFFORD ANYTHING NICE ON MY ALLOWANCE...
I DON'T WANT ANYTHING EXPEN-SIVE.
I JUST WANT SOME-THING...
...FROM YOU.

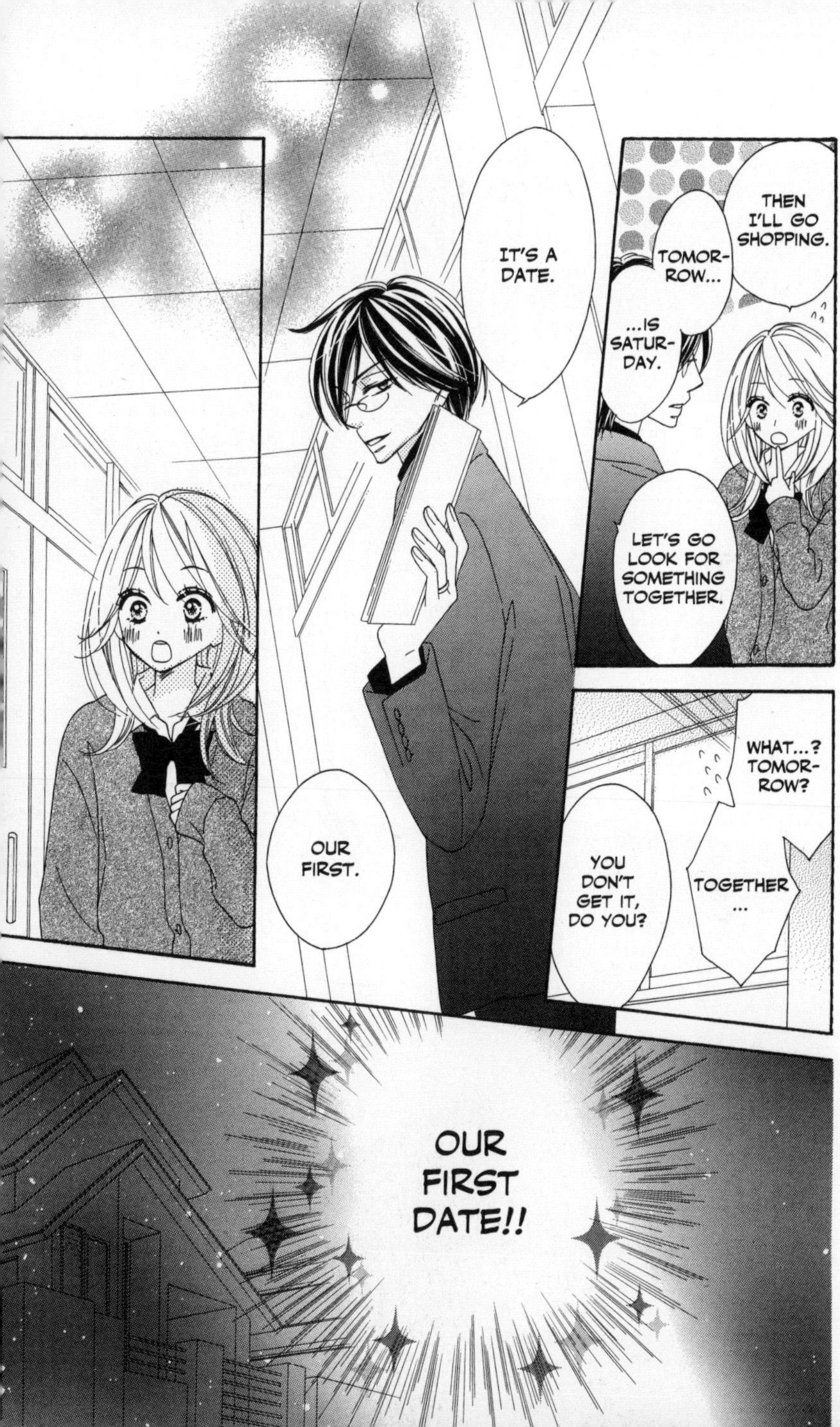
THEN I'LL GO SHOPPING.
TOMOR-ROW...
...IS SATUR-DAY.
LET'S GO LOOK FOR SOMETHING TOGETHER.
WHAT...? TOMOR-ROW?
TOGETHER...
YOU DON'T GET IT, DO YOU?
IT'S A DATE.
OUR FIRST.
OUR FIRST DATE!!

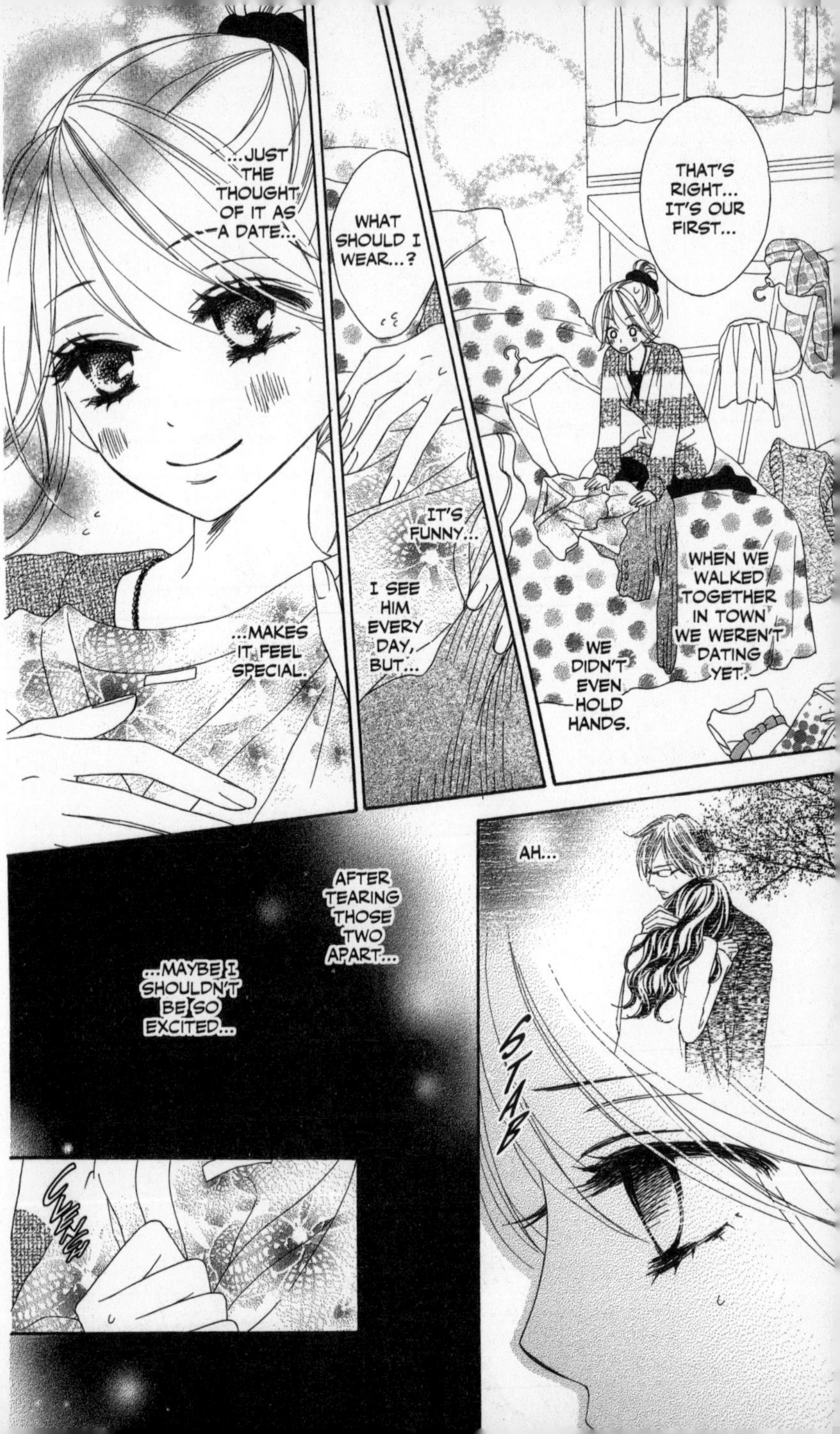
THAT'S RIGHT... IT'S OUR FIRST...
WHEN WE WALKED TOGETHER IN TOWN WE WEREN'T DATING YET.
WE DIDN'T EVEN HOLD HANDS.
WHAT SHOULD I WEAR...?
IT'S FUNNY...
I SEE HIM EVERY DAY, BUT...
...JUST THE THOUGHT OF IT AS A DATE...
...MAKES IT FEEL SPECIAL.
AH...
STAB
AFTER TEARING THOSE TWO APART...
...MAYBE I SHOULDN'T BE SO EXCITED...

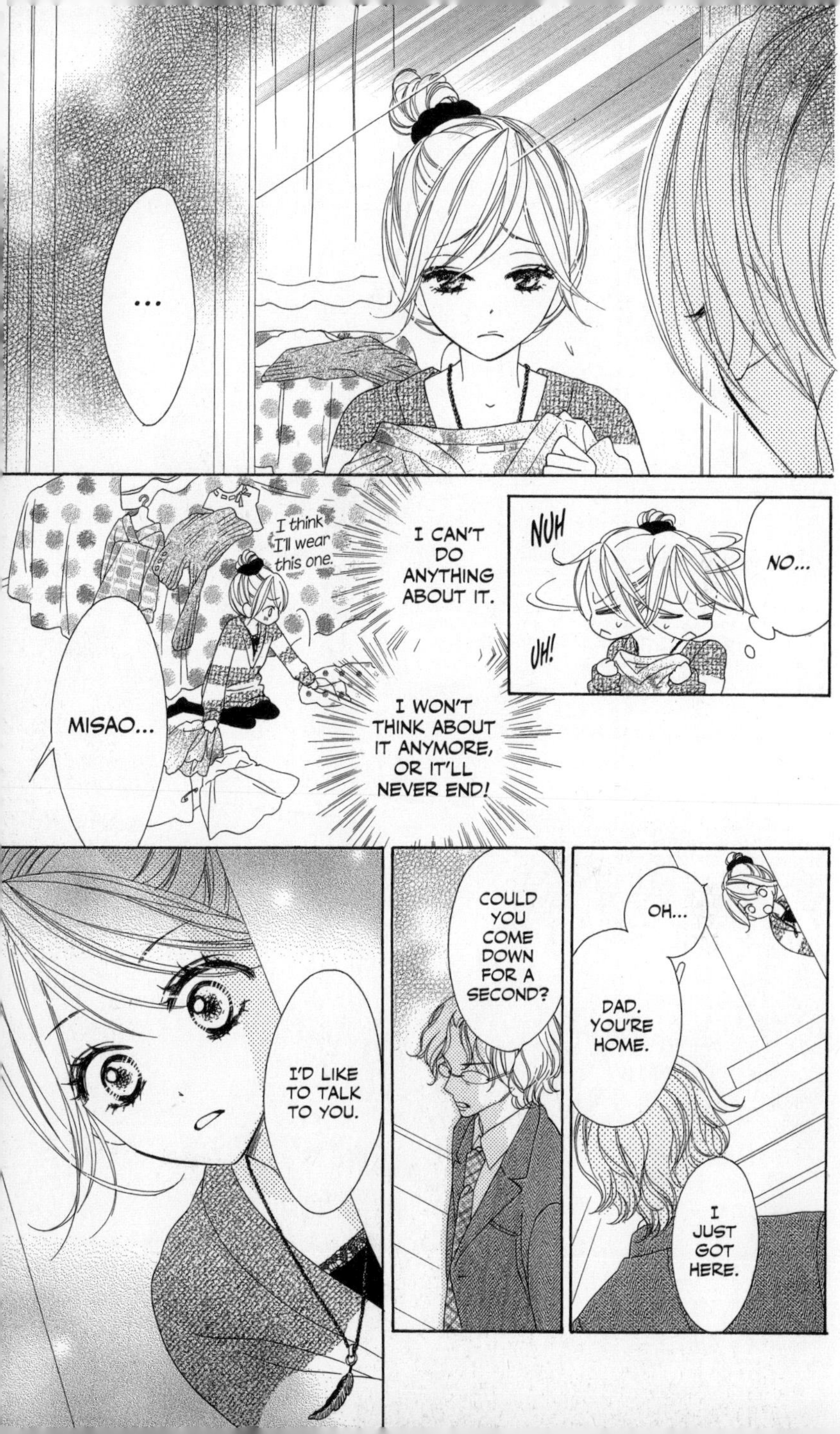
...
NO...
NUH
UH!
I CAN'T DO ANYTHING ABOUT IT.
I think I'll wear this one.
I WON'T THINK ABOUT IT ANYMORE, OR IT'LL NEVER END!
MISAO...
OH...
DAD. YOU'RE HOME.
I JUST GOT HERE.
COULD YOU COME DOWN FOR A SECOND?
I'D LIKE TO TALK TO YOU.

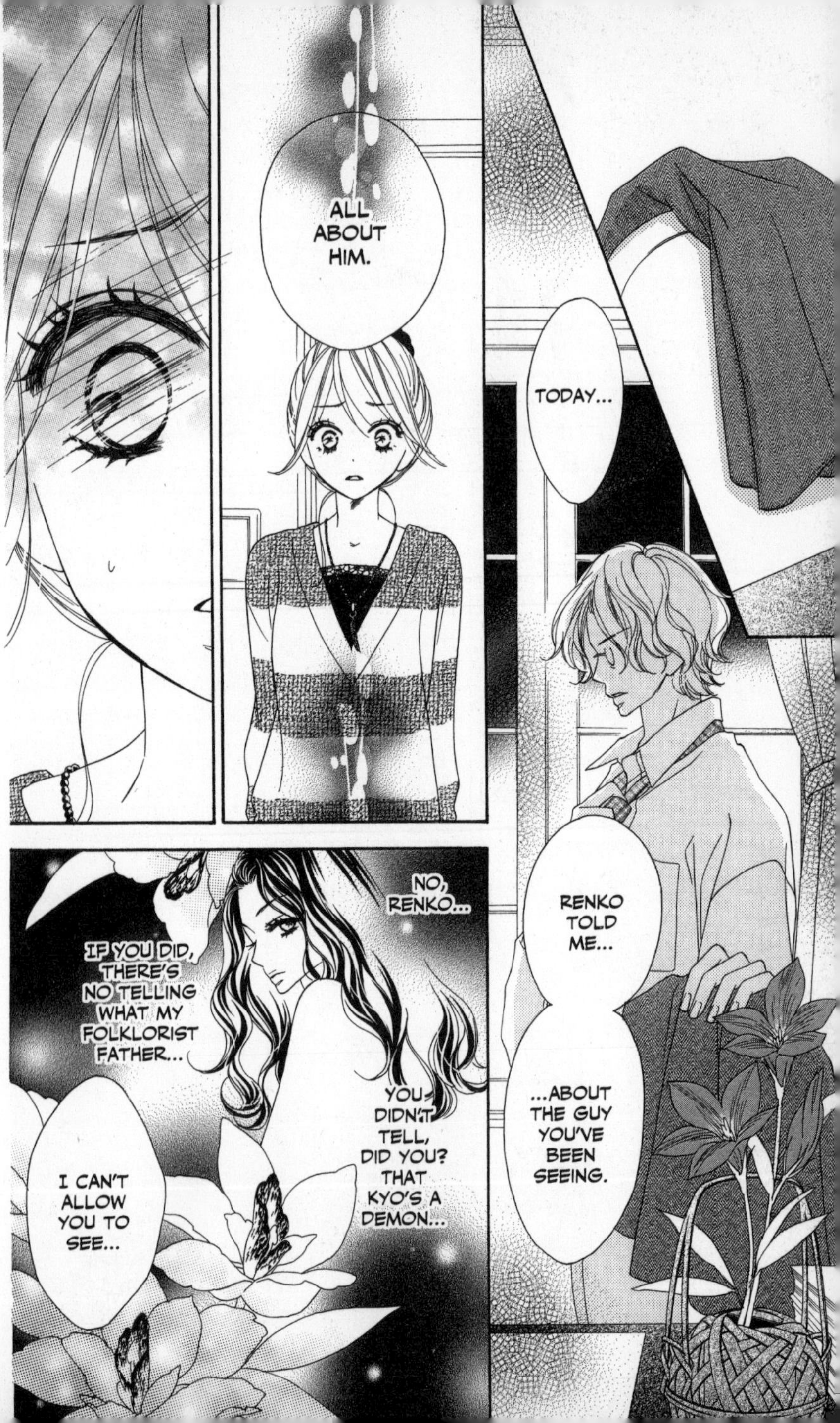
TODAY...
RENKO TOLD ME...
...ABOUT THE GUY YOU'VE BEEN SEEING.
ALL ABOUT HIM.
NO, RENKO...
YOU DIDN'T TELL, DID YOU? THAT KYO'S A DEMON...
IF YOU DID, THERE'S NO TELLING WHAT MY FOLKLORIST FATHER...
I CAN'T ALLOW YOU TO SEE...

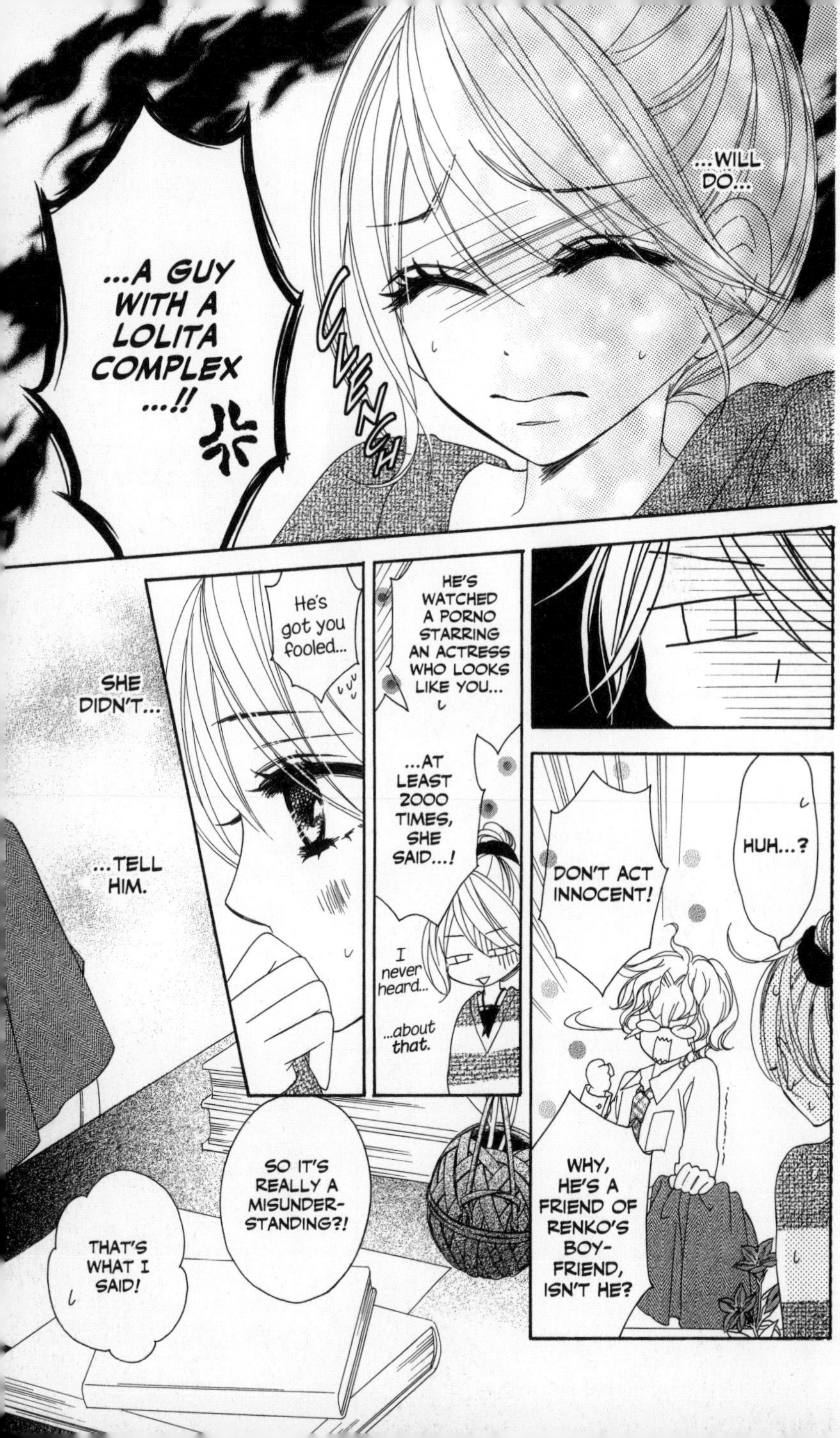
...WILL DO...
UWENGH
...A GUY WITH A LOLITA COMPLEX ...!!
HUH...?
DON'T ACT INNOCENT!
WHY, HE'S A FRIEND OF RENKO'S BOY-FRIEND, ISN'T HE?
HE'S WATCHED A PORNO STARRING AN ACTRESS WHO LOOKS LIKE YOU...
...AT LEAST 2000 TIMES, SHE SAID...!
I never heard...
...about that.
He's got you fooled...
SHE DIDN'T...
...TELL HIM.
SO IT'S REALLY A MISUNDER-STANDING?!
THAT'S WHAT I SAID!

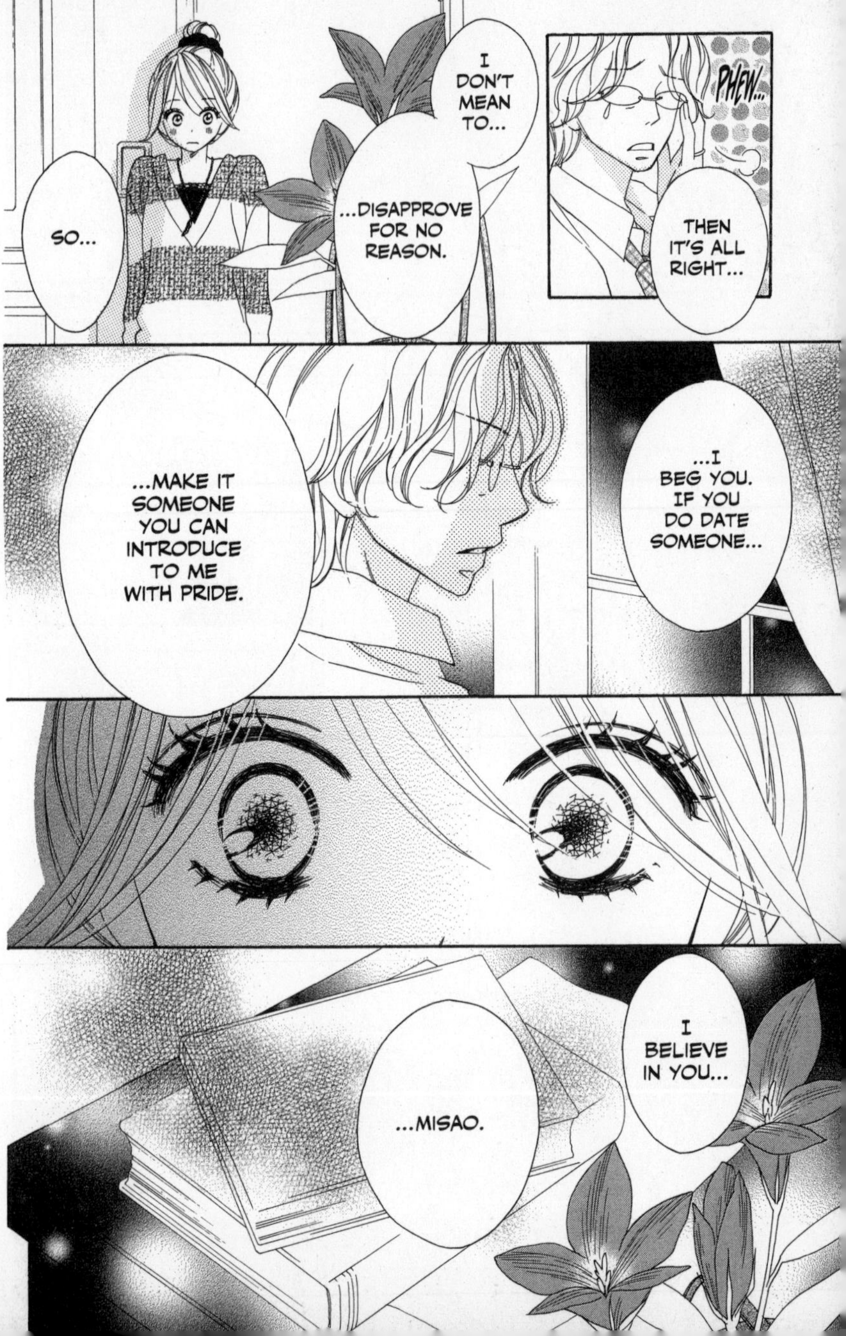
PHEW...
THEN IT'S ALL RIGHT...
I DON'T MEAN TO...
...DISAPPROVE FOR NO REASON.
SO...
...I BEG YOU. IF YOU DO DATE SOMEONE...
...MAKE IT SOMEONE YOU CAN INTRODUCE TO ME WITH PRIDE.
I BELIEVE IN YOU...
...MISAO.

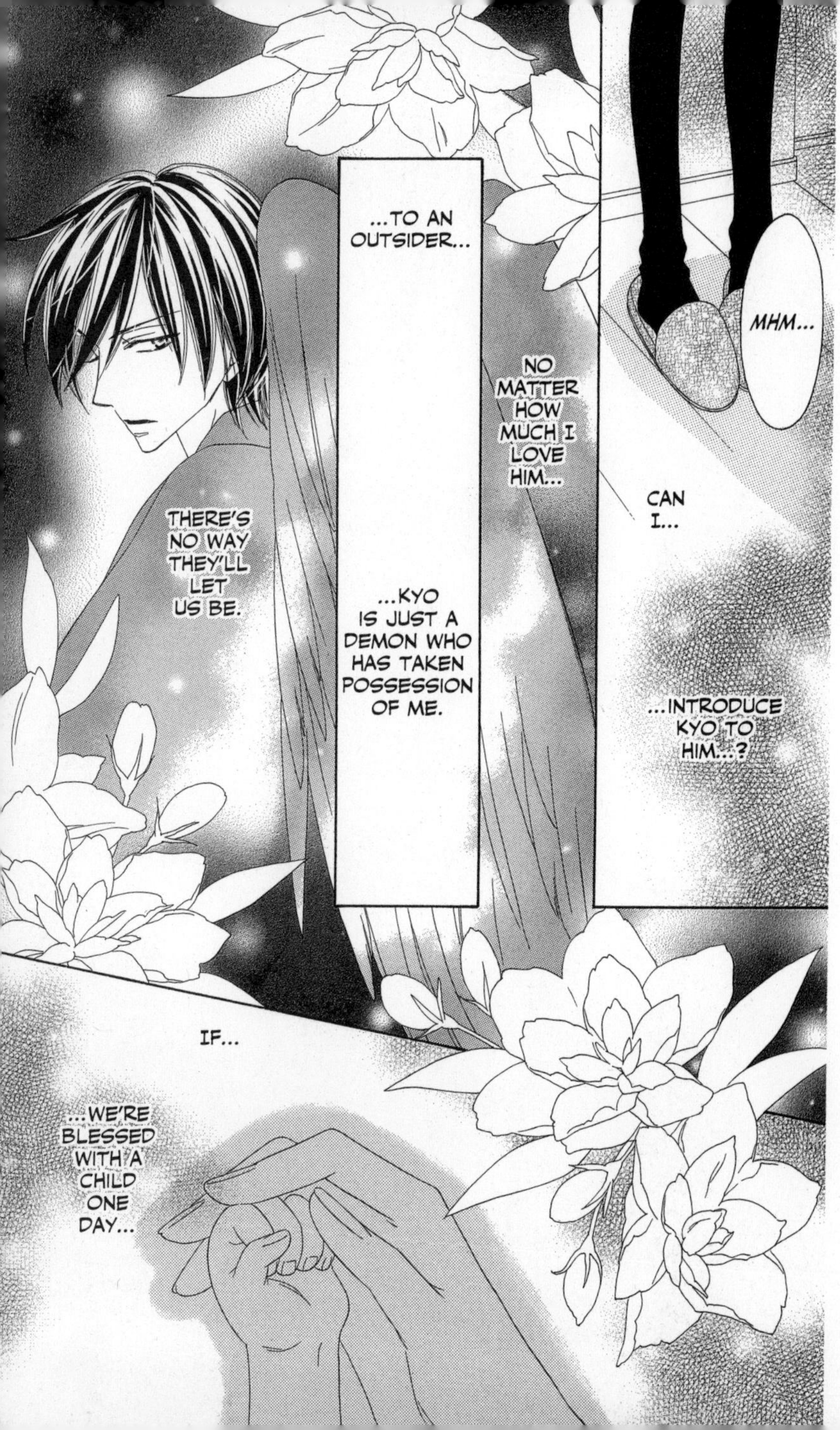
MHM...
CAN I...
...INTRODUCE KYO TO HIM...?
NO MATTER HOW MUCH I LOVE HIM...
...TO AN OUTSIDER...
...KYO IS JUST A DEMON WHO HAS TAKEN POSSESSION OF ME.
THERE'S NO WAY THEY'LL LET US BE.
IF...
...WE'RE BLESSED WITH A CHILD ONE DAY...

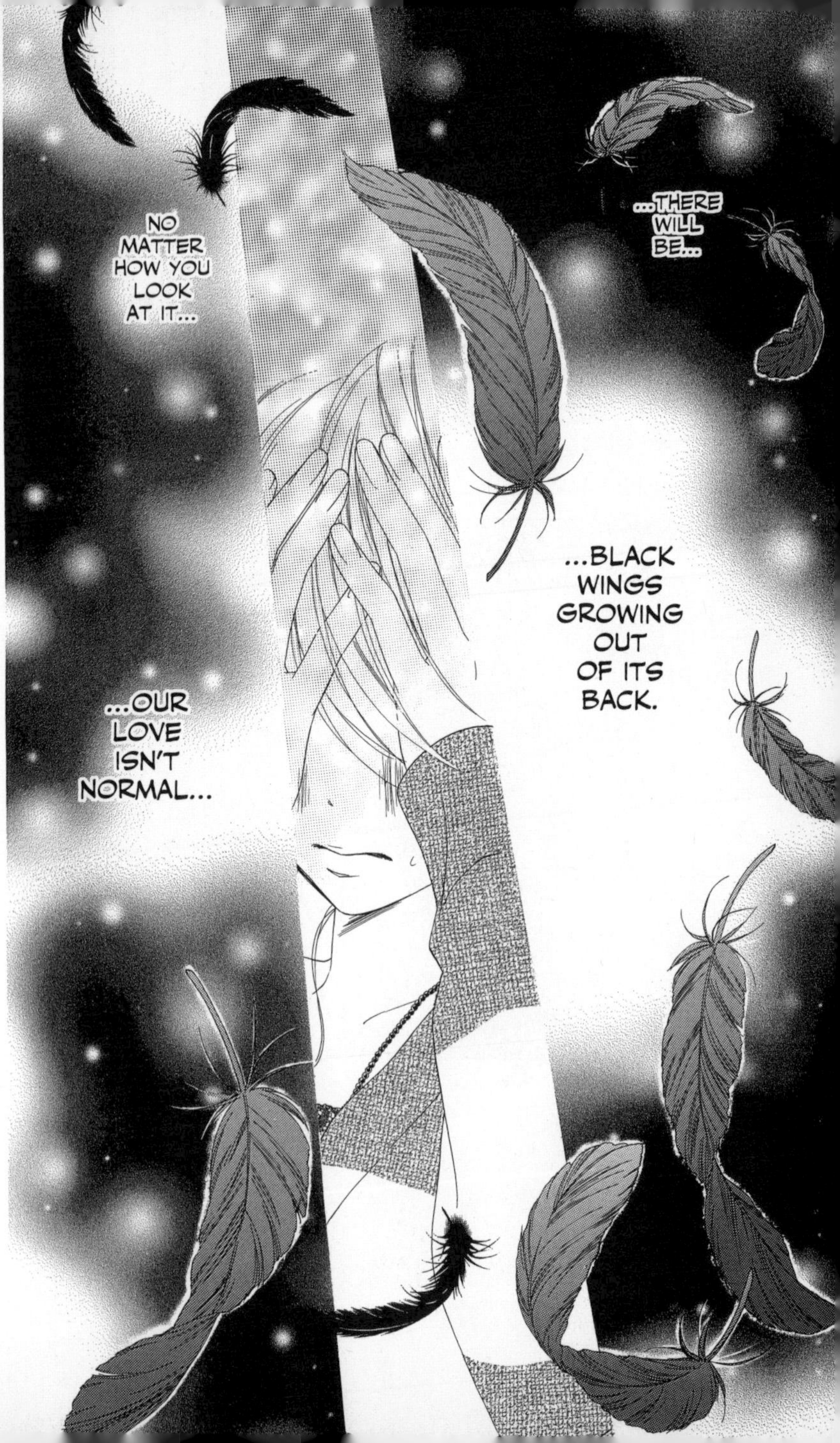
NO MATTER HOW YOU LOOK AT IT...
...OUR LOVE ISN'T NORMAL...
...THERE WILL BE...
...BLACK WINGS GROWING OUT OF ITS BACK.

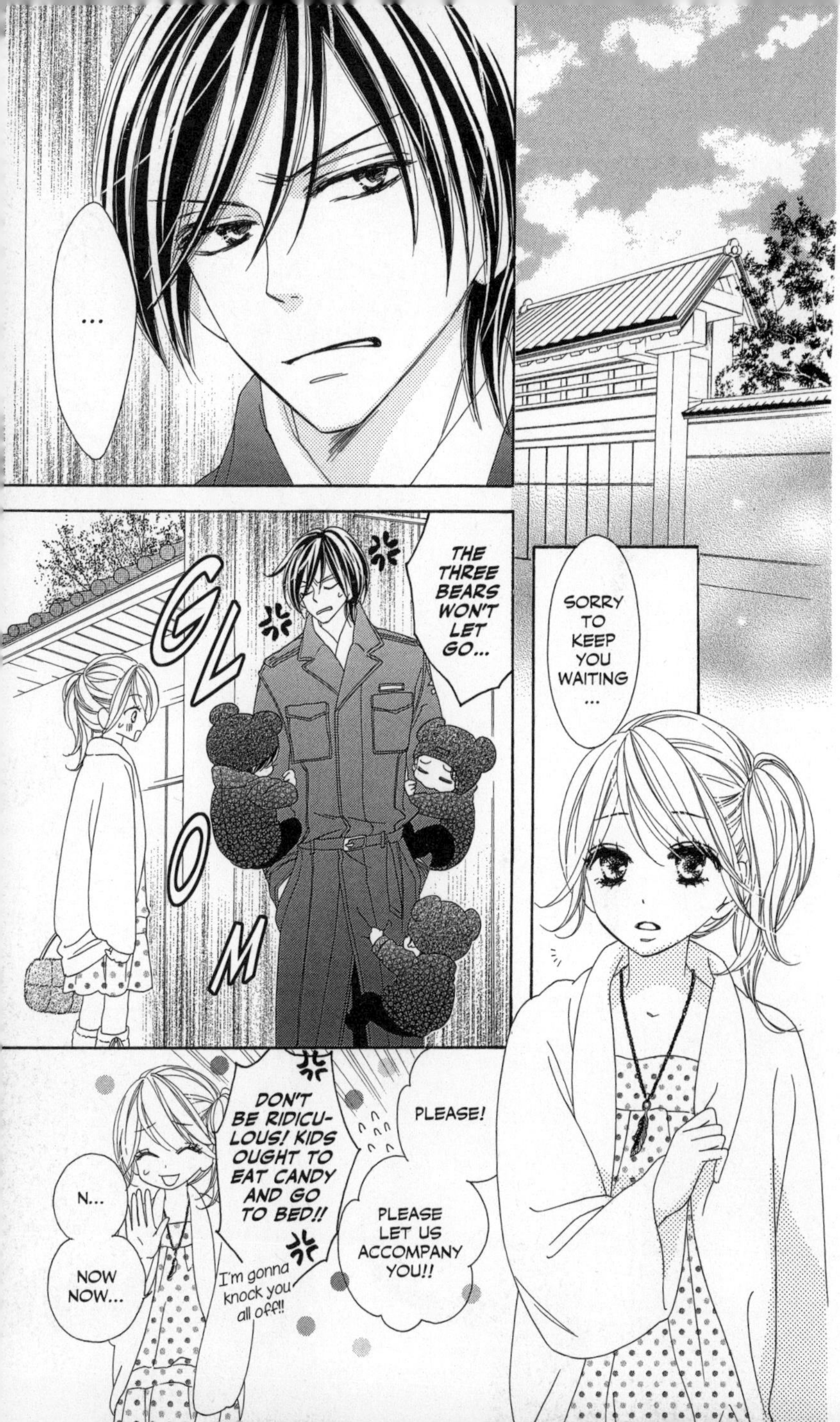
SORRY TO KEEP YOU WAITING ...
...
THE THREE BEARS WON'T LET GO...
GLOOM
PLEASE!
PLEASE LET US ACCOMPANY YOU!!
DON'T BE RIDICULOUS! KIDS OUGHT TO EAT CANDY AND GO TO BED!!
I'm gonna knock you all off!!
N...
NOW NOW...

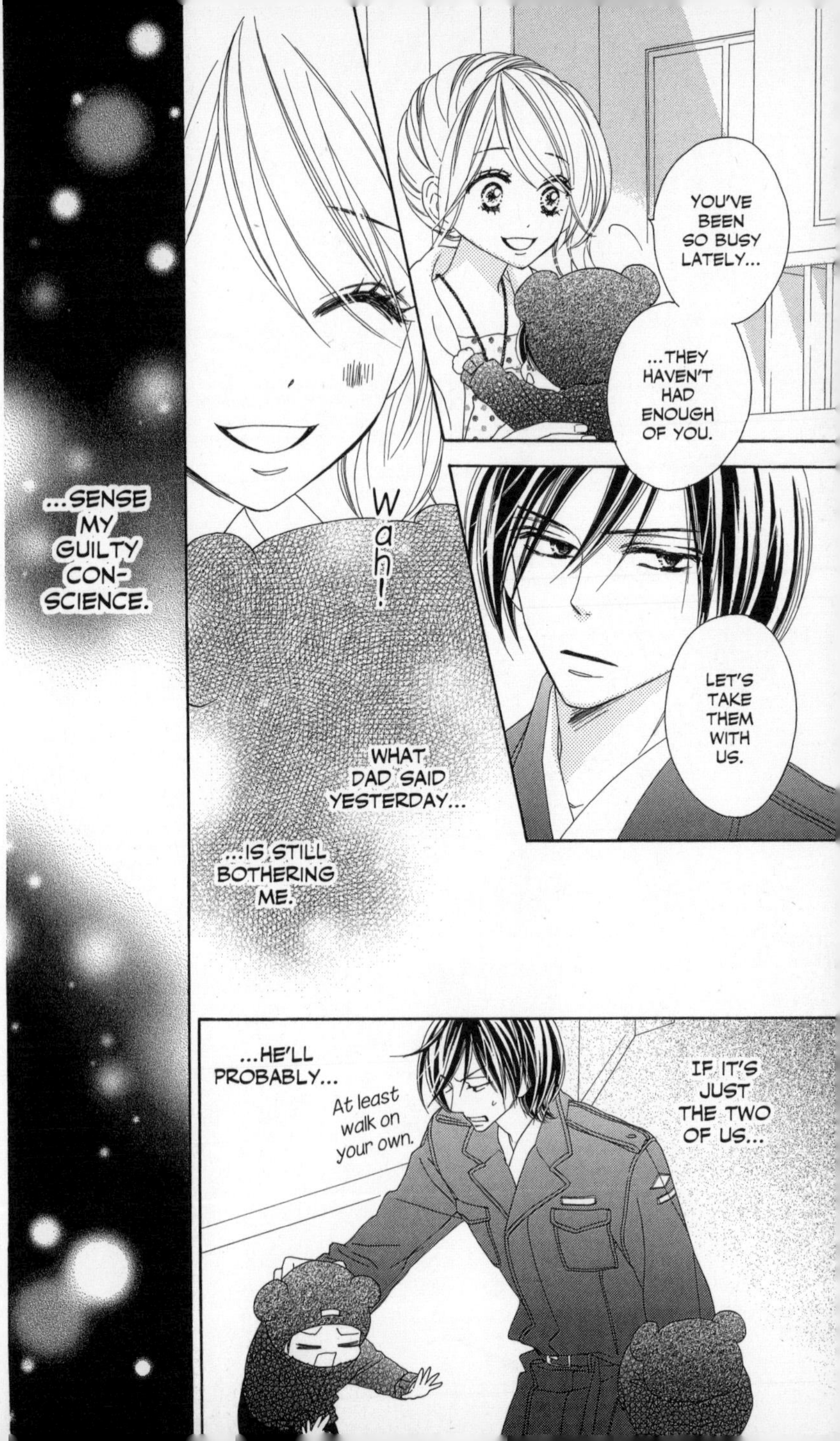
YOU'VE BEEN SO BUSY LATELY...
...THEY HAVEN'T HAD ENOUGH OF YOU.
LET'S TAKE THEM WITH US.
Wah!
WHAT DAD SAID YESTERDAY...
...IS STILL BOTHERING ME.
IF IT'S JUST THE TWO OF US...
At least walk on your own.
...HE'LL PROBABLY...
...SENSE MY GUILTY CON-SCIENCE.

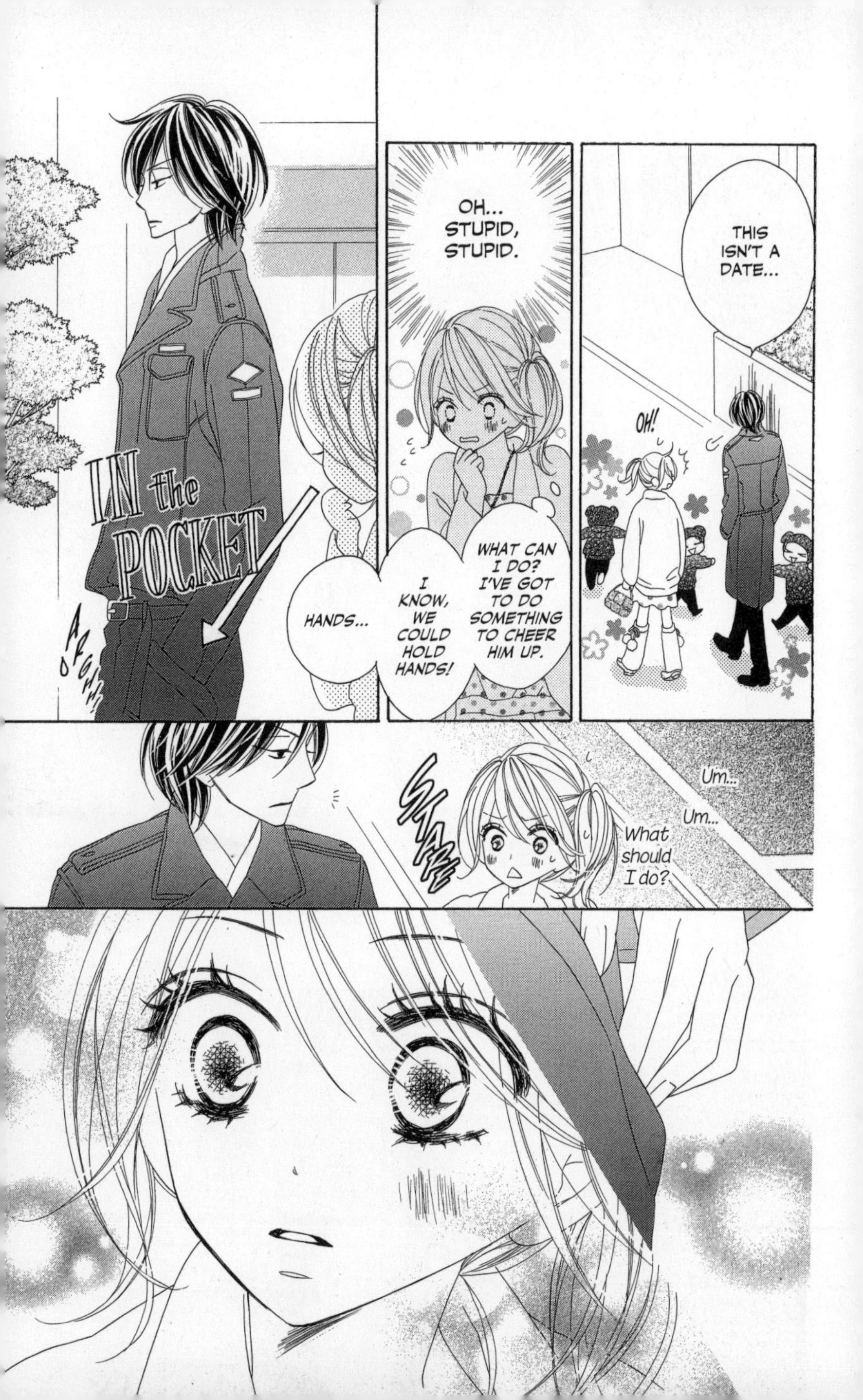
THIS ISN'T A DATE...
OH!
OH... STUPID, STUPID.
WHAT CAN I DO? I'VE GOT TO DO SOMETHING TO CHEER HIM UP.
I KNOW, WE COULD HOLD HANDS!
HANDS...
IN the POCKET
Um...
Um...
What should I do?

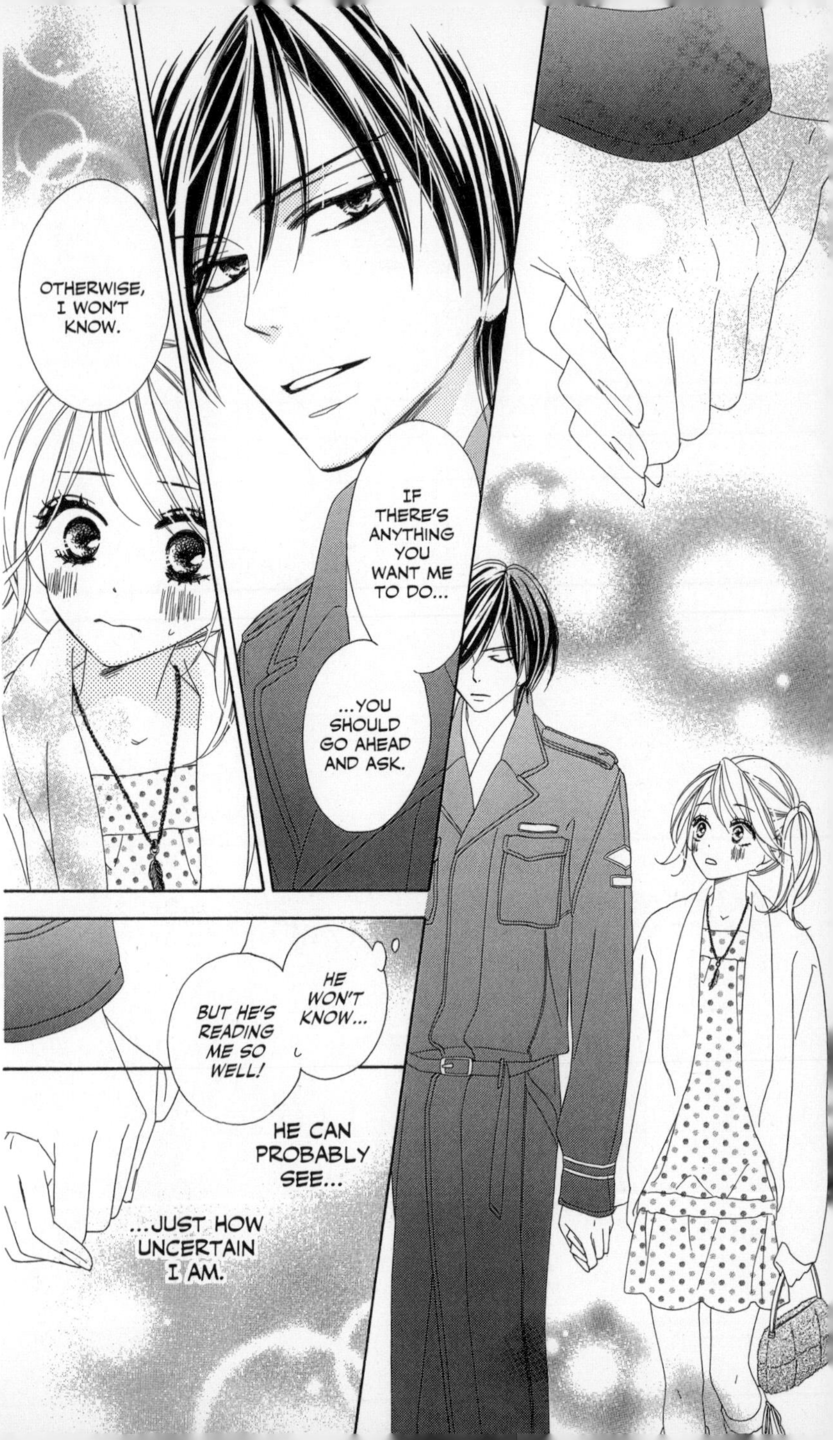
IF THERE'S ANYTHING YOU WANT ME TO DO...
...YOU SHOULD GO AHEAD AND ASK.
OTHERWISE, I WON'T KNOW.
HE WON'T KNOW...
BUT HE'S READING ME SO WELL!
HE CAN PROBABLY SEE...
...JUST HOW UNCERTAIN I AM.

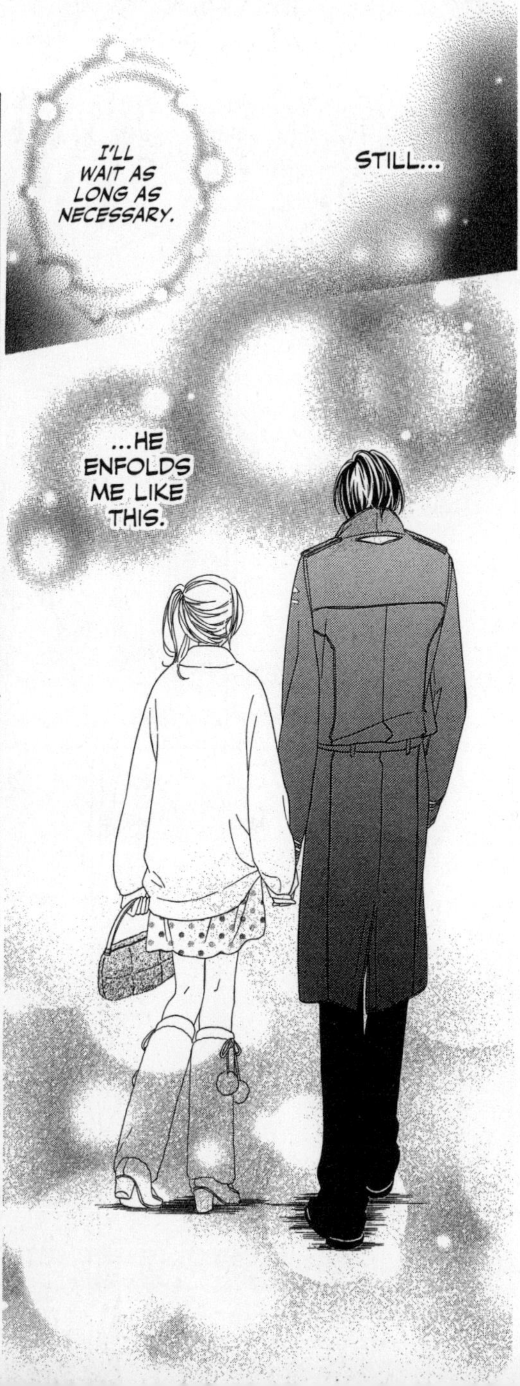
STILL...
I'LL WAIT AS LONG AS NECESSARY.
...HE ENFOLDS ME LIKE THIS.

Character Introduction

Tadanobu Kuzunoha
age: 20 height: 182cm

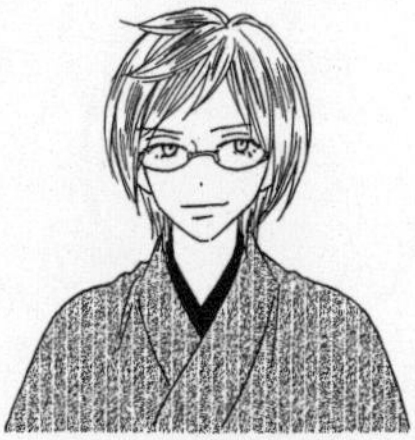

The same goes for this one. There is almost no name more appropriate for a fox! Both "Tadanobu" and "Kuzunoha" are names of foxes that appear in Kabuki plays. Kabuki again....

Although he is more powerful than his younger brother Shuhei, he doesn't have the drive. Perhaps he and Kyo got along so well because they were such opposites. Actually, I never thought he would be appearing here....

On a side note, after I finally came to the decision to announce Kyo's age the last time, I got so many comments saying, "He doesn't look it," "I thought he was in his late 20s." That's what I thought too, and that's why I was hesitant to announce it! You probably think the same about Tadanobu, don't you?

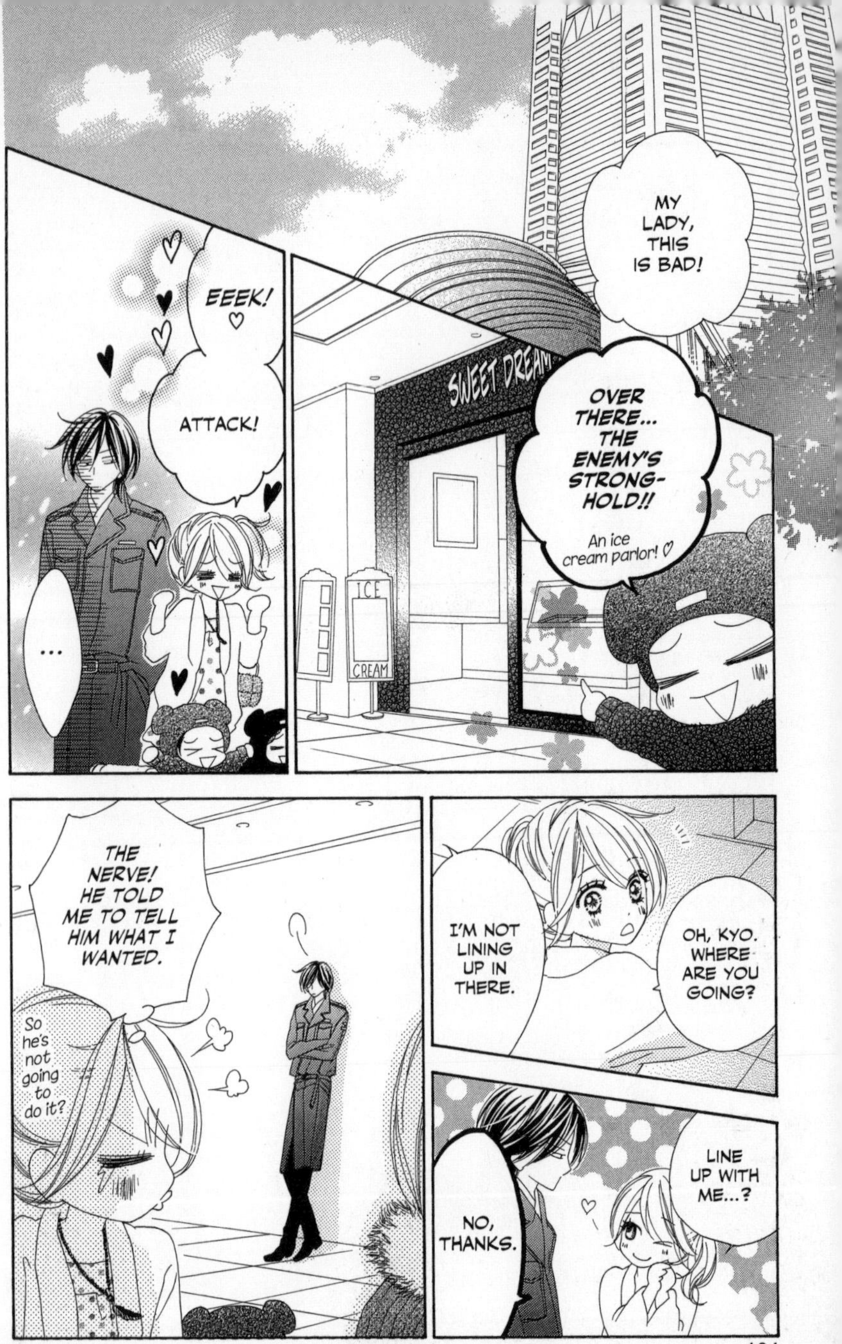
MY LADY, THIS IS BAD!
SWEET DREAM
OVER THERE... THE ENEMY'S STRONG-HOLD!!
An ice cream parlor! ♡
ICE CREAM
EEEK! ♡
ATTACK!
...
OH, KYO. WHERE ARE YOU GOING?
I'M NOT LINING UP IN THERE.
LINE UP WITH ME...?
NO, THANKS.
THE NERVE! HE TOLD ME TO TELL HIM WHAT I WANTED.
So he's not going to do it?

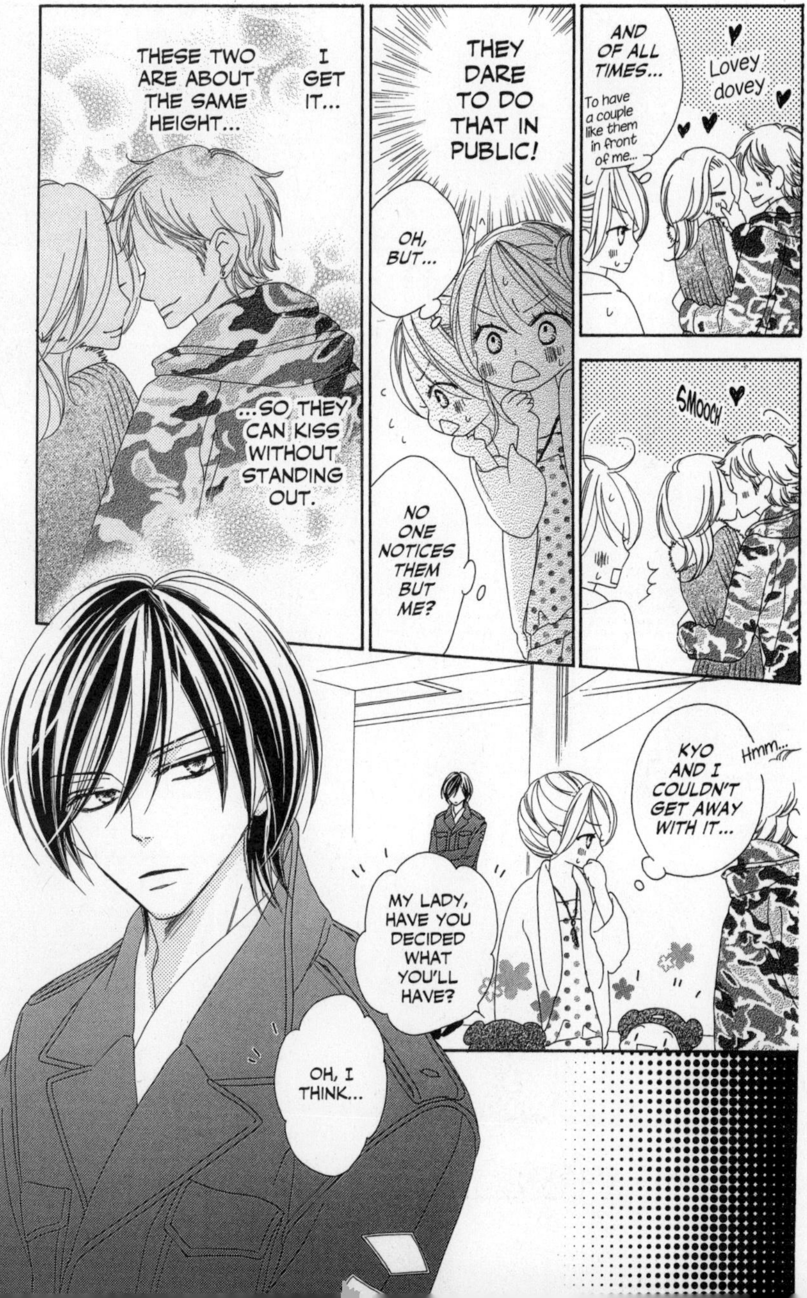
AND OF ALL TIMES...
To have a couple like them in front of me...
Lovey dovey
SMOOCH
THEY DARE TO DO THAT IN PUBLIC!
OH, BUT...
NO ONE NOTICES THEM BUT ME?
I GET IT...
THESE TWO ARE ABOUT THE SAME HEIGHT...
...SO THEY CAN KISS WITHOUT STANDING OUT.
Hmm...
KYO AND I COULDN'T GET AWAY WITH IT...
MY LADY, HAVE YOU DECIDED WHAT YOU'LL HAVE?
OH, I THINK...

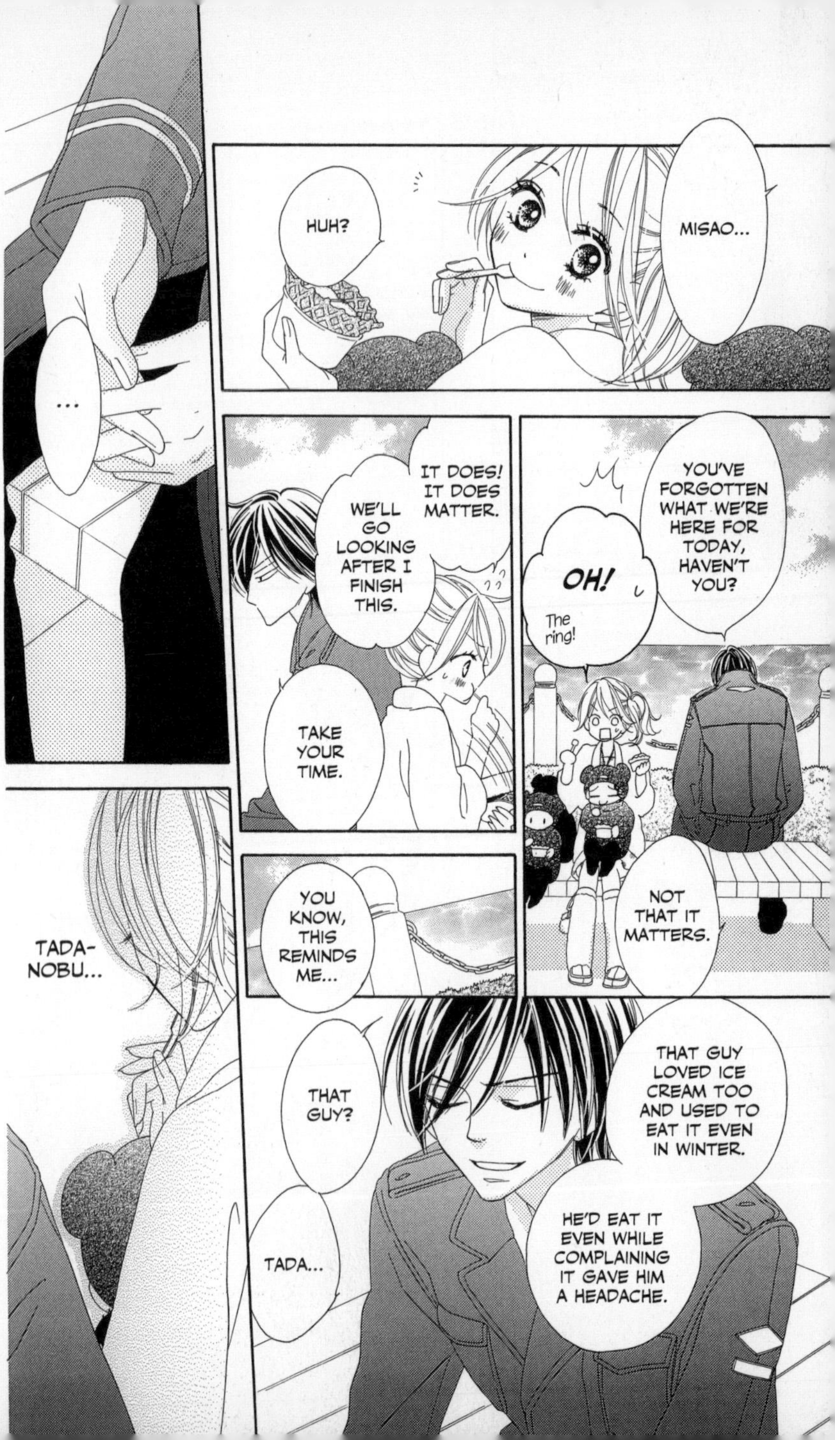
MISAO...
HUH?
YOU'VE FORGOTTEN WHAT WE'RE HERE FOR TODAY, HAVEN'T YOU?
OH!
The ring!
NOT THAT IT MATTERS.
IT DOES! IT DOES MATTER.
WE'LL GO LOOKING AFTER I FINISH THIS.
TAKE YOUR TIME.
...
YOU KNOW, THIS REMINDS ME...
THAT GUY LOVED ICE CREAM TOO AND USED TO EAT IT EVEN IN WINTER.
HE'D EAT IT EVEN WHILE COMPLAINING IT GAVE HIM A HEADACHE.
THAT GUY?
TADA...
TADA-NOBU...

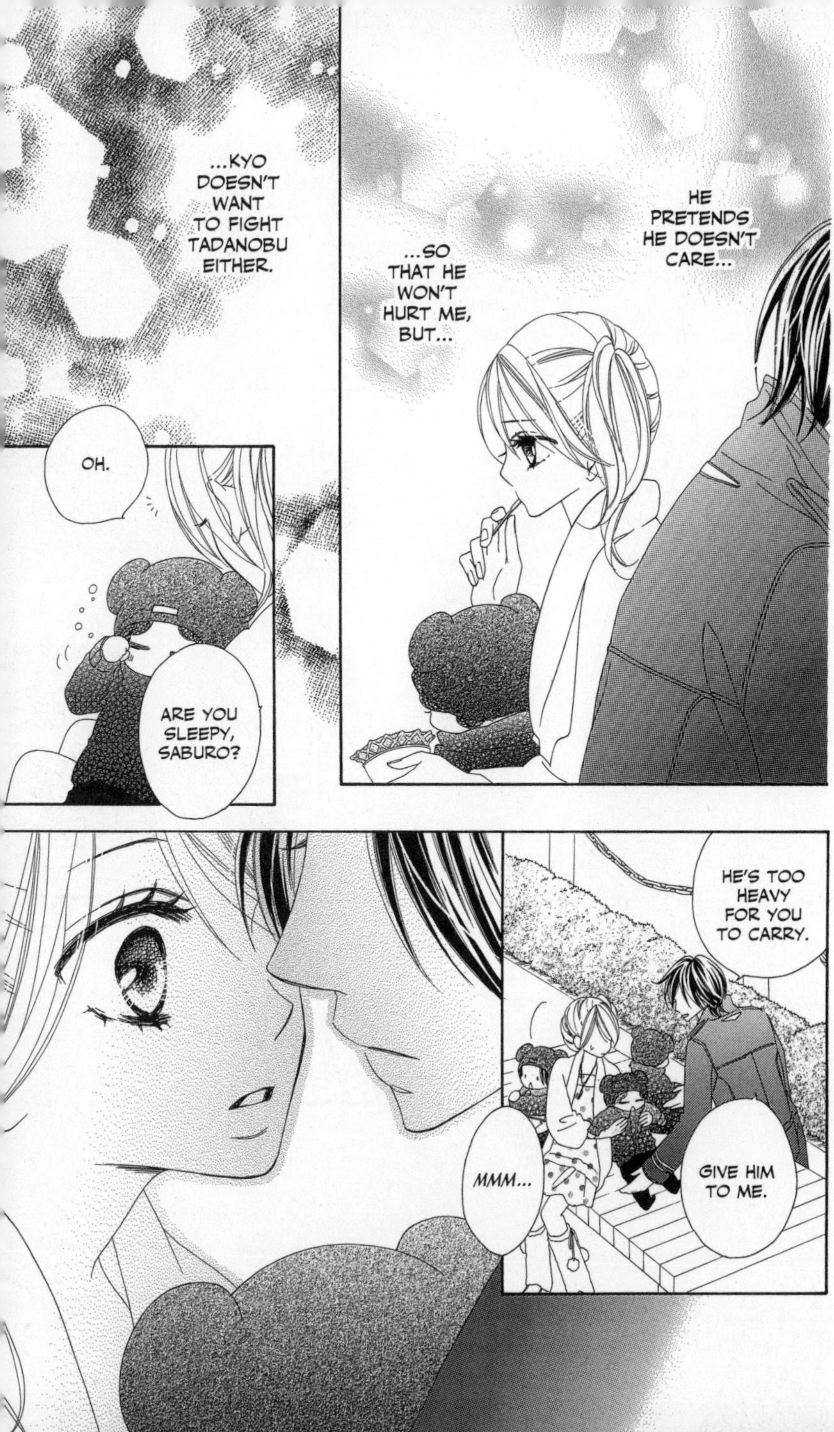
HE PRETENDS HE DOESN'T CARE...
...SO THAT HE WON'T HURT ME, BUT...
...KYO DOESN'T WANT TO FIGHT TADANOBU EITHER.
OH.
ARE YOU SLEEPY, SABURO?
HE'S TOO HEAVY FOR YOU TO CARRY.
GIVE HIM TO ME.
MMM...

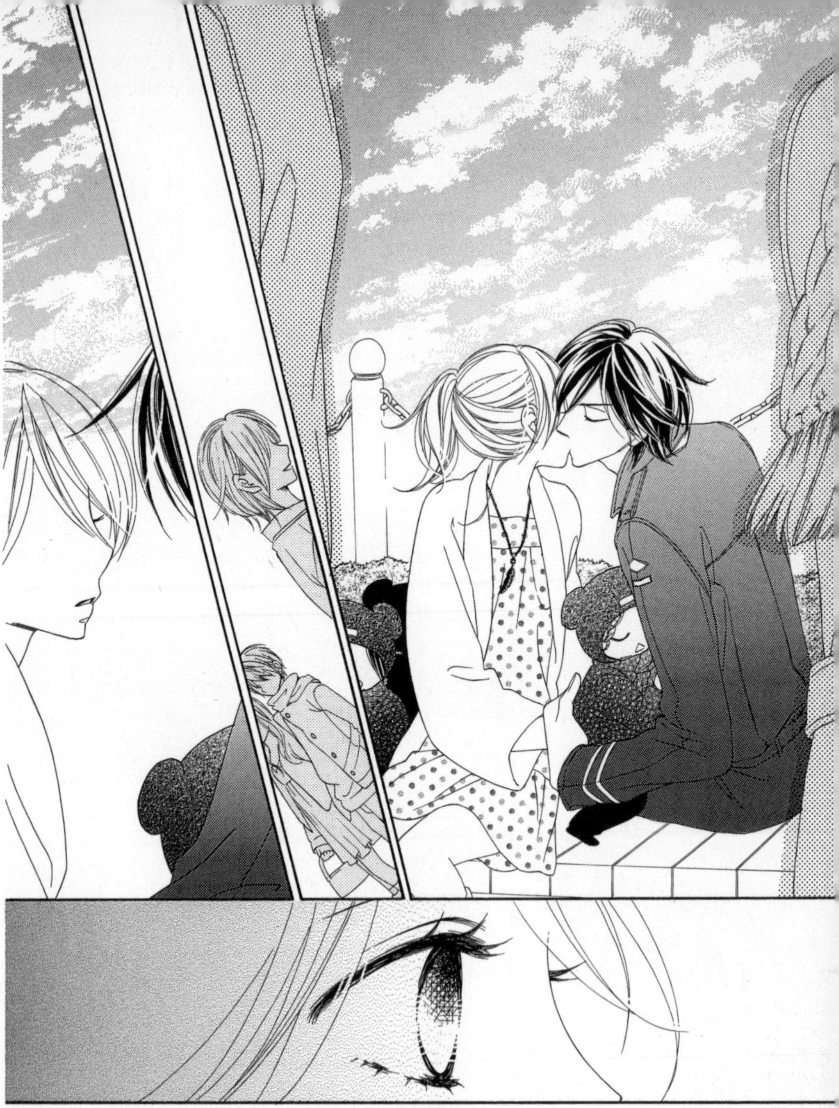

BUT I
CAN'T
LET HIM
GO.

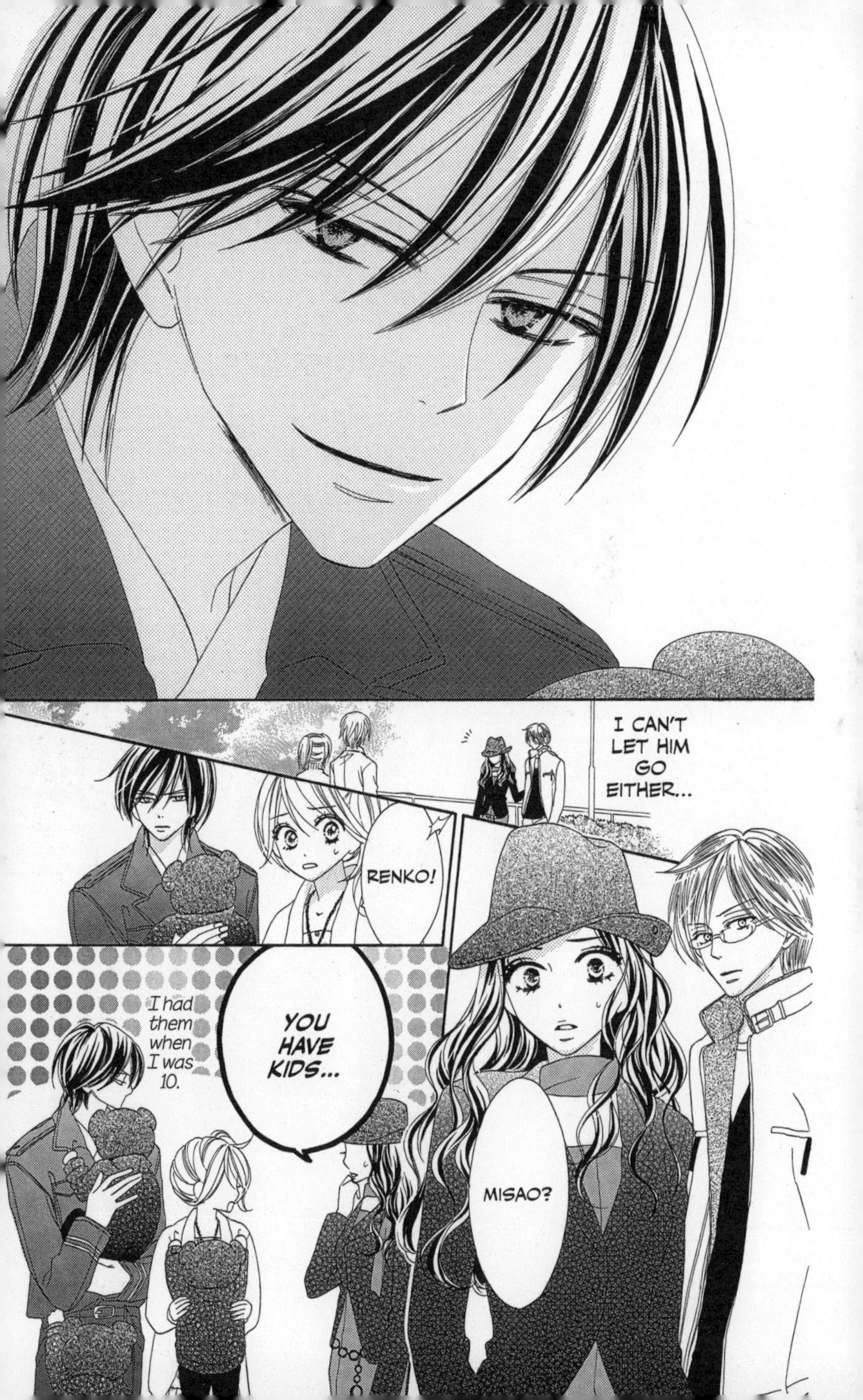
I CAN'T LET HIM GO EITHER...
RENKO!
MISAO?
YOU HAVE KIDS...
I had them when I was 10.

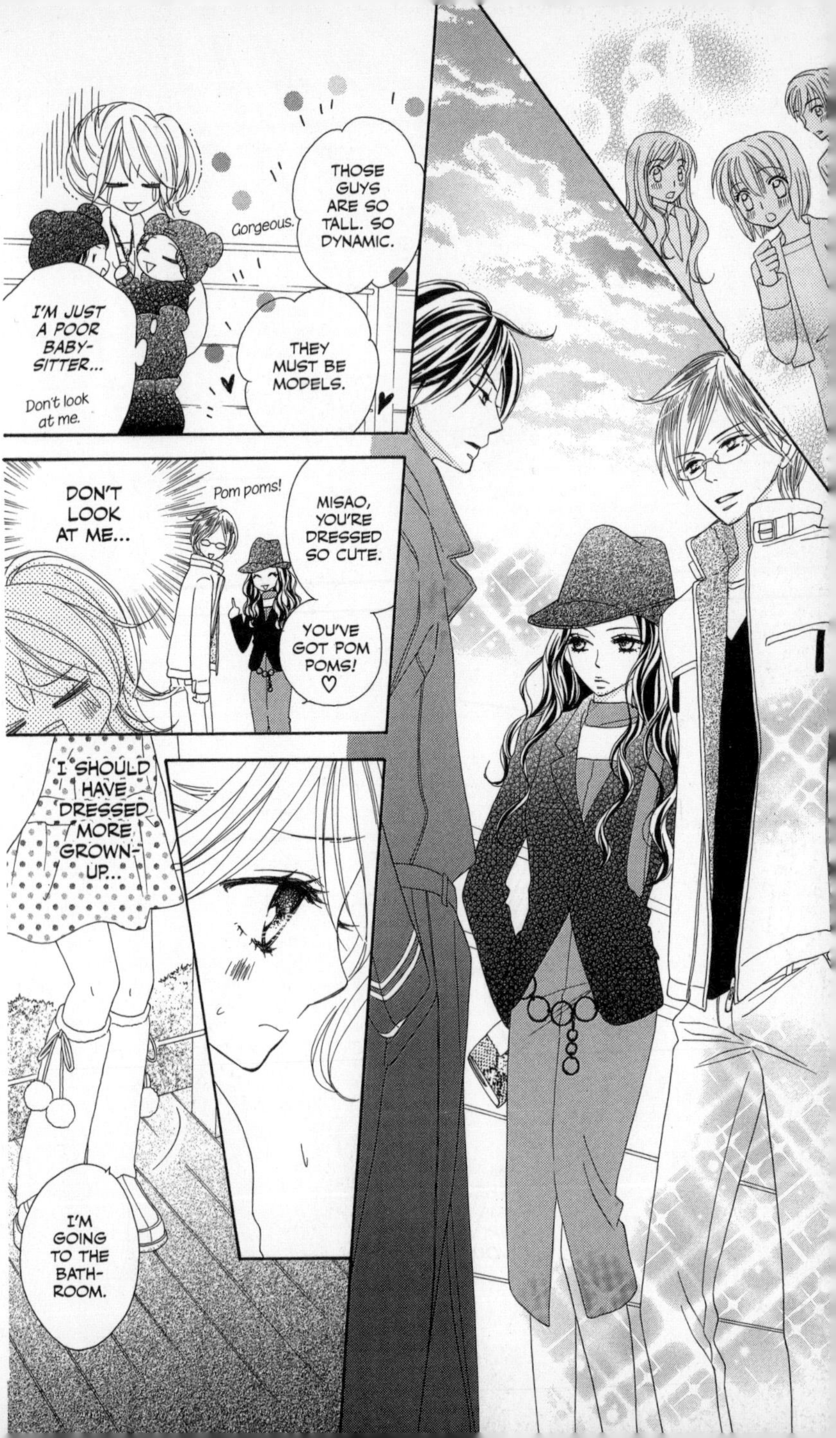
THOSE GUYS ARE SO TALL. SO DYNAMIC.
Gorgeous.
THEY MUST BE MODELS.
I'M JUST A POOR BABY-SITTER...
Don't look at me.
MISAO, YOU'RE DRESSED SO CUTE.
Pom poms!
YOU'VE GOT POM POMS! ♡
DON'T LOOK AT ME...
I SHOULD HAVE DRESSED MORE GROWN-UP...
I'M GOING TO THE BATH-ROOM.

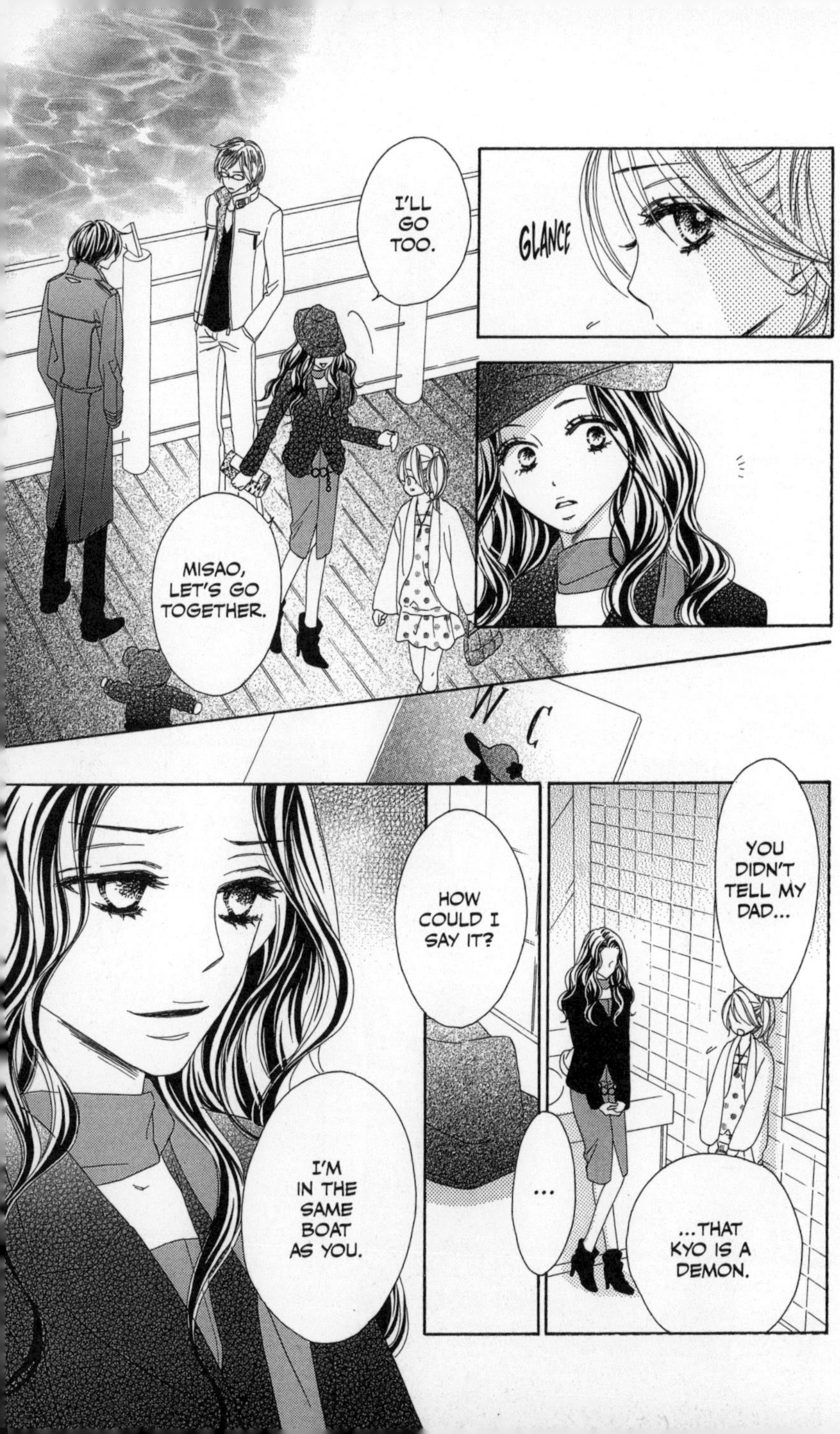
GLANCE
I'LL GO TOO.
MISAO, LET'S GO TOGETHER.
YOU DIDN'T TELL MY DAD...
...THAT KYO IS A DEMON.
...
HOW COULD I SAY IT?
I'M IN THE SAME BOAT AS YOU.

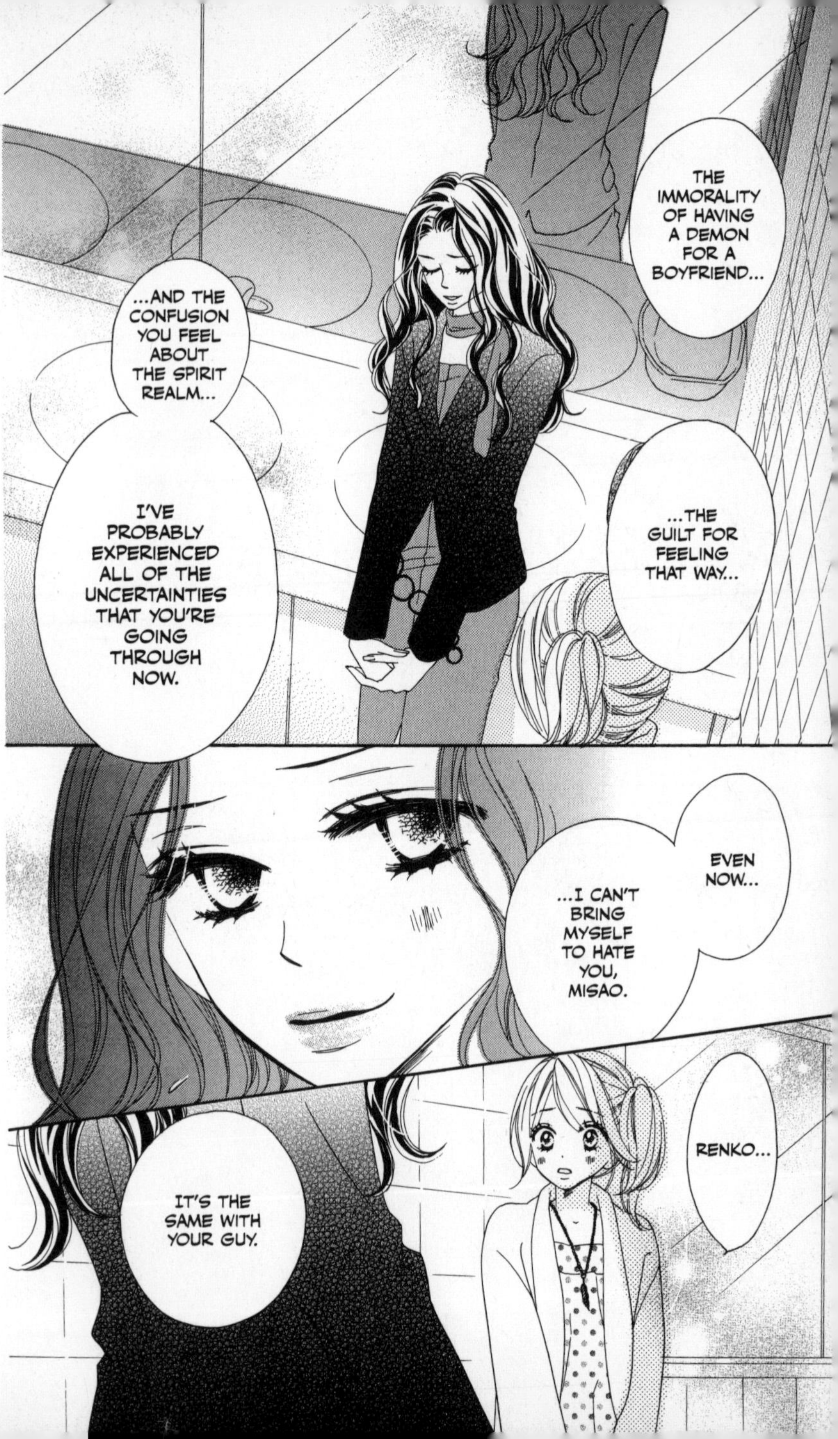
THE IMMORALITY OF HAVING A DEMON FOR A BOYFRIEND...
...THE GUILT FOR FEELING THAT WAY...
...AND THE CONFUSION YOU FEEL ABOUT THE SPIRIT REALM...
I'VE PROBABLY EXPERIENCED ALL OF THE UNCERTAINTIES THAT YOU'RE GOING THROUGH NOW.
EVEN NOW...
...I CAN'T BRING MYSELF TO HATE YOU, MISAO.
RENKO...
IT'S THE SAME WITH YOUR GUY.

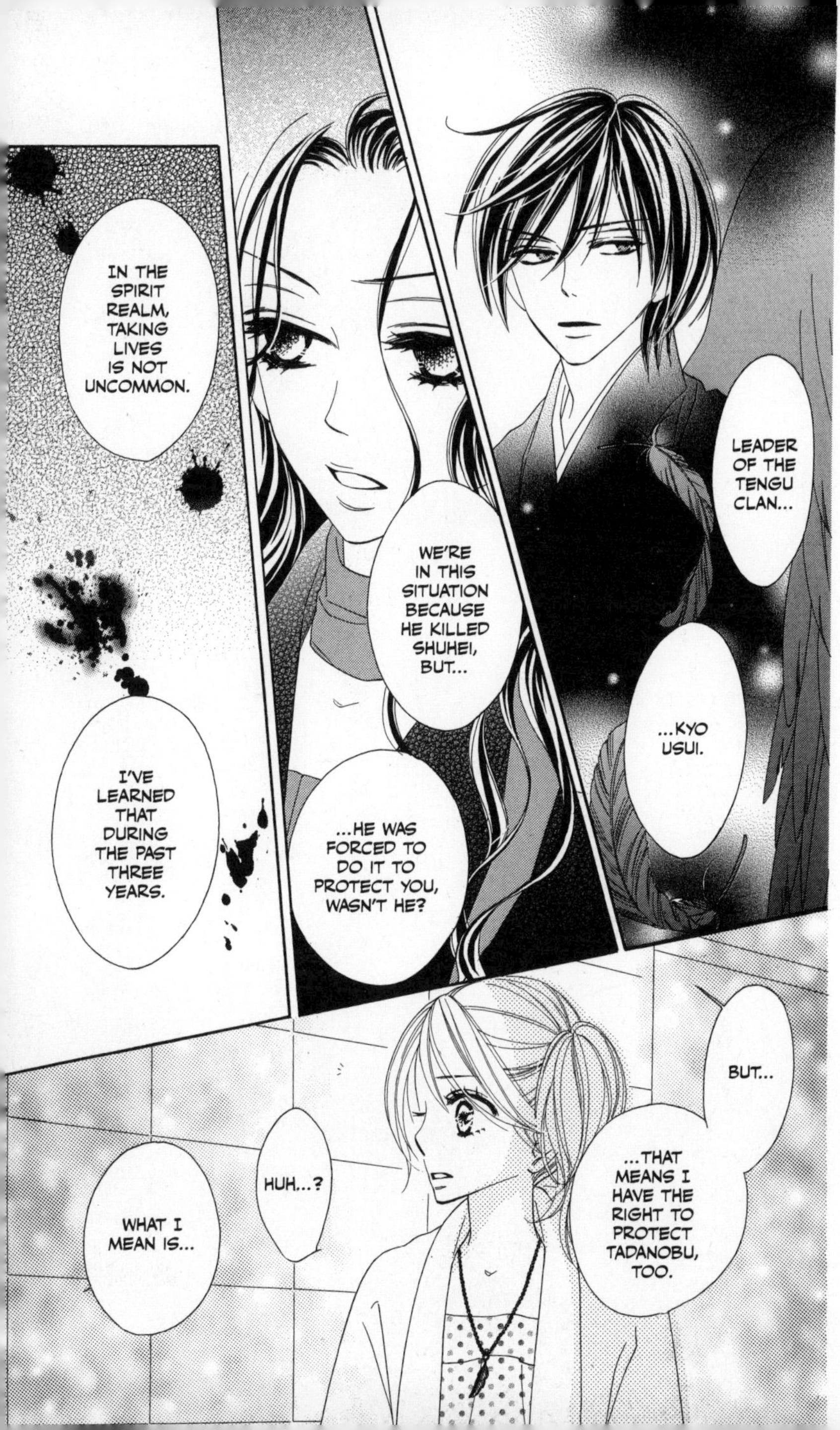
LEADER OF THE TENGU CLAN...
...KYO USUI.
WE'RE IN THIS SITUATION BECAUSE HE KILLED SHUHEI, BUT...
...HE WAS FORCED TO DO IT TO PROTECT YOU, WASN'T HE?
IN THE SPIRIT REALM, TAKING LIVES IS NOT UNCOMMON.
I'VE LEARNED THAT DURING THE PAST THREE YEARS.
BUT...
...THAT MEANS I HAVE THE RIGHT TO PROTECT TADANOBU, TOO.
HUH...?
WHAT I MEAN IS...

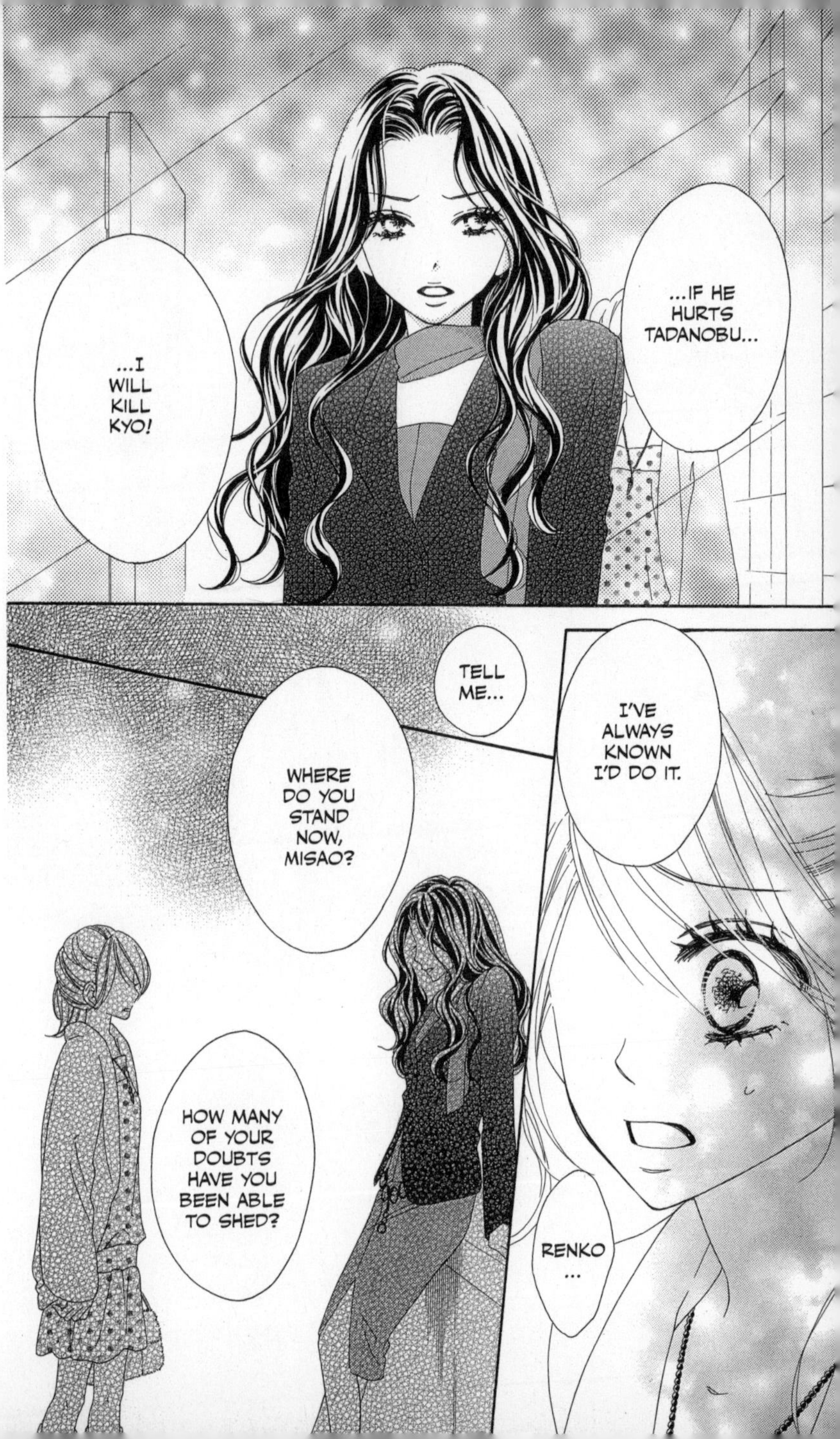
...IF HE HURTS TADANOBU...
...I WILL KILL KYO!
I'VE ALWAYS KNOWN I'D DO IT.
RENKO ...
TELL ME...
WHERE DO YOU STAND NOW, MISAO?
HOW MANY OF YOUR DOUBTS HAVE YOU BEEN ABLE TO SHED?

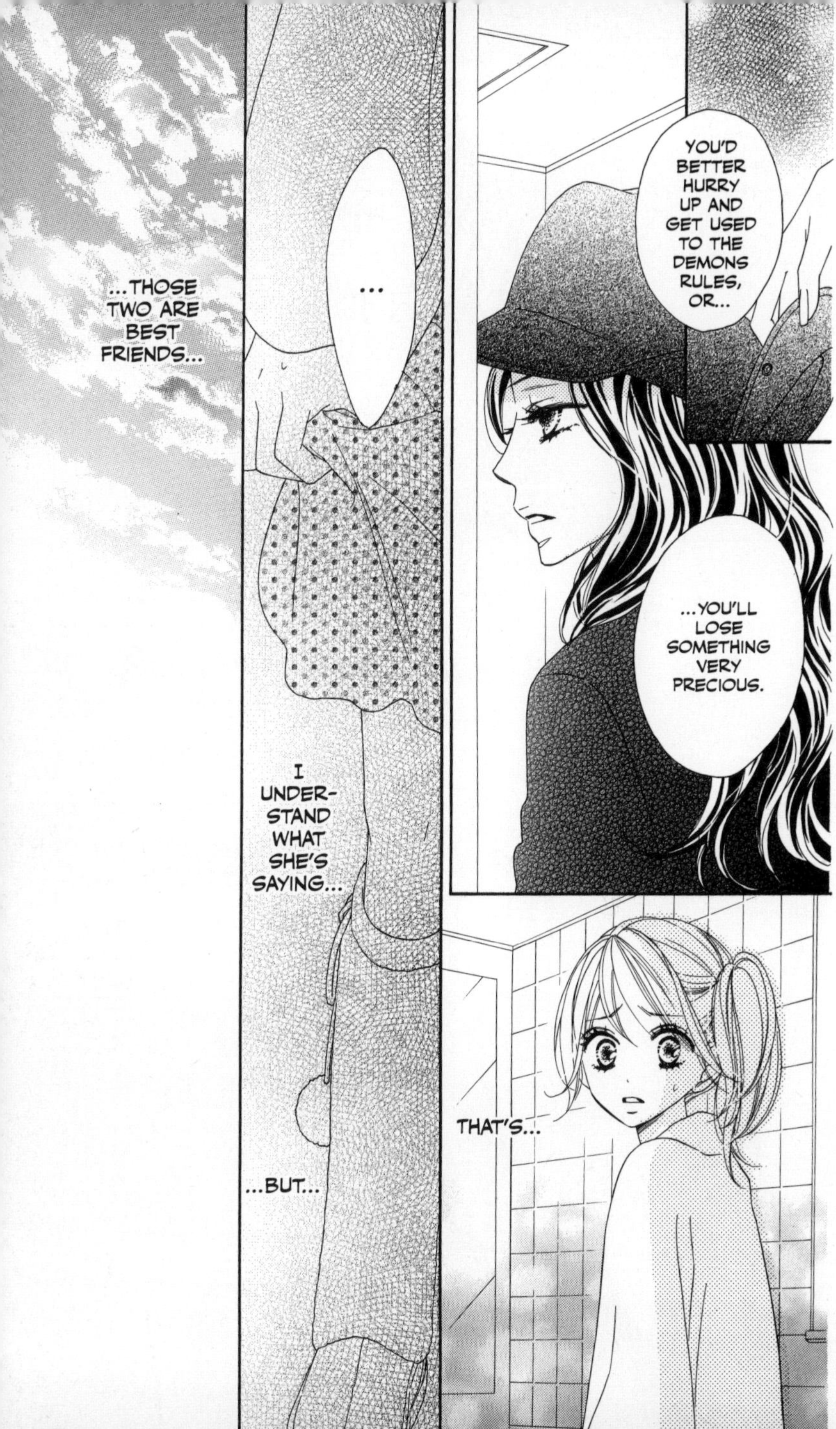
YOU'D BETTER HURRY UP AND GET USED TO THE DEMONS RULES, OR...
...YOU'LL LOSE SOMETHING VERY PRECIOUS.
THAT'S...
...
I UNDERSTAND WHAT SHE'S SAYING...
...BUT...
...THOSE TWO ARE BEST FRIENDS...

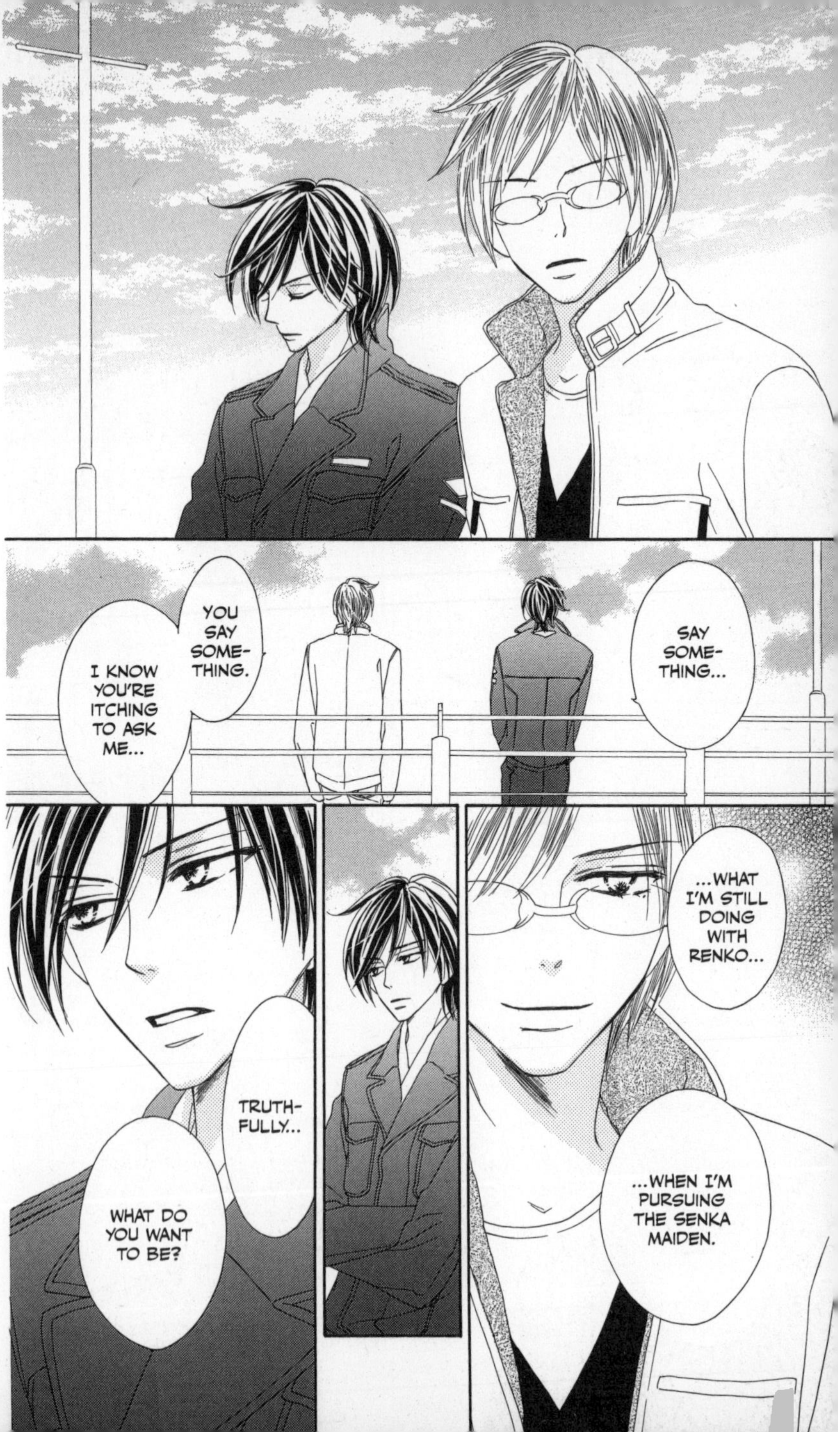
SAY SOMETHING...
YOU SAY SOMETHING.
I KNOW YOU'RE ITCHING TO ASK ME...
...WHAT I'M STILL DOING WITH RENKO...
...WHEN I'M PURSUING THE SENKA MAIDEN.
TRUTHFULLY...
WHAT DO YOU WANT TO BE?

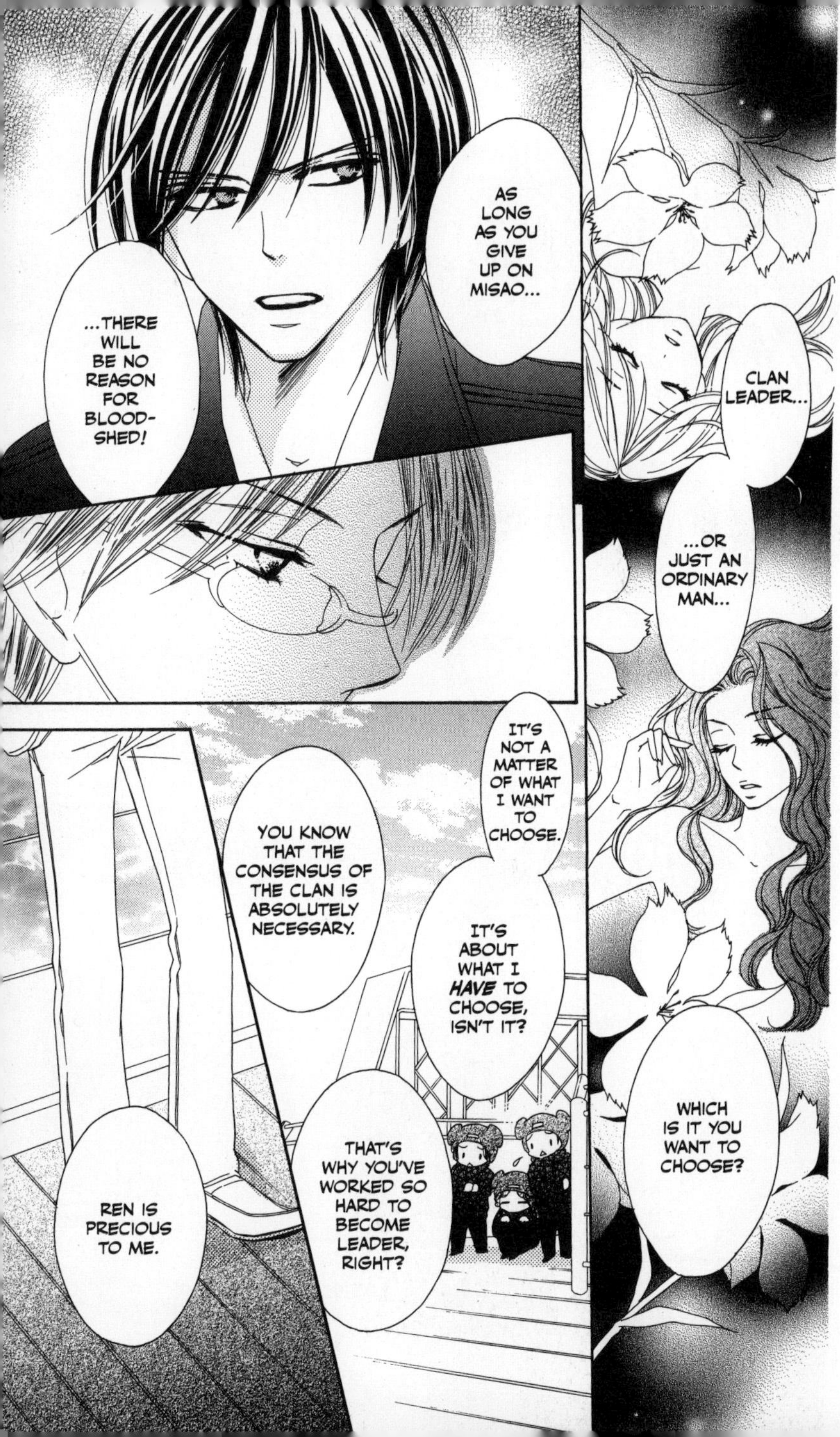
CLAN LEADER...
...OR JUST AN ORDINARY MAN...
WHICH IS IT YOU WANT TO CHOOSE?
AS LONG AS YOU GIVE UP ON MISAO...
...THERE WILL BE NO REASON FOR BLOOD-SHED!
IT'S NOT A MATTER OF WHAT I WANT TO CHOOSE.
IT'S ABOUT WHAT I *HAVE* TO CHOOSE, ISN'T IT?
YOU KNOW THAT THE CONSENSUS OF THE CLAN IS ABSOLUTELY NECESSARY.
THAT'S WHY YOU'VE WORKED SO HARD TO BECOME LEADER, RIGHT?
REN IS PRECIOUS TO ME.

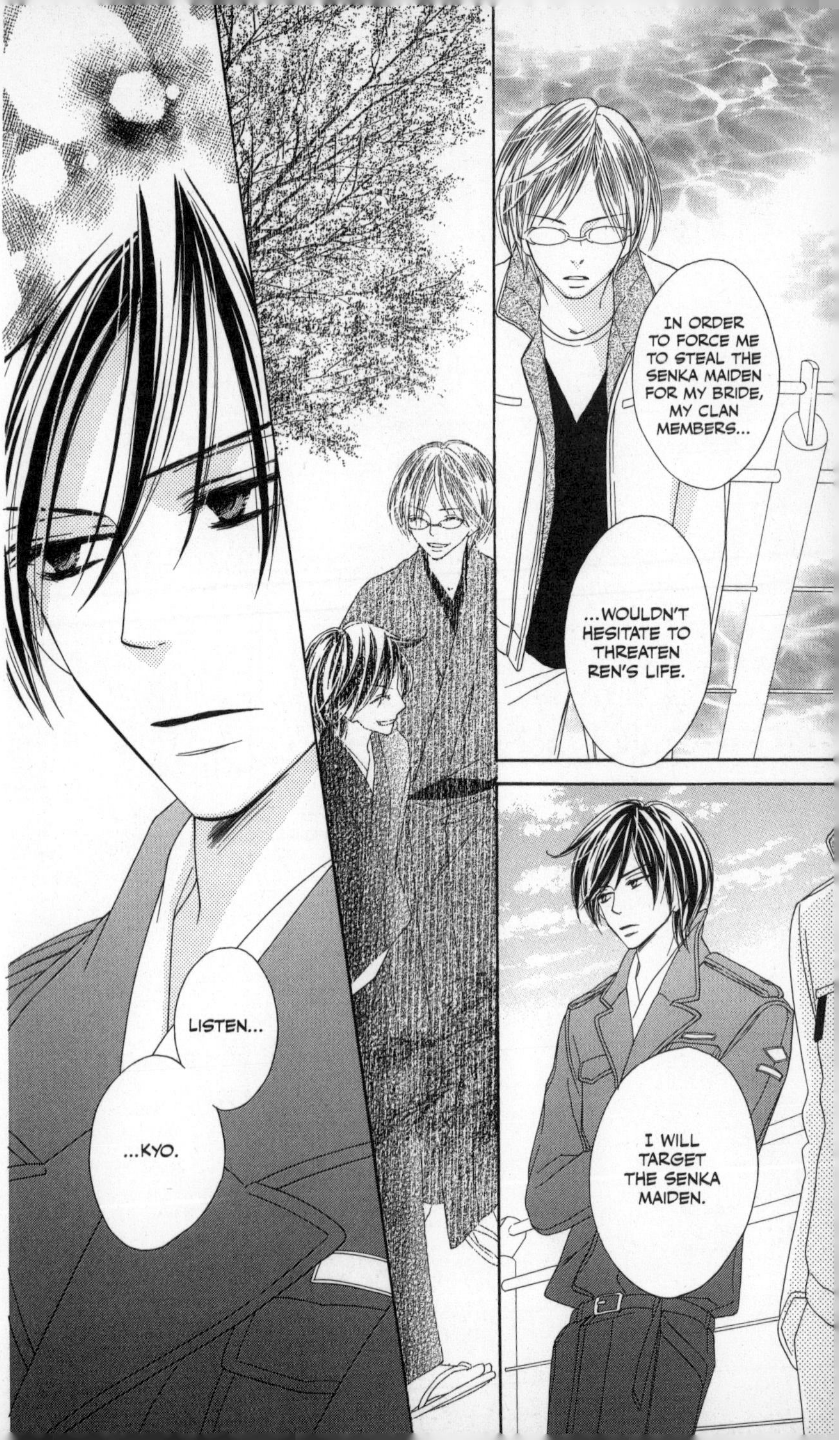
IN ORDER TO FORCE ME TO STEAL THE SENKA MAIDEN FOR MY BRIDE, MY CLAN MEMBERS...
...WOULDN'T HESITATE TO THREATEN REN'S LIFE.
I WILL TARGET THE SENKA MAIDEN.
LISTEN...
...KYO.

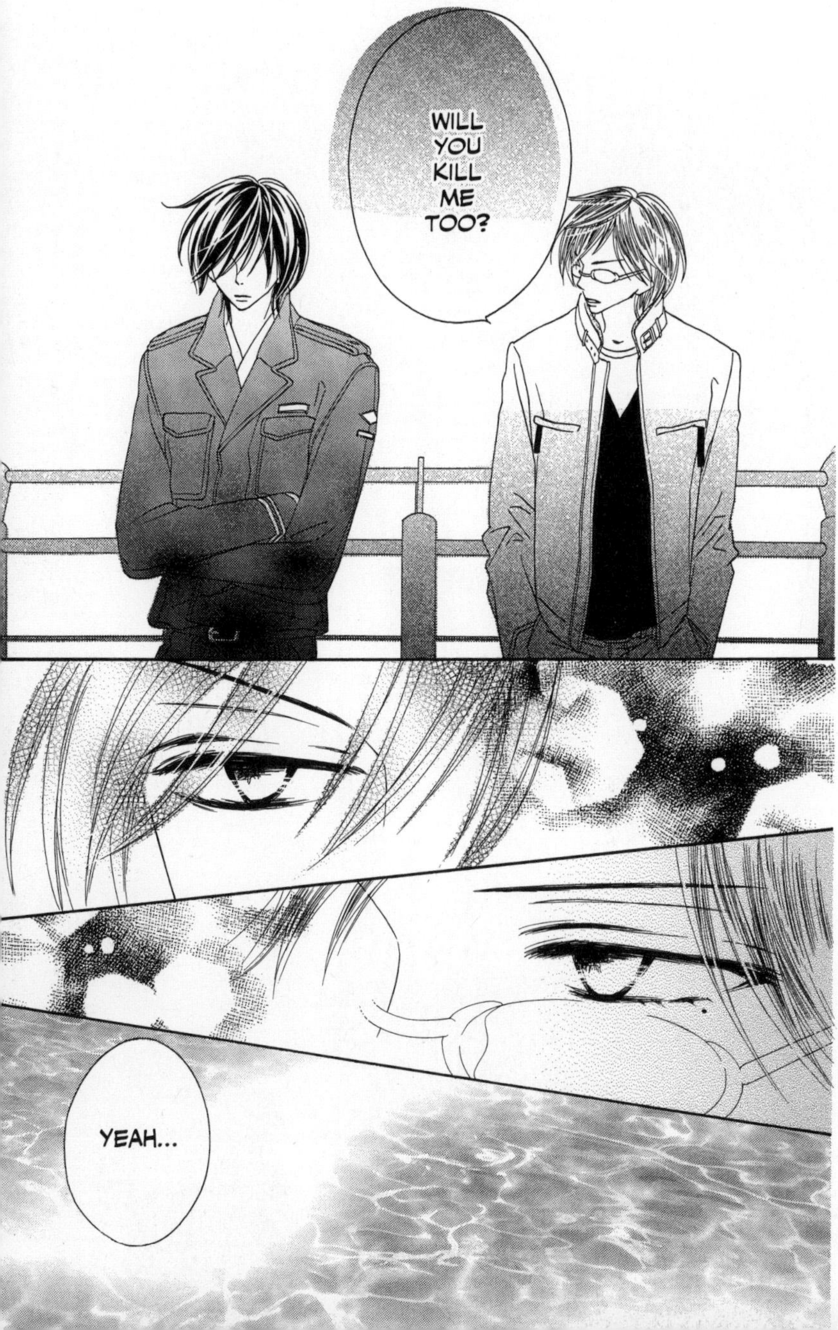
WILL YOU KILL ME TOO?
YEAH...

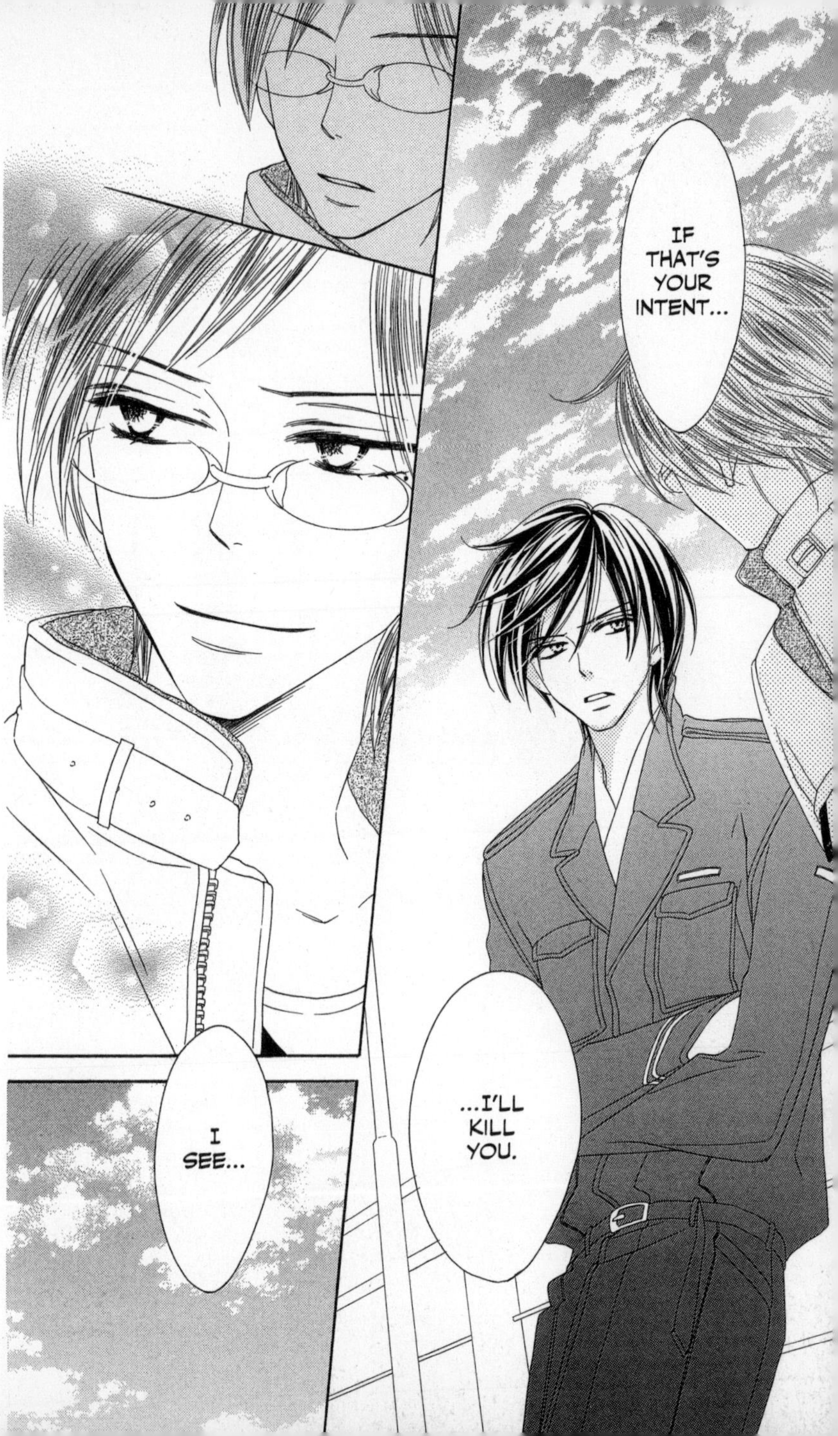
IF THAT'S YOUR INTENT...
...I'LL KILL YOU.
I SEE...

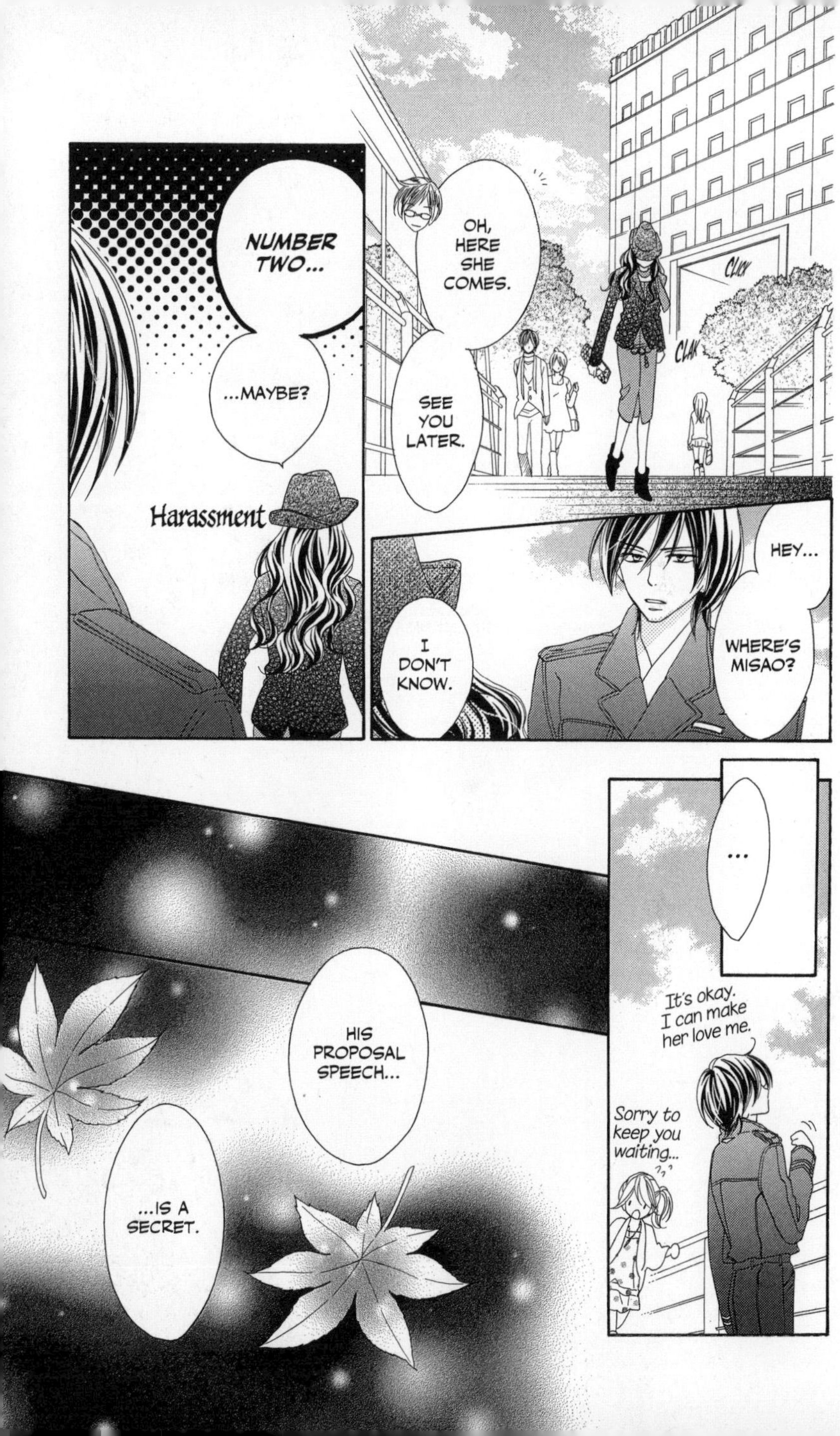

CLICK
OH, HERE SHE COMES.
CLAK
SEE YOU LATER.
HEY...
WHERE'S MISAO?
I DON'T KNOW.
NUMBER TWO...
...MAYBE?
Harassment
...
It's okay. I can make her love me.
Sorry to keep you waiting...
HIS PROPOSAL SPEECH...
...IS A SECRET.

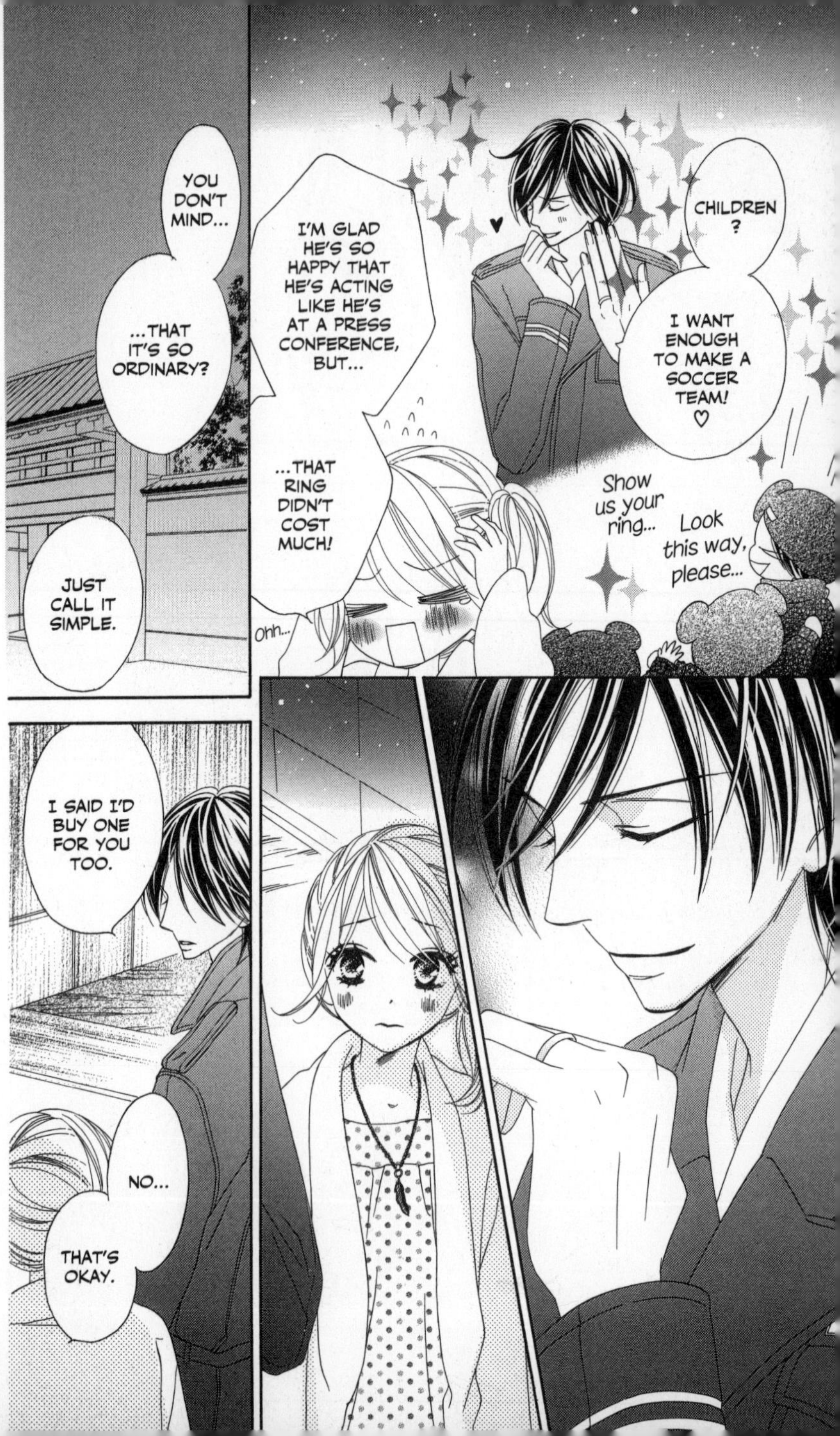
CHILDREN?
I WANT ENOUGH TO MAKE A SOCCER TEAM! ♡
Show us your ring...
Look this way, please...
I'M GLAD HE'S SO HAPPY THAT HE'S ACTING LIKE HE'S AT A PRESS CONFERENCE, BUT...
...THAT RING DIDN'T COST MUCH!
Ohh...
YOU DON'T MIND...
...THAT IT'S SO ORDINARY?
JUST CALL IT SIMPLE.
I SAID I'D BUY ONE FOR YOU TOO.
NO...
THAT'S OKAY.

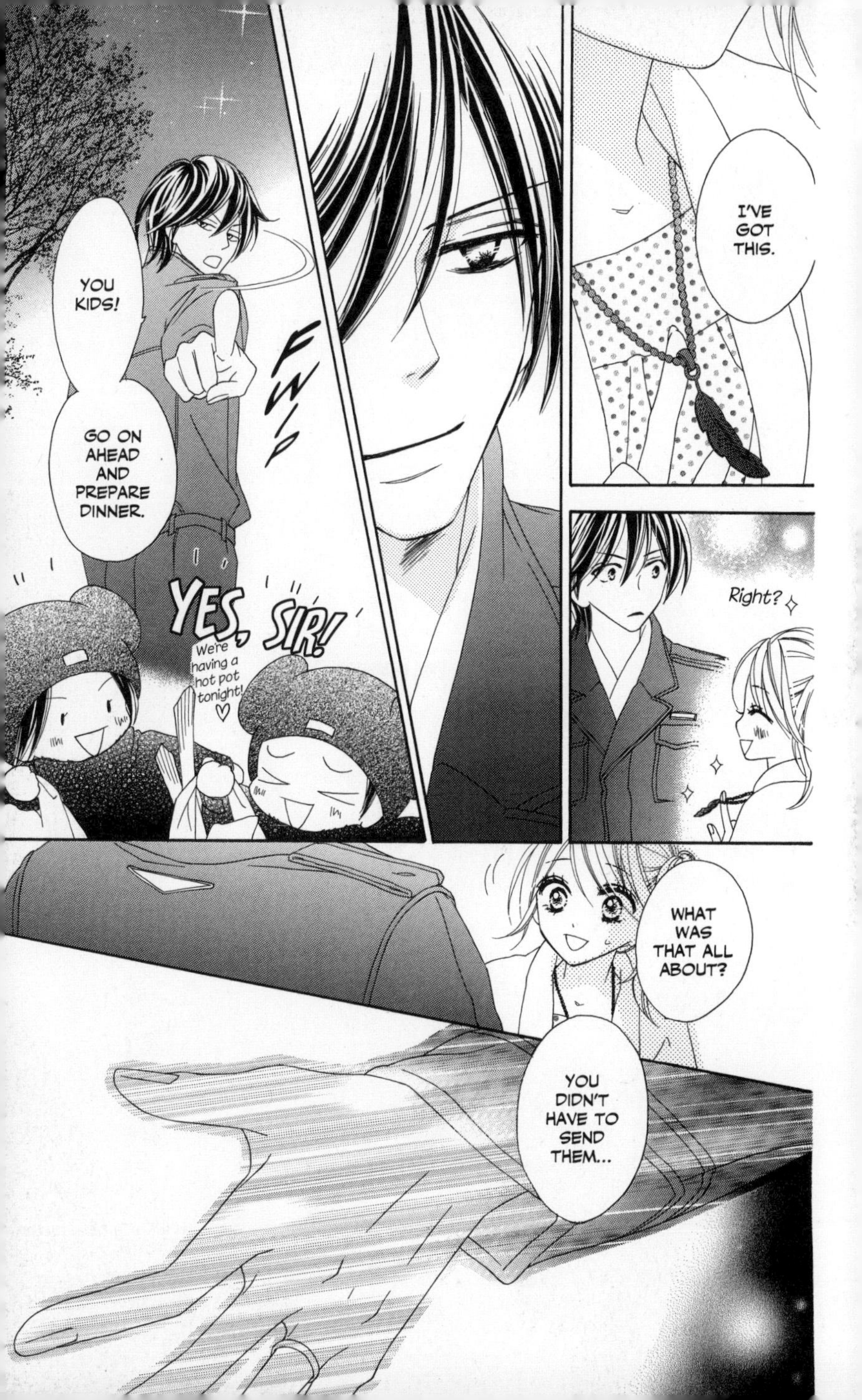
I'VE GOT THIS.
Right?
FWIP
YOU KIDS!
GO ON AHEAD AND PREPARE DINNER.
YES, SIR!
We're having a hot pot tonight! ♡
WHAT WAS THAT ALL ABOUT?
YOU DIDN'T HAVE TO SEND THEM...

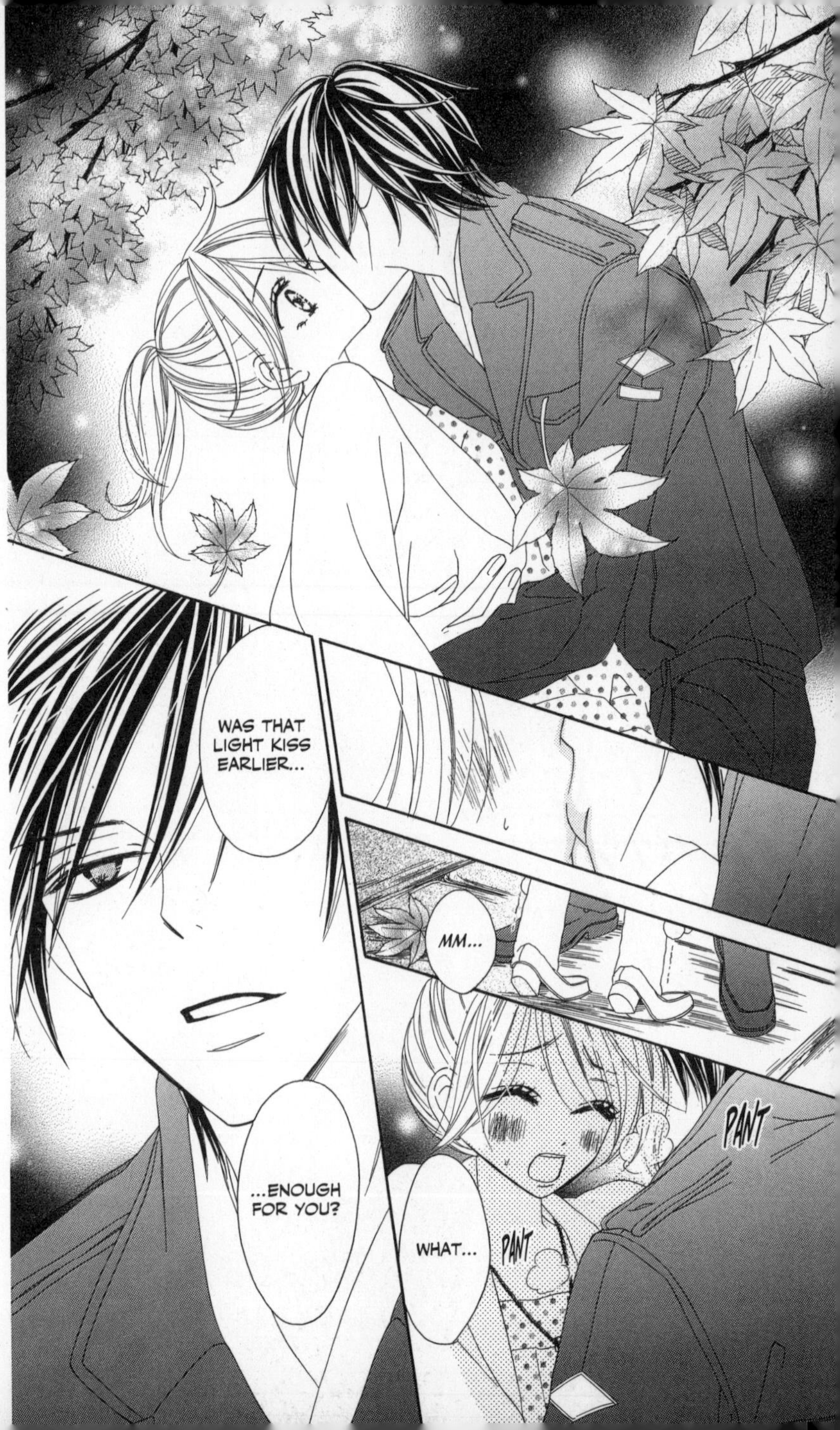

MM...
PANT
PANT
WHAT...
WAS THAT LIGHT KISS EARLIER...
...ENOUGH FOR YOU?

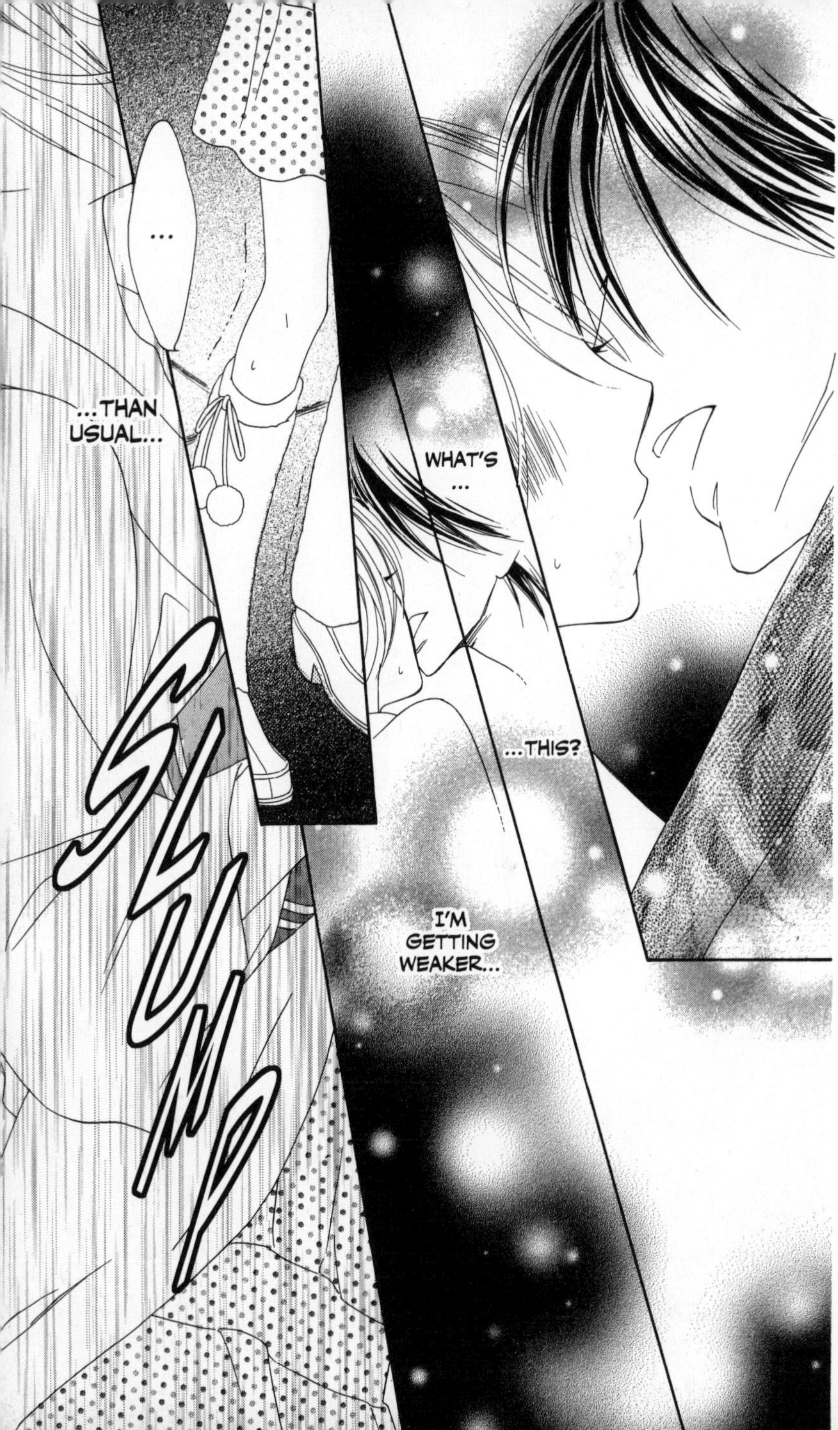
WHAT'S ...
...THIS?
I'M GETTING WEAKER...
...
...THAN USUAL...
SLUMP

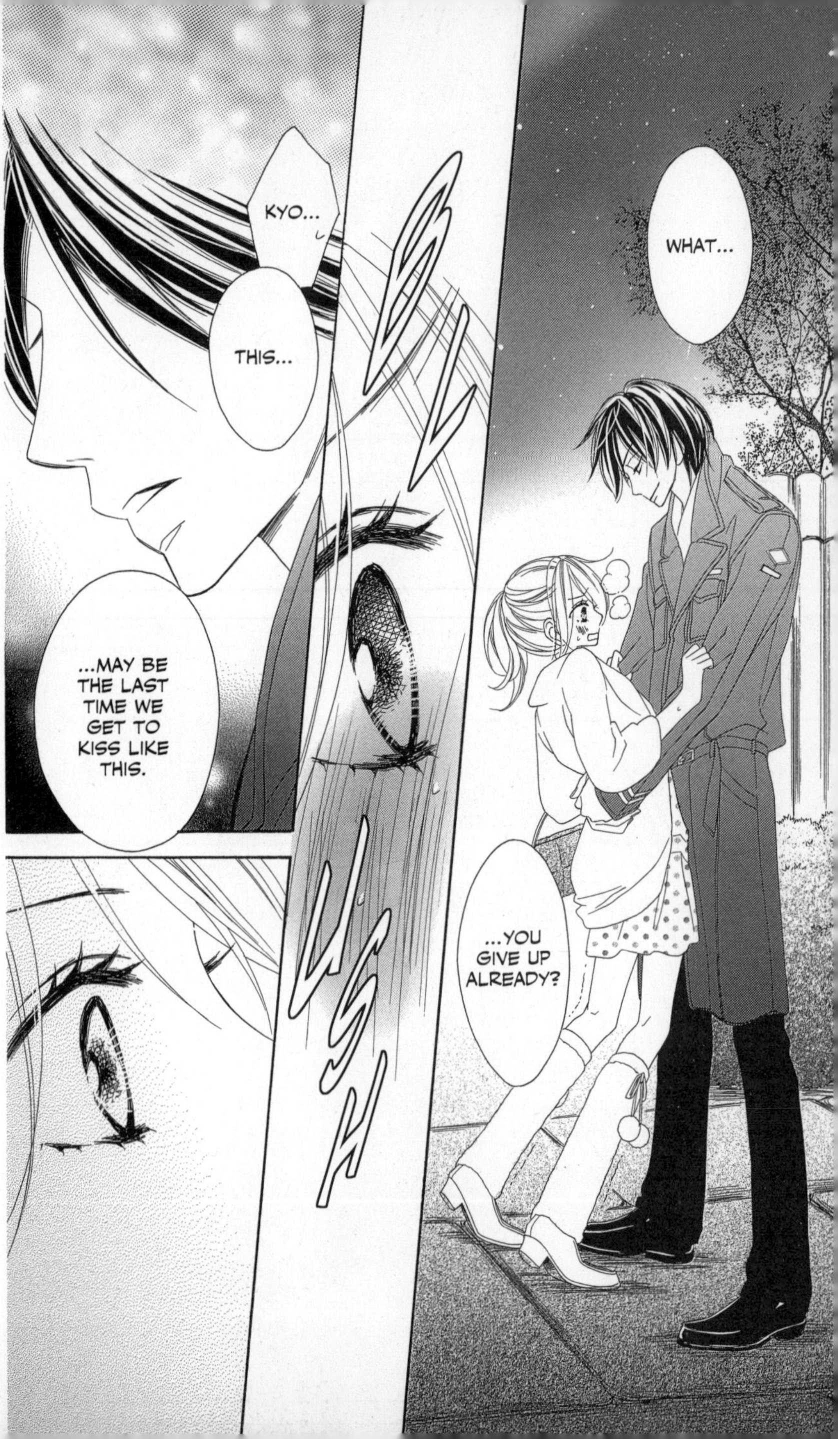
WHAT...
...YOU GIVE UP ALREADY?
KYO...
THIS...
...MAY BE THE LAST TIME WE GET TO KISS LIKE THIS.

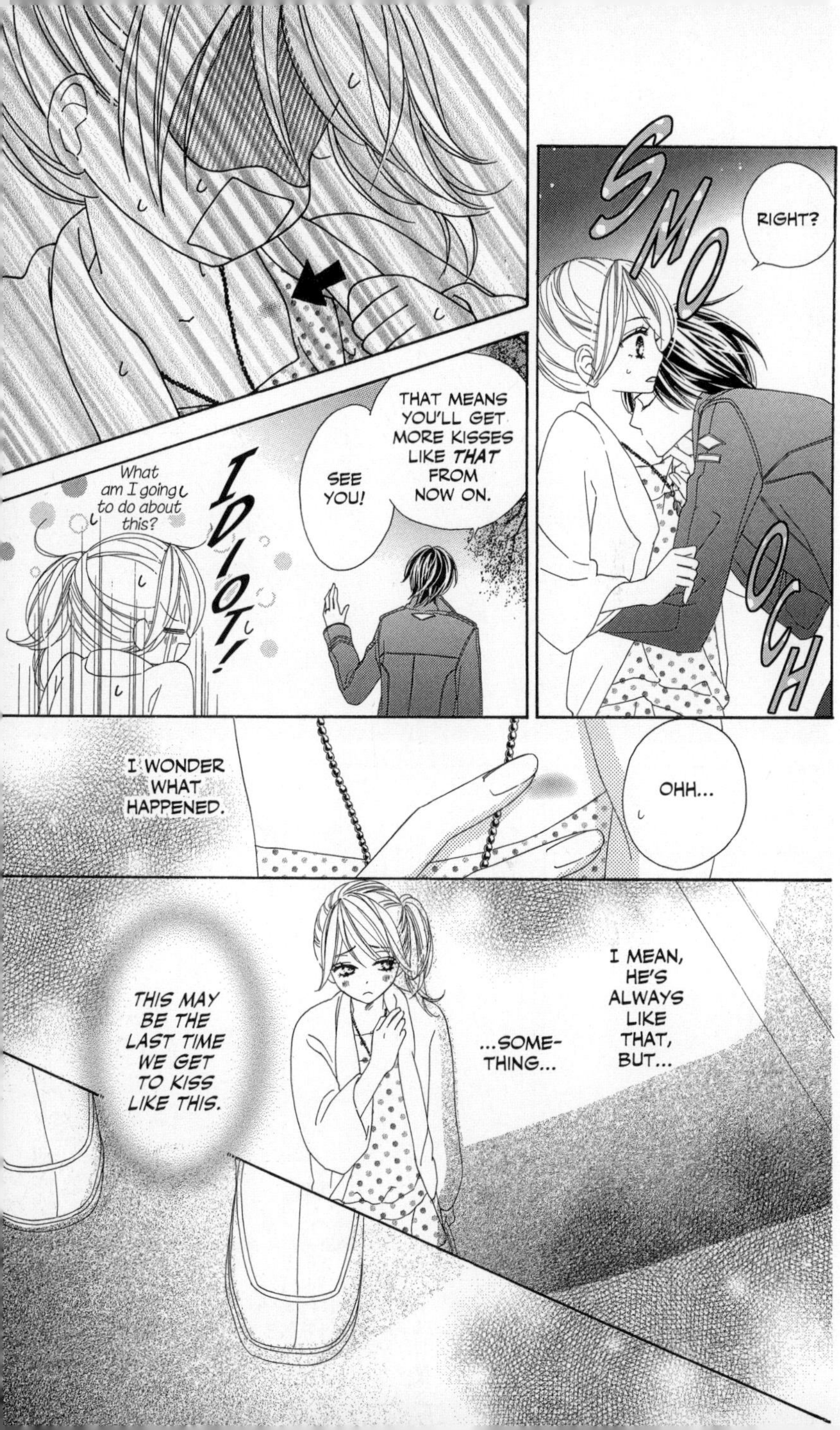
RIGHT?
SMOOCH
THAT MEANS YOU'LL GET MORE KISSES LIKE *THAT* FROM NOW ON.
SEE YOU!
IDIOT!
What am I going to do about this?
OHH...
I WONDER WHAT HAPPENED.
I MEAN, HE'S ALWAYS LIKE THAT, BUT...
...SOMETHING...
THIS MAY BE THE LAST TIME WE GET TO KISS LIKE THIS.

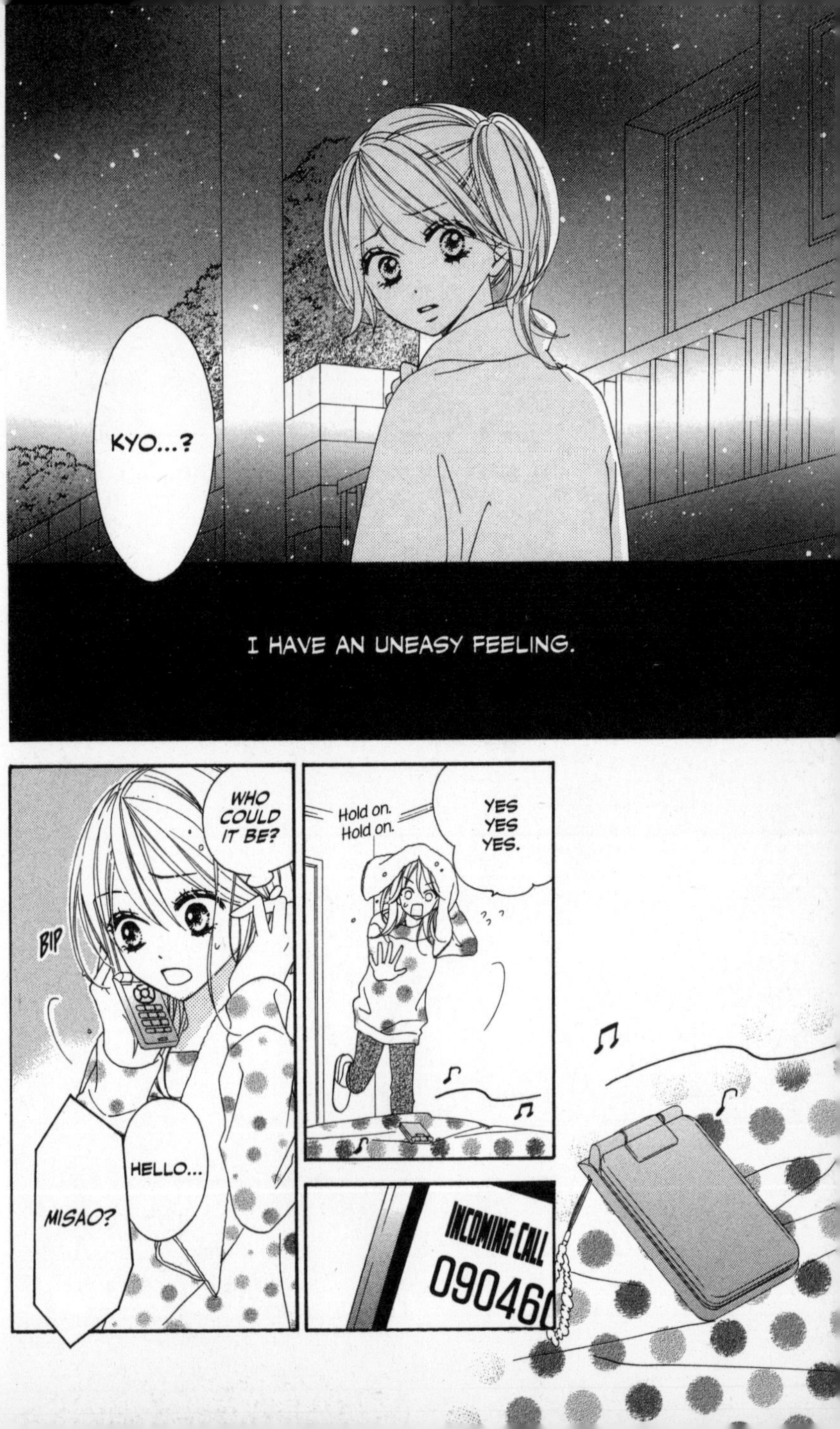
KYO...?
I HAVE AN UNEASY FEELING.
YES YES YES.
Hold on. Hold on.
INCOMING CALL
090460
WHO COULD IT BE?
BIP
HELLO...
MISAO?

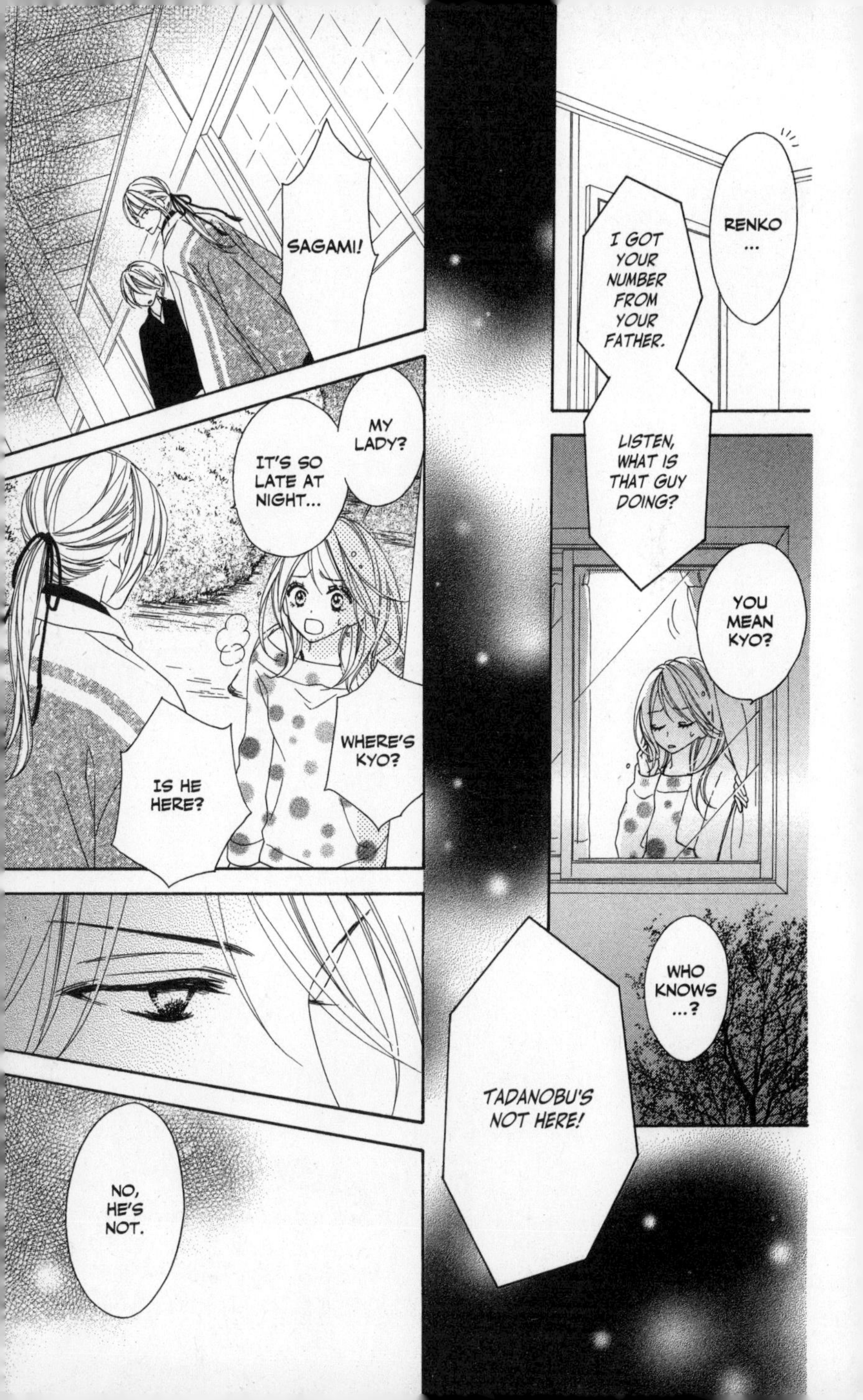
RENKO...
I GOT YOUR NUMBER FROM YOUR FATHER.
LISTEN, WHAT IS THAT GUY DOING?
YOU MEAN KYO?
WHO KNOWS...?
TADANOBU'S NOT HERE!
SAGAMI!
MY LADY?
IT'S SO LATE AT NIGHT...
WHERE'S KYO?
IS HE HERE?
NO, HE'S NOT.

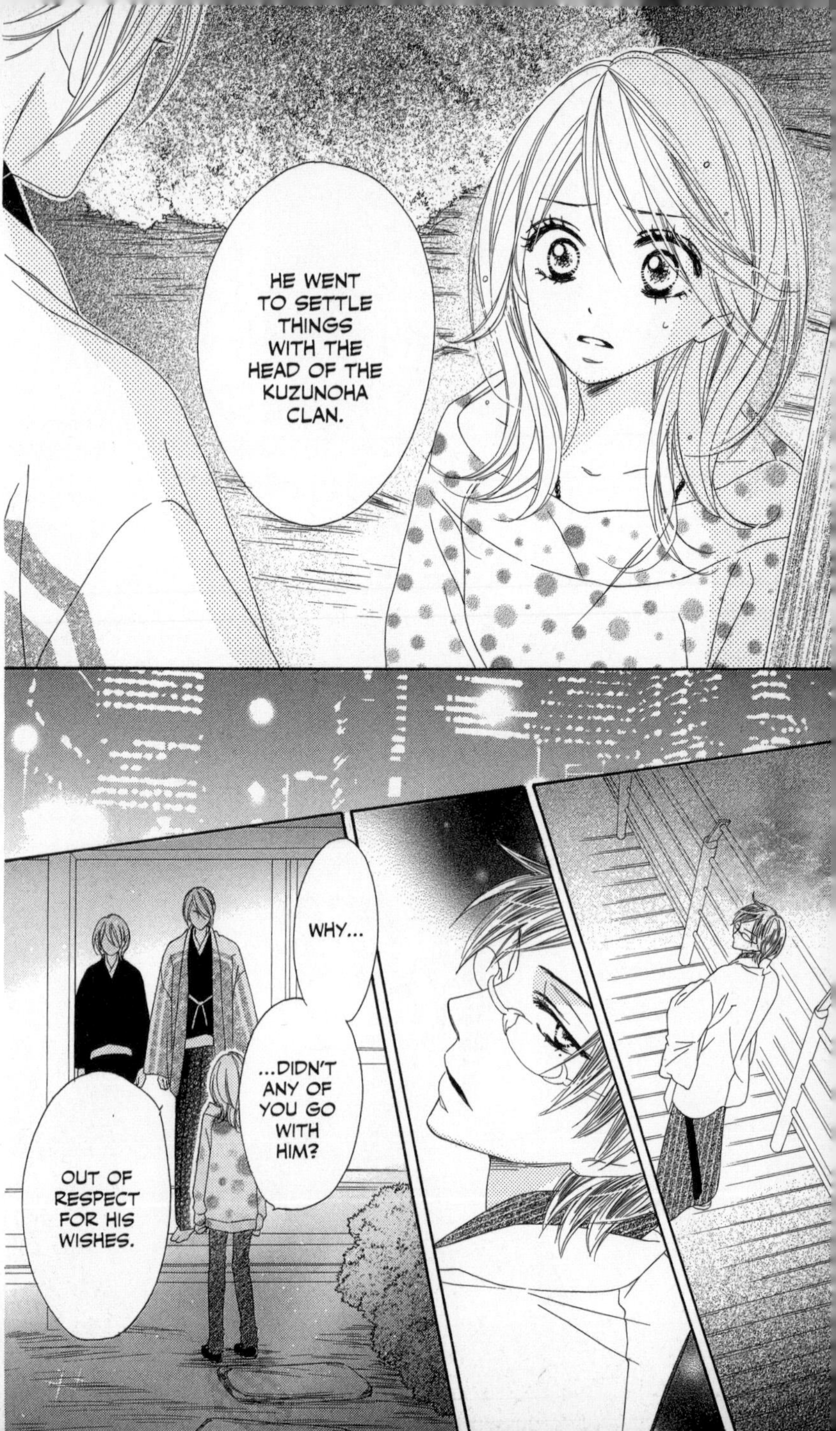
HE WENT TO SETTLE THINGS WITH THE HEAD OF THE KUZUNOHA CLAN.
WHY...
...DIDN'T ANY OF YOU GO WITH HIM?
OUT OF RESPECT FOR HIS WISHES.

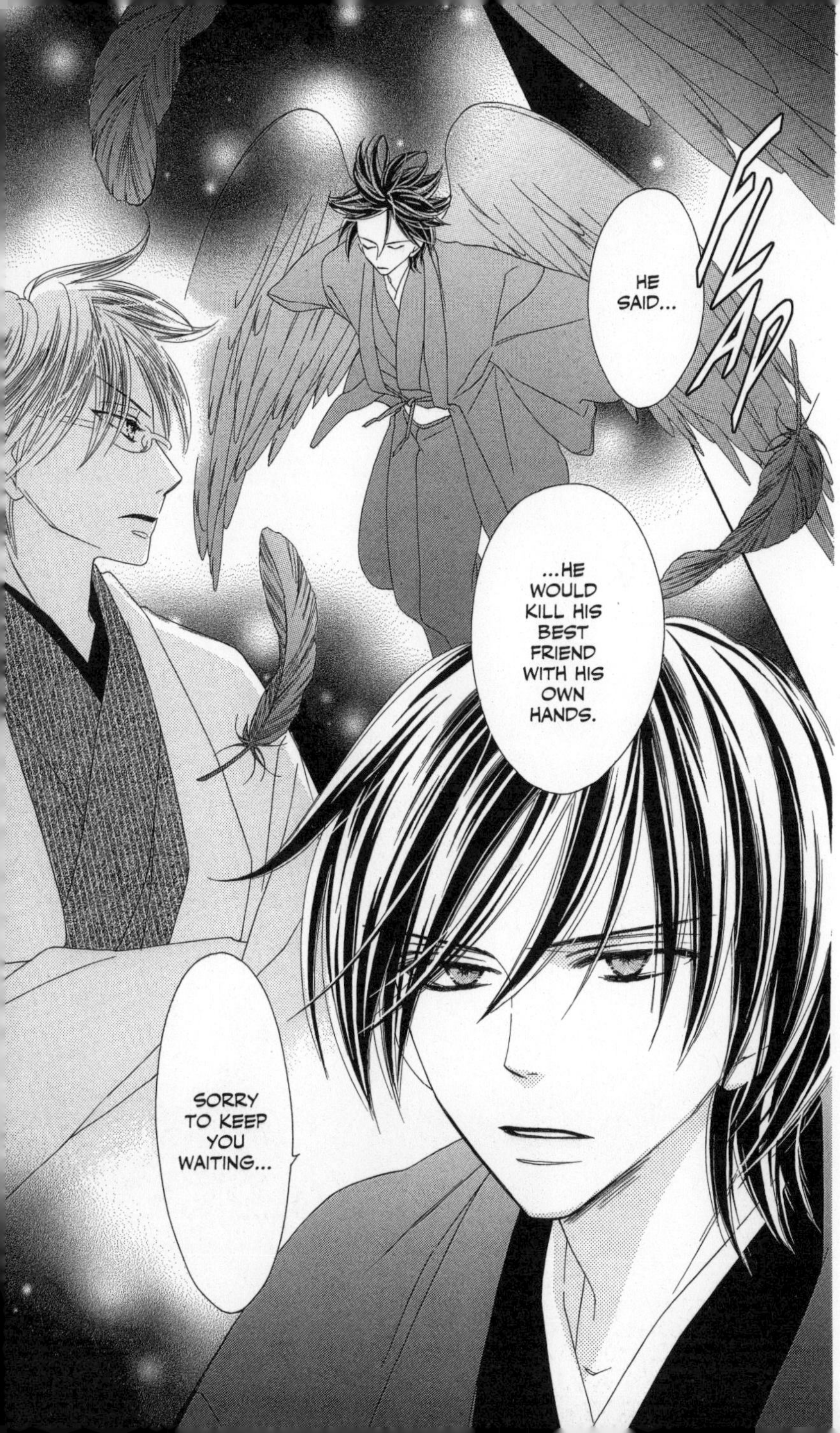
HE SAID...
...HE WOULD KILL HIS BEST FRIEND WITH HIS OWN HANDS.
SORRY TO KEEP YOU WAITING...

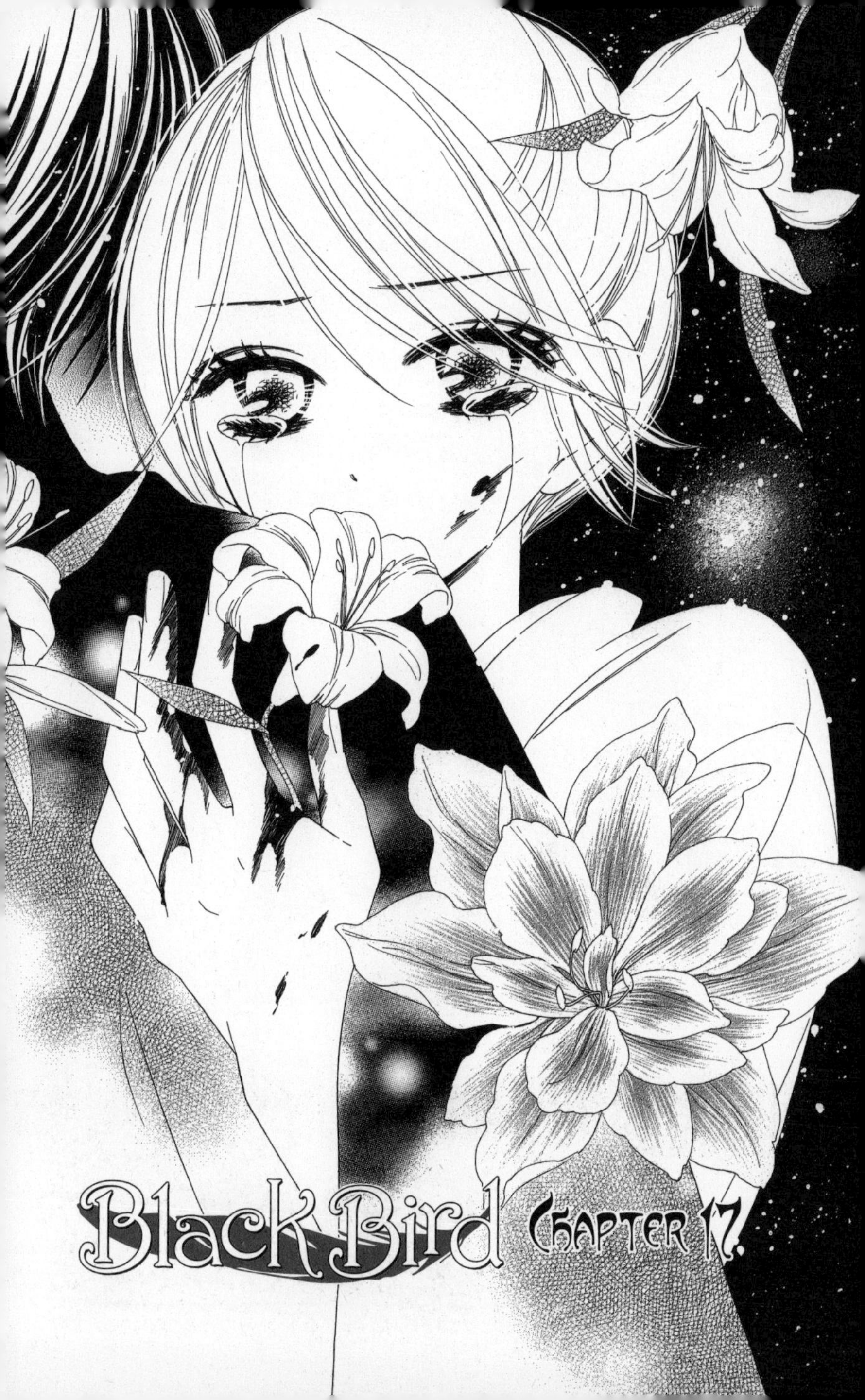
Black Bird
Chapter 17

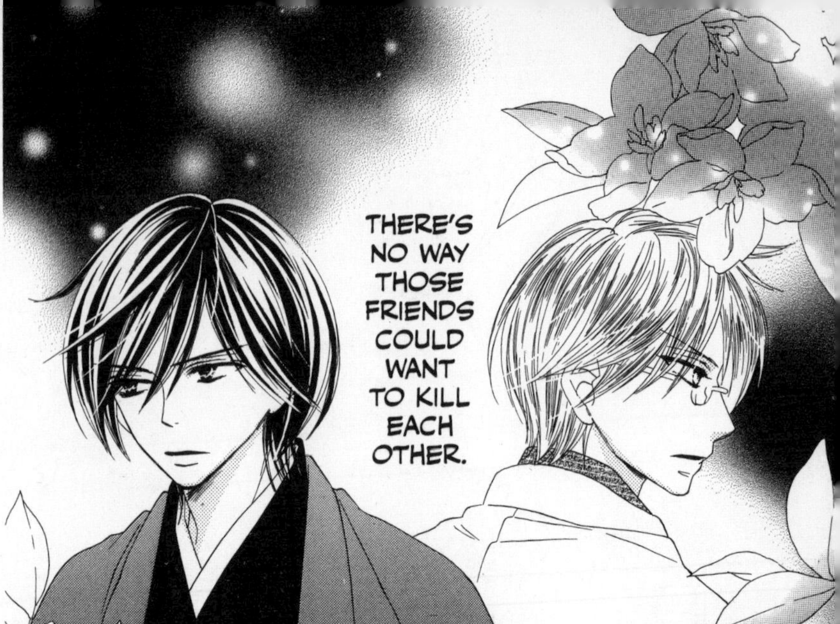
THERE'S NO WAY THOSE FRIENDS COULD WANT TO KILL EACH OTHER.

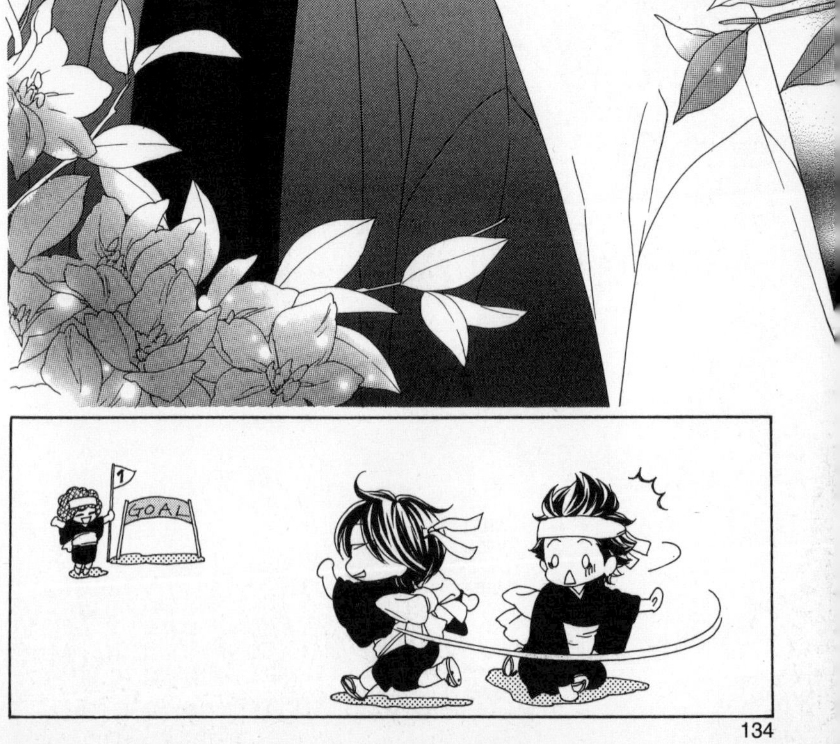
1
GOAL

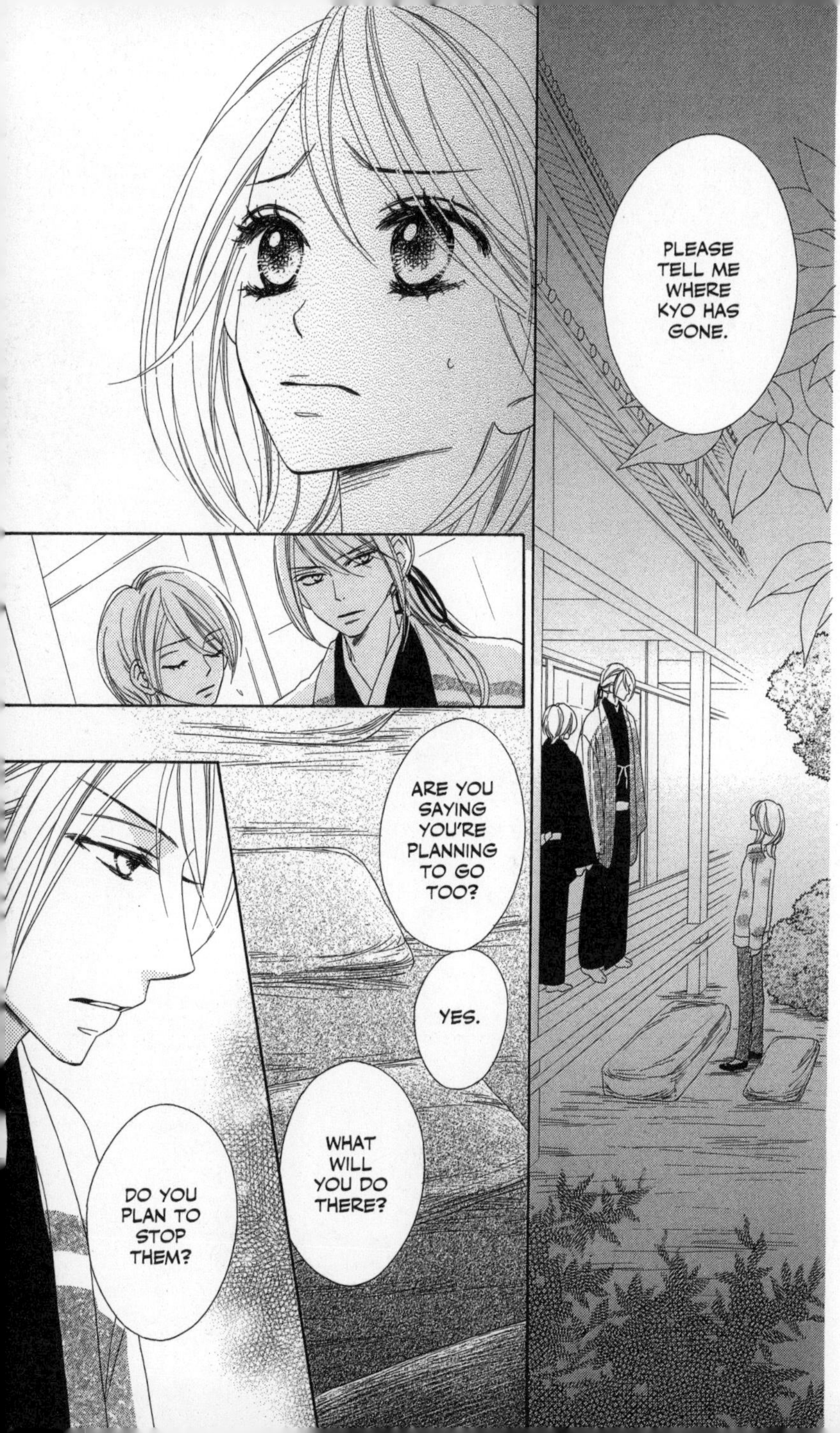
PLEASE TELL ME WHERE KYO HAS GONE.
ARE YOU SAYING YOU'RE PLANNING TO GO TOO?
YES.
WHAT WILL YOU DO THERE?
DO YOU PLAN TO STOP THEM?

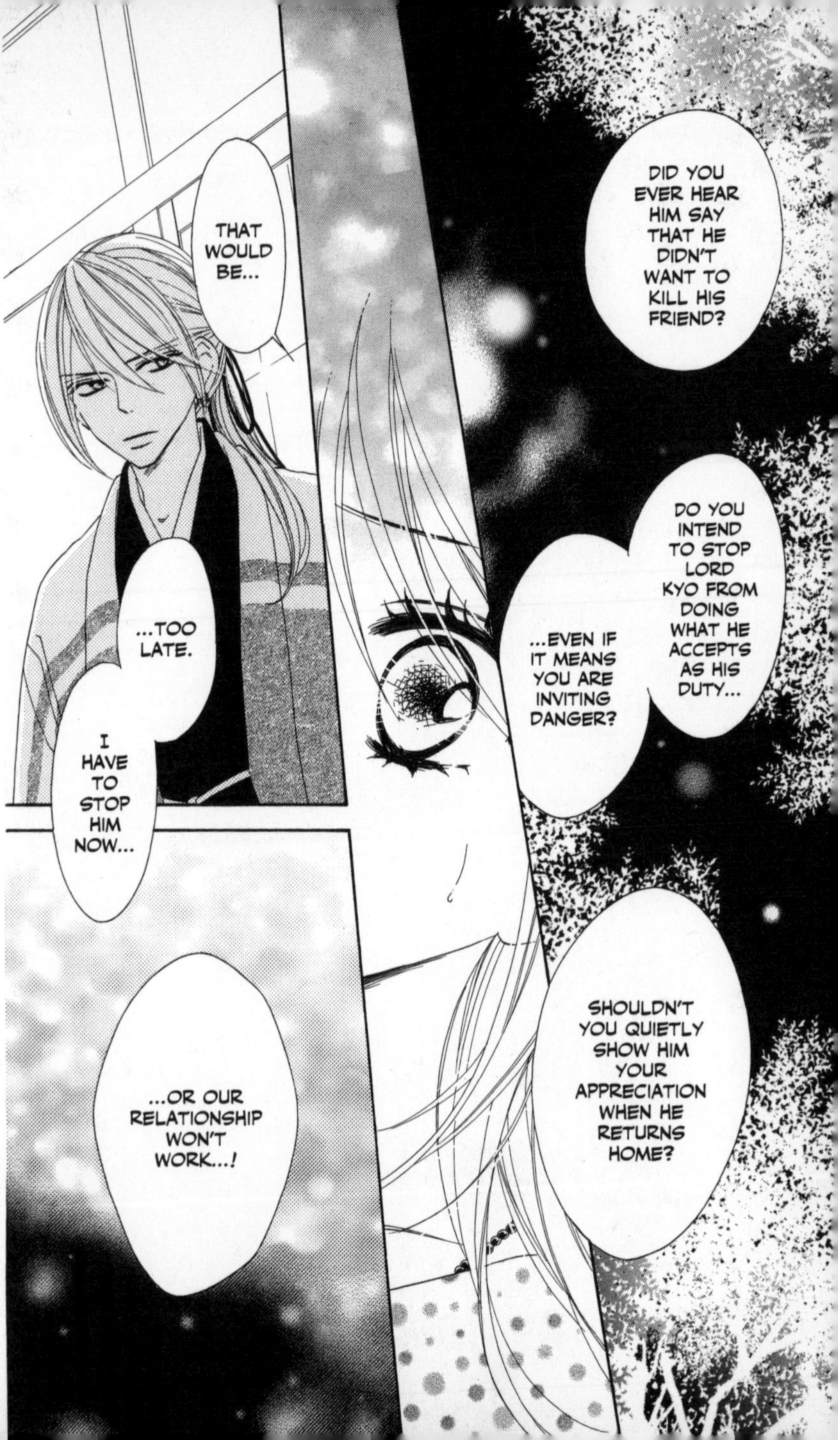
DID YOU EVER HEAR HIM SAY THAT HE DIDN'T WANT TO KILL HIS FRIEND?
DO YOU INTEND TO STOP LORD KYO FROM DOING WHAT HE ACCEPTS AS HIS DUTY...
...EVEN IF IT MEANS YOU ARE INVITING DANGER?
SHOULDN'T YOU QUIETLY SHOW HIM YOUR APPRECIATION WHEN HE RETURNS HOME?
THAT WOULD BE...
...TOO LATE.
I HAVE TO STOP HIM NOW...
...OR OUR RELATIONSHIP WON'T WORK...!

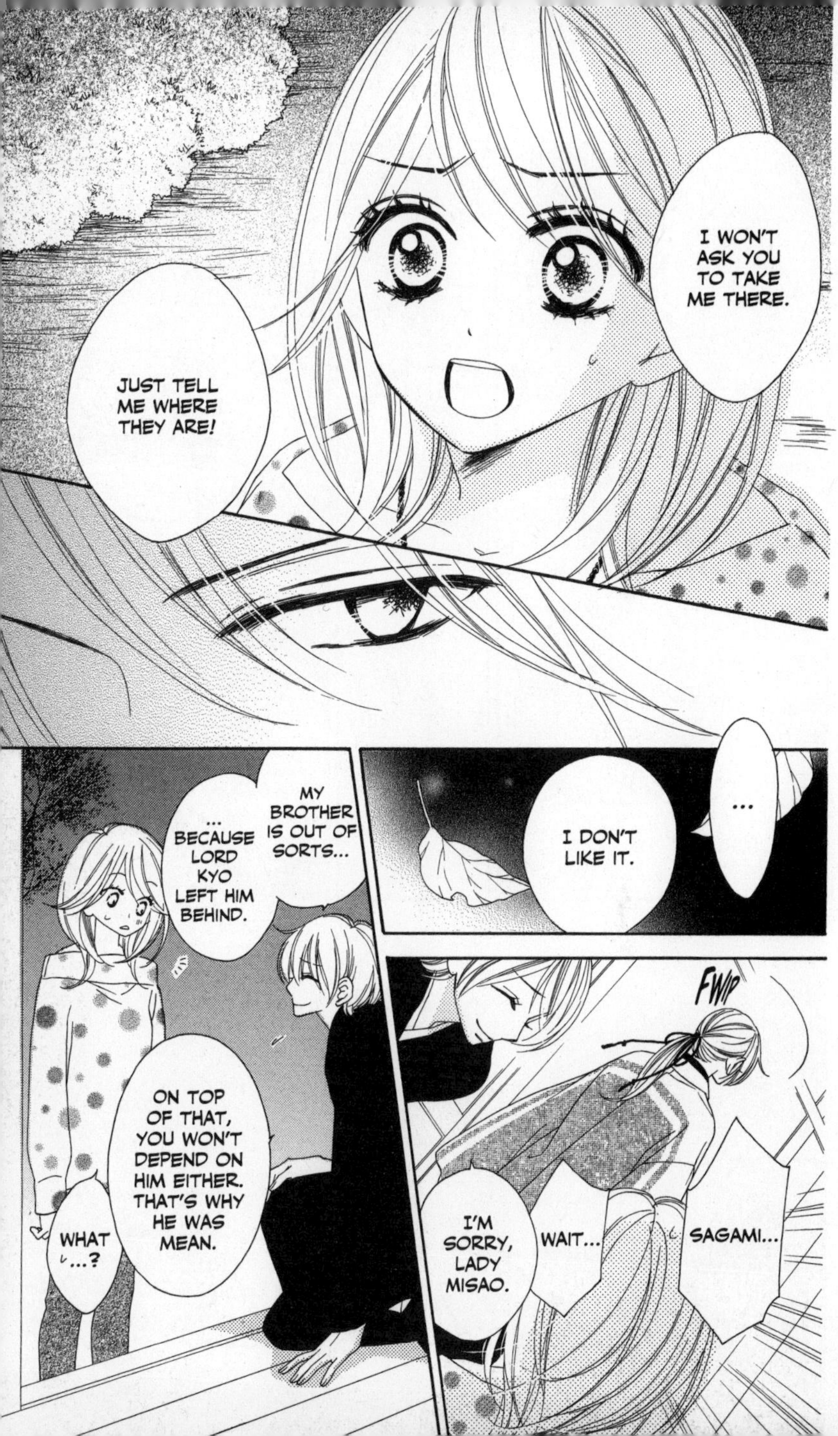
I WON'T ASK YOU TO TAKE ME THERE.
JUST TELL ME WHERE THEY ARE!
...
I DON'T LIKE IT.
FWIP
SAGAMI...
WAIT...
I'M SORRY, LADY MISAO.
MY BROTHER IS OUT OF SORTS...
... BECAUSE LORD KYO LEFT HIM BEHIND.
ON TOP OF THAT, YOU WON'T DEPEND ON HIM EITHER. THAT'S WHY HE WAS MEAN.
WHAT ...?

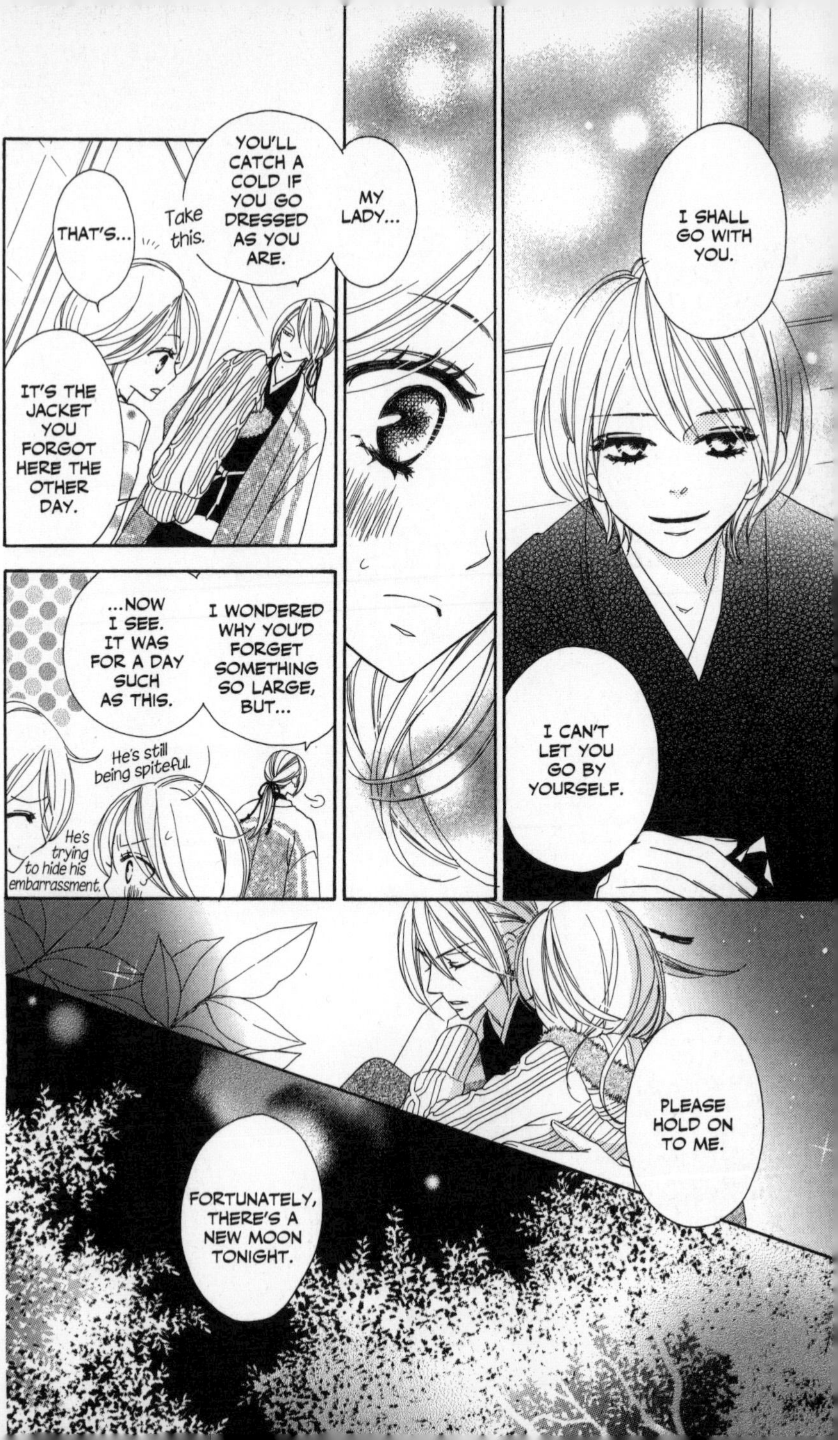
I SHALL GO WITH YOU.
I CAN'T LET YOU GO BY YOURSELF.
MY LADY...
YOU'LL CATCH A COLD IF YOU GO DRESSED AS YOU ARE.
Take this.
THAT'S...
IT'S THE JACKET YOU FORGOT HERE THE OTHER DAY.
I WONDERED WHY YOU'D FORGET SOMETHING SO LARGE, BUT...
...NOW I SEE. IT WAS FOR A DAY SUCH AS THIS.
He's still being spiteful.
He's trying to hide his embarrassment.
PLEASE HOLD ON TO ME.
FORTUNATELY, THERE'S A NEW MOON TONIGHT.

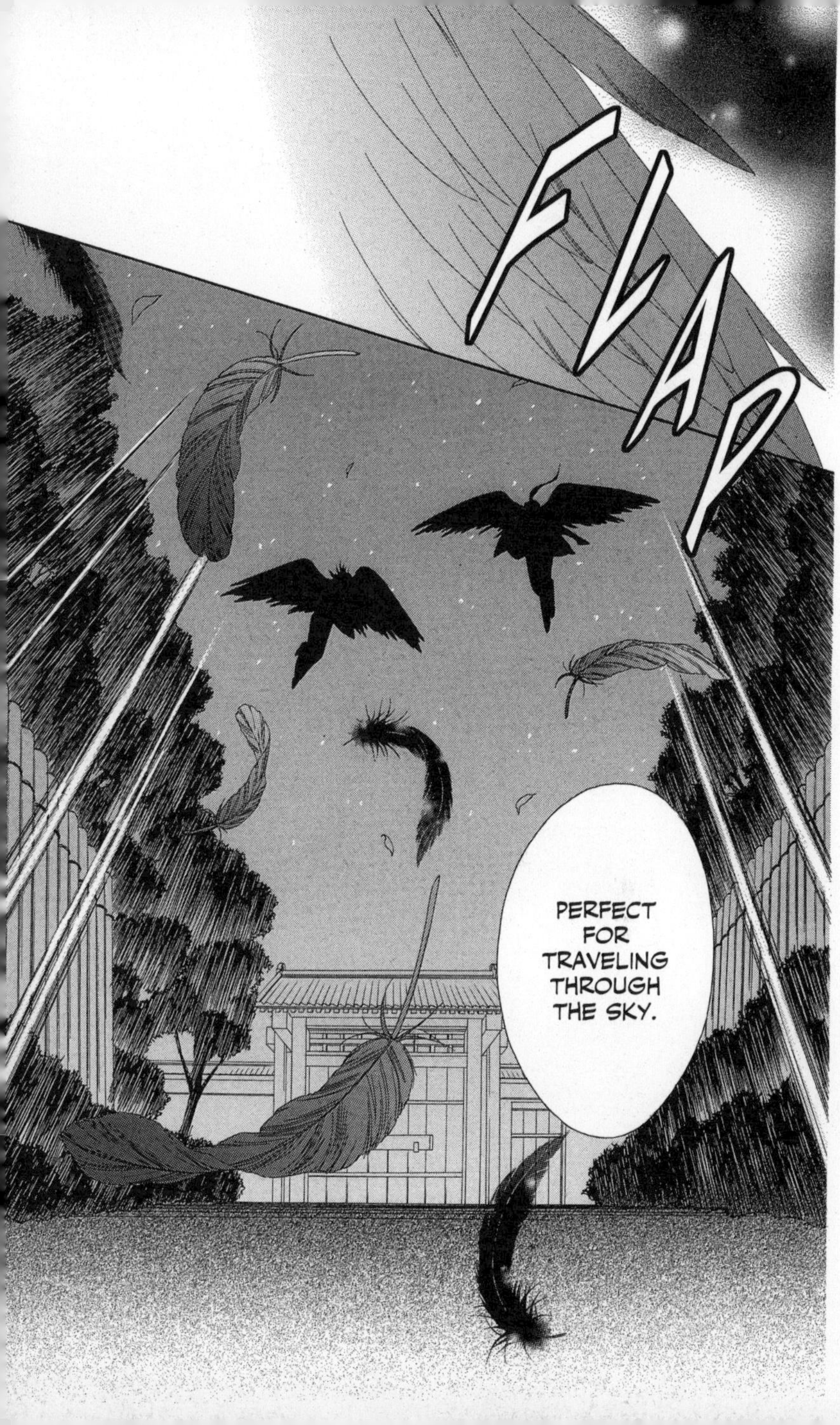
FLAP
PERFECT FOR TRAVELING THROUGH THE SKY.

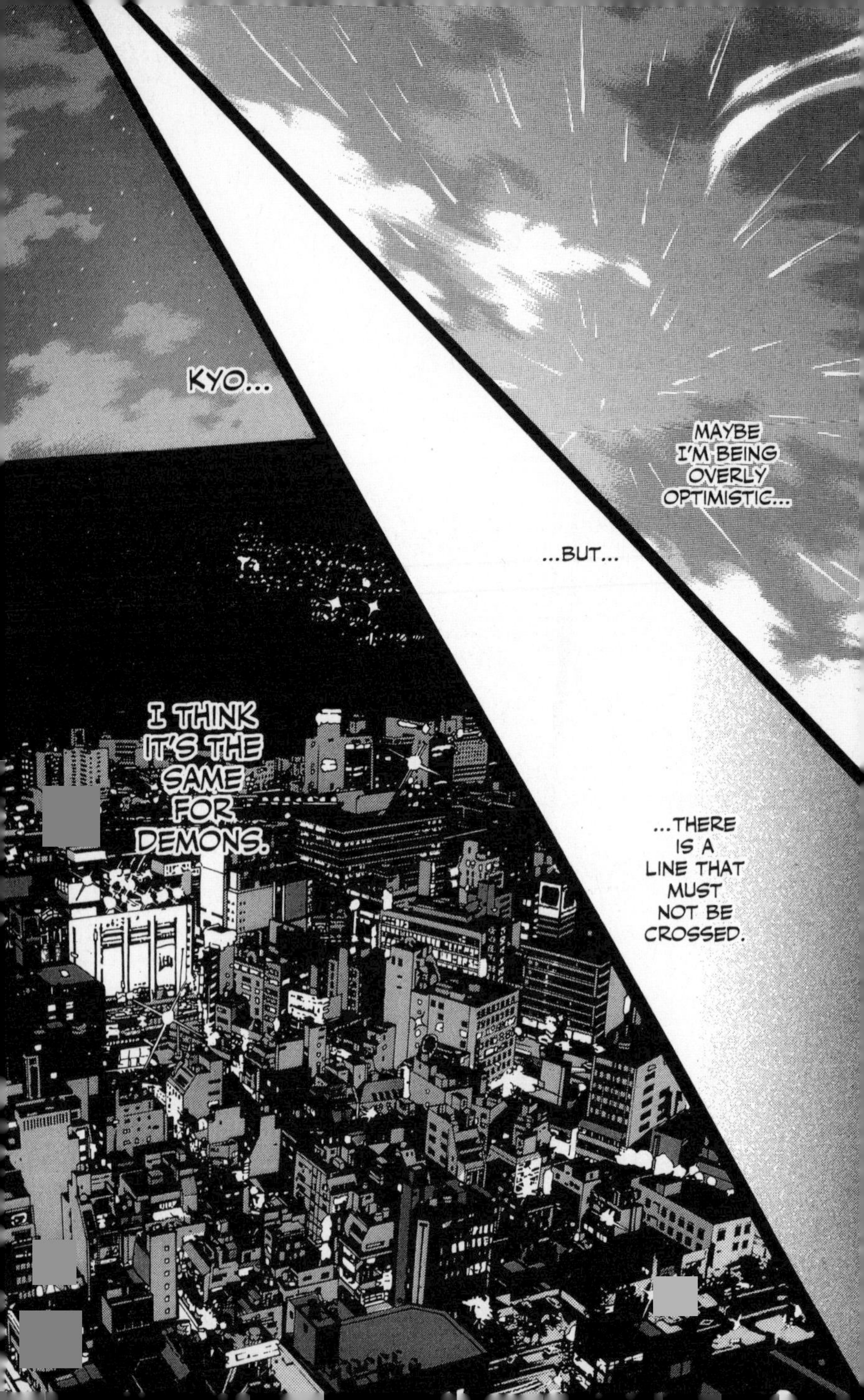
MAYBE I'M BEING OVERLY OPTIMISTIC...
...BUT...
...THERE IS A LINE THAT MUST NOT BE CROSSED.
KYO...
I THINK IT'S THE SAME FOR DEMONS.

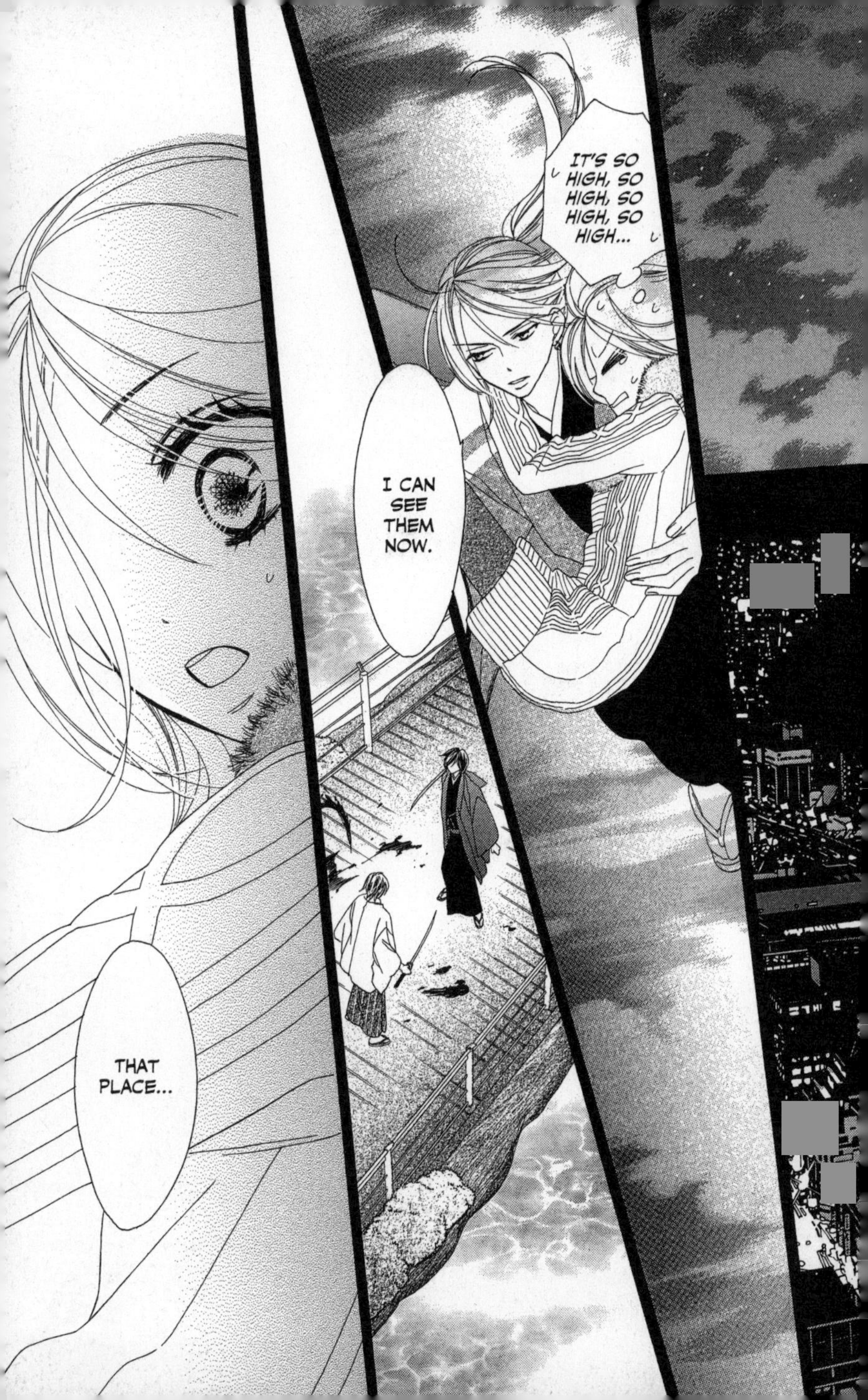
IT'S SO HIGH, SO HIGH, SO HIGH, SO HIGH...
I CAN SEE THEM NOW.
THAT PLACE...

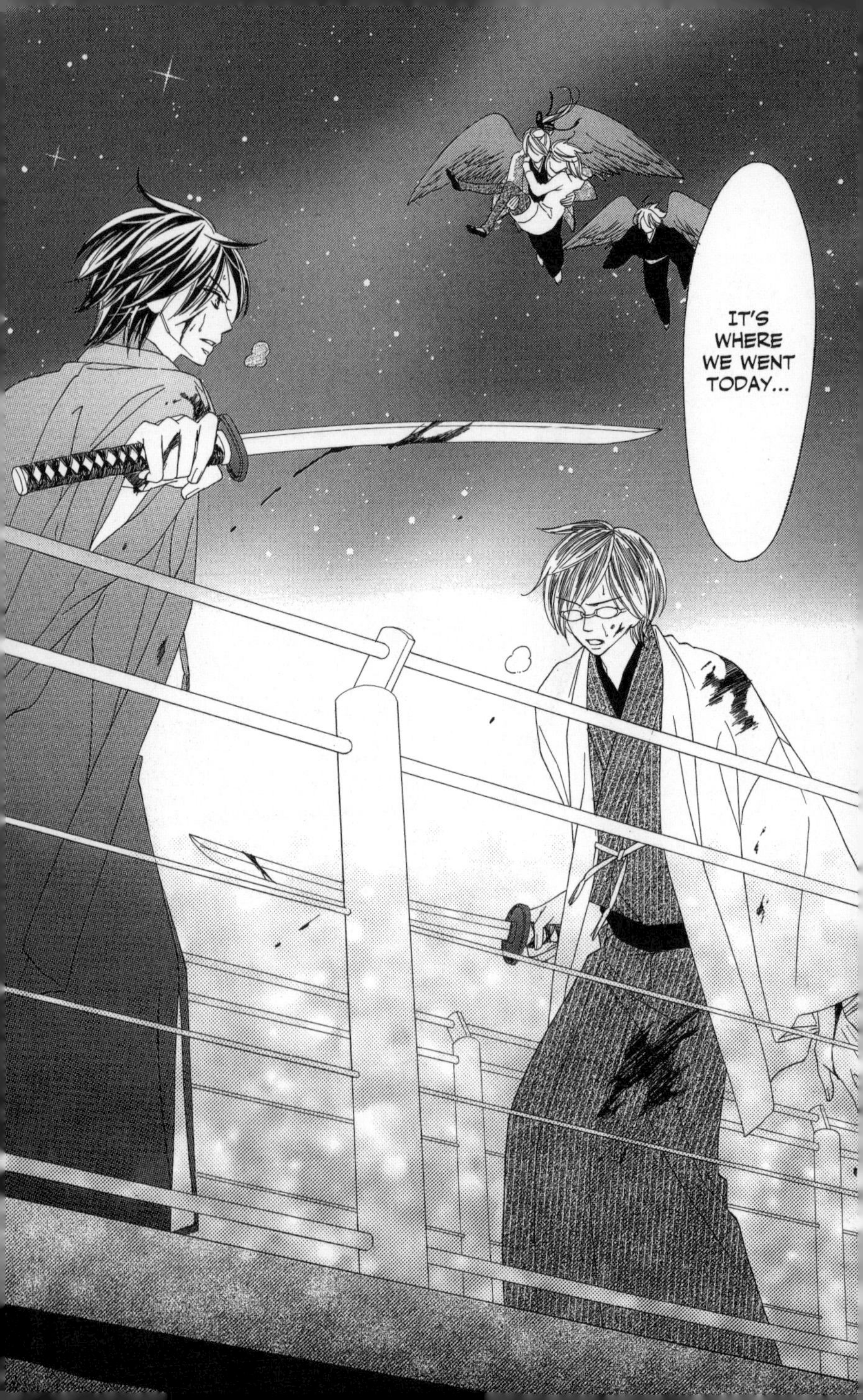
IT'S WHERE WE WENT TODAY...

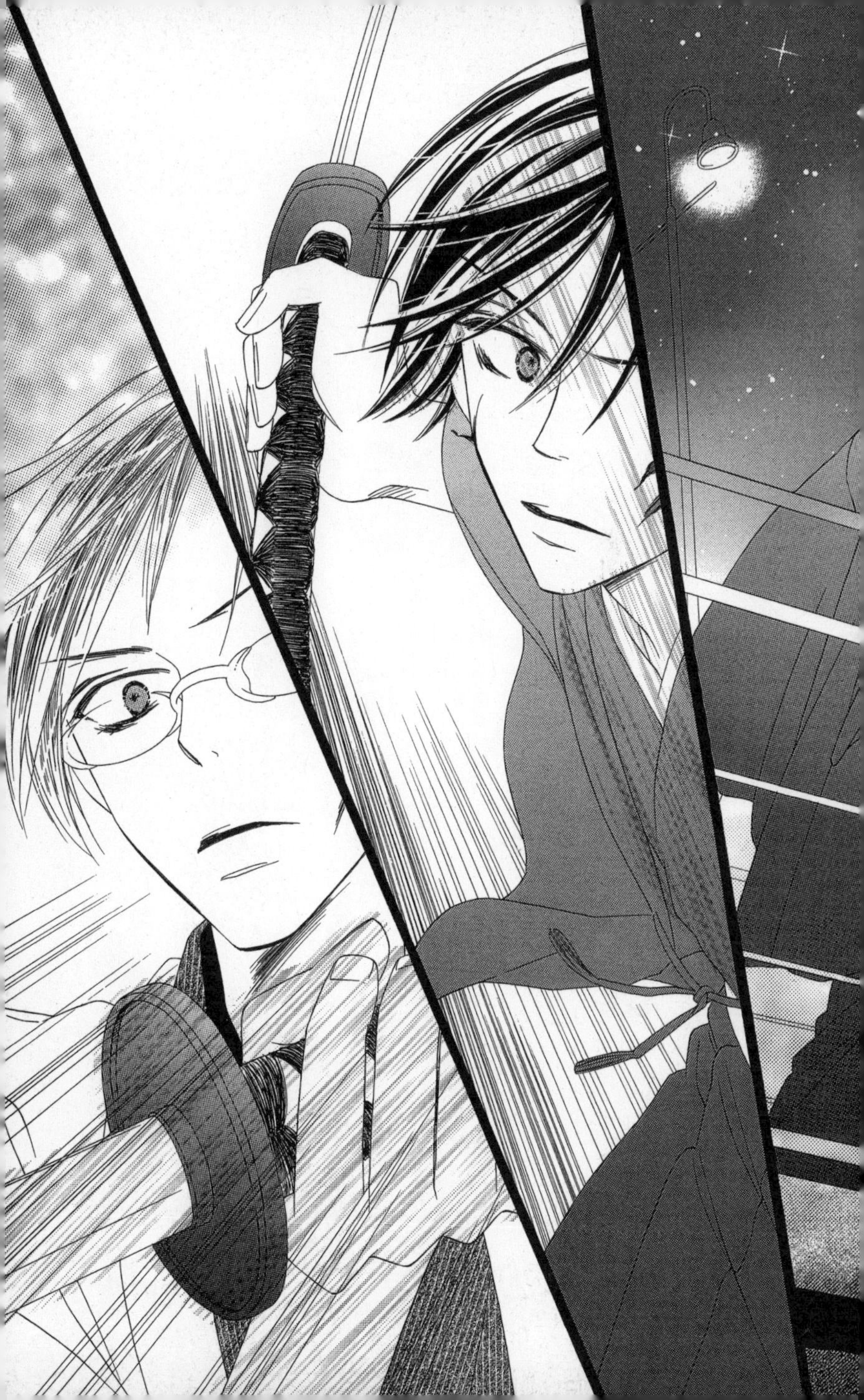

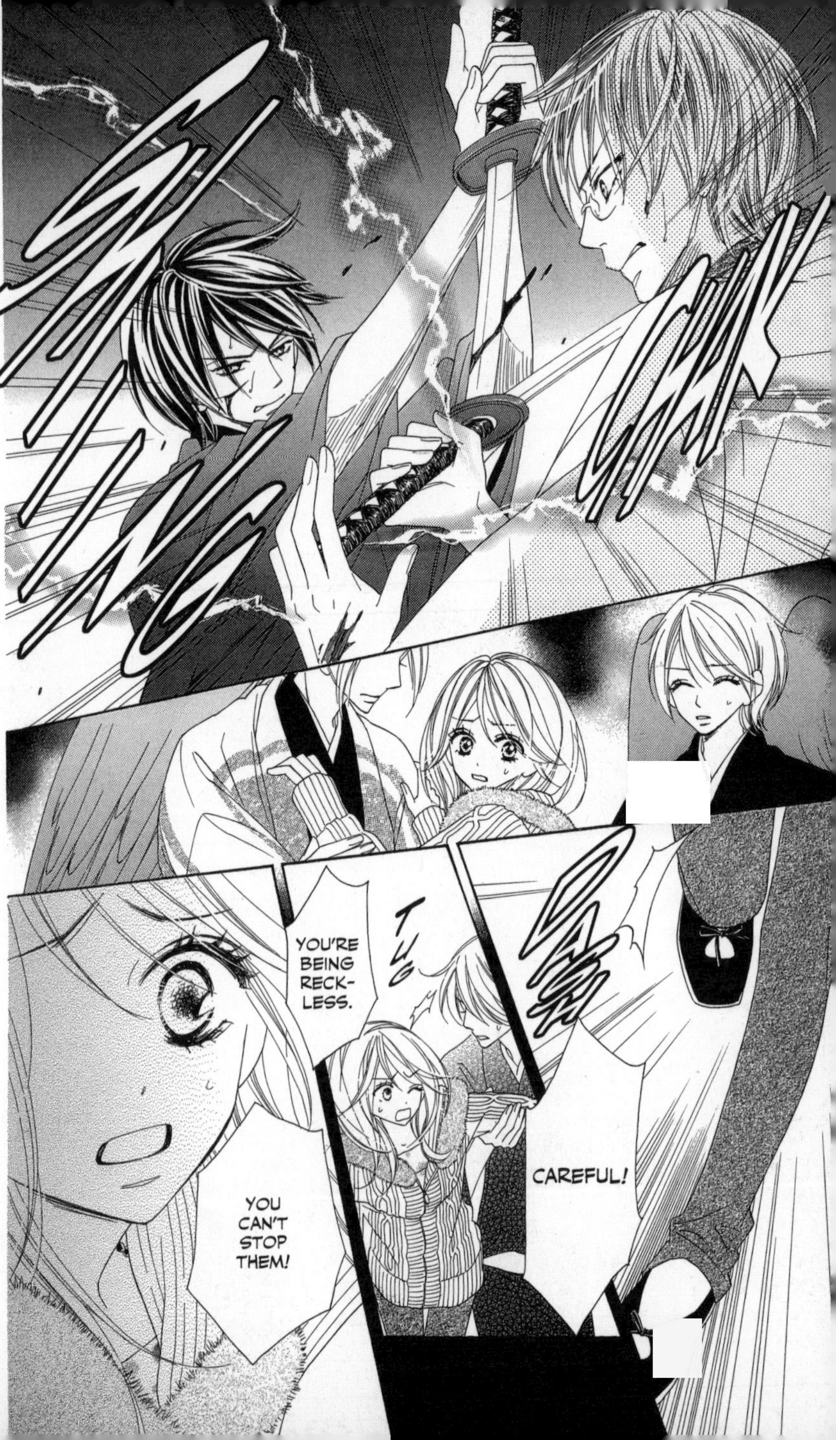
CAREFUL!
TUG
YOU'RE BEING RECK-LESS.
YOU CAN'T STOP THEM!

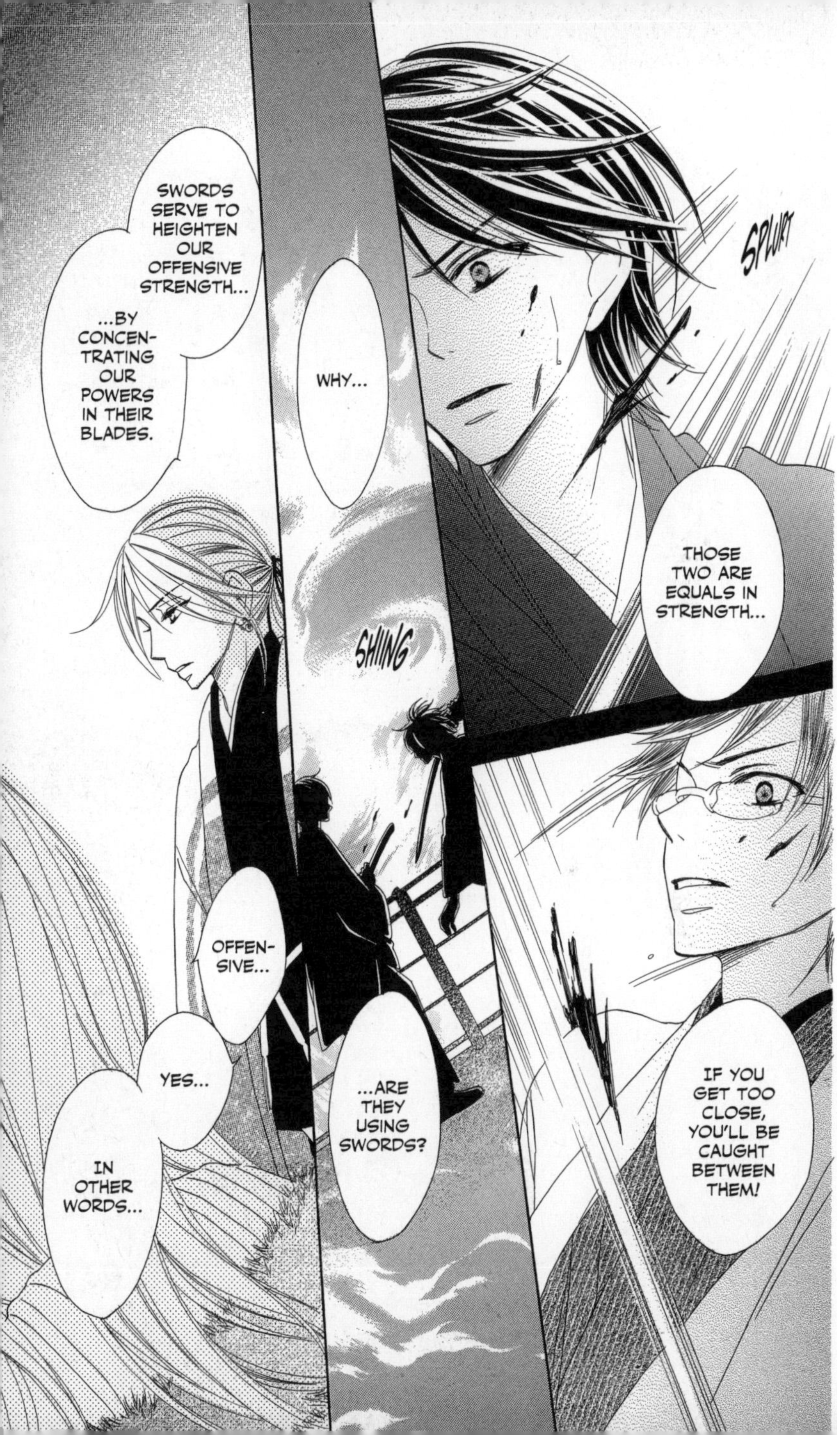
SPLURT
THOSE TWO ARE EQUALS IN STRENGTH...
IF YOU GET TOO CLOSE, YOU'LL BE CAUGHT BETWEEN THEM!
WHY...
SHIING
...ARE THEY USING SWORDS?
SWORDS SERVE TO HEIGHTEN OUR OFFENSIVE STRENGTH...
...BY CONCEN-TRATING OUR POWERS IN THEIR BLADES.
OFFEN-SIVE...
YES...
IN OTHER WORDS...

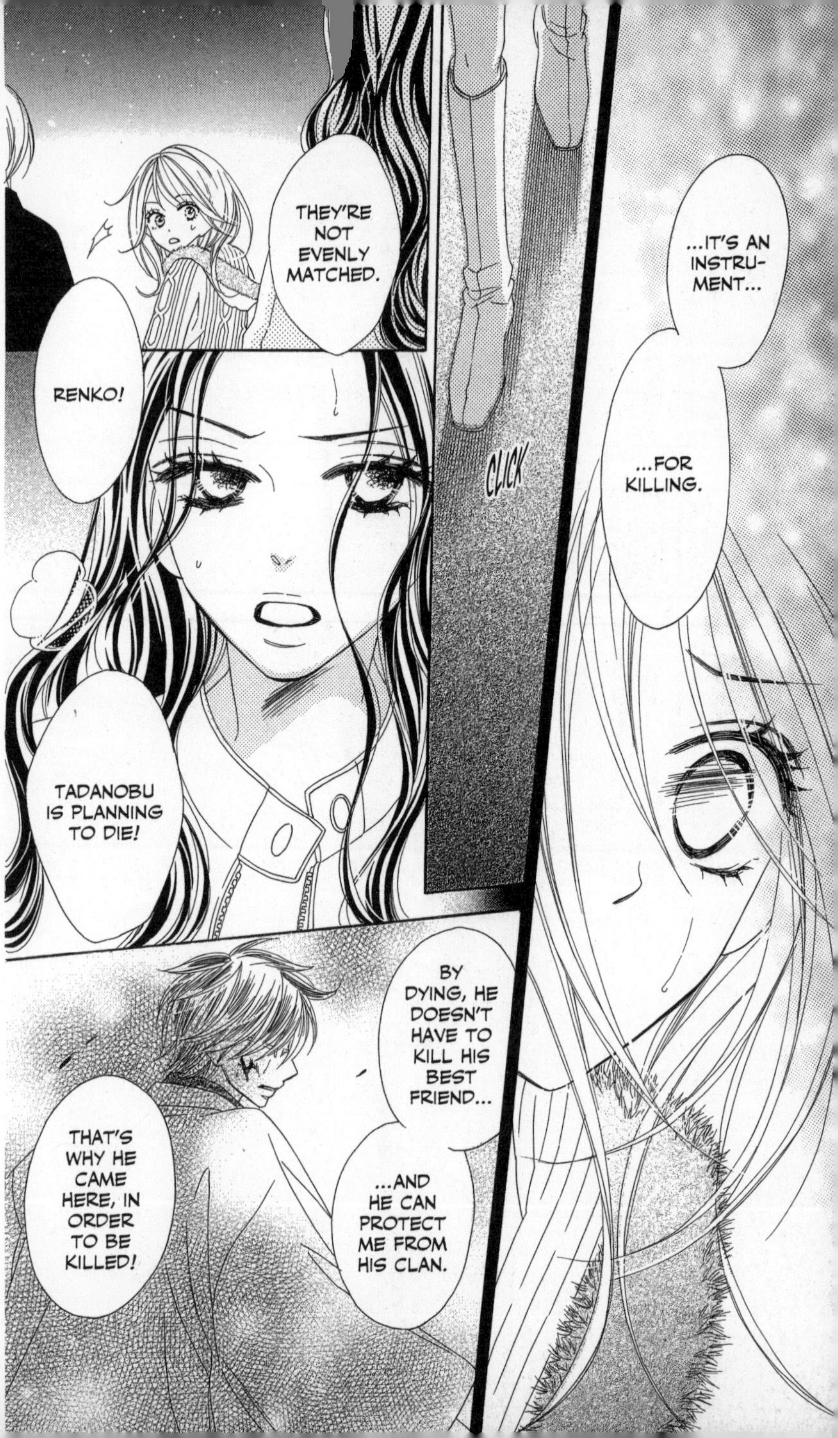

...IT'S AN INSTRU-MENT...
...FOR KILLING.
CLICK
THEY'RE NOT EVENLY MATCHED.
RENKO!
TADANOBU IS PLANNING TO DIE!
BY DYING, HE DOESN'T HAVE TO KILL HIS BEST FRIEND...
...AND HE CAN PROTECT ME FROM HIS CLAN.
THAT'S WHY HE CAME HERE, IN ORDER TO BE KILLED!

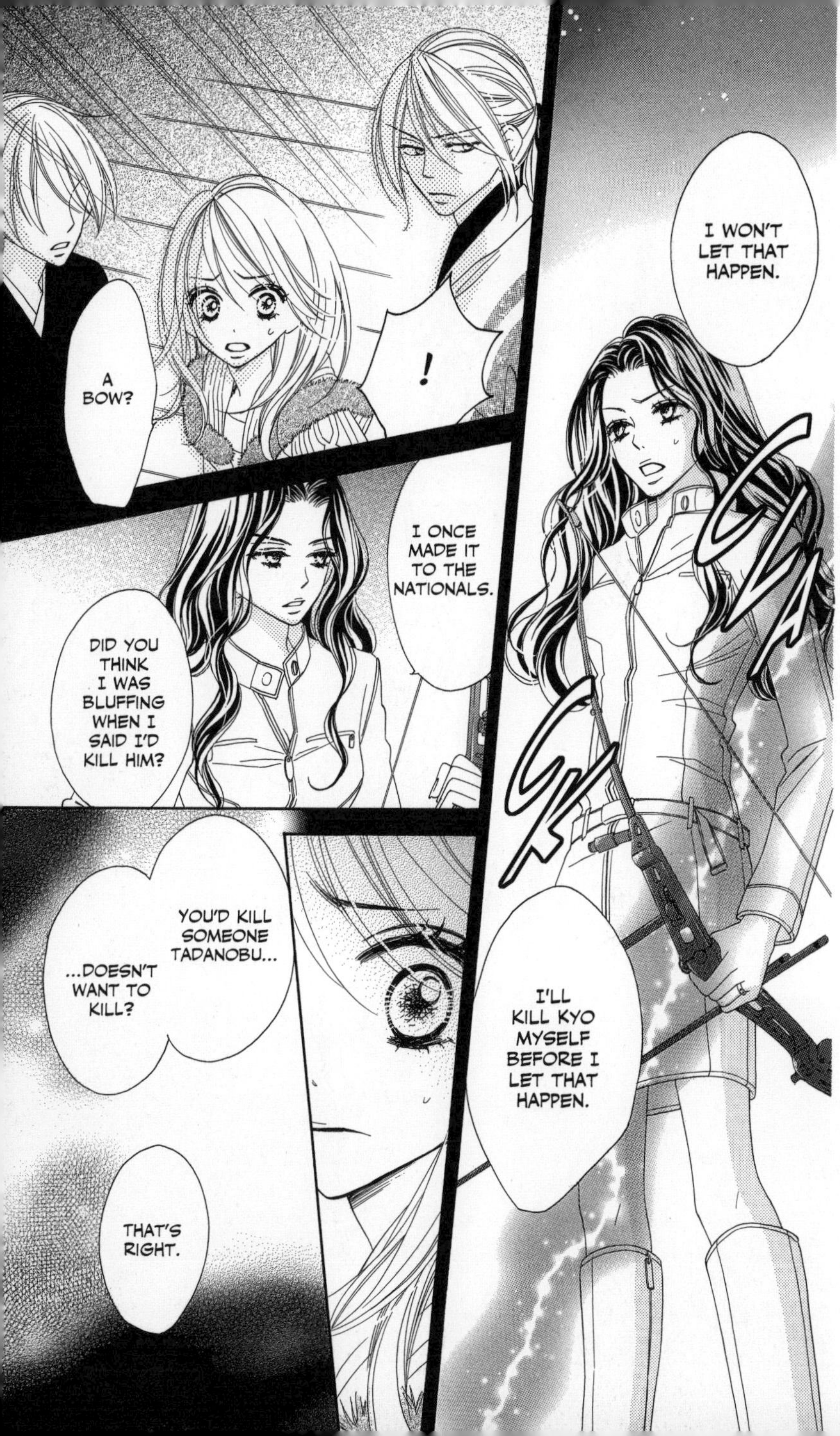
I WON'T LET THAT HAPPEN.
I'LL KILL KYO MYSELF BEFORE I LET THAT HAPPEN.
!
A BOW?
I ONCE MADE IT TO THE NATIONALS.
DID YOU THINK I WAS BLUFFING WHEN I SAID I'D KILL HIM?
YOU'D KILL SOMEONE TADANOBU...
...DOESN'T WANT TO KILL?
THAT'S RIGHT.

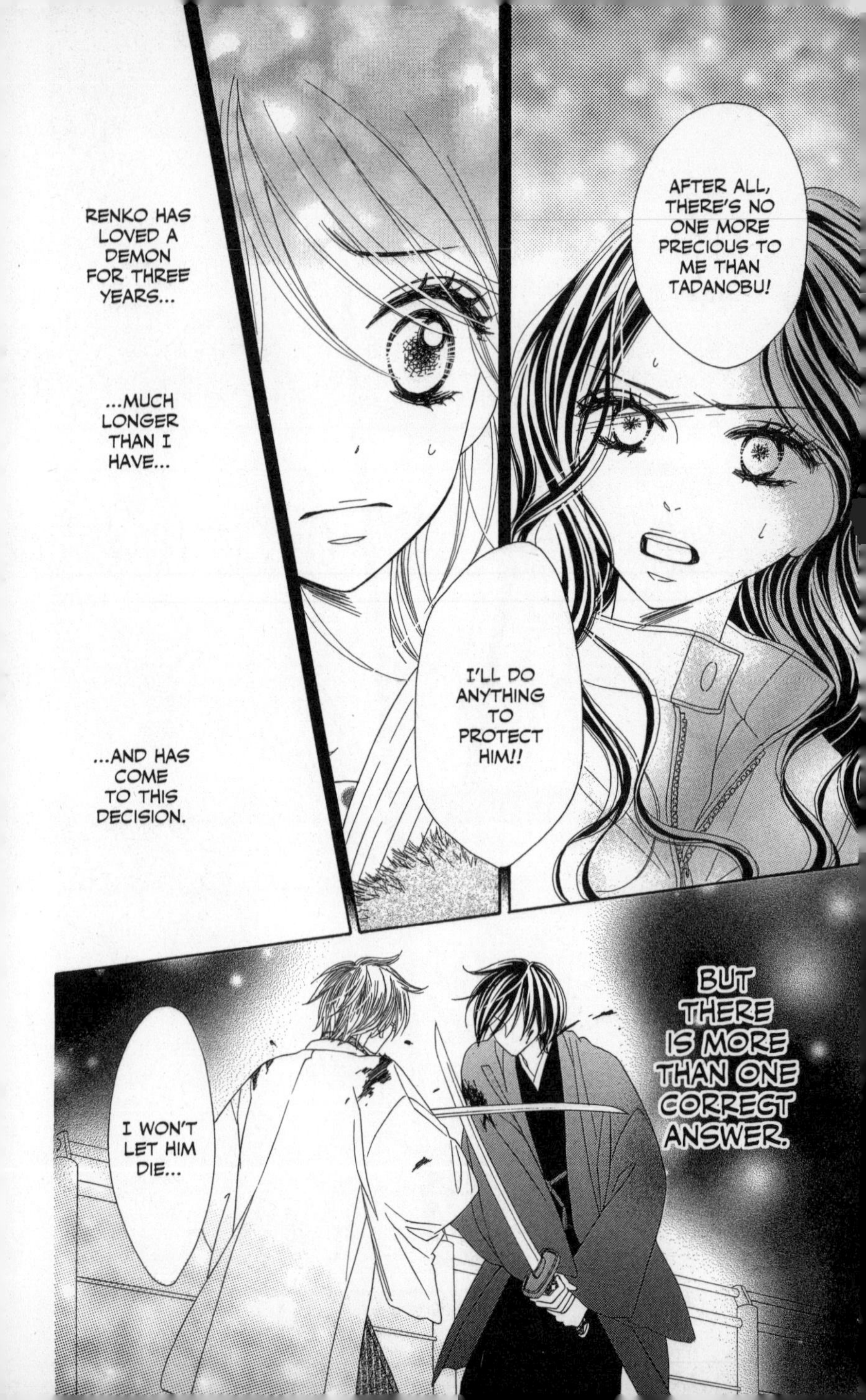
AFTER ALL, THERE'S NO ONE MORE PRECIOUS TO ME THAN TADANOBU!
I'LL DO ANYTHING TO PROTECT HIM!!
RENKO HAS LOVED A DEMON FOR THREE YEARS...
...MUCH LONGER THAN I HAVE...
...AND HAS COME TO THIS DECISION.
BUT THERE IS MORE THAN ONE CORRECT ANSWER.
I WON'T LET HIM DIE...

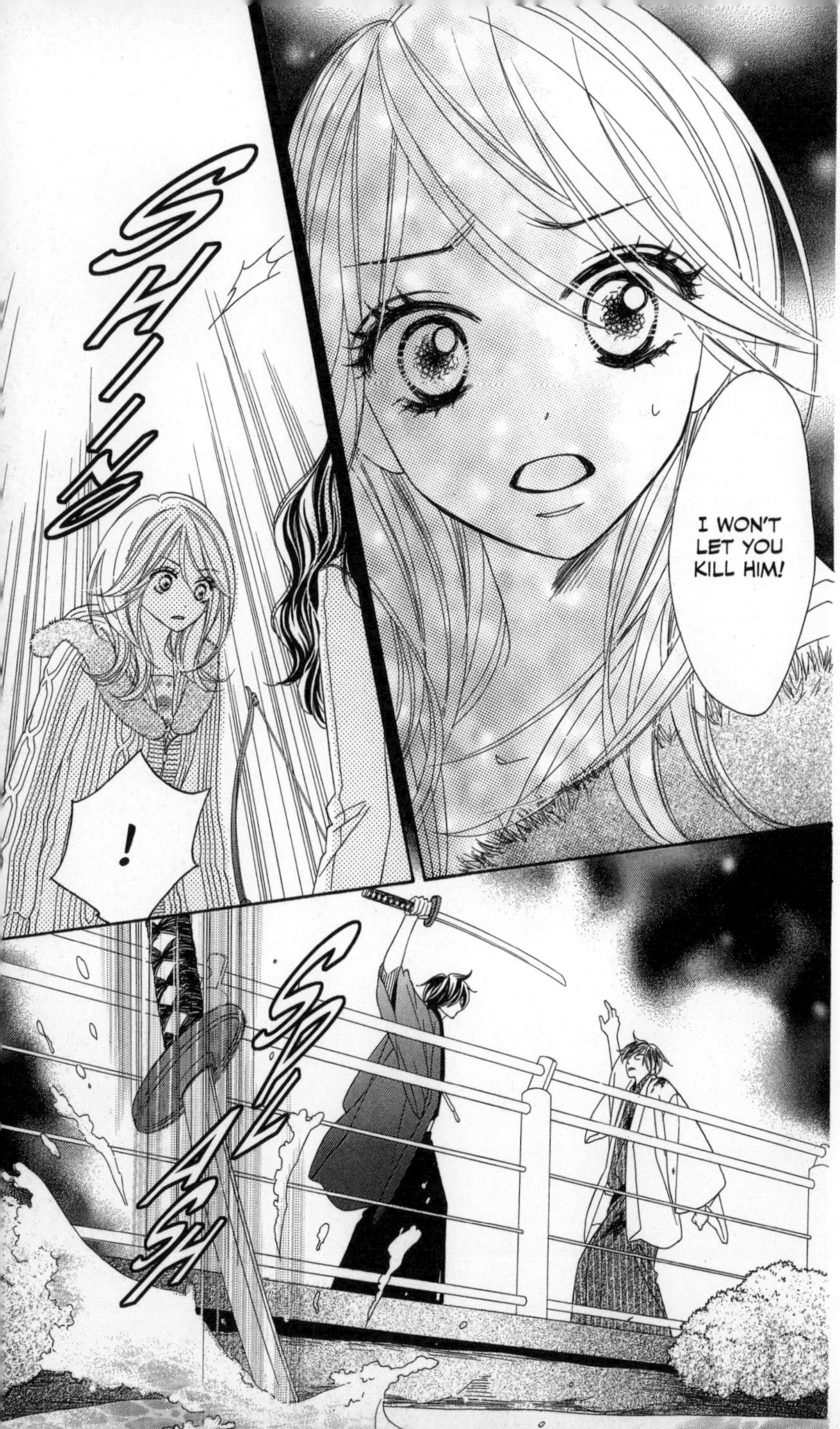
I WON'T LET YOU KILL HIM!
SHIIING
!
SPLASH

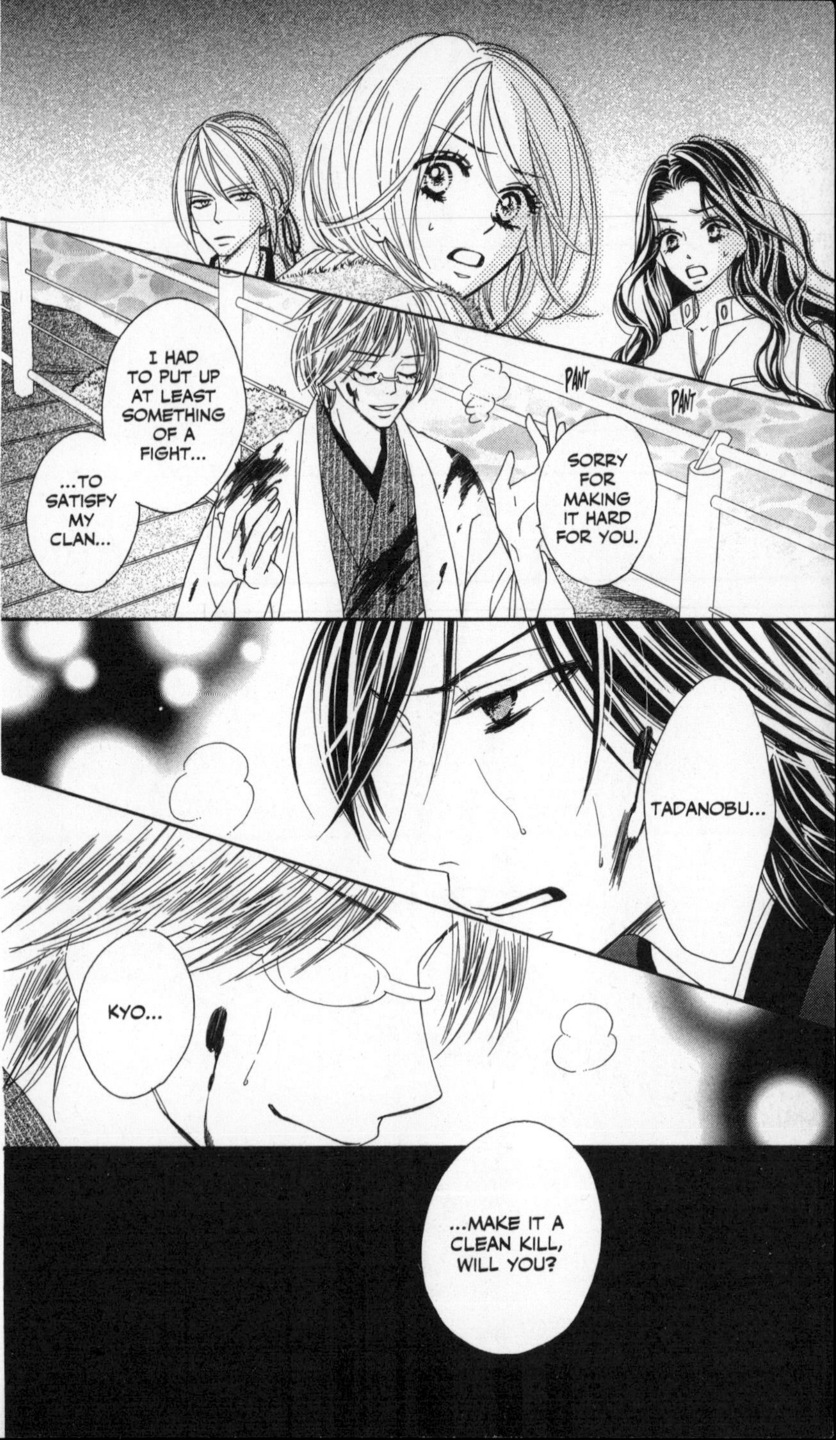

PANT
PANT
SORRY FOR MAKING IT HARD FOR YOU.
I HAD TO PUT UP AT LEAST SOMETHING OF A FIGHT...
...TO SATISFY MY CLAN...
TADANOBU...
KYO...
...MAKE IT A CLEAN KILL, WILL YOU?

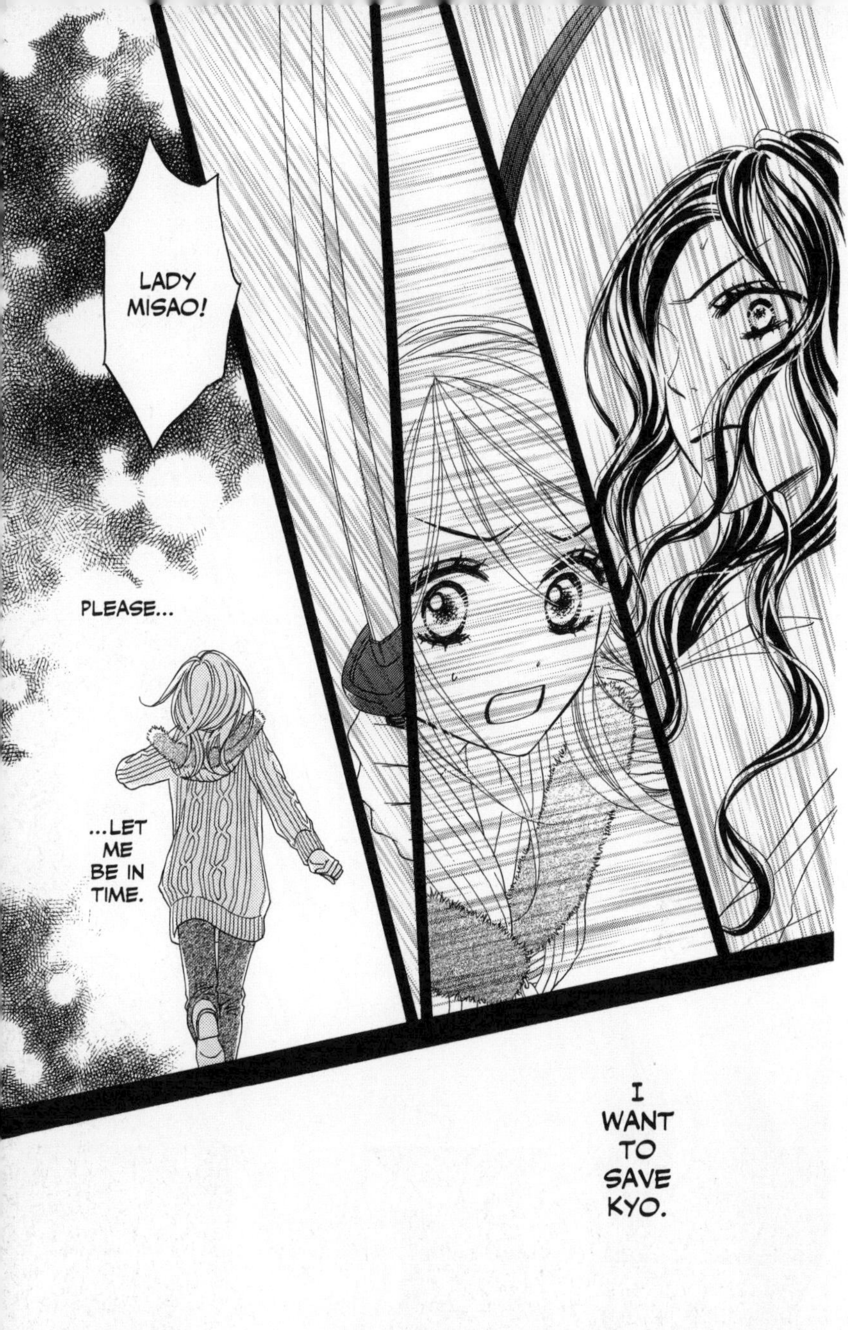
LADY MISAO!
PLEASE...
...LET ME BE IN TIME.
I WANT TO SAVE KYO.

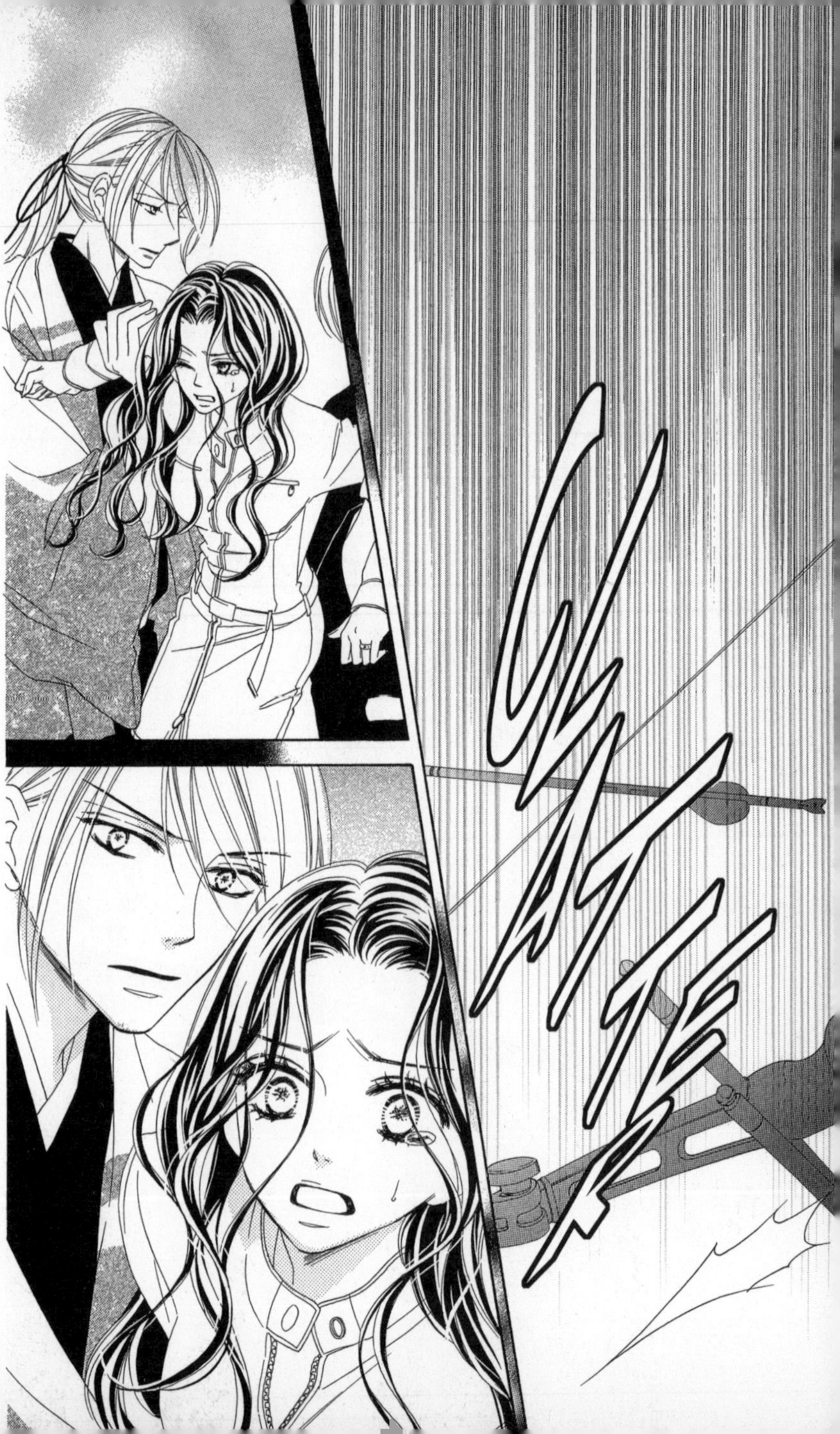
CLATTER

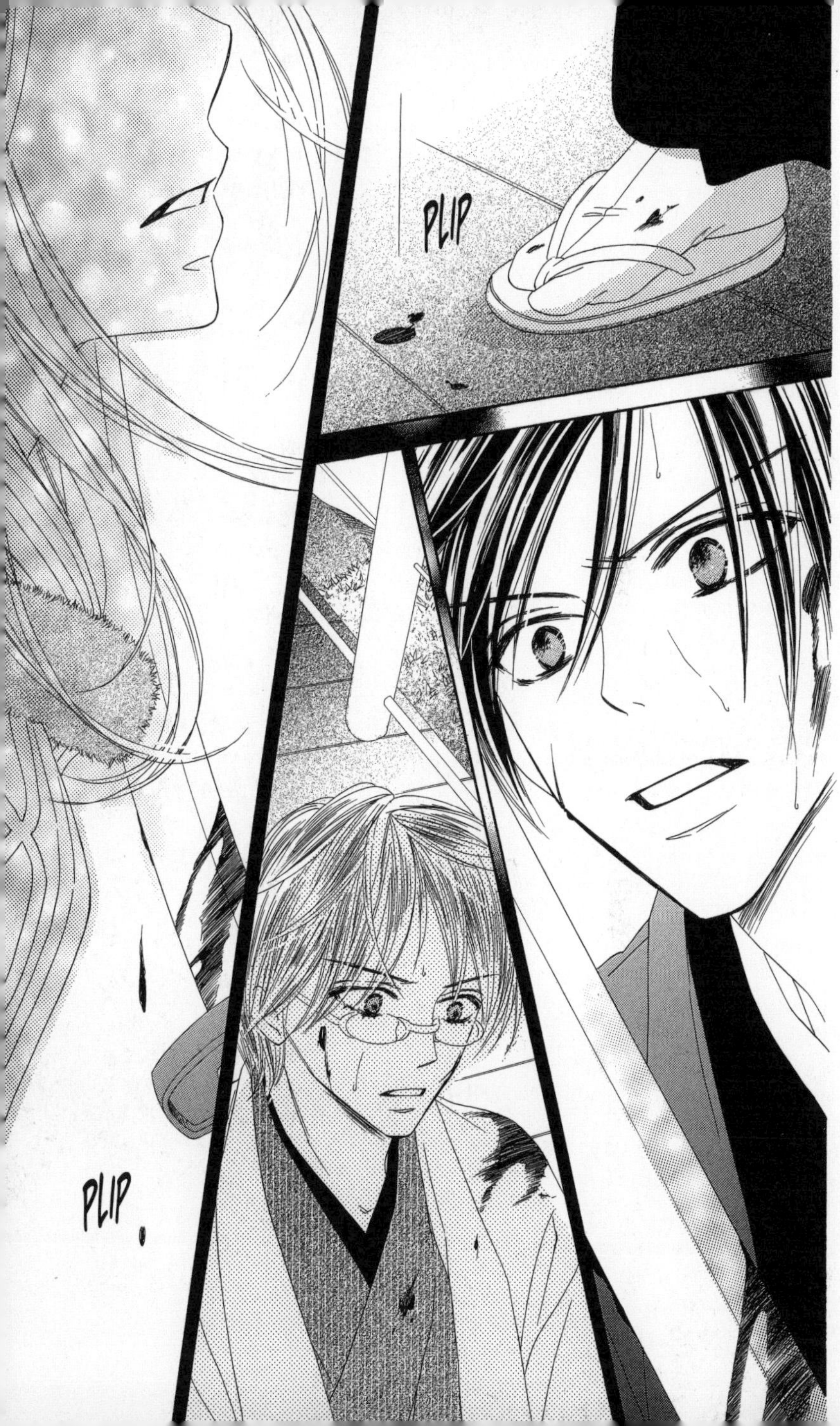
PLIP
PLIP

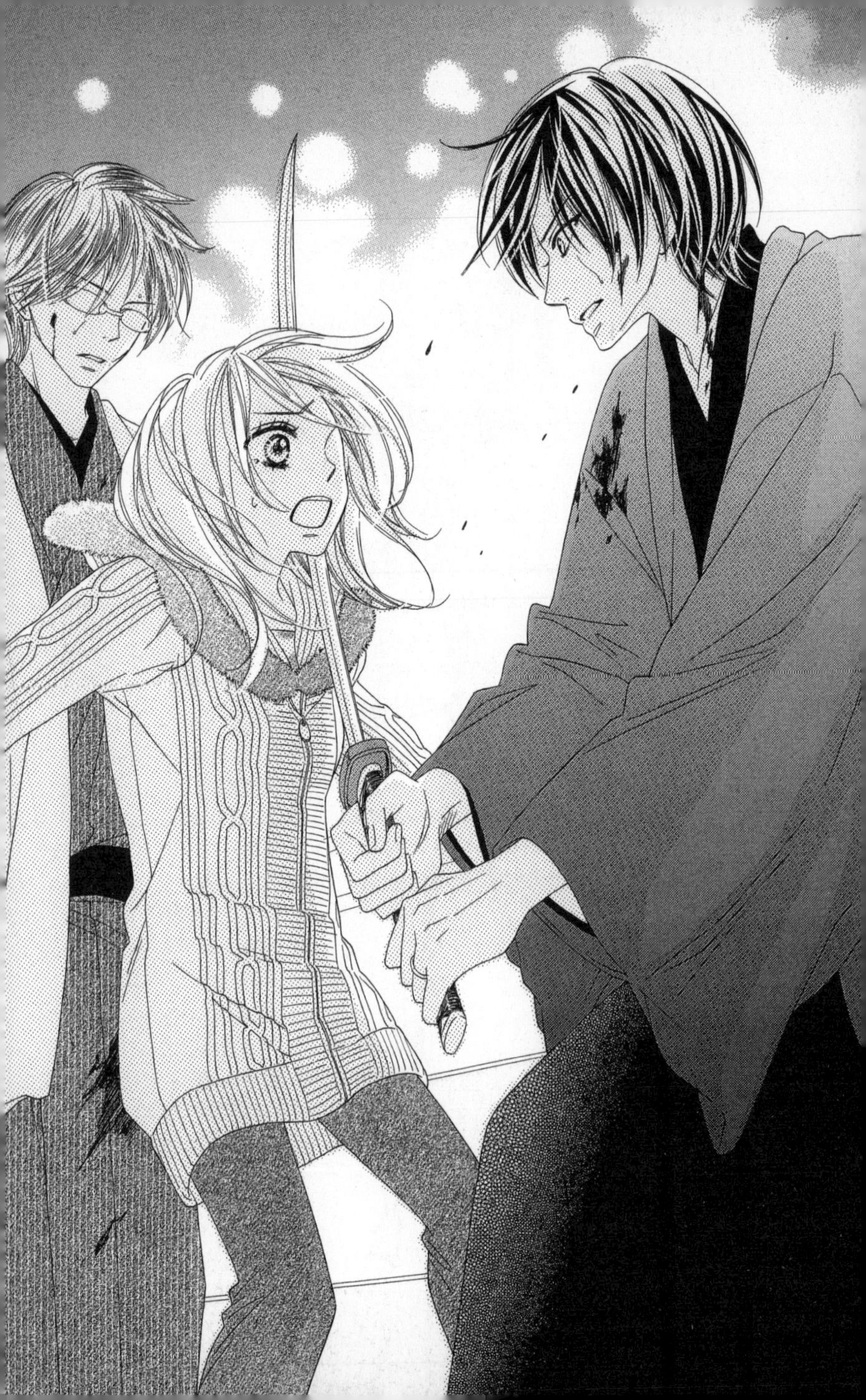

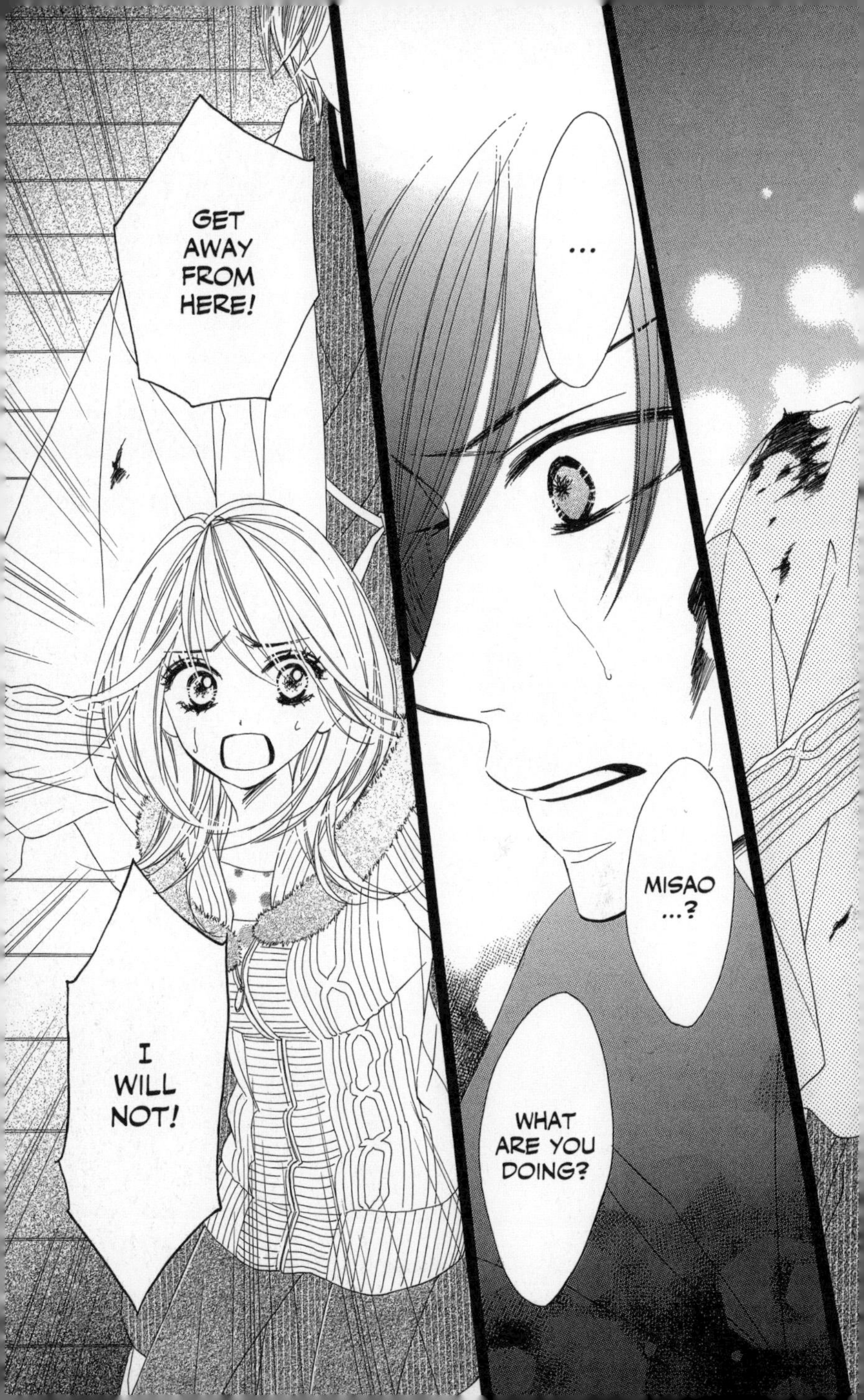
...
MISAO ...?
WHAT ARE YOU DOING?
GET AWAY FROM HERE!
I WILL NOT!

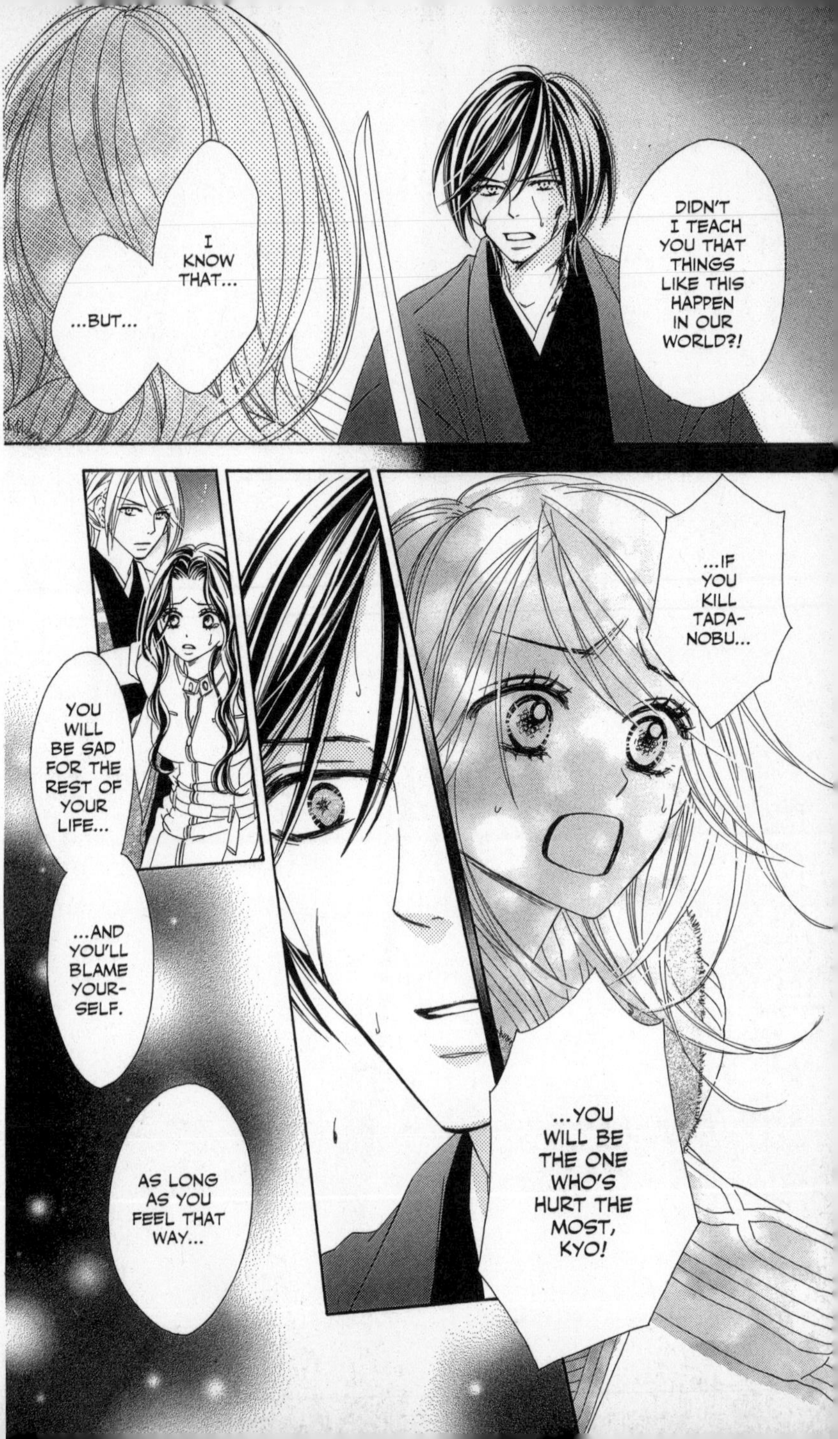
DIDN'T I TEACH YOU THAT THINGS LIKE THIS HAPPEN IN OUR WORLD?!
I KNOW THAT...
...BUT...
...IF YOU KILL TADA-NOBU...
YOU WILL BE SAD FOR THE REST OF YOUR LIFE...
...AND YOU'LL BLAME YOUR-SELF.
AS LONG AS YOU FEEL THAT WAY...
...YOU WILL BE THE ONE WHO'S HURT THE MOST, KYO!

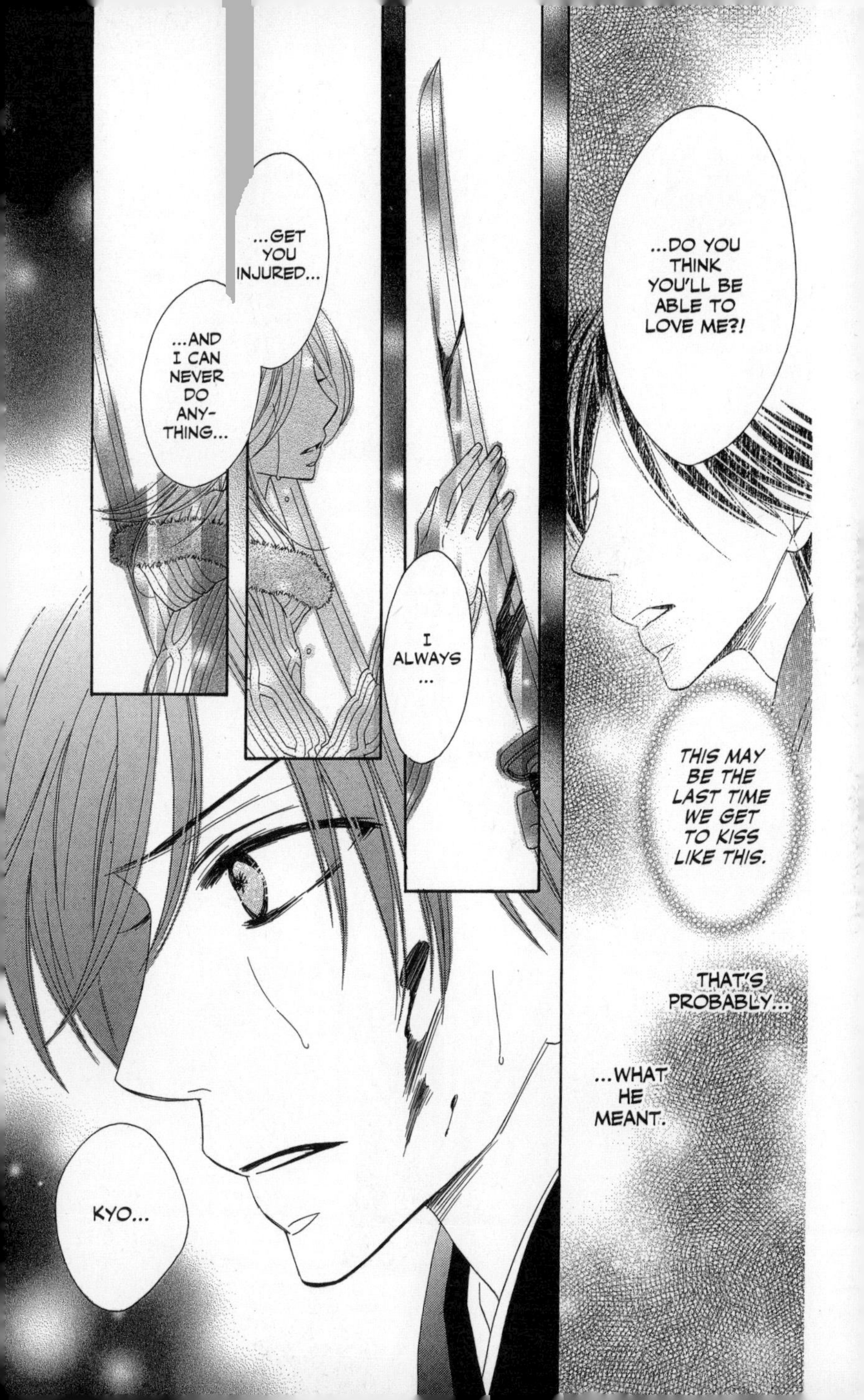
...DO YOU THINK YOU'LL BE ABLE TO LOVE ME?!
THIS MAY BE THE LAST TIME WE GET TO KISS LIKE THIS.
THAT'S PROBABLY...
...WHAT HE MEANT.
I ALWAYS ...
...GET YOU INJURED...
...AND I CAN NEVER DO ANY-THING...
KYO...

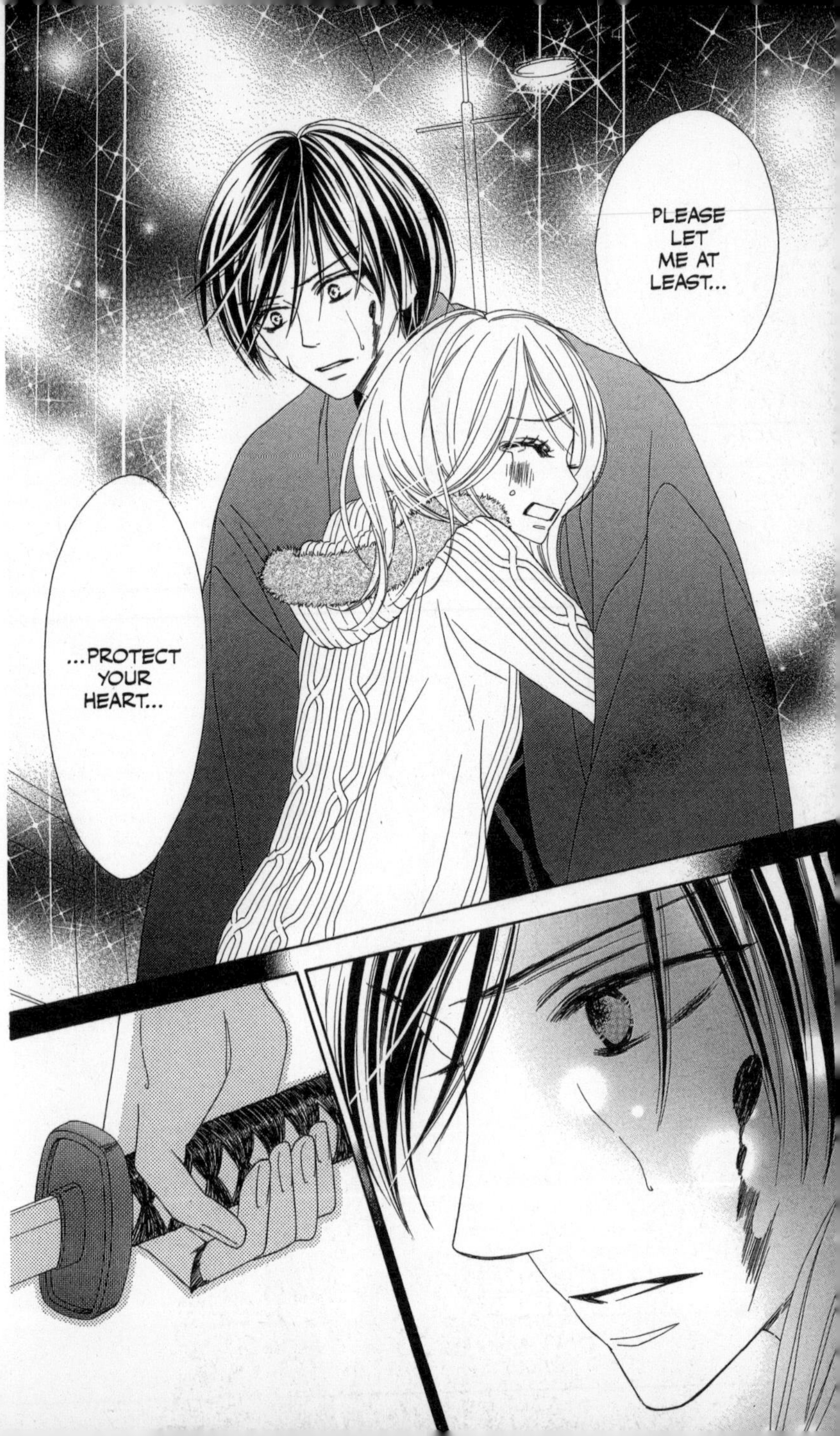
PLEASE LET ME AT LEAST...
...PROTECT YOUR HEART...

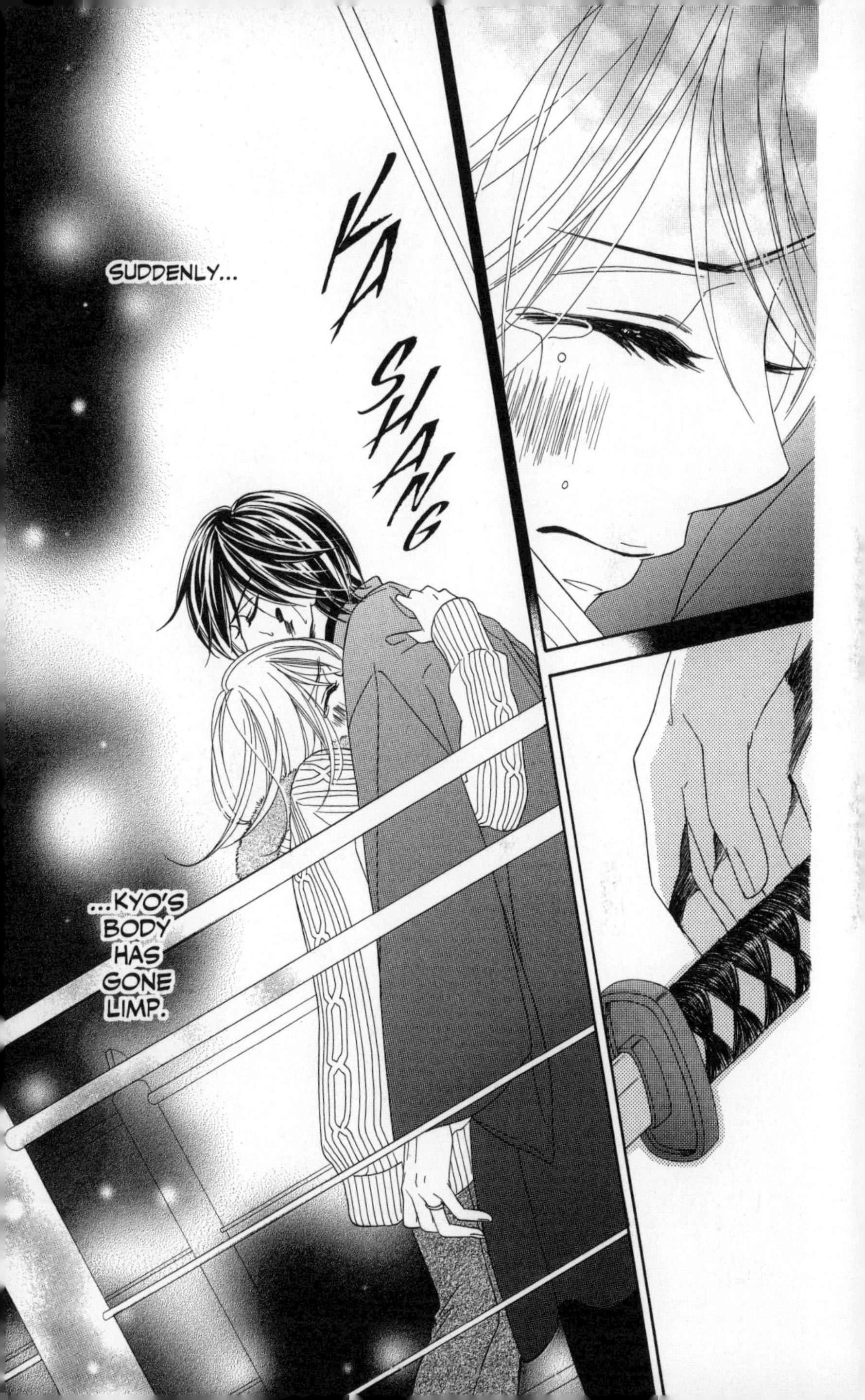
KA SHANG
SUDDENLY...
...KYO'S BODY HAS GONE LIMP.

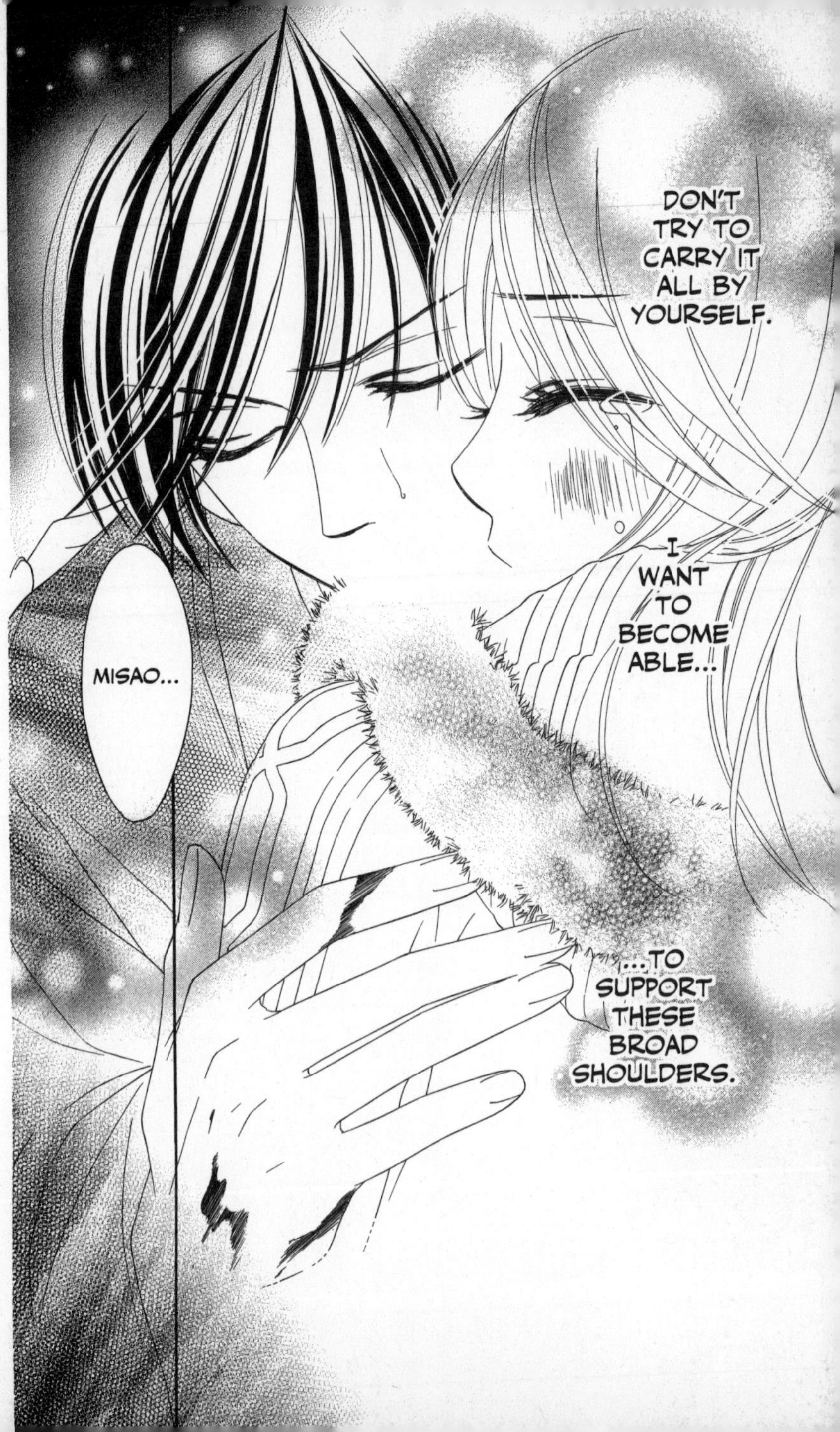
DON'T TRY TO CARRY IT ALL BY YOURSELF.
I WANT TO BECOME ABLE...
...TO SUPPORT THESE BROAD SHOULDERS.
MISAO...

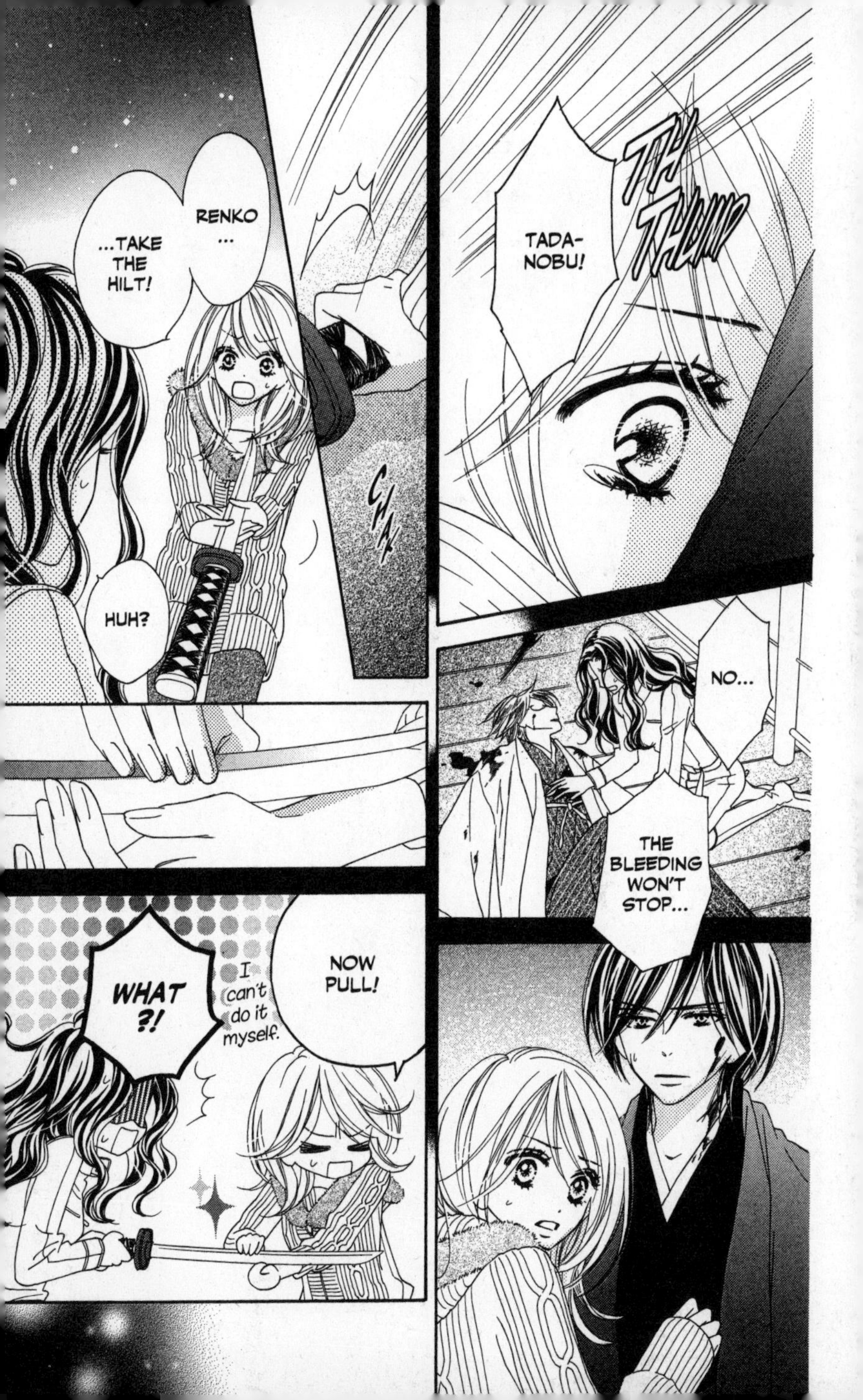
TADA-NOBU!
NO...
THE BLEEDING WON'T STOP...
RENKO ...
...TAKE THE HILT!
HUH?
NOW PULL!
I can't do it myself.
WHAT?!

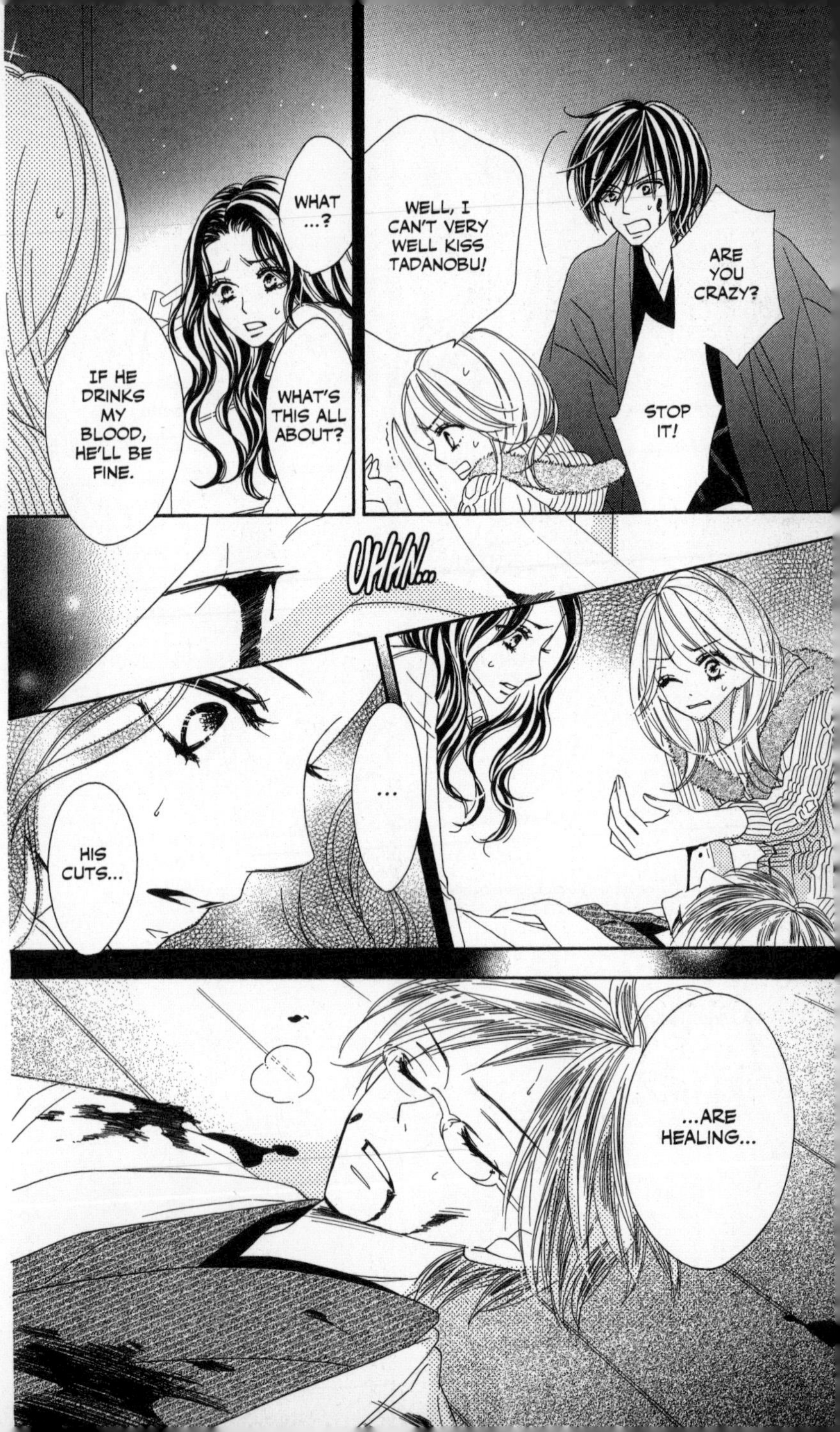
ARE YOU CRAZY?
WELL, I CAN'T VERY WELL KISS TADANOBU!
STOP IT!
WHAT ...?
WHAT'S THIS ALL ABOUT?
IF HE DRINKS MY BLOOD, HE'LL BE FINE.
UHHN...
...
HIS CUTS...
...ARE HEALING...

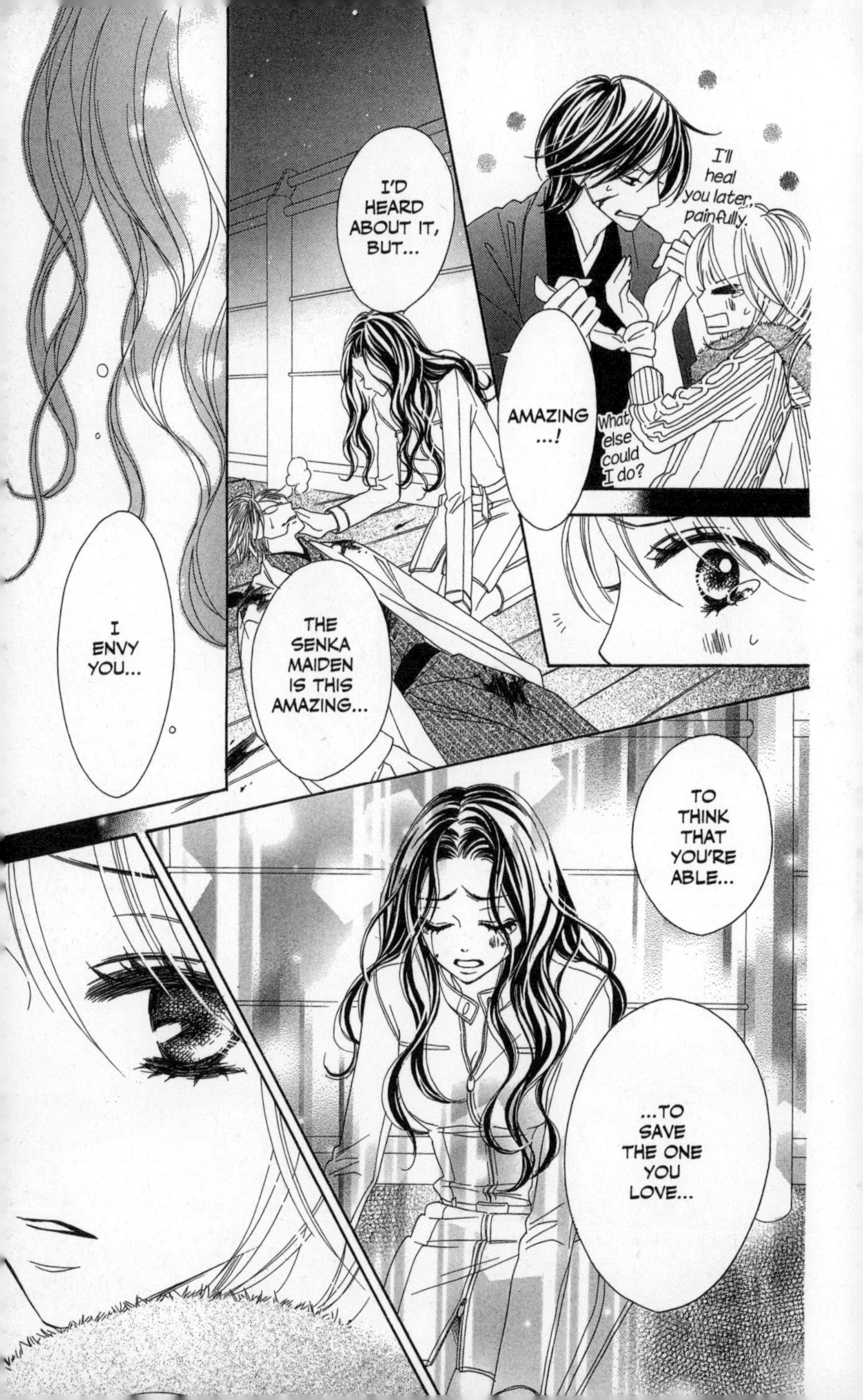
I'll heal you later, painfully.
What else could I do?
AMAZING ...!
I'D HEARD ABOUT IT, BUT...
THE SENKA MAIDEN IS THIS AMAZING...
I ENVY YOU...
TO THINK THAT YOU'RE ABLE...
...TO SAVE THE ONE YOU LOVE...

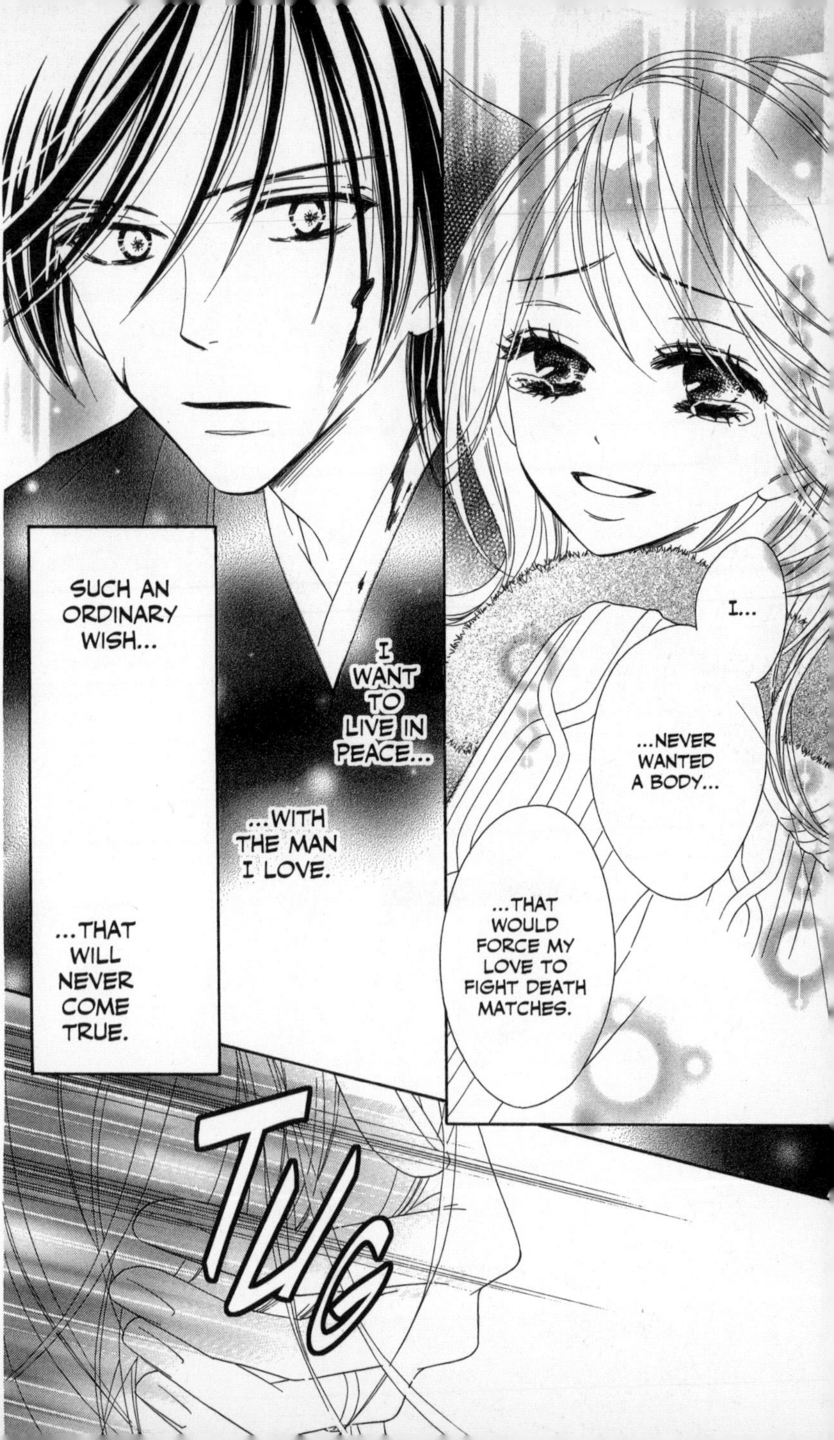
I...
...NEVER WANTED A BODY...
...THAT WOULD FORCE MY LOVE TO FIGHT DEATH MATCHES.
I WANT TO LIVE IN PEACE...
...WITH THE MAN I LOVE.
SUCH AN ORDINARY WISH...
...THAT WILL NEVER COME TRUE.
TUG

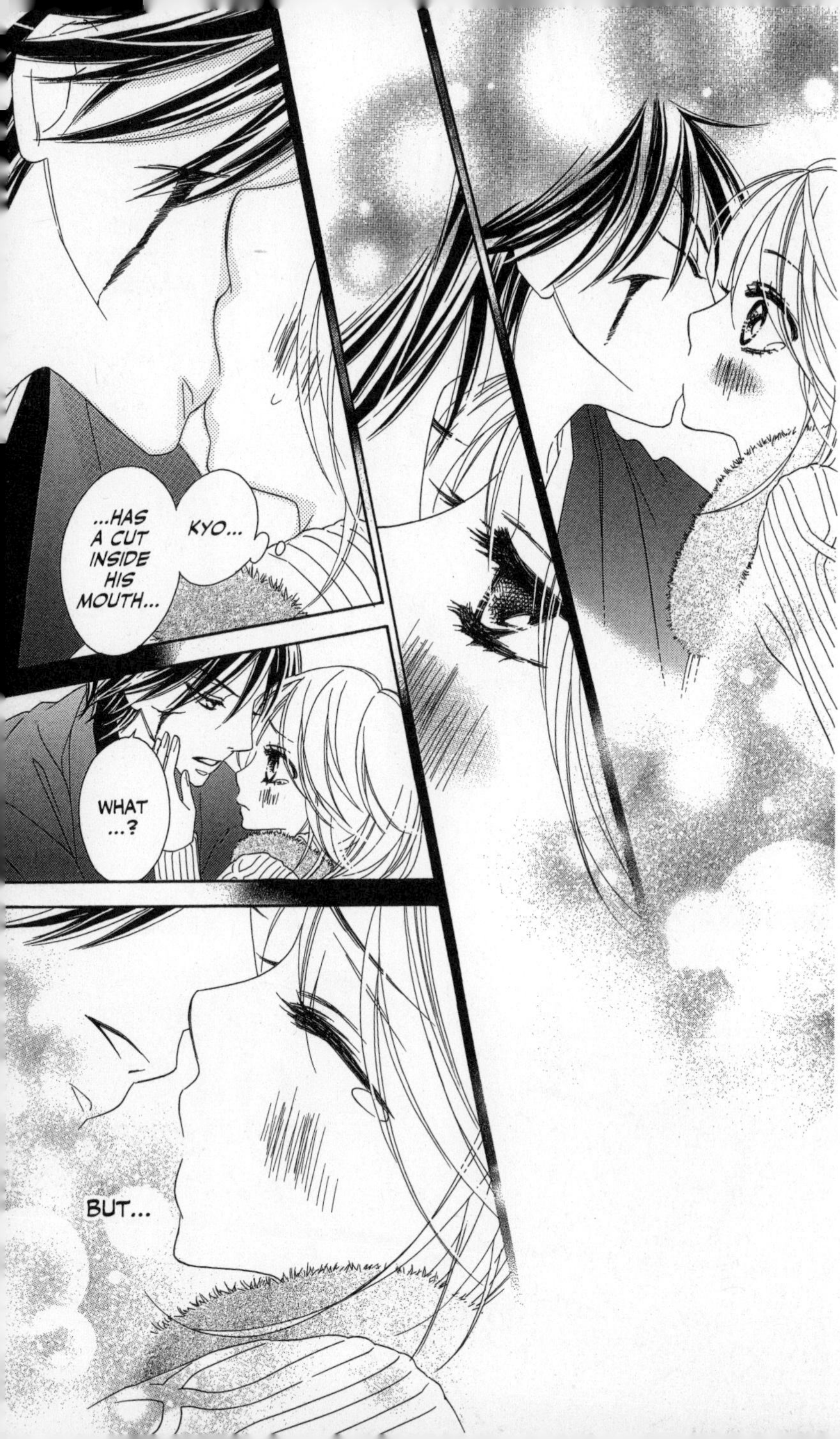
KYO...
...HAS A CUT INSIDE HIS MOUTH...
WHAT ...?
BUT...

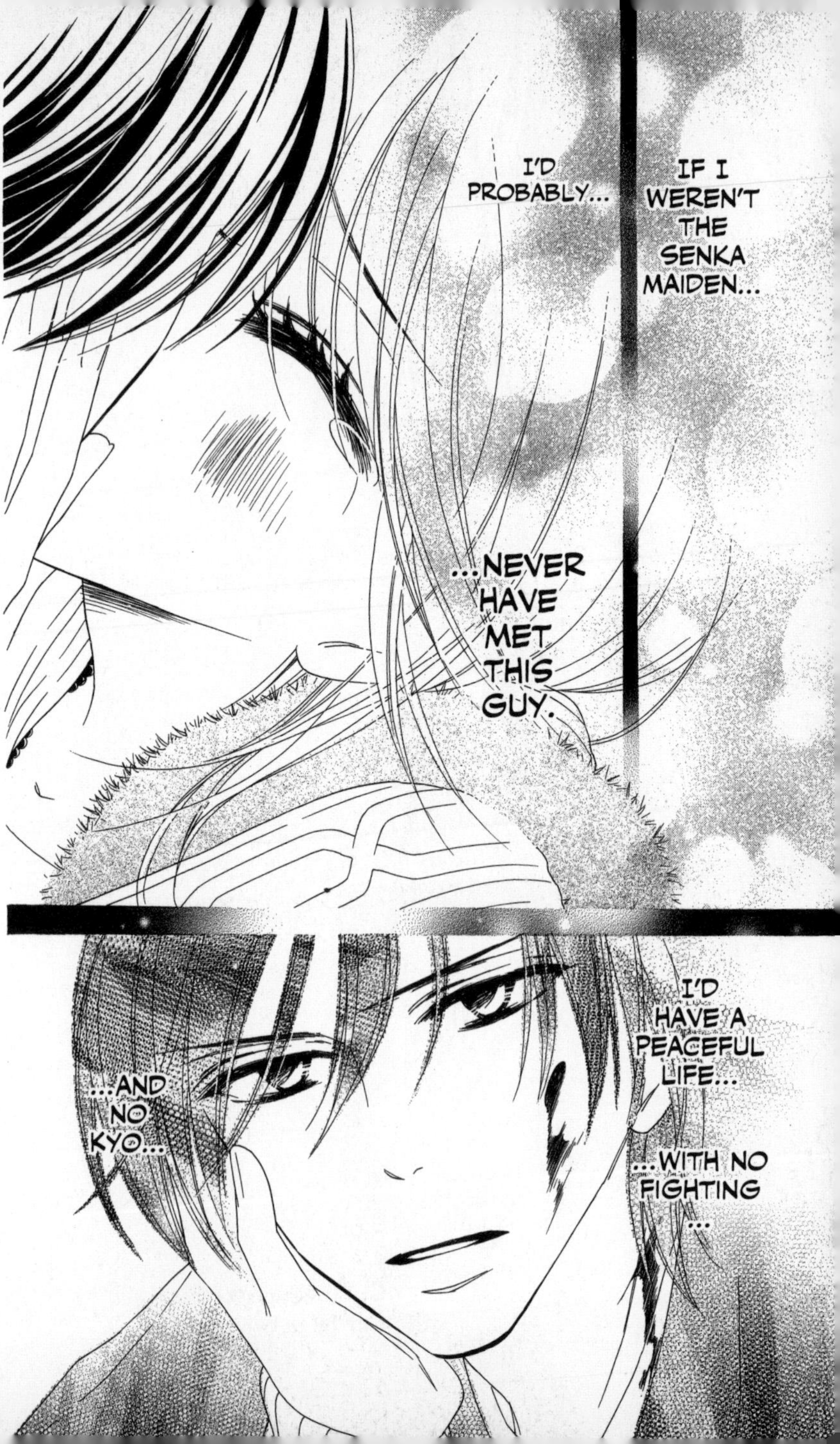
IF I WEREN'T THE SENKA MAIDEN...
I'D PROBABLY...
...NEVER HAVE MET THIS GUY.
I'D HAVE A PEACEFUL LIFE...
...WITH NO FIGHTING...
...AND NO KYO...

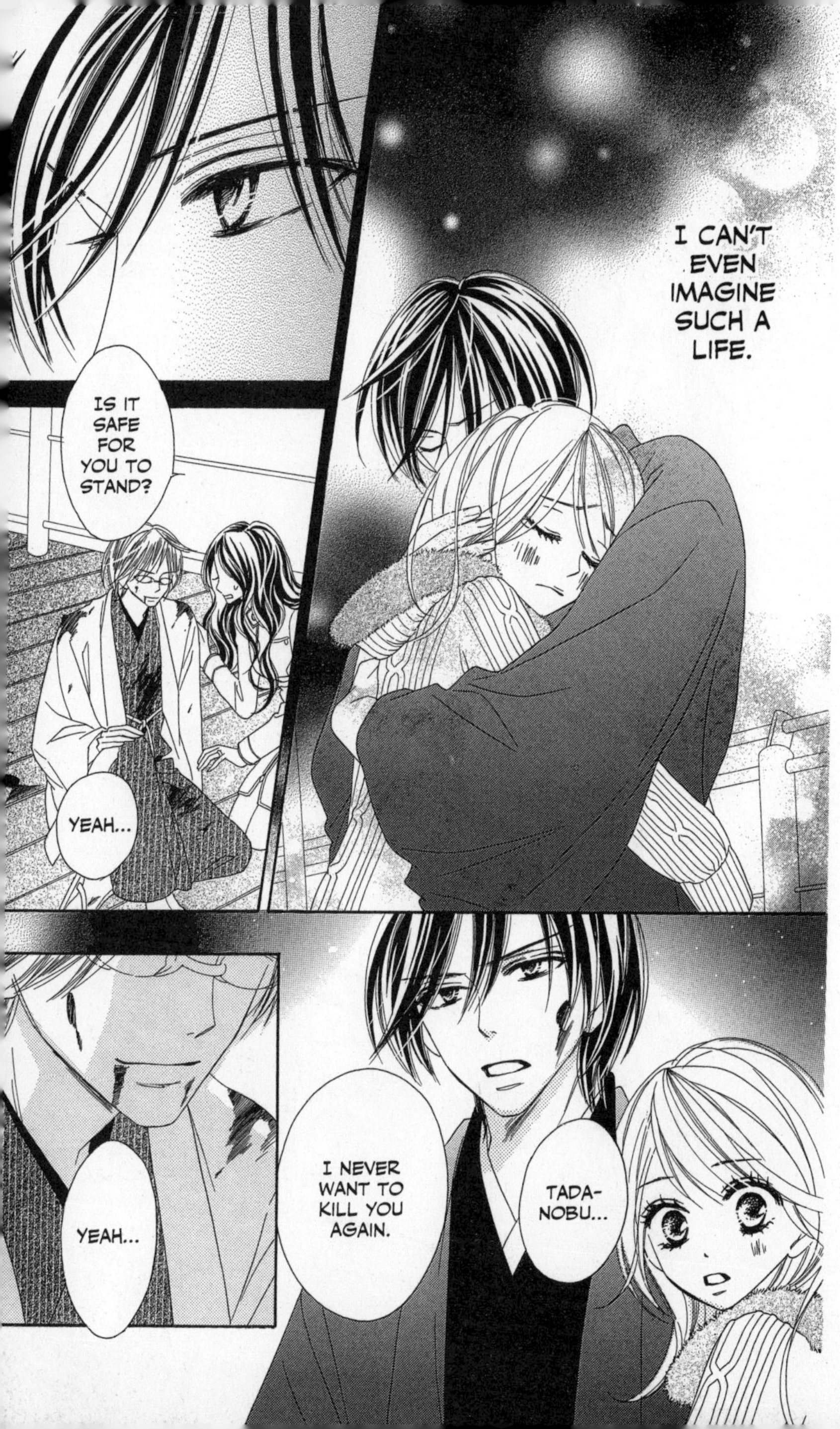
I CAN'T EVEN IMAGINE SUCH A LIFE.
IS IT SAFE FOR YOU TO STAND?
YEAH...
TADA-NOBU...
I NEVER WANT TO KILL YOU AGAIN.
YEAH...

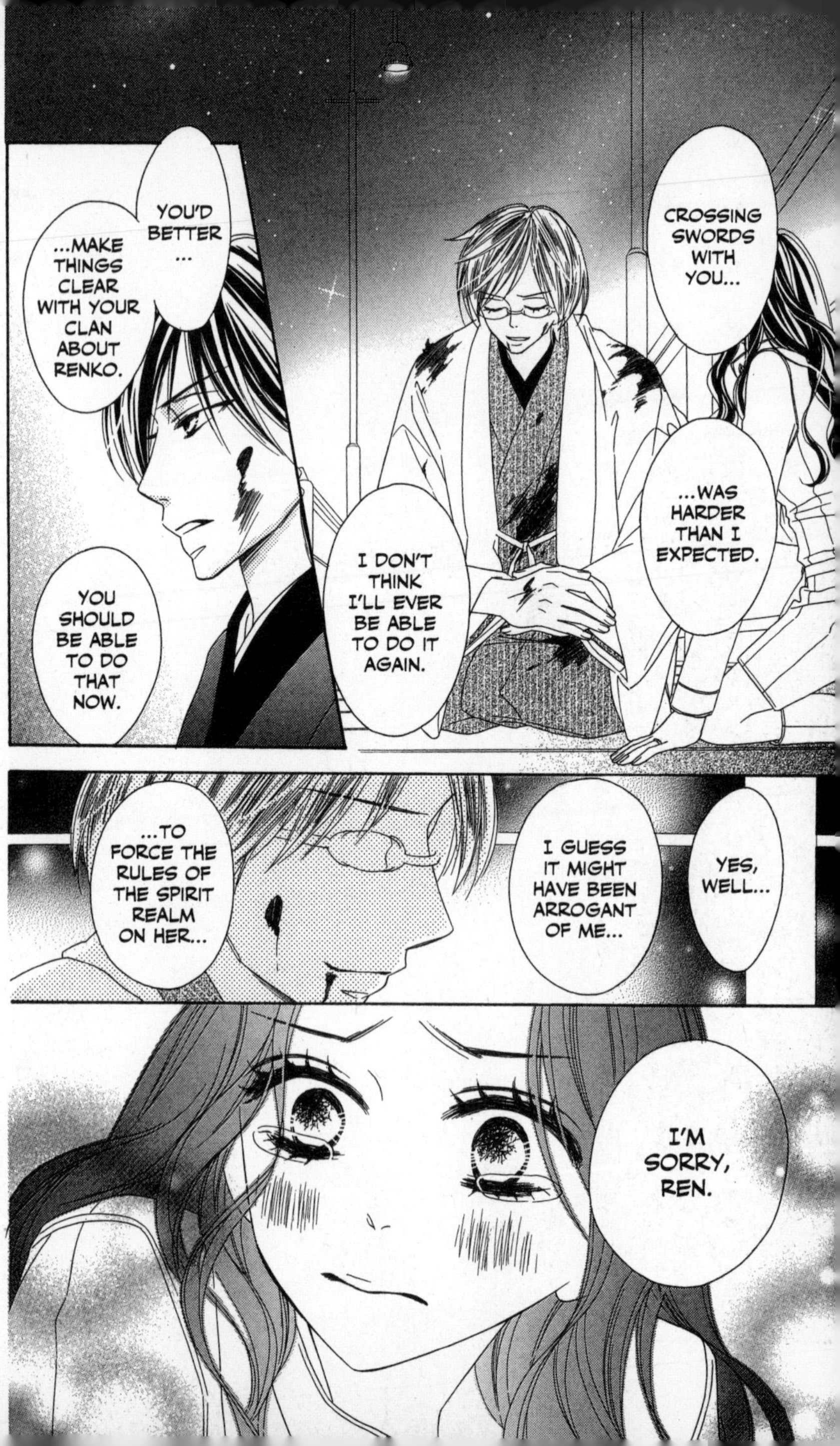
CROSSING SWORDS WITH YOU...
...WAS HARDER THAN I EXPECTED.
I DON'T THINK I'LL EVER BE ABLE TO DO IT AGAIN.
YOU'D BETTER...
...MAKE THINGS CLEAR WITH YOUR CLAN ABOUT RENKO.
YOU SHOULD BE ABLE TO DO THAT NOW.
YES, WELL...
I GUESS IT MIGHT HAVE BEEN ARROGANT OF ME...
...TO FORCE THE RULES OF THE SPIRIT REALM ON HER...
I'M SORRY, REN.

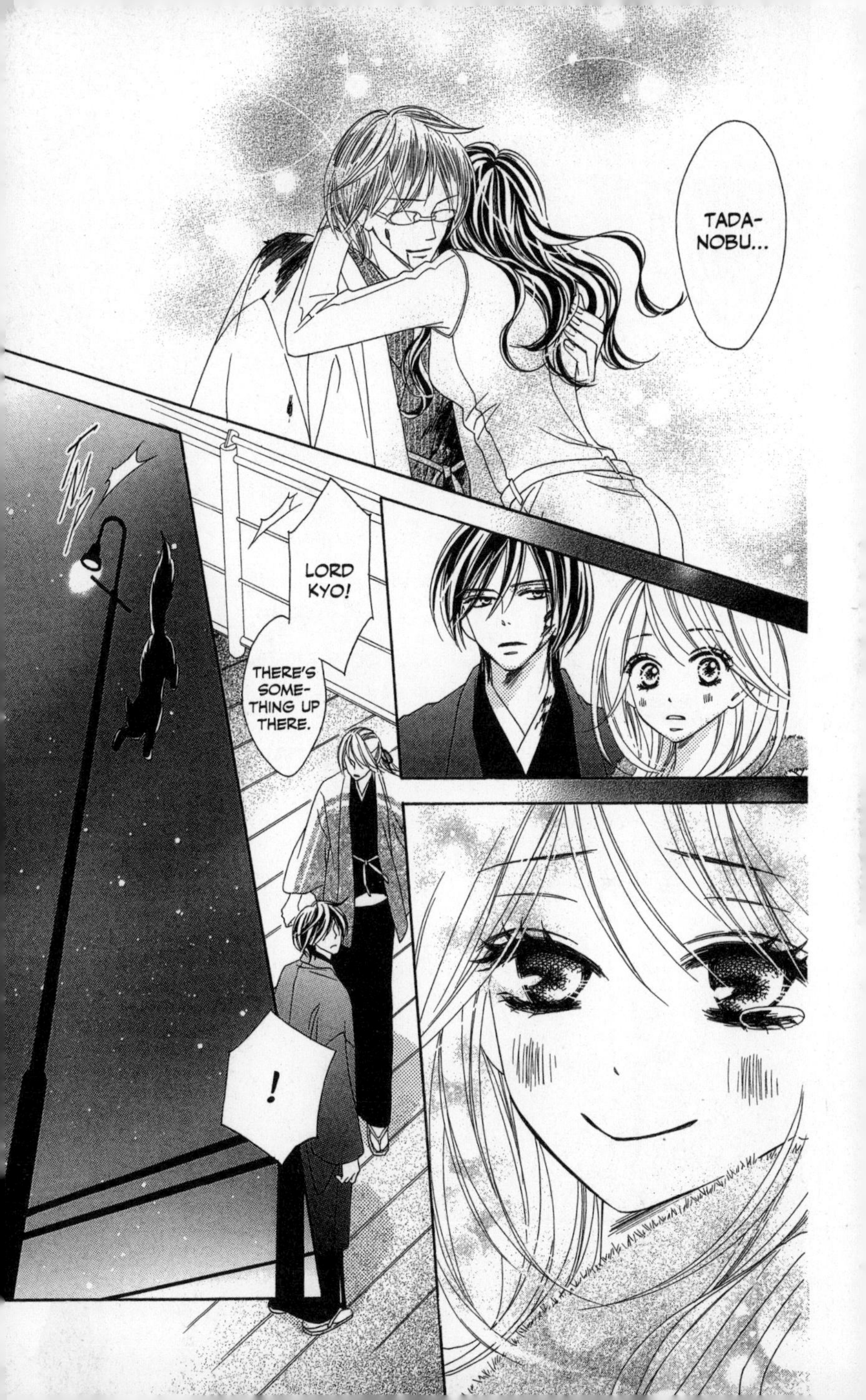
TADA-NOBU...
LORD KYO!
THERE'S SOME-THING UP THERE.
!

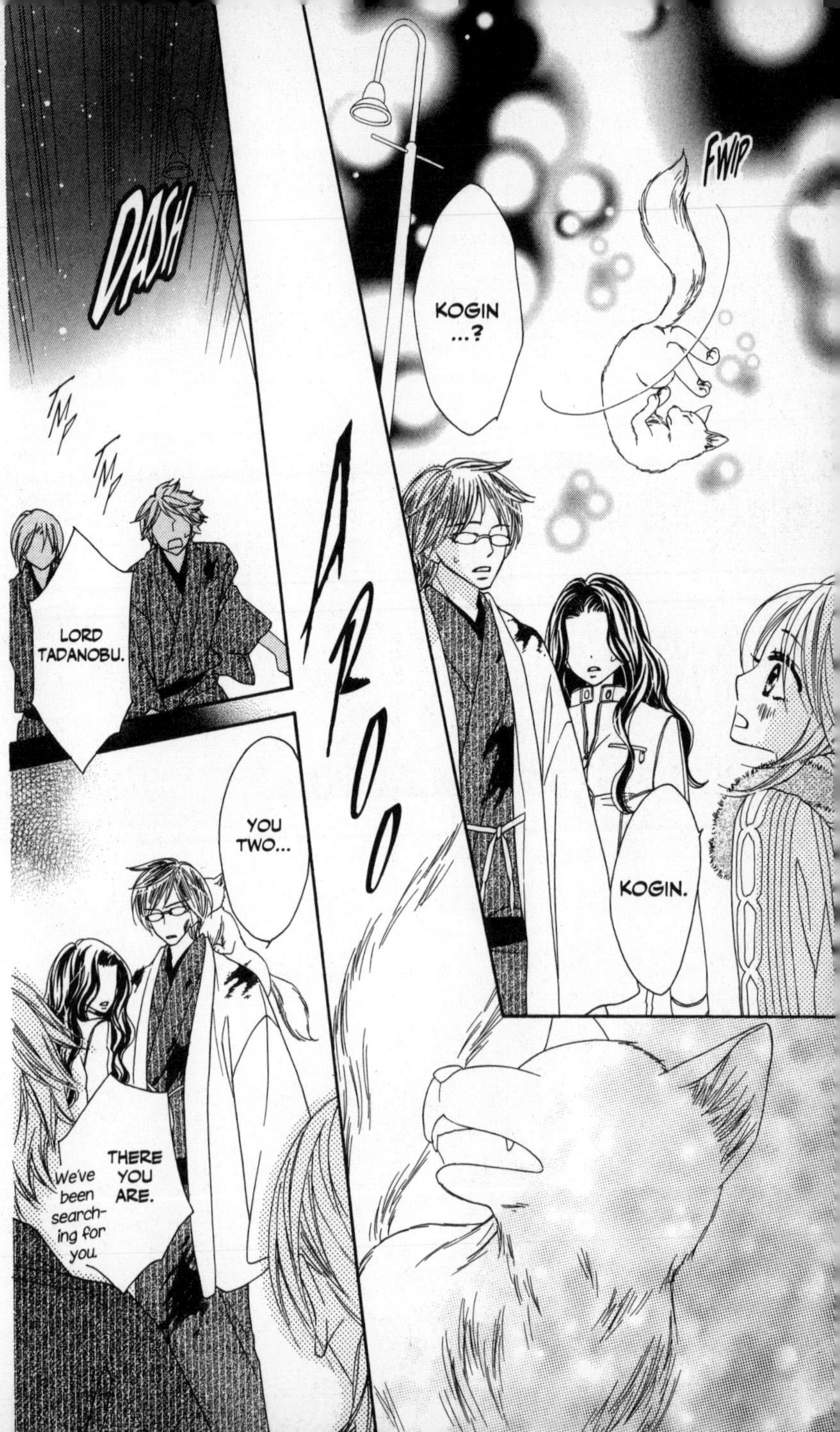
FWIP
KOGIN ...?
KOGIN.
DASH
TMP
TMP
LORD TADANOBU.
YOU TWO...
THERE YOU ARE.
We've been searching for you.

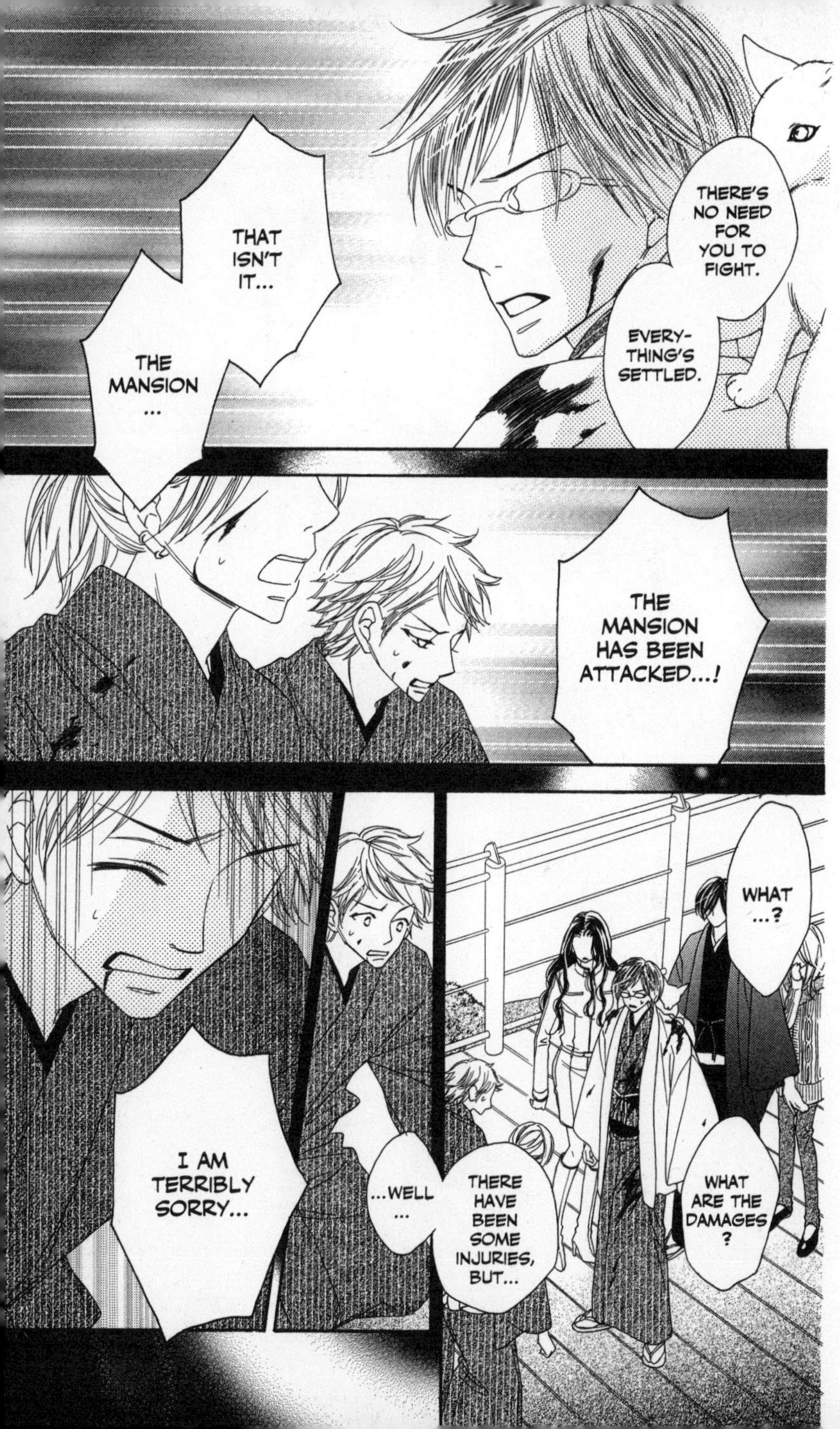
THERE'S NO NEED FOR YOU TO FIGHT.
EVERY-THING'S SETTLED.
THAT ISN'T IT...
THE MANSION ...
THE MANSION HAS BEEN ATTACKED...!
WHAT ...?
WHAT ARE THE DAMAGES ?
THERE HAVE BEEN SOME INJURIES, BUT...
...WELL ...
I AM TERRIBLY SORRY...

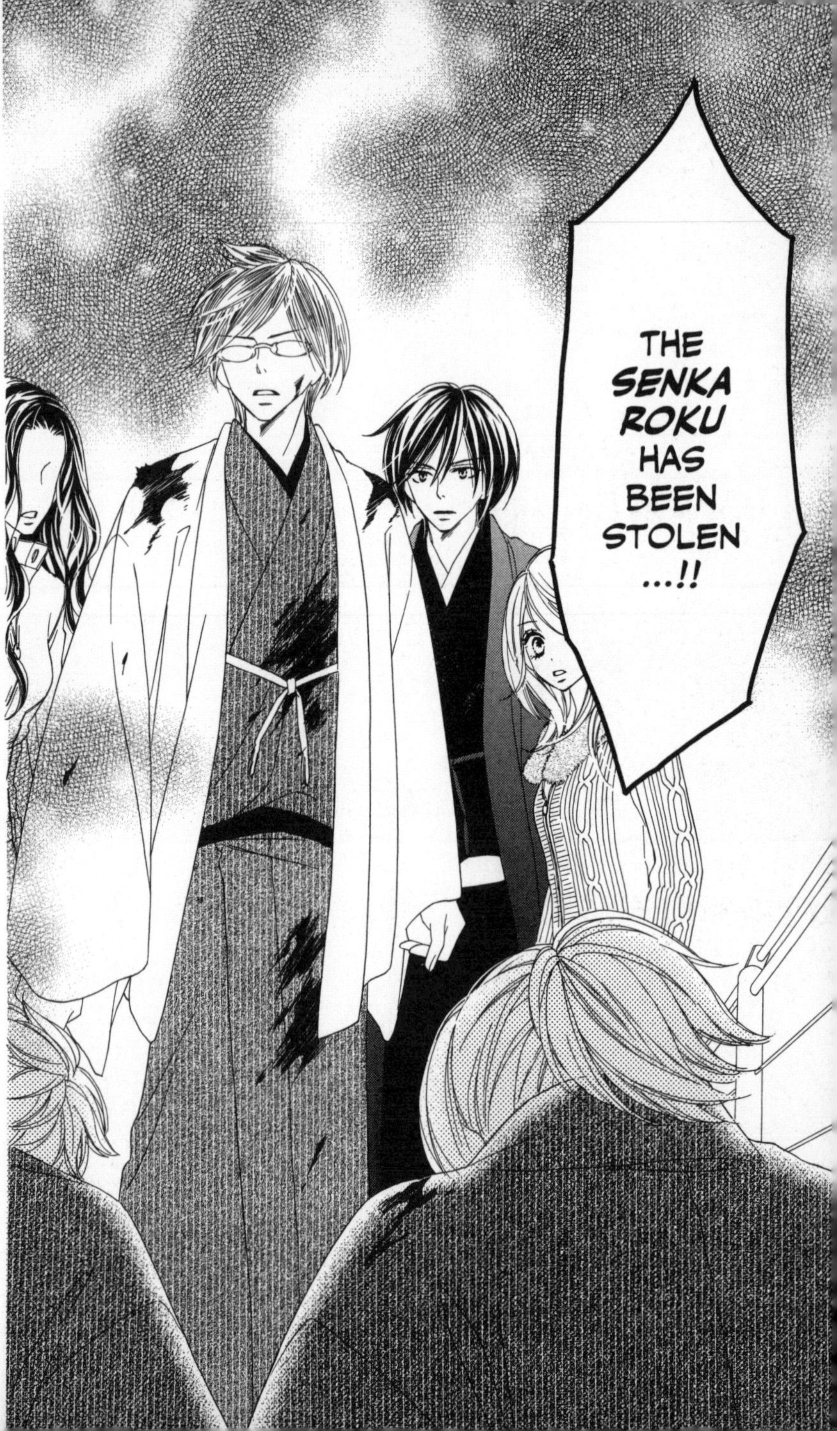
THE SENKA ROKU HAS BEEN STOLEN ...!!

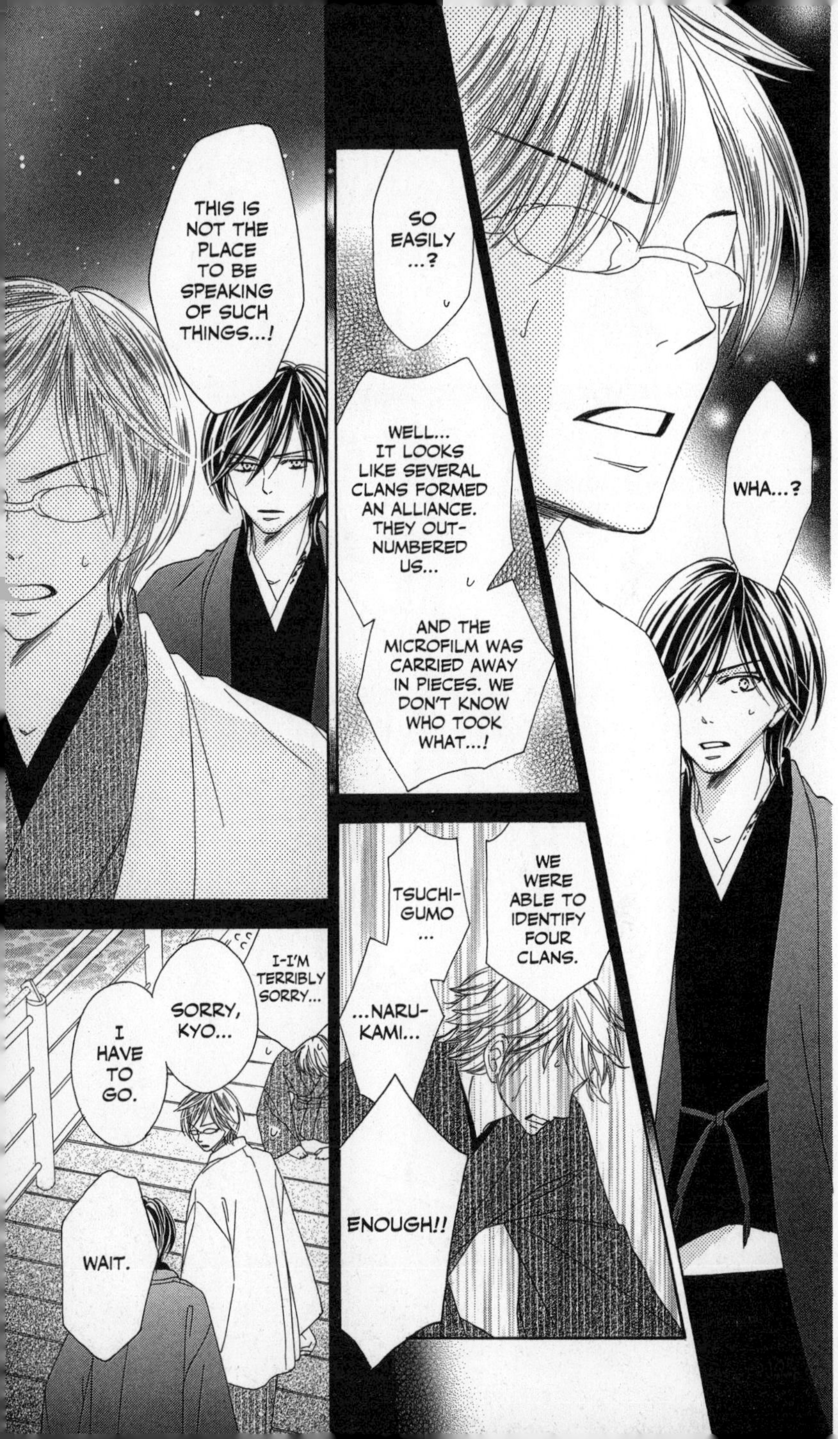
WHA...?
SO EASILY ...?
WELL... IT LOOKS LIKE SEVERAL CLANS FORMED AN ALLIANCE. THEY OUT-NUMBERED US...
AND THE MICROFILM WAS CARRIED AWAY IN PIECES. WE DON'T KNOW WHO TOOK WHAT...!
WE WERE ABLE TO IDENTIFY FOUR CLANS.
TSUCHI-GUMO ...
...NARU-KAMI...
ENOUGH!!
THIS IS NOT THE PLACE TO BE SPEAKING OF SUCH THINGS...!
I-I'M TERRIBLY SORRY...
SORRY, KYO...
I HAVE TO GO.
WAIT.

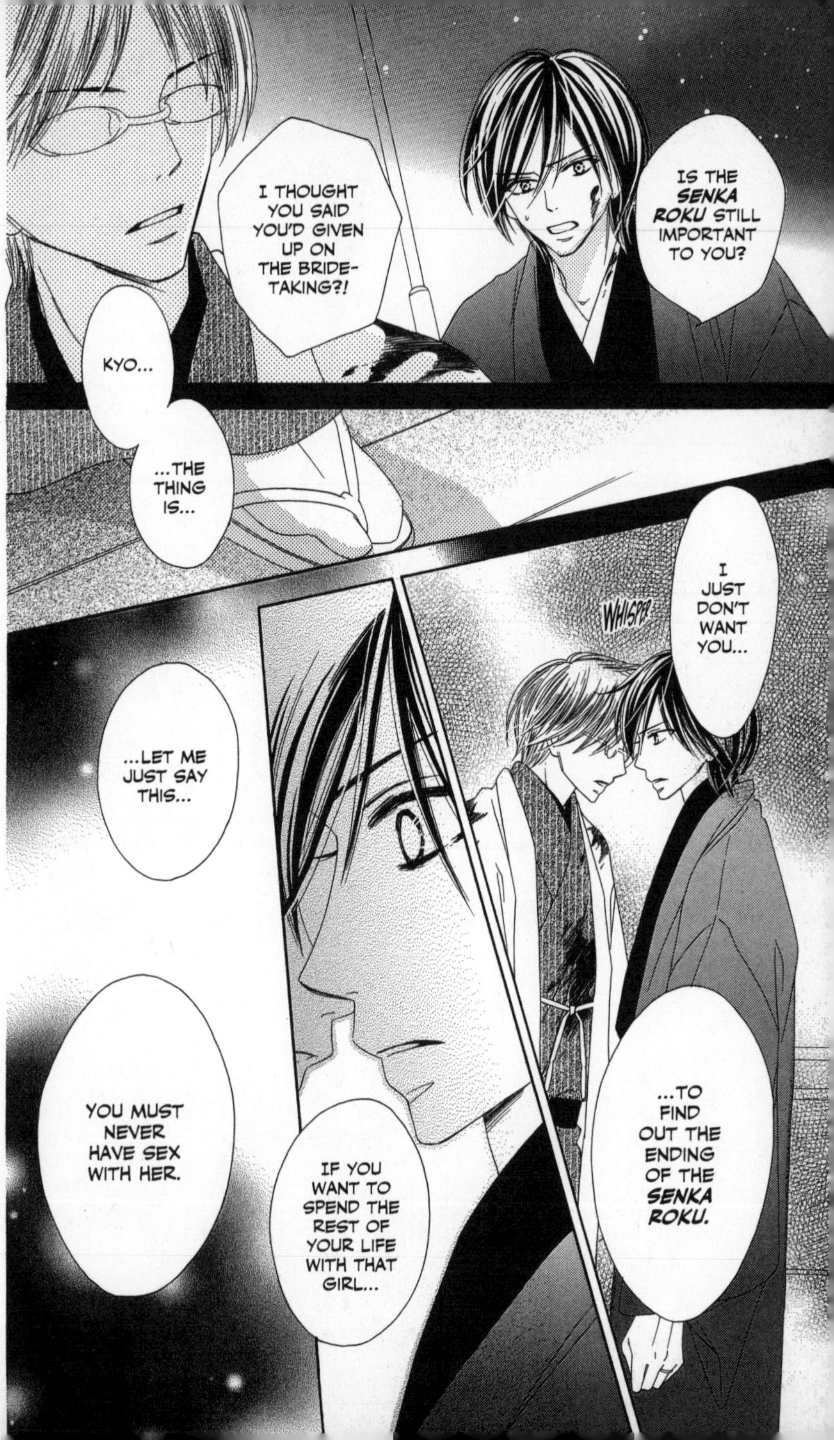
IS THE *SENKA ROKU* STILL IMPORTANT TO YOU?
I THOUGHT YOU SAID YOU'D GIVEN UP ON THE BRIDE-TAKING?!
KYO...
...THE THING IS...
WHISPER
I JUST DON'T WANT YOU...
...TO FIND OUT THE ENDING OF THE *SENKA ROKU.*
...LET ME JUST SAY THIS...
IF YOU WANT TO SPEND THE REST OF YOUR LIFE WITH THAT GIRL...
YOU MUST NEVER HAVE SEX WITH HER.

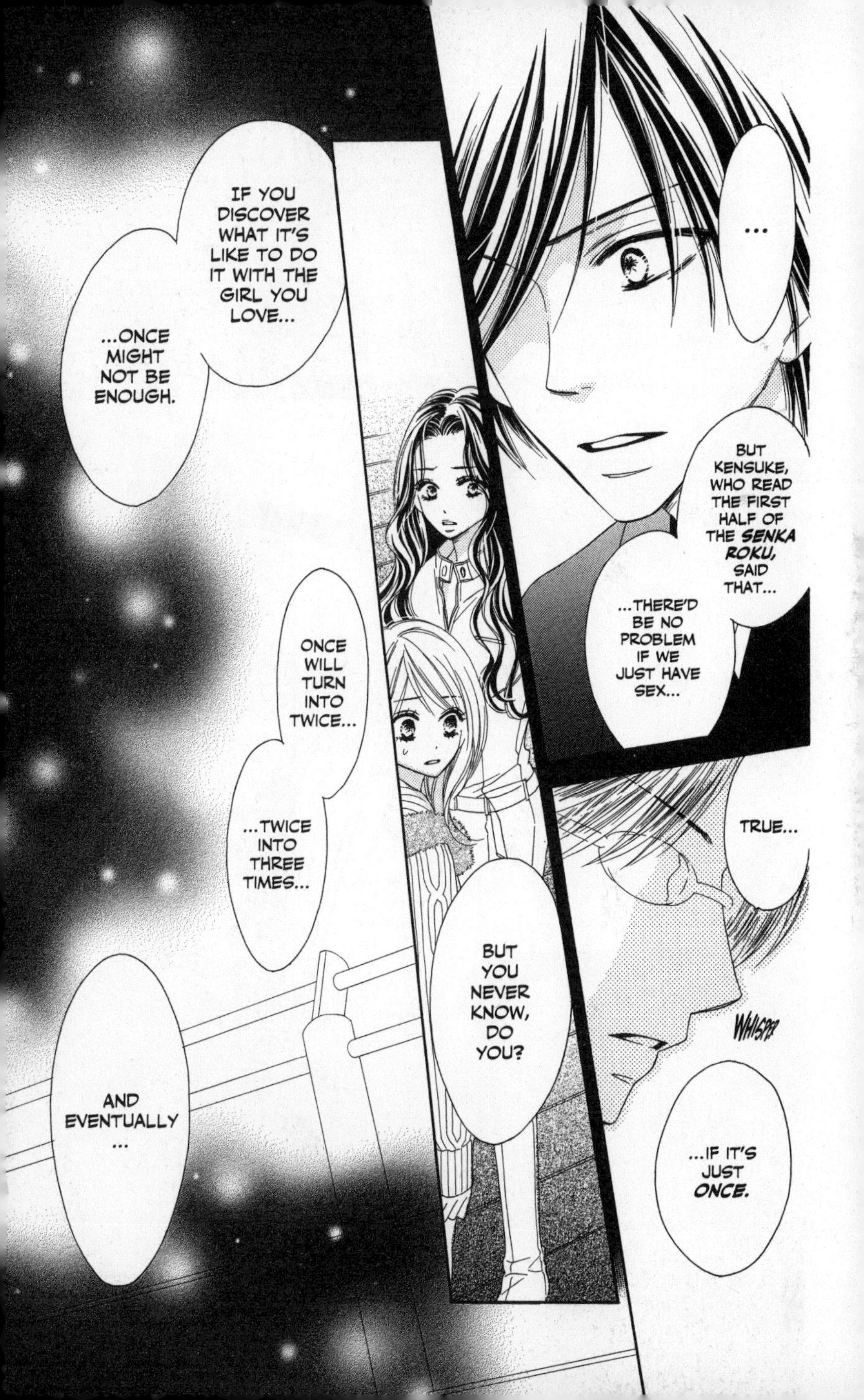
...
BUT KENSUKE, WHO READ THE FIRST HALF OF THE **SENKA ROKU,** SAID THAT...
...THERE'D BE NO PROBLEM IF WE JUST HAVE SEX...
TRUE...
WHISPER
...IF IT'S JUST **ONCE.**
BUT YOU NEVER KNOW, DO YOU?
IF YOU DISCOVER WHAT IT'S LIKE TO DO IT WITH THE GIRL YOU LOVE...
...ONCE MIGHT NOT BE ENOUGH.
ONCE WILL TURN INTO TWICE...
...TWICE INTO THREE TIMES...
AND EVENTUALLY ...

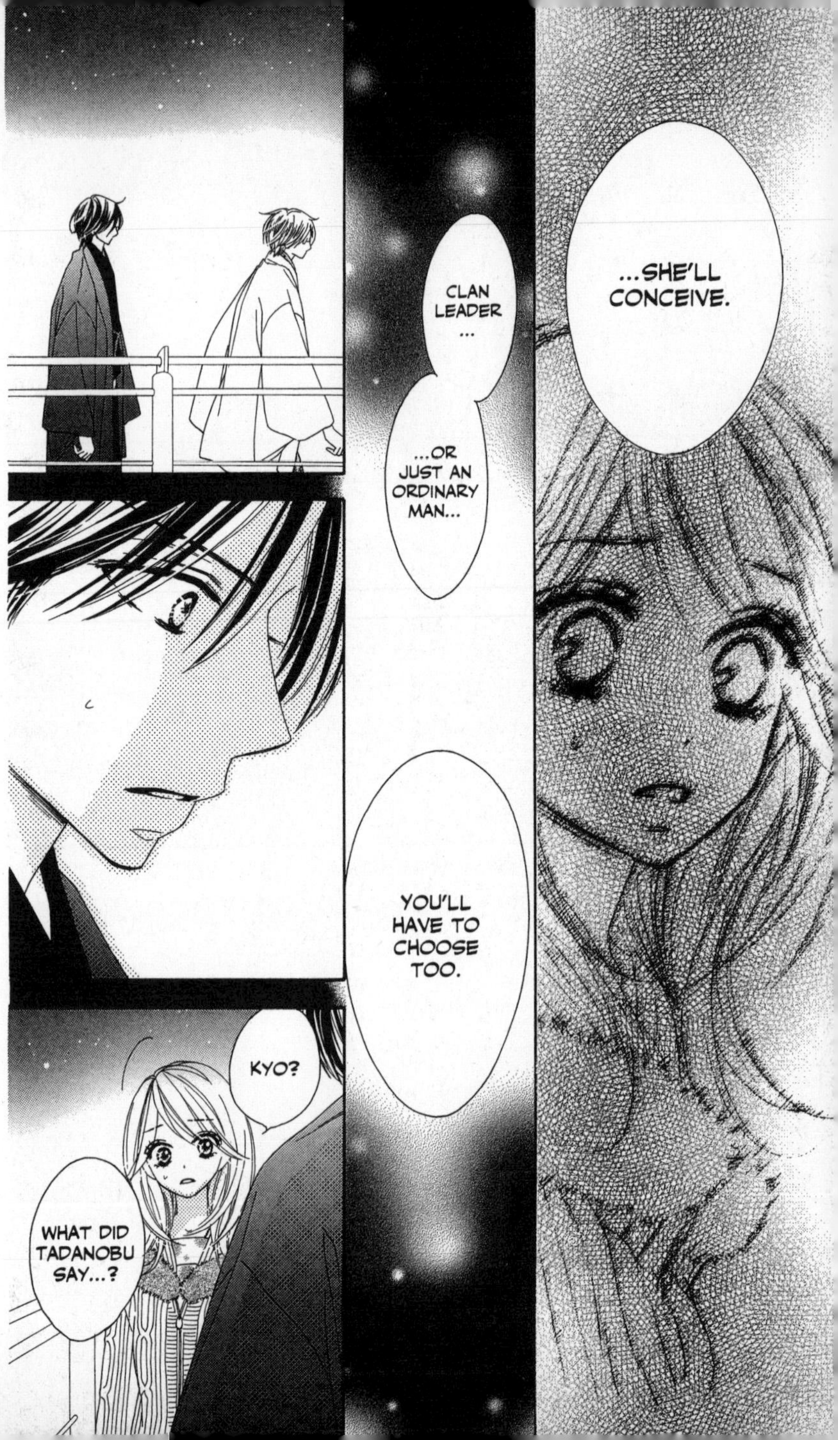
...SHE'LL CONCEIVE.
CLAN LEADER ...
...OR JUST AN ORDINARY MAN...
YOU'LL HAVE TO CHOOSE TOO.
KYO?
WHAT DID TADANOBU SAY...?

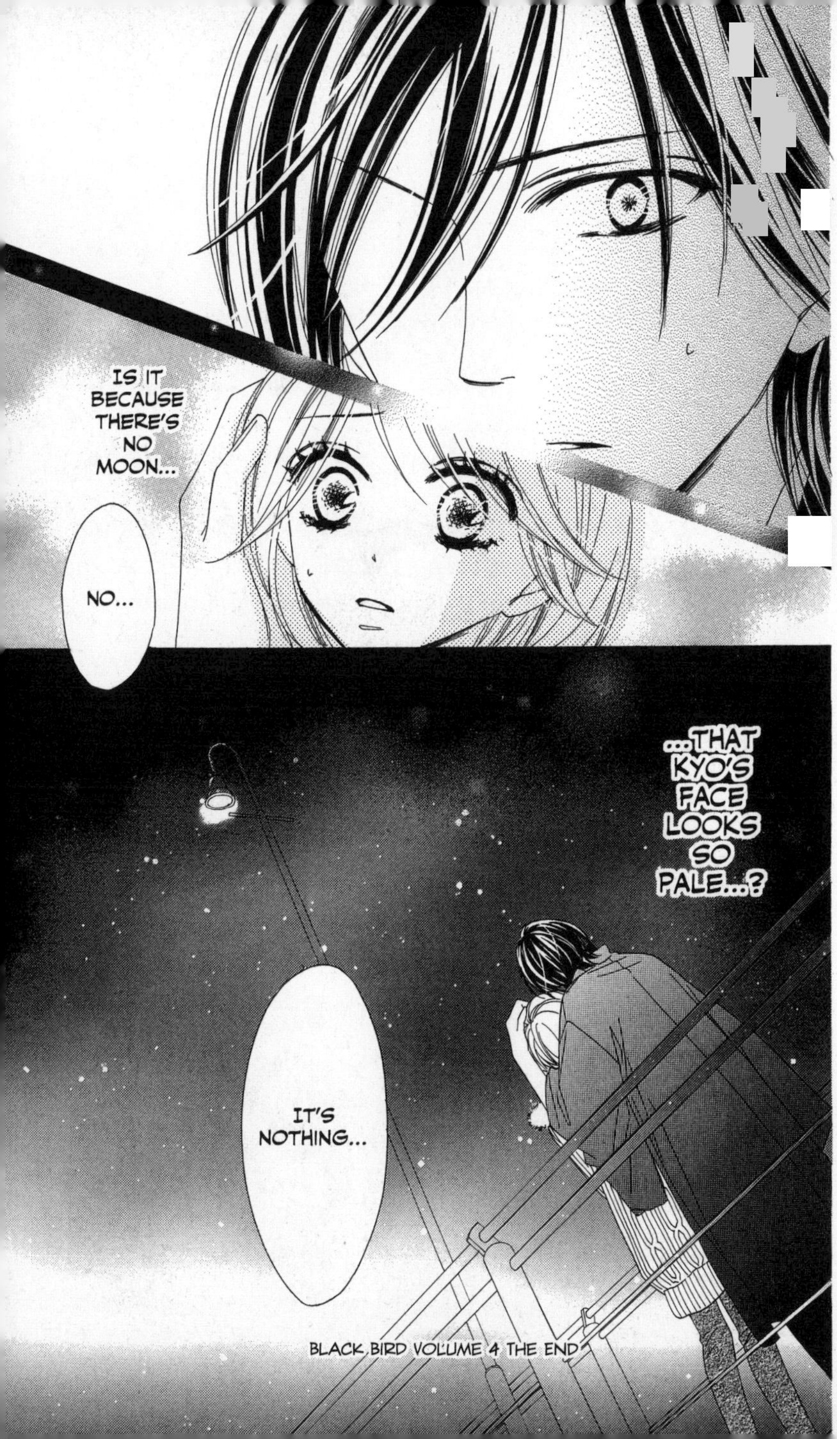
IS IT BECAUSE THERE'S NO MOON...
NO...
...THAT KYO'S FACE LOOKS SO PALE...?
IT'S NOTHING...
BLACK BIRD VOLUME 4 THE END

About the Magazine That Carries *Black Bird*

I often receive questions about this, but this manga is serialized in the Shogakukan magazine called ***Betsucomi.*** It is issued in Japan about the 13th of each month. By the time the Japanese graphic novel come out, the magazine should be about two chapters ahead. If there's anyone who is curious about how the story progresses at the end of a graphic novel volume, I suggest you check out the magazine.♡ There are lots of prizes being offered too!

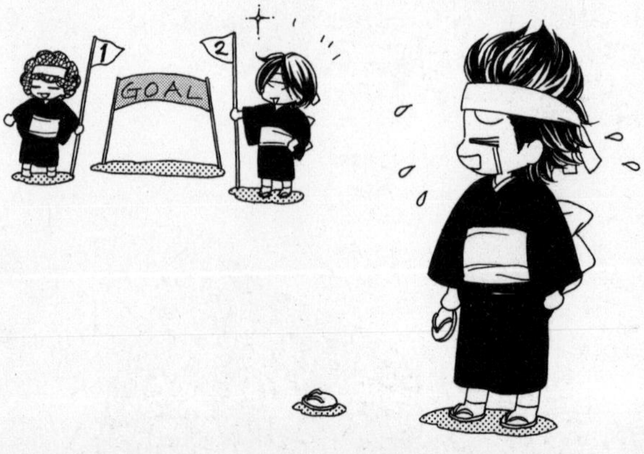
2
1
GOAL

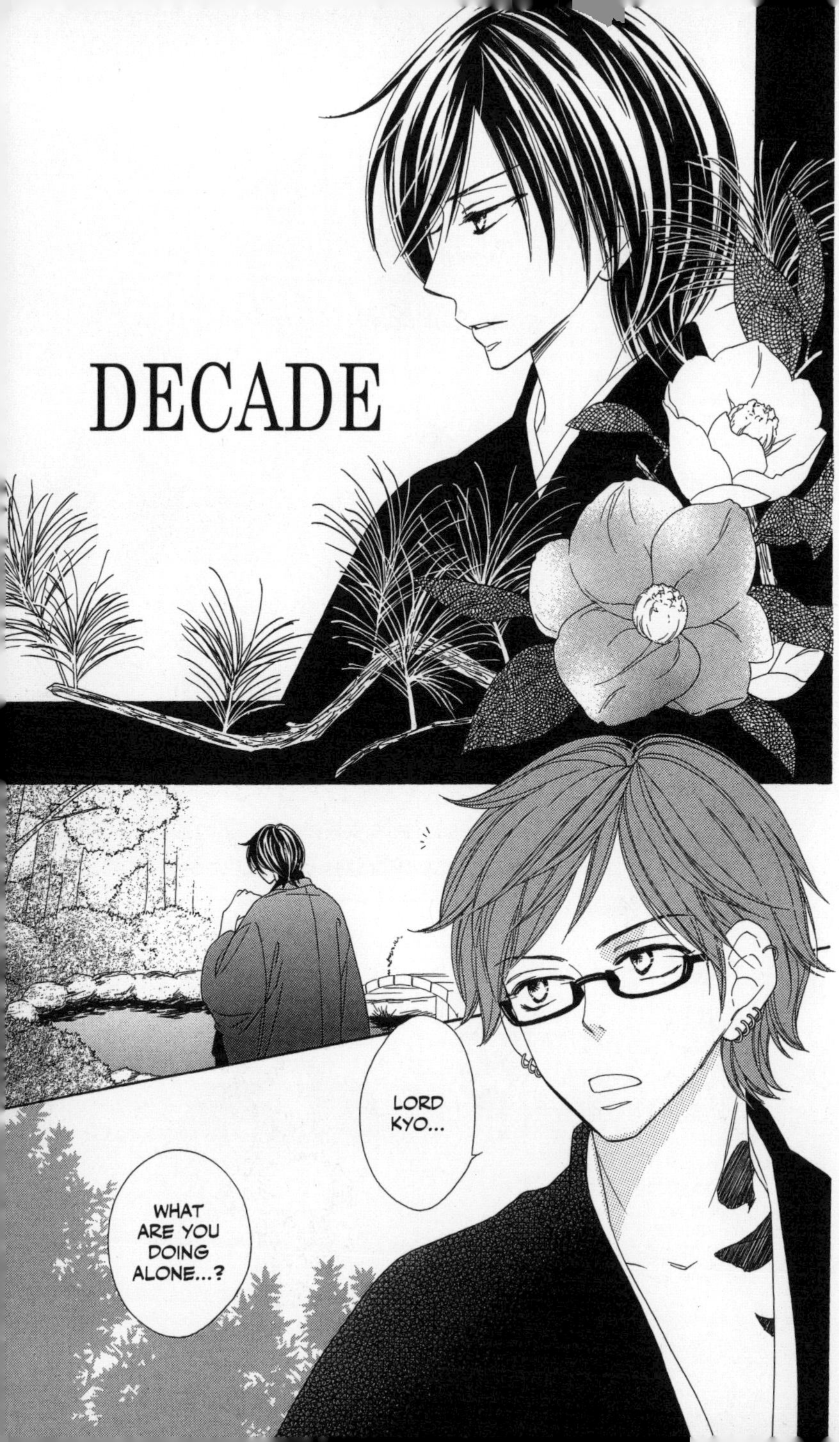
DECADE
LORD KYO...
WHAT ARE YOU DOING ALONE...?

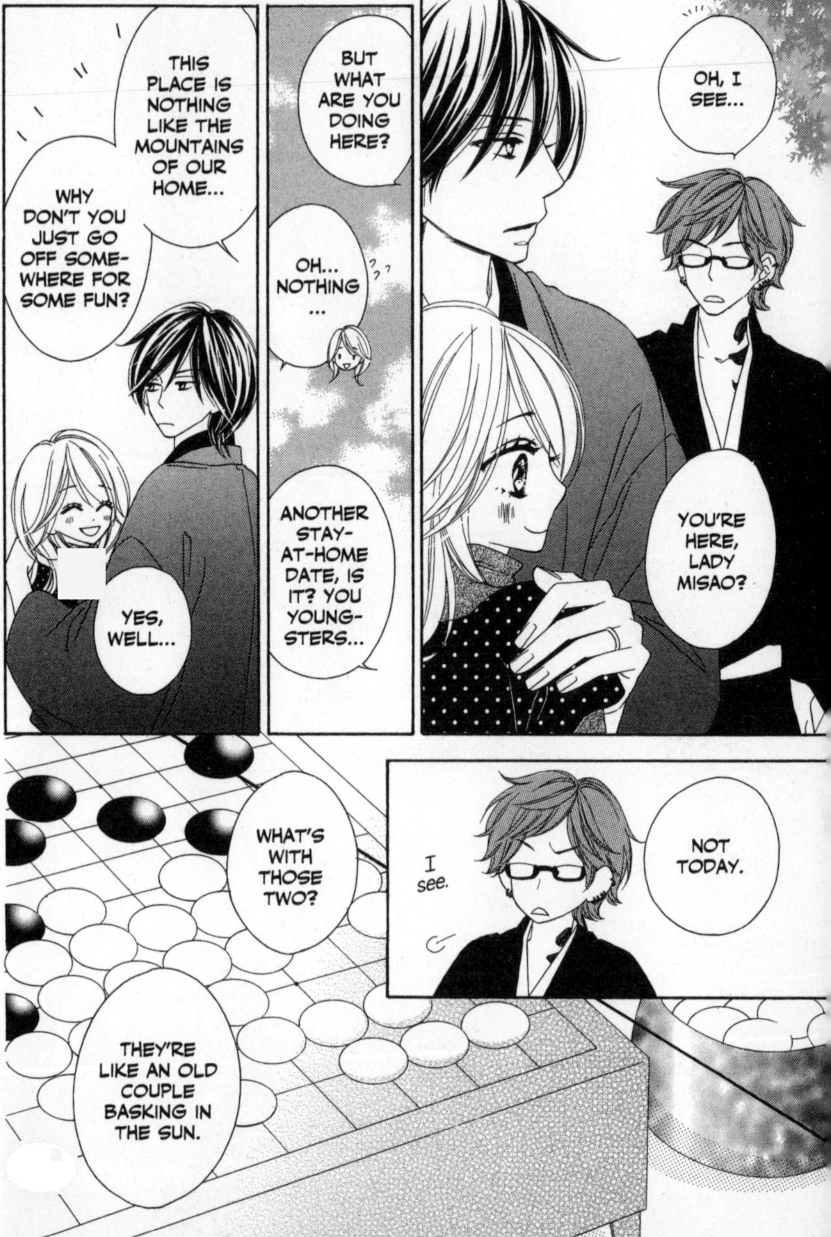
OH, I SEE...
YOU'RE HERE, LADY MISAO?
BUT WHAT ARE YOU DOING HERE?
OH... NOTHING ...
ANOTHER STAY-AT-HOME DATE, IS IT? YOU YOUNGSTERS...
THIS PLACE IS NOTHING LIKE THE MOUNTAINS OF OUR HOME...
WHY DON'T YOU JUST GO OFF SOME-WHERE FOR SOME FUN?
YES, WELL...
NOT TODAY.
I see.
WHAT'S WITH THOSE TWO?
THEY'RE LIKE AN OLD COUPLE BASKING IN THE SUN.

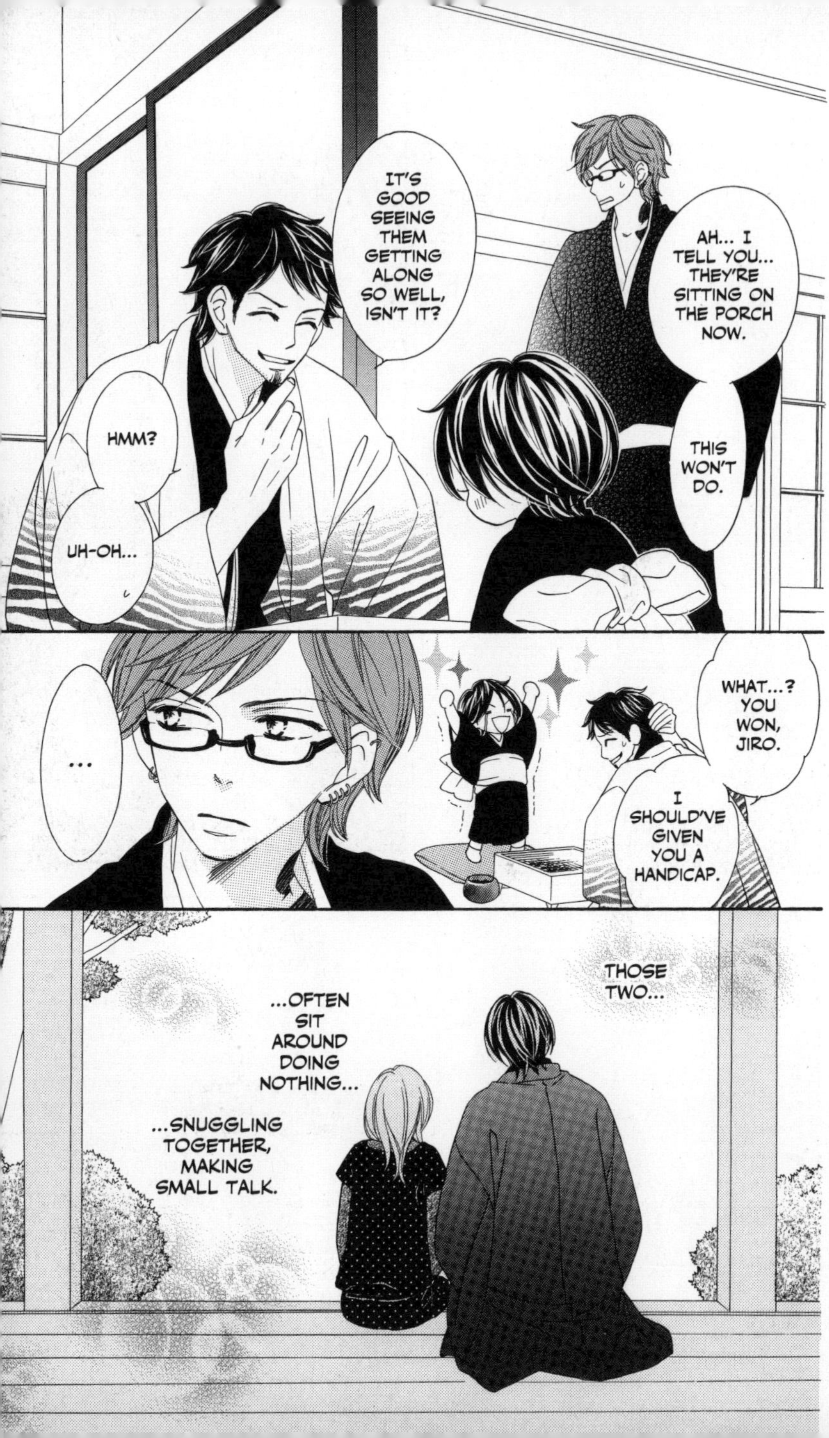
AH... I TELL YOU... THEY'RE SITTING ON THE PORCH NOW.
THIS WON'T DO.
IT'S GOOD SEEING THEM GETTING ALONG SO WELL, ISN'T IT?
HMM?
UH-OH...
WHAT...? YOU WON, JIRO.
I SHOULD'VE GIVEN YOU A HANDICAP.
...
THOSE TWO...
...OFTEN SIT AROUND DOING NOTHING...
...SNUGGLING TOGETHER, MAKING SMALL TALK.

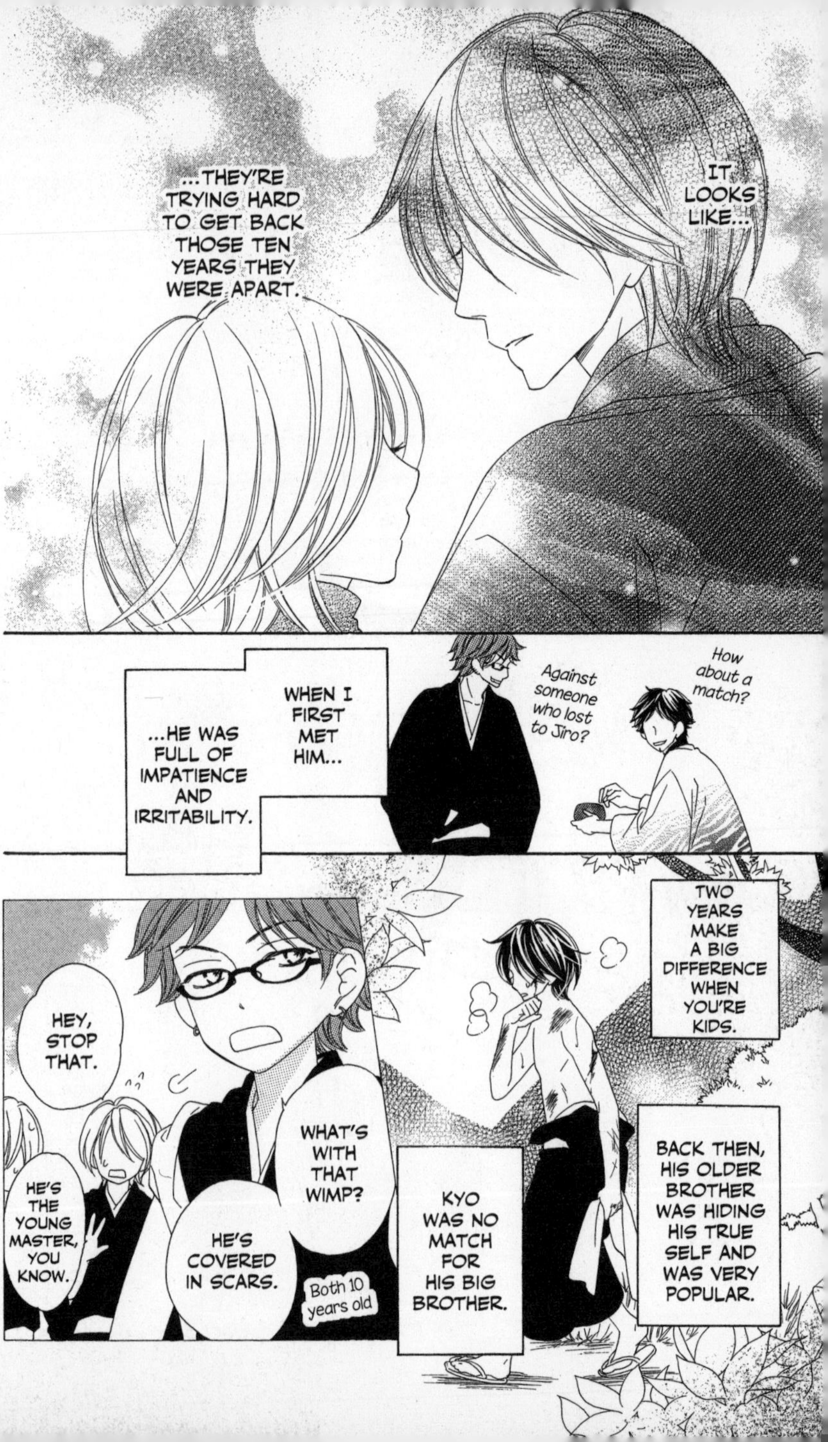
IT LOOKS LIKE...
...THEY'RE TRYING HARD TO GET BACK THOSE TEN YEARS THEY WERE APART.
How about a match?
Against someone who lost to Jiro?
WHEN I FIRST MET HIM...
...HE WAS FULL OF IMPATIENCE AND IRRITABILITY.
TWO YEARS MAKE A BIG DIFFERENCE WHEN YOU'RE KIDS.
BACK THEN, HIS OLDER BROTHER WAS HIDING HIS TRUE SELF AND WAS VERY POPULAR.
KYO WAS NO MATCH FOR HIS BIG BROTHER.
HEY, STOP THAT.
WHAT'S WITH THAT WIMP?
HE'S COVERED IN SCARS.
Both 10 years old
HE'S THE YOUNG MASTER, YOU KNOW.

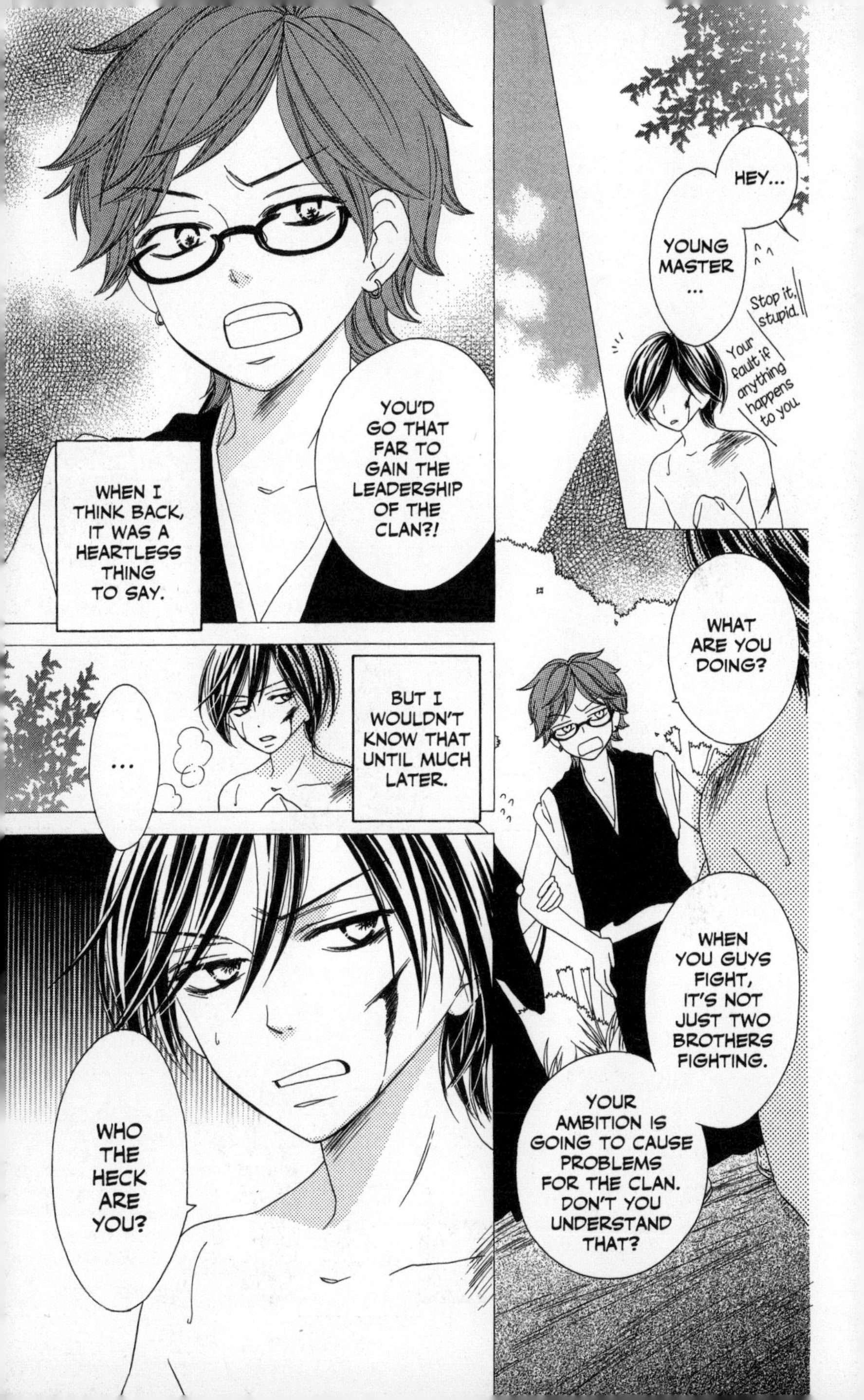
HEY...
YOUNG MASTER ...
Stop it, stupid.
Your fault if anything happens to you.
WHAT ARE YOU DOING?
WHEN YOU GUYS FIGHT, IT'S NOT JUST TWO BROTHERS FIGHTING.
YOUR AMBITION IS GOING TO CAUSE PROBLEMS FOR THE CLAN. DON'T YOU UNDERSTAND THAT?
YOU'D GO THAT FAR TO GAIN THE LEADERSHIP OF THE CLAN?!
WHEN I THINK BACK, IT WAS A HEARTLESS THING TO SAY.
BUT I WOULDN'T KNOW THAT UNTIL MUCH LATER.
...
WHO THE HECK ARE YOU?

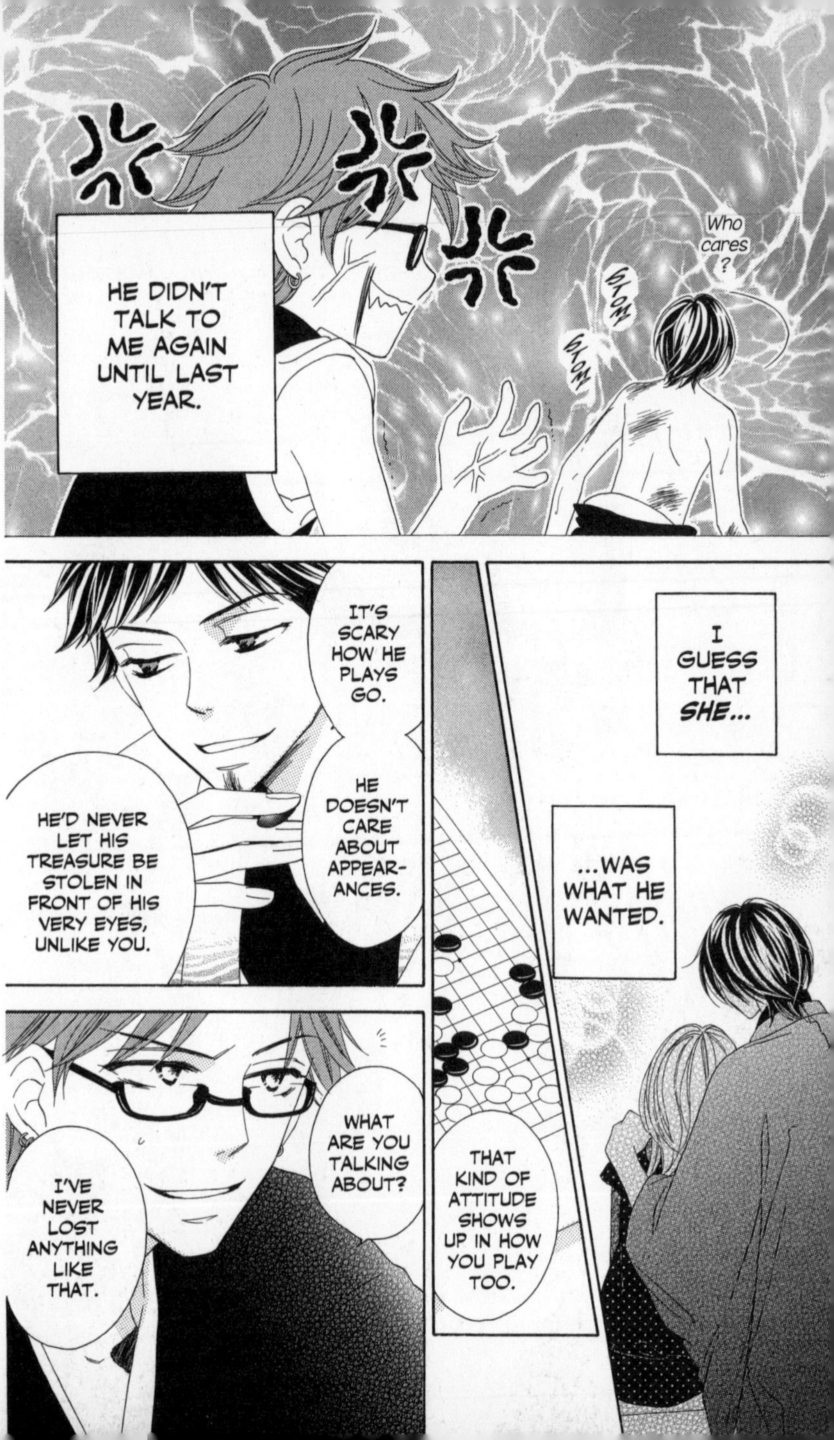
Who cares?
SLOM
SLOM
HE DIDN'T TALK TO ME AGAIN UNTIL LAST YEAR.
I GUESS THAT *SHE*...
...WAS WHAT HE WANTED.
THAT KIND OF ATTITUDE SHOWS UP IN HOW YOU PLAY TOO.
IT'S SCARY HOW HE PLAYS GO.
HE DOESN'T CARE ABOUT APPEARANCES.
HE'D NEVER LET HIS TREASURE BE STOLEN IN FRONT OF HIS VERY EYES, UNLIKE YOU.
WHAT ARE YOU TALKING ABOUT?
I'VE NEVER LOST ANYTHING LIKE THAT.

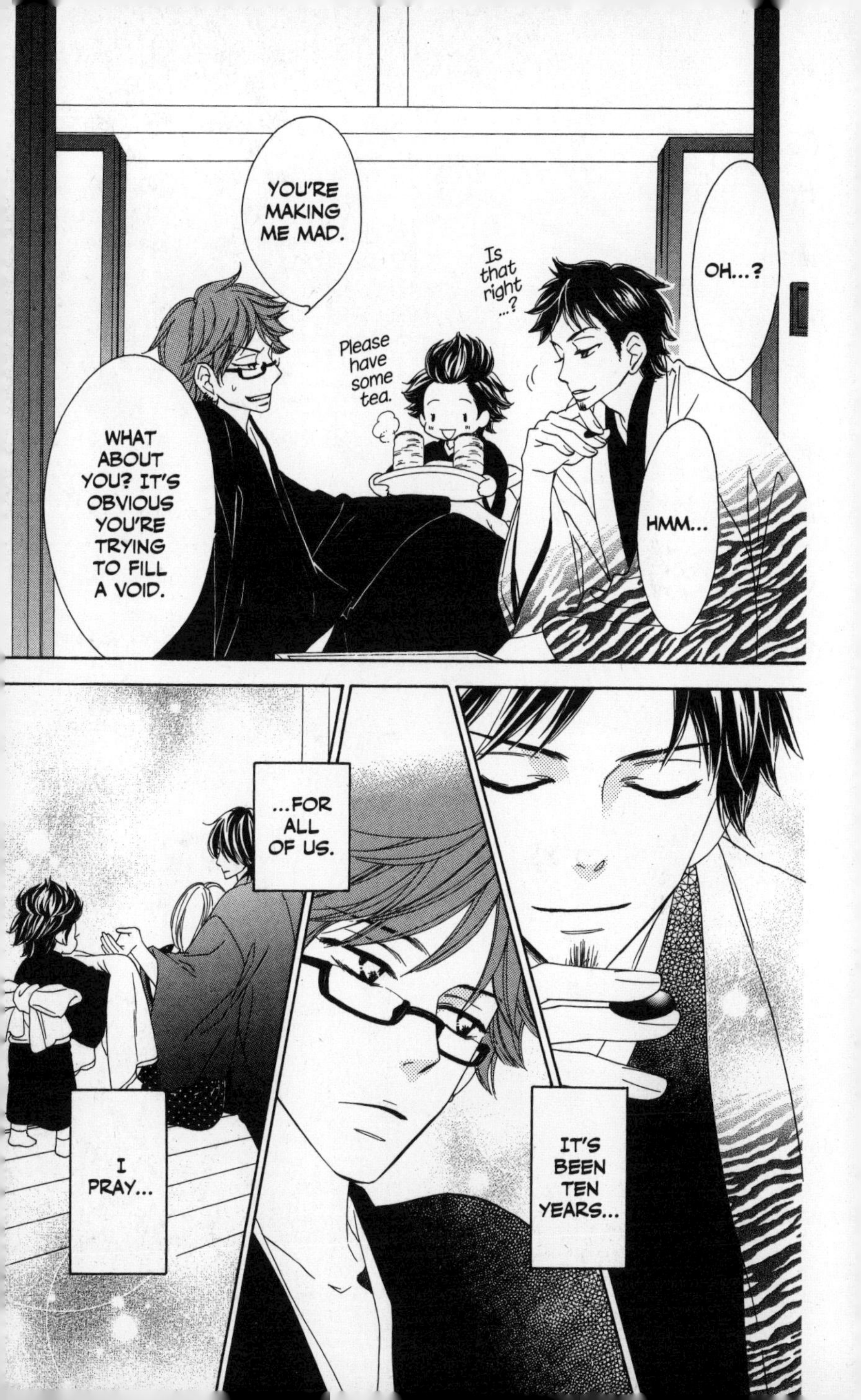
OH...?
YOU'RE MAKING ME MAD.
Is that right...?
Please have some tea.
HMM...
WHAT ABOUT YOU? IT'S OBVIOUS YOU'RE TRYING TO FILL A VOID.
IT'S BEEN TEN YEARS...
...FOR ALL OF US.
I PRAY...

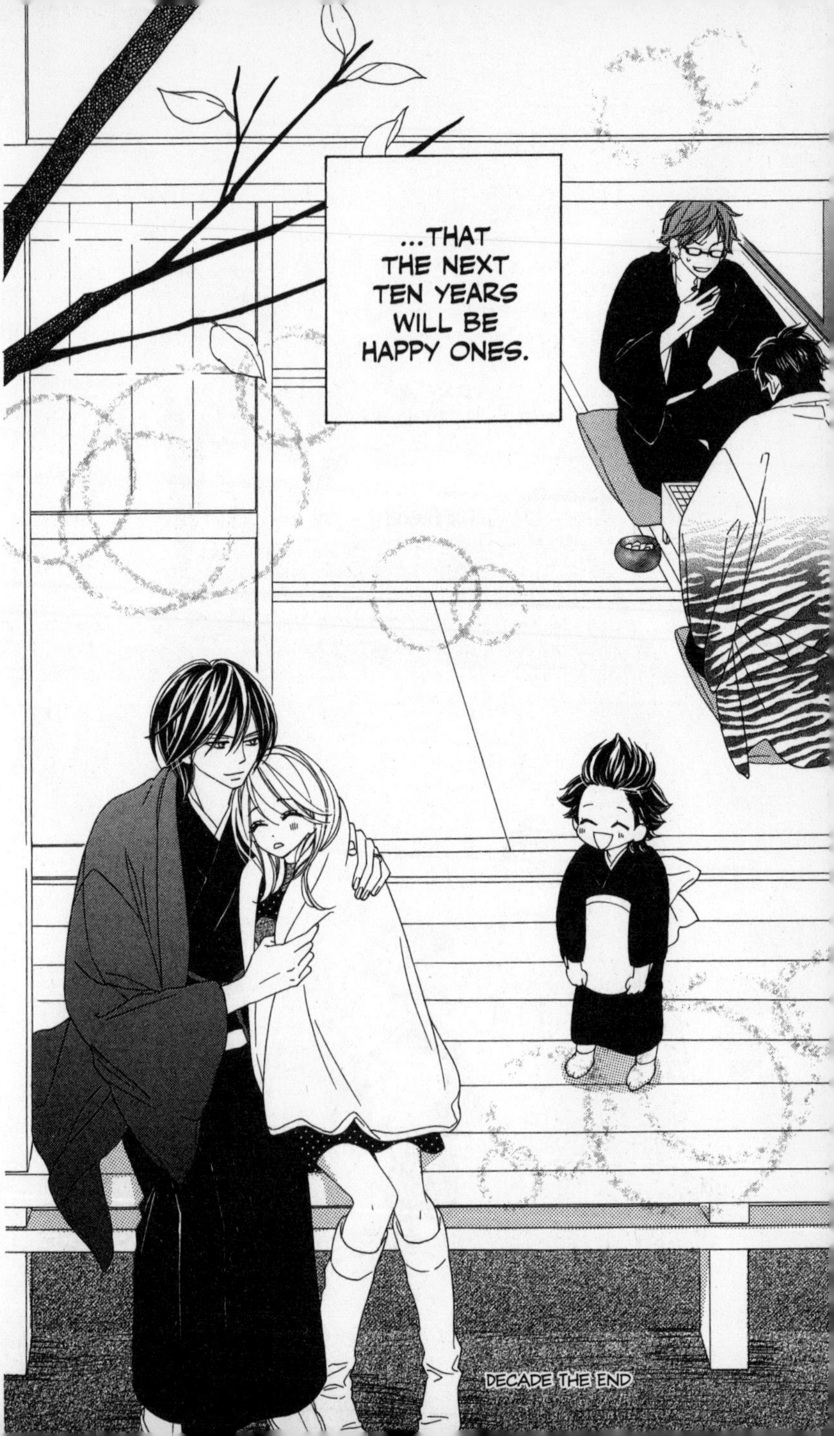
...THAT THE NEXT TEN YEARS WILL BE HAPPY ONES.
DECADE THE END

The title of the special feature is "DECADE," which means ten years. I drew the same scene in a special feature from Misao's viewpoint for Volume 5, so I hope you will read them together.

This is my homepage! ↓
    http://Sakurakoujien.lolipop.jp

I am thinking of showing you the steps involved in creating the cover illustration for Volume 4. Don't expect too much, or you'll be disappointed.

To everyone who has helped me, and everyone who reads this, I send my thanks. ♡

An auspicious day, January 2008 Kanoko Sakurakouji

GLOSSARY

PAGE 11, PANEL 4: *Senka Roku*
This literally means "The Peach Records." Here it is a record of wives taken by members of the Kuzunoha clan. It is passed down from generation to generation.

PAGE 15, PANEL 3: *Genroku Era*
From 1688 to 1704, during the reign of the Emperor Higashiyama.

PAGE 15, PANEL 5: *Edo Period*
From 1603 to 1867, also known as the Tokugawa period. It ended when the Meiji Restoration brought an end to the shogunate style of government and reinstated imperial rule.

PAGE 27, PANEL 5: *Can you not see this seal?!*
A reference to a popular samurai TV series call *Mito Komon*, in which an influential retired samurai goes around incognito and, at the climax of almost every episode, shows his seal case and sends all the evildo-ers cowering at the sight of the seal of the powerful ruling family.

PAGE 31, side note: *Hakama and haori*
Both are traditional Japanese gar-ments worn with kimono. The hakama resembles pants or a skirt and is worn below the waist. The haori is a kimono jacket, like the one Kyo is wearing here.

PAGE 184, PANEL 4: *Go*
A strategic board game that is said to have originated in ancient China. It is still popular in east Asian countries like Japan, China and Korea.

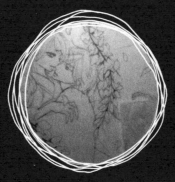

Kanoko Sakurakouji was born in downtown Tokyo, and her hobbies include reading, watching plays, traveling and shopping. Her debut title, *Raibu ga Hanetara*, ran in *Bessatsu Shojo Comic* (currently called *Bestucomi*) in 2000, and her 2004 *Bestucomi* title *Backstage Prince* was serialized in VIZ Media's *Shojo Beat* magazine. She won the 54th Shogakukan Manga Award for *Black Bird*.

BLACK BIRD

VOL. 4
Shojo Beat Edition

Story and Art by KANOKO SAKURAKOUJI

© 2007 Kanoko SAKURAKOUJI/Shogakukan
All rights reserved.
Original Japanese edition "BLACK BIRD" published by SHOGAKUKAN Inc.

TRANSLATION JN Productions
TOUCH-UP ART & LETTERING Gia Cam Luc
DESIGN Courtney Utt
EDITOR Pancha Diaz

The rights of the author(s) of the work(s) in this publication
to be so identified have been asserted in accordance with
the Copyright, Designs and Patents Act 1988. A CIP catalogue
record for this book is available from the British Library.

The stories, characters and incidents mentioned
in this publication are entirely fictional.

Printed in the U.S.A.

Published by VIZ Media, LLC
P.O. Box 77010
San Francisco, CA 94107

10 9 8 7 6 5 4
First printing, May 2010
Fourth printing, August 2012

www.shojobeat.com   www.viz.com

9